Basic Skills in English

Purple Level

Yellow Level

Blue Level

Orange Level

Green Level

Red Level

Basic Skills in English

Green Level

Joy Littell, EDITORIAL DIRECTOR

McDougal, Littell & Company
Evanston, Illinois
New York   Dallas   Sacramento

AUTHORS

Joy Littell, Editorial Director, McDougal, Littell & Company

Edward Hagelin Pearson, Lincoln Junior High School, Park Ridge, Illinois

Kraft and Kraft, Developers of Educational Materials, Newburyport, Massachusetts

CONSULTANTS

Carole B. Bencich, Coordinator of Secondary Language Arts, Brevard County School Board, Rockledge, Florida

Dr. Sheila F. S. Ford, Coordinator for Secondary Language Arts, Spring Branch Independent School District, Houston, Texas

Marietta H. Hickman, English Department Chairman, Wake Forest-Rolesville High School, Wake Forest, North Carolina

Mary Evans Roberts, Supervisor of English and Language Arts, Savannah-Chatham Public Schools, Savannah, Georgia

ISBN: 0-86609-482-2   TE ISBN: 0-86609-483-0

Acknowledgments

Simon & Schuster: for entries from *Webster's New World Dictionary*, Students Edition; copyright © 1981 by Simon & Schuster, Inc. Macmillan Publishing Company: the Handbook section contains, in revised form, some materials that appeared originally in *The Macmillan English Series, Grade 6,* by Thomas Clark Pollock et. al., © 1963 by Macmillan Company. Used by arrangement. (Acknowledgments are continued on page 624.)

11,39

Composition

Handbook

Words: Developing Your Vocabulary

Part 1

Alive and Well

Learning About Language

Here's the Idea English is a living language. It grows and changes. **Modern English** is different from **Middle English,** which was spoken until about 500 years ago. It is even more different from **Old English,** which was spoken until about 900 years ago. Many of the words you use today come from Middle and Old English words. For example, the word *seven* comes from the Middle English *seoven. Seoven* came from the Old English word *seofon.* Words that come from older forms of English are native English words. There are also several other sources for words in the English language.

Borrowed Words Many English words come from other languages. For example, *antenna* comes from Latin. *Chili* is a Spanish word. *Coupon* is French. *Boss* comes from Dutch. *Moccasin* is an American Indian word.

Compound Words Two words are often combined to make a new word. Some examples are *basketball, headache,* and *sunrise.*

Blends Sometimes a part of one word and a part of another word are combined to make a new word. For example, the word *smog* comes from *smoke* and *fog.*

Acronyms An acronym is a word made from the first letters of several words. The acronym *scuba* comes from the words *self contained underwater breathing apparatus.*

Echoic Words Some words imitate sounds. *Buzz, meow,* and *zap* are examples of words that echo sounds.

English is a continually changing language. In this lesson, you have seen how some changes occur. You can now see why learning English is a continual process for everyone.

Check It Out Read the following sentences.

1. We spent the *day* at Hampton Beach.
2. Ken likes *pizza* with mushrooms and sausage.
3. The Sears Tower is Chicago's tallest *skyscraper*.
4. The Thompsons enjoy *brunch* every Sunday.
5. *NASA* officials cheered the launching.
6. The parrot *squawked* as we neared its cage.

- Which word comes from the Old English word *daeg*? Which word is borrowed from Italian? Which word is a compound word? Which word is a blend of *breakfast* and *lunch*? Which word is an acronym for *National Aeronautics and Space Administration*? Which word echoes a sound?
- Do you see how English is enriched by new words?

Try Your Skill Using a dictionary, try to find out how each of these words came into modern English.

boy   slim   snowplow   UNICEF   sizzle   patio

Keep This in Mind

- English continually grows and changes. New words are formed as others fall out of use.
- Some modern English words come from Middle and Old English. Others are borrowed words, compound words, blends, acronyms, and echoic words.

Now Write Write four of these words: *Saturday, antenna, sleigh, liftoff, chortle,* and *sonar.* Using a dictionary, check the meanings of the words and find out how they came into English. Write a sentence for each of them. Label your paper **Alive and Well.** Keep your paper in your writing folder.

Part 2

Future Talk

New Language for Special Fields

Here's the Idea You have already learned several ways in which new words enter the language. There is another way that is becoming more and more common.

The world is always changing. Every day, people have new ideas and create new inventions. The English language also grows and changes. New ideas and inventions require new words to describe them. Also, old words take on new meanings as people use them in connection with these new ideas.

The space industry, for example, has added a whole new vocabulary to the English language. Not many years ago, no one knew what *astronaut* meant. The words *countdown* and *launch pad* were not in any dictionary.

Also, computers are changing our world so quickly that many people speak of the *computer revolution*. Here are some words from that revolution that are now a part of the English language:

software	printout	interface
chip	floppy disc	byte

Science and technology have also added new words to the language with their inventions. How many of these words do you know?

magnetic	laser	hardware
relay	digital	black hole

Because the world is always changing, you want to be aware of these changes and the words that describe them.

Check It Out Look at the following words. They are all terms used in the space industry, with computers, or in science and technology. Some have older, familiar meanings. Some are made up of two familiar words.

chip	keyboard	videotape	bionic
word processor	memory	liftoff	monitor

- Do you see how words can take on new meanings to describe new ideas and inventions?
- Are there any relationships between the old meanings and the new meanings?

Try Your Skill In class, list on the blackboard as many terms used in the space industry, with computers, or in science and technology as your class can think of. Go through the list and decide which words have both a new and an old meaning. See how many definitions you know for these words. Can you tell how the old and new meanings are related?

Keep This in Mind

- The English language changes as the world changes.
- New words are created for new ideas and inventions. Old words take on new meanings.

Now Write Look carefully through a newspaper or magazine for terms used in the space industry, with computers, or in science and technology. List three of each kind of word. Also, write the sentence you found each word in. Then write the meaning of each word. Share your words with your classmates. Label your paper **Future Talk.** Save your work in your folder.

Part 3

Say It Again, Sam

Context: Definition and Restatement

Here's the Idea   When you see an unfamiliar word, you may be able to learn its meaning from its context. **Context** means the words surrounding a word. The context may hold clues to the meaning of the word. The most direct context clues are definition and restatement.

When **definition** is used, the meaning of a word is stated directly.

> The sheets were made of *muslin. Muslin* is a strong, cotton cloth.

When **restatement** is used, the meaning of a word is usually signaled by key words, like *or, is called, that is, which is,* or *in other words*. Sometimes the meaning of the unfamiliar word is signaled by a comma or a pair of commas.

> The butter had a *rancid* smell; in other words, it was spoiled.
> I just want a *morsel*, a tiny piece, of that delicious cake.

When you read, look for a definition or a restatement of an unfamiliar word. These clues help you learn words more easily.

Check It Out   Look at the examples below.

1. The minister stood behind a *lectern*. A lectern is a tall stand used to hold a book or notes to be read.
2. My Uncle Bob works as a *mason*, or bricklayer.
3. Al's writing is not *legible*; that is, it is difficult to read.
4. The carpenter needed an *awl*, a small pointed tool for making holes in wood.

- What is the meaning of each italicized word?
- What clue in each sentence indicates a definition or restatement?

Try Your Skill Using context clues, decide what each italicized word means. Write a definition for each word.

1. In Georgia, we saw beautiful *jasmine*. Jasmine is a plant with fragrant yellow flowers.

2. My father gave a *noncommital* answer, which was neither a yes nor a no.

3. The ring was made of *garnets*, deep red stones, set in gold.

4. New England has some of the most *fickle*, or changeable, weather in the country.

5. More than five hundred American cities have *city managers*. A city manager is a person who is hired to run a city as a business is run.

6. The bird dog never *deviated*, or turned aside, from the trail it was following.

Keep This in Mind

- Context, the words surrounding a word, often gives clues to the meaning of that word.
- Definition and restatement are the most direct context clues.
- Several words or phrases alert you to definition or restatement. These include *or*, *is called*, *that is*, *which is*, or *in other words*. A definition or restatement may also be set off by commas.

Now Write On your paper, write the title of this lesson, **Say It Again, Sam.** Choose four of the following words: *chard, escalator, lease, neon, secretary,* and *umpire*. Write a sentence for each of the four words. Use definition or restatement in the context. Use a dictionary, if necessary, to help you. Check your sentences by having a reader see if your meaning is clear. When you have checked your sentences, put the paper into your folder.

Part 4

A Good Example

Using Context Clues: Examples

Here's the Idea An unfamiliar word is not always defined or restated. However, sometimes you may be able to understand the meaning of a word through examples. By studying the examples, you can often determine what the unfamiliar word means.

In this type of context clue, a general term is given along with specific examples. Sometimes the general term will be unfamiliar to you. At other times, one of the specific examples might be the unfamiliar word. In either case, you can use the sentence as a whole to figure out the meaning of the word you don't know.

Read these sentences:

I wrote a report on the *lynx* and other wildcats.
Amphibians, such as frogs and toads, are cold-blooded.

You may not know exactly what a lynx looks like. However, the word *other* signals that a lynx is a wildcat. Similarly, you may not know exactly what an amphibian is, but the phrase *such as* signals that frogs and toads are amphibians.

Many key words and phrases signal the use of examples. These include *especially, like, other, this, these, for example, for instance,* and *such as.*

Check It Out Read the following sentences.

1. All *citrus fruits*, especially oranges, are good sources of the Vitamin C you need.

2. The scientists were experimenting with *diesels* and other engines.

3. The music of classical *composers*, Beethoven and Mozart for example, has been used in recent movies.

4. The values of units of money, such as the *yen* and the *franc*, change almost daily.

- What is the meaning of each of the italicized words?
- Which words or phrases signal an example?

Try Your Skill Try to get the meaning of the italicized words in these sentences from the use of examples in context. Write the definition of each italicized word.

1. A large, open porch, like a *veranda*, is often found at the back of older houses.

2. Some large birds, the *emu* for instance, are unable to fly.

3. I enjoy eating all kinds of salad greens, like *endive* and *chicory*.

4. Turkeys, chickens, and other *fowl* can be bought fresh at this market.

Keep This in Mind

- An example may be used as a context clue.
- Certain key words signal examples. Key words and phrases include *especially, like, other, this, these, for example, for instance,* and *such as.*

Now Write On your paper, write the title of this lesson, **A Good Example.** Choose three of the following words and use them in sentences: *clothing, succulents, citrus fruit, annual flowers,* and *aerobic exercise.* If any of these words are unfamiliar to you, look them up in the dictionary. Make the meaning of each word clear by using an example as a context clue. Check your sentences by having a reader see if your meaning is clear. When you have checked your sentences, put your work into your folder.

Part 5

Like and Unlike

Context Clues: Comparison and Contrast

Here's the Idea Comparison and contrast are two other types of context clues. You can understand the meaning of an unfamiliar word by learning what it is like or not like.

When **comparison** is used, a word is compared with another word or phrase that you already know. Try to discover the meaning of the word *crimson* from the following context.

> Her *crimson* dress was like the red of a brilliant sunset.

The word *like* signals that *crimson* is being compared to the red of a sunset. From this comparison, you know that crimson is a red color. Key words used to signal comparisons include *as, like, in the same way,* and *similar to.*

When **contrast** is used, a word is contrasted with another word or phrase opposite that is familiar to you. If you know the opposite of an unfamiliar word, you can often understand the meaning you do not know. Read this example.

> Dad found the trip *enthralling*, even though Uncle Al thought it was boring.

Enthralling is contrasted with *boring.* The phrase *even though* suggests that bored Uncle Al did not find the trip enthralling. *Enthralling* must mean the opposite of *boring.*

Key words that signal contrast as a context clue include *though, but, unlike, while, on the contrary,* and *on the other hand.*

Check It Out Read the sentences below.

1. The mood was as *sinister* as that of a haunted house on a stormy night.
2. Ted's *impudent* behavior was like that of a spoiled child.
3. Unlike Laura, who believes all she hears, Meg is *skeptical.*

4. Parking is *prohibited* on Sunday from 7:00 A.M. until noon, but it is allowed at all other times.

- What is the meaning of each italicized word?
- Which key words signal that comparison is used?
- Which key words signal that contrast is used?

Try Your Skill   Write a definition for each italicized word.

1. Unlike Jay, who congratulated me, Larry *scoffed* at my prize.
2. The cheers *resonated* throughout the hall like bells chiming in a tower.
3. Unlike many other nuts, *filberts* grow on bushes instead of trees.
4. Like most *extroverts*, Dot was friendly and outgoing.
5. I found the movie interesting, but Ben said it was *tedious*.

Keep This in Mind

- Comparison and contrast provide context clues to the meanings of unfamiliar words.
- Key words and phrases that signal a comparison include *as, like, in the same way,* and *similar to.*
- Key words that signal a contrast include *although, but, unlike, while, on the contrary,* and *on the other hand.*

Now Write   On your paper, write the title of this lesson, **Like and Unlike.** Use four of these words in sentences: *careless, valuable, sparkling, generous, prodigious,* and *efficient.* If any of these words are unfamiliar to you, look them up in a dictionary. Write two sentences using comparison as a context clue. Then write two more sentences using contrast as a clue. Use key words to signal which context clue you are using. Check your sentences by having a reader see if your meaning is clear. Put your paper into your folder.

Part 6

Be Precise

Using Synonyms and Antonyms

Here's the Idea   Words with similar meanings are called **synonyms.** Synonyms do not mean exactly the same thing. However, they do mean almost the same thing.

Think about the words *chuckle* and *giggle*, for instance. They mean almost the same things, but not quite. *Chuckle* means a soft, low laugh made at what is mildly funny. *Giggle* means a quick, high-pitched laugh made in a silly or nervous way. You can see that one synonym would be more accurate than the other in a specific situation.

Eat is a word with many synonyms. Two of these are *gulp* and *nibble*. Which would you use to describe how a hungry person was eating? You would probably use *gulp*, since it means "to swallow greedily or in large amounts."

Antonyms are words that have almost opposite meanings. *Hot* and *cold* are antonyms. So are *fat* and *thin*. Words often have more than one antonym, just as they often have more than one synonym. Other antonyms for hot are *cool, chilly,* and *frozen*.

Synonyms and antonyms will help you when you write. Check to see if a synonym might be more accurate than a word you are using. Check to see if an antonym might help you to make a contrast. If you are precise with words, you will be able to express your ideas more clearly.

Check It Out   Read the following sentences.

1. "Be quiet," *said* Tanya, "we don't want them to hear us."
   barked   called   shrieked   whispered
2. Is your job *dull*, or is it _____?" asked Ron.
   busy   exciting   important   valuable

- Which is the best synonym for *said*? Why?
- Which is the best antonym for *dull*? Why?
- Do the words you selected express the ideas as clearly as possible?

Try Your Skill   Read each sentence below. Choose the word that best replaces the italicized word. Number your paper from 1 to 5 and write the correct word.

1. We *went* home to avoid the approaching storm.
    dashed   strolled   walked   wandered
2. Ms. Moyers said my report was *good* and deserved an A.
    fine   kind   nice   superior
3. The library kept all of its magazines in one *big* room.
    generous   important   spacious   wide
4. This story is so *interesting*, I just can't put it down.
    attractive   curious   fascinating   tantalizing
5. For three weeks Carl had looked for a job, so he felt *sad* when he was turned down again.
    dejected   gloomy   mournful   sorrowful

Keep This in Mind

- Synonyms are words with similar meanings.
- Antonyms are words with opposite meanings.
- Choose synonyms and antonyms that are accurate and appropriate for what you want to say.

Now Write   On your paper, write the title of this lesson, **Be Precise.** The words *chatter, comment, recite,* and *talk* are synonyms. Use each in a sentence. Write each sentence so that the precise meaning of each synonym is clear. Check your sentences by having a reader see if your meaning is clear. When you have finished, put your work into your folder.

Part 7

Get on Base

Using Word Parts: Base Words

Here's the Idea   One way to add new words to your vocabulary is to learn about base words and word parts. A **base word** is a word on which other words are based. *Trust*, for example, is a base word.

Sometimes word parts are added at the beginning of a base word. When *mis-* is added to *trust*, the new word *mistrust* is formed. The new word has a different meaning from the base word. Other word parts are added at the end of a base word. Add *-ful* to *trust*, and the new word *trustful* is formed. Sometimes, more than one word part is added to a base word. *Mis-* and *-ful* can both be added to *trust* to make *mistrustful*.

Sometimes the spelling of a base word changes when a word part is added. The spelling is more likely to change when a word part is added at the end of a base word. When the word part *-able* is added to the base word *move*, the new word *movable* is formed. Notice that the *e* in *move* is dropped.

In the next two lessons, you will learn some word parts and their meanings. This knowledge will help you enlarge your vocabulary. You'll be able to add the meaning of the word part to the meaning of the base word. That will give you the meaning of a new word. For example, suppose that you bought a *nontaxable* item. *Non-* means "not," and *-able* means "can." The base word is *tax*. *Nontaxable* means "cannot be taxed."

Check It Out   Read each group of words below.

return	adventurous	useful
returnable	misadventure	misuse
nonreturnable	unadventurous	useless

- What is the base word in each group of words?
- Which base word changed its spelling slightly when a word part was added at the end?
- Which words are new to you?

Try Your Skill   Read the following list. Write the base word in each word. You may want to check a dictionary for correct spelling.

1. sleepless	5. illegal	9. refillable
2. nonprofit	6. ungraceful	10. misplace
3. unthinkable	7. imperfect	11. survivor
4. dangerous	8. unjust	12. preschooler

Keep This in Mind

- Word parts may be added at the beginning or end of base words to make new words.
- Sometimes the spelling of a base word changes when a part is added.
- Knowing base words and word parts will help you to enlarge your vocabulary.

Now Write   Using any one of your textbooks, find five words that have base words and word parts. The word part may be at the beginning or end of the word. Try to choose words that are unfamiliar to you.

On your paper, write the title of this lesson, **Get on Base.** Then write the words you have found. Next to each word, write the base word. If you know the meaning of the base word, write it on your paper. If not, look it up in a dictionary and then write it. Try to figure out the entire word.

Put your work into your folder.

Part 8

What's First?

Using Word Parts: Prefixes

Here's the Idea   You know that word parts can be added to base words. A word part added at the beginning of a base word is called a **prefix**. *Pre-* means "before" and *fix* means "attach," so *prefix* means "to attach before."

The word part *un-*, for example, is a common prefix. Sometimes *un-* means "not," as it does in the word *unlike*. If you are unlike someone, you are not like her or him. Sometimes *un-* means "the opposite of," as it does in the word *unchain*. If you *unchain* the door, you can open it.

Some prefixes have one meaning. Others have two. Once you learn to recognize these prefixes, they will help you to understand many unfamiliar words. Here are some prefixes.

Prefix	Meaning	Examples
in- (also **il-**, **im-**, and **ir-**)	"not"	indefinite, illegal immature, irregular
mis-	"wrong"	misbehave, miscount
non-	"not"	nonprofit, nonstop
pre-	"before"	prefix, prewash
re-	"again" or "back"	rebuild, recall
sub-	"under" or "less than"	subway, substandard
super-	"above" or "more than"	supernatural
un-	"not" or "opposite of"	untested, uneven

Some words seem to start with a prefix but really do not. At first glance, the word *region* may look as though it starts with the prefix *re-*. Does it? To find out, look for the base word. If you cover the letters *re*, you are left with *gion*, which isn't a word. Since there is no base word, the letters *re* are not a prefix in *region*.

Check It Out   Look at the words below.

immodest	disagree	misunderstand	substation
submarine	irregular	illogical	incomplete
nonfiction	repay	supermarket	preview

- What is the prefix in each word? What does each prefix mean?
- What does each word mean?

Try Your Skill   Read the words below. Some of the words have prefixes. Others do not. If a word has a prefix, write the meaning of the prefix plus the base word. For example, for the word *recall*, you would write this: again + call.

1. subhuman	6. improper	11. untie
2. superior	7. illogical	12. invisible
3. input	8. preflight	13. united
4. nonviolent	9. rectangle	14. refit
5. imagine	10. unmarked	15. supertanker

Keep This in Mind

- A prefix is a word part that is added at the beginning of a word.
- Each prefix has one or more meanings. The prefix changes the meaning of the base word, making a new word.
- Some words seem to begin with a prefix but do not. Check to see if the base word makes sense without the prefix.

Now Write   On your paper, write **What's First?** Find eight words, each containing one of the eight prefixes explained in this lesson. Use a dictionary to help you. Next to each word, write its definition. Keep all your work in your folder.

Part 9

The End

Using Word Parts: Suffixes

Here's the Idea A word part added at the end of a base word is called a **suffix.** One common suffix, for example, is -*less*, which means "without." If a situation is *hopeless*, it is "without a hope." Notice how the meaning of a suffix combines with the meaning of a base word to make a new word with a different meaning.

Sometimes the spelling of the base word changes when a suffix is added. Someone who *runs* is a *runner.* You can see that the final *n* is doubled. A person having *fame* is *famous.* A scene full of *beauty* is *beautiful.* Notice that the final *e* in *fame* is dropped in *famous.* Notice also that the final *y* in *beauty* is changed to *i* in *beautiful.*

Sometimes the change involves more than one letter. For example, something belonging to *Ireland* is *Irish.* You can see that when the suffix -*ish* is added, the whole word changes. Use a dictionary to check the spelling of a word if necessary.

Below are some of the more commonly used suffixes.

Suffix	Meaning	Examples
-able or **-ible**	"can be, having this quality"	likable, forcible
-er or **-or**	"a person or thing that does something"	singer, elevator
-ful	"full of, having"	graceful
-ish	"belonging to or like"	Spanish, childish
-less	"without"	homeless
-ness	"the state or quality of being"	sickness, sadness
-ous	"full of, having"	poisonous

Check It Out   Look at the words below.

priceless	truthful	English
operator	carrier	movable
mysterious	gentleness	sensible

- What is the suffix in each word? What does each word mean?
- In which words is the spelling of the base word changed?

Try Your Skill   Number your paper from 1 to 15. Find the suffix in each word below. If you aren't sure about the spelling of the base word, check a dictionary. Write the base word and the meaning of the suffix for each word. For example, for the word *joyous*, you would write this: joy + full of.

1. youthful	6. Scottish	11. studious
2. avoidable	7. miner	12. sizable
3. deafness	8. pitiful	13. brightness
4. courageous	9. soundless	14. wasteful
5. trainer	10. convertible	15. devilish

Keep This in Mind

- A suffix is a word part added at the end of a base word. A suffix combines with a base word to make a new word.
- Sometimes the spelling of a base word changes when a suffix is added.
- Use a dictionary to check the spelling of a word when you add a suffix.

Now Write   On your paper, write **The End.** Write seven words, each containing one of the seven suffixes explained in this lesson. Next to each word write its definition. Use a dictionary to help you. Put your work into your folder.

Using a Dictionary

Part 1

Word for Word

Using a Dictionary

Here's the Idea A **dictionary** is a book containing a list of words and information about those words. The listing itself is valuable because it shows you that a word exists. The information shows you how to use words correctly.

In a dictionary, words are listed in alphabetical order. Words that begin with *a* come before words that begin with *b*, and so on. If two words begin with the same letter, they are alphabetized by the second letter. If the first and second letters are the same, the words are alphabetized by the third letter. These words are in alphabetical order: *on, once, one, tea, teach,* and *team.*

There are many kinds of dictionaries. Some list words for special fields. For example, you can find a dictionary of medical terms or a crossword puzzle dictionary. Some dictionaries list the words in one language and their definitions in another.

Some of the biggest dictionaries are *unabridged*. That is, they contain nearly all the words in the language. Most of the time a desk or pocket-size dictionary, which is *abridged*, will contain the information you need.

The abbreviations, symbols, and organization may vary from one dictionary to another. For this reason, you should become familiar with the dictionary you use. Study the explanations in the front of the dictionary that tell you what the abbreviations and symbols mean.

Check It Out Look at the bottom portion of a dictionary page on page 23. Answer these questions.
- How are the words listed?
- What special symbols are used?
- What words are new to you?

☆chic·le (chik′'l) *n.* [AmSp. < Nahuatl *chictli*] a gumlike substance made from the milky juice of the sapodilla tree, used in making chewing gum

Chic·o·pee (chik′ə pē) [< AmInd., lit., swift river] city in SW Mass.: pop. 67,000

chic·o·ry (chik′ə rē) *n., pl.* **-ries** [< OFr. < L. < Gr. *kichora*] **1.** a weedy plant of the composite family, with blue flowers: the leaves are used in salads **2.** its root, roasted and ground for mixing with coffee or for use as a coffee substitute

chide (chīd) *vt., vi.* **chid′ed** or **chid** (chid), **chid′ed** or **chid** or **chid·den** (chid′'n), **chid′ing** [OE. *cidan*] to scold, esp. in a mild way —**chid′ing·ly** *adv.*

chief (chēf) *n.* [< OFr. < L. *caput*, the head: for IE. base see HEAD] **1.** the head or leader of a group, organization, etc. **2.** *Heraldry* the upper third of a shield — *adj.* **1.** highest in rank, office, etc. *[the chief executive]* **2.** main; principal *[the chief advantages]* —**in chief** in the chief position *[commander in chief]*

☆**Chief Executive** the President of the U.S.

chief justice the presiding judge of a court made up of several judges

chief·ly (chēf′lē) *adv.* **1.** most of all; above all *[chiefly interested in science]* **2.** mainly; mostly *[a melon is chiefly water]* —*adj.* of or like a chief

CHICORY

child·ish (-ish) *adj.* **1.** of or like a child **2.** not fit for an adult; immature; silly —see SYN. at CHILDLIKE —**child′ish·ly** *adv.* — **child′ish·ness** *n.*

child labor the regular, full-time employment in factories, stores, offices, etc. of children who are less than a legally defined age: in the U.S., it is against Federal law to employ children under the age of 16 (or under 18 in occupations that are dangerous)

child·like (-līk′) *adj.* like a child, esp. in being innocent, trusting, etc. —**child′like′ness** *n.*

SYN.—**childlike** and **childish** are both applied to persons of any age in referring to qualities considered typical of a child, **childlike** suggesting the favorable qualities such as innocence, honesty, curiosity, zest, etc., and **childish** the unfavorable ones such as immaturity, foolishness, lack of self-control, self-centeredness, etc.

chil·dren (chil′drən) *n. pl. of* CHILD

children of Israel the Jews; Hebrews

child's play (chīldz) anything simple to do

Chil·e (chil′ē) country on the SW coast of S. America: 286,397 sq. mi.; pop. 9,780,000; cap. Santiago —**Chil′e·an** *adj., n.*

☆ chil·e (chil′ē) *n. same as* CHILI

☆ chil·e con car·ne (chil′ē kən kär′nē, kän′) *same as* CHILI CON CARNE

Chile saltpeter native sodium nitrate, esp. as found naturally in Chile and Peru

☆ chil·i (chil′ē) *n., pl.* **chil′ies** [MexSp. < Nahuatl *chilli*] **1.** the dried pod of red pepper, a very hot seasoning **2.** the tropical American plant, of the nightshade family, that bears this pod **3.** *same as* CHILI CON CARNE

---

fat, āpe, cär; ten, ēven; is, bīte; gō, hôrn, tōͧol, lͧook; oil, out; up, fur; get; joy; yet; chin; she; thin, then; zh, leisure; ŋ, ring; ə for *a* in *ago*, *e* in *agent*, *i* in *sanity*, *o* in *comply*, *u* in *focus*; ′ as in *able* (ā′b'l); Fr. bal; ë, Fr. coeur; ö, Fr. feu; Fr. mon; ô, Fr. coq; ü, Fr. duc; *r*, Fr. cri; H, G. ich; kh, G. doch; ‡foreign; ☆ Americanism; < derived from. See inside front cover.

Try Your Skill

Write each group of words in alphabetical order. Then, use a dictionary to find a word to add to each list.

1. turn, tape, teeth, tile, toe, try
2. thank, there, the, thaw, theater, thin
3. throw, throat, three, thread, through, throne

Keep This in Mind

- Dictionaries are reference books that list words alphabetically and give explanations for each word.
- Use a dictionary when you're reading and writing.
- Become familiar with the abbreviations, symbols, and organization of the dictionaries you use.

Now Write

Label your paper **Word for Word.** Find ten words that begin with the same letter. Alphabetize them and write a definition for each. Use a dictionary.

Part 2

Follow the Signs

Using Guide Words

Here's the Idea Open a dictionary and look at the top of any page. You will see two words written in large, bold print. They are **guide words.** The guide word on the left is the same as the first entry word on the page. The guide word on the right is the same as the last entry word on the page. All the other words on the page are arranged alphabetically between the guide words. Look at this top portion of a dictionary page.

mushroom	632	**musty**

to start or to go faster —*vi.* to travel on foot over snow, usually with a dog sled —*n.* a journey by mushing
mush·room (mush′room′, -room′) *n.* [OFr. *moisseron* < LL. *mussirio*] **1.** any of various rapid-growing, fleshy fungi having a stalk with an umbrellalike top; popularly, any edible variety, as distinguished from the poisonous ones (*toadstools*) **2.** anything like a mushroom in shape or rapid growth —*adj.* **1.** of or made with mushrooms **2.** like a mushroom in shape or rapid growth —*vi.* **1.** to grow or spread rapidly **2.** to flatten out at the end so as to resemble a mushroom
mush·y (mush′ē) *adj.* mush′i·er, mush′i·est **1.** like mush; thick and soft **2.** [Colloq.] affectionate or sentimental in a way that seems silly or overdone —**mush′i·ly** *adv.* —**mush′i·ness** *n.*
mu·sic (myoo′zik) *n.* [< OFr. < L. < Gr. *mousikē* (*technē*), musical (art) < *mousa*, a Muse] **1.** the art of putting tones together in various melodies, rhythms, and harmonies to form compositions for singing or for playing on instruments **2.** the tones so arranged, or their arrangement **3.** any rhythmic sequence of pleasing sounds [the *music* of the birds] **4.** *a)* a musical composition, esp. in the form of a written or printed score *b)* the musical compositions of a particular style, period, or composer **5.** ability to respond to or take pleasure in music —☆**face the music** [Colloq.] to accept the consequences, however unpleasant —**set to music** to compose music for (a poem, etc.)
mu·si·cal (myoo′zi k′l) *adj.* **1.** of or for the creation or performance of music **2.** melodious or harmonious **3.** fond of or skilled in music **4.** set to music —*n.* ☆a theatrical or film production with dialogue and a musical score with popular songs and dances: in full, **musical comedy** (or **play,** or **drama**) —**mu·si·cal′i·ty** (-kal′ə tē) *n.* —**mu′si·cal·ly** *adv.*

☆**musk·rat** (musk′rat′) *n., pl.* **-rats′, -rat′:** see PLURAL, II, D, l **1.** a N. American rodent living in water and having glossy brown fur, webbed hind feet, and a musklike odor **2.** its fur
musk·y (mus′kē) *adj.* musk′i·er, musk′i·est of, like, or smelling of musk —**musk′i·ness** *n.*
Mus·lim (muz′ləm, mooz′-) *n., adj. same as* MOSLEM
mus·lin (muz′lin) *n.* [< Fr. < It. *mussolino* < *Mussolo*, Mosul, city in Iraq] a strong, often sheer cotton cloth of plain weave; esp., a heavy variety used for sheets, pillowcases, etc.
muss (mus) *n.* [prob. var. of MESS] **1.** [Now Rare] a mess **2.** [Old Slang or Dial.] a squabble —*vt.* to make messy or untidy; disarrange (often with *up*)
mus·sel (mus′'l) *n.* [< OE., ult. < L. *musculus*, mussel, MUSCLE] any of various bivalve mollusks; specif., *a)* an edible saltwater variety *b)* a large freshwater variety with a pearly shell formerly made into buttons
Mus·set (mü se′), (**Louis Charles**) **Al·fred de** (àl fred′ də) 1810-57; Fr. poet & writer
Mus·so·li·ni (moos′ə lē′nē; *E.* moos′ə lē′nē, mus′-), **Be·ni·to** (be nē′tō) 1883-1945; It. dictator; Fascist prime minister of Italy (1922-43): executed
Mus·sorg·sky (moo sôrg′skē), **Mo·dest Pe·tro·vich** (mô dyest′ pyi trô′vich) 1839-81; Russ. composer
Mus·sul·man (mus′'l mən) *n., pl.* **-mans** [< Per. < Ar. *muslim*] [Now Rare] a Moslem

MUSKRAT
(body 9-13 in. long; tail 7-11 in. long)

Guide words tell you at a glance the range of words that appear on the page. They make it quicker and easier to find words. Refer to them as you flip the dictionary pages in search of your word. Keep looking for guide words that are more and more like the word you want.

Check It Out   Look at the portion of a dictionary page on page 24.

- What are the guide words for this page? Would you find the word *museum* on this page? Would you turn the pages forward or backward to find *muscle*?

Try Your Skill   Write the following sets of guide words on your paper: *dinner/dirty, disagree/discover, few/figure,* and *file/fire.* Write each word below under the appropriate set of guide words. Then put the words in each list in alphabetical order.

fight	disc	discomfort	fiction
discover	diploma	direct	fiddle
direction	field	film	dinosaur
final	discount	dirt	disconnect
fine	fifth	directory	filter
disaster	fill	fierce	finish

Keep This in Mind

- Dictionary guide words show the alphabetical range of words on each page. The left guide word is the same as the first word on the page. The right guide word is the same as the last word on the page.

Now Write   If you were writing a composition about outer space, you might have to look up the following words: *astronaut, galaxy, meteor, nebula, planet,* and *satellite.* On your paper, write the title of this lesson, **Follow the Signs.** List the words above. Find each word in the dictionary and read its meaning. Next to each word, write the guide words that appear at the top of the page where the word is found. Then write six sentences. Use one of the words in each sentence.

   Put your work into your folder.

Part 3

Read All About It

Reading a Dictionary Entry

Here's the Idea   A dictionary entry explains the meaning of a word. An entry also gives other helpful information about a word. Not every entry will include all information. However, most dictionaries will give you the following information in a single entry:

The **entry word** itself is in bold type and divided into syllables. For example, *neighborhood* is entered as **neigh·bor·hood.**

The **pronunciation** of the word often appears inside parentheses. Symbols help you to sound out the word. The word is divided into syllables, and an accent mark tells you which syllable to stress.

The **part of speech** is given by an abbreviation in bold print. For example, *noun* is abbreviated *n.;* adverb is abbreviated *adv.*

If a word has **special forms** or **endings,** they will be included next in the entry. For example, the entry for the irregular verb *run* includes the forms **ran, run,** and **running.**

The **origin,** or **history,** of a word is given next, often in brackets. Symbols and abbreviations are used. The symbol < means "came from." Look up unfamiliar abbreviations in the complete list at the front of the dictionary.

Definitions are given in a numbered list. Usually the most common definition is given first.

A word may have a meaning that is used only in casual conversation. This is called a *colloquial*, or informal, meaning. It is followed by the abbreviation [colloq.]. The dictionary also indicates slang, which is very informal, popular language.

Synonyms and **antonyms** may also be listed. Some entries may include a *synonymy*—a group of synonyms and their shades of meaning. Or, the notation "*see* **SYN.** at . . ." may refer you to a synonymy in another entry.

Look at the dictionary entry below.

> **gar·den** (gär′d'n) *n.* [< ONormFr. *gardin* < Frank.: for IE. base see GIRD] **1.** a piece of ground, usually close to a house, for the growing of fruits, flowers, or vegetables **2.** an area of fertile, well-cultivated land: also **garden spot 3.** [*often pl.*] a parklike place for public enjoyment, sometimes having special displays of animals or plants —*vi.* to work in or take care of a garden, lawn, etc.—*vt.* to make a garden of —*adj.* **1.** of, for, or grown in a garden **2.** ordinary; commonplace *[*a *garden* variety of poet*]* —**lead (someone) down the garden path** to mislead or deceive (someone)— **gar′ den·er** *n.*

- How many syllables are there in *garden*? Where is the pronunciation given? What abbreviations for parts of speech do you see? What part of the entry tells you the languages the word came from? What is the most common definition?

Try Your Skill   Turn back to the sample dictionary page in the last lesson, **Follow the Signs.** Answer the following questions.

1. How do you pronounce *mussel*?
2. What parts of speech are listed for *mushroom*?
3. What are the other forms of the adjective *mushy*?
4. Where does the word *muslin* come from?
5. What is the most common definition of *mushroom*?

Keep This in Mind

- A dictionary entry contains the meanings of a word and other helpful information.
- Dictionary entries may differ from book to book.

Now Write   Label your paper **Read All About It.** Using a dictionary, find examples of words with these characteristics:

1. has four syllables
2. has two pronunciations
3. has three parts of speech
4. has come from French

Write the examples on your paper. Save your work.

Part 4

A Good Fit

Finding the Meaning of a Word

Here's the Idea   What do you do if an entry word has several meanings listed? How can you tell which is the right one? In most cases, the sentence in which you found the word, the context, will help you out.

In each sentence below, the context helps you to determine the meaning of the word *eye*.

1. There is something in my *eye*. (In this context, *eye* means "organ of sight.")

2. The *eye* of the hurricane passed over our house. (In this context, *eye* means "calm center.")

3. Can you thread the *eye* of this needle? (In this context *eye* means "hole.")

First read through the definitions given in the dictionary. Then try to find the meaning that fits the particular context.

Check It Out   Read this sentence and dictionary entry.

Will your bicycle fit in this *space*?

> **space** (spas) *n.* [< OFr. < L. *spatium*]   **1.** *a)* the area that stretches in all directions, has no limits, and contains all things in the universe   *b) same as* OUTER SPACE   **2.** *a)* the distance, expanse, or area between, over, or within things [the *space* between desks]   *b)* area or room for something [parking *space;* advertising *space* in a newspaper, etc.]   **3.** length or period of time [the *space* of a week]   ☆**4.** accommodations that can be had or reserved on a train, airplane, etc.   **5.** *Math.* a set of points or elements that can be represented in a coordinate system by a single real number, a pair of numbers, etc.   **6.** *Music* the open area between any two lines of a staff   **7.** *Printing*   *a)* a blank piece of type metal used to separate words, letters, etc.   *b)* the area left vacant by this in a printed or typed line —*adj.* of space, esp. outer space —*vt.* **spaced, spac'ing** to arrange with spaces in between [trees *spaced* evenly; concerts *spaced* throughout the season] —**space'less** *adj.* —**spac'er** *n.*

• Which definition fits the context of the sentence?

Try Your Skill Read this dictionary entry for the word *grade*. You can see that there are many meanings. Some meanings are for *grade* as a noun, and some are for *grade* as a verb.

Each of the meanings is used in one of the sentences that follows. Write the number of each sentence. After it, write the meaning that matches the use of the word *grade*.

> **grade** (grad) *n.* [Fr. < L. *gradus*, a step < *gradi*, to step < IE. base *ghredh-*, to stride] **1.** any of the stages in a series; step; degree [civil service jobs arranged in *grades*] **2.** *a*) a degree in a scale of quality, rank, etc. [*grade* A eggs] *b*) any of the official ranks or ratings of officers or enlisted men [an army colonel and a navy captain are in *grade* 0-6] *c*) an accepted standard or level [up to *grade*] *d*) a group of the same rank, merit, etc. ☆**3.** *a*) the degree of rise or descent of a slope, as of a road *b*) the slope itself [climbing a steep *grade*] **4.** the ground level around a building ☆**5.** a division in a school curriculum, usually equal to one year ☆**6.** a mark or rating on an examination, in a school course, etc. —*vt.* **grad′ed, grad′ing** **1.** to arrange in grades; sort [to *grade* apples] ☆**2.** to give a grade (sense 6) to **3.** to gradate ☆**4.** to level or slope (ground) evenly for a road, etc. —*vi.* **1.** to be of a certain grade **2.** to change gradually [green *grading* into blue] —☆**make the grade** **1.** to get to the top of a steep incline **2.** to overcome obstacles and succeed

1. Ronnie's *grade* on the math quiz was 88.
2. Mom bought one dozen extra large *grade* A eggs.
3. The driver slowed down as she approached the steep *grade*.
4. My sister Bonnie is in the ninth *grade*.
5. The sunset you painted is realistic, especially where the yellow *grades* into orange.

Keep This in Mind

- If you are not sure what a word means, look it up. Read all the definitions of the word. Use the context of the sentence to help you find the appropriate definition.

Now Write Look up the word *run* in the dictionary. Copy five meanings of *run*. For each meaning, write a sentence. Label your paper **A Good Fit** and put it in your folder.

The Right Language at the Right Time

Part 1

On Occasion

Standard and Nonstandard English

Here's the Idea Suppose you were going to play a game of baseball. Would you dress and act as you do in English class? Probably not. Instead, you would suit your clothes and actions to the situation. In the same way, different situations call for different ways of speaking and writing. There are two kinds of language that you can use. These are standard English and nonstandard English.

Standard English is language that follows the rules of good grammar and usage. It is correct in any situation. When you use standard English, everyone can understand you. That is why most salespeople, teachers, reporters, and politicians use standard English.

Nonstandard English is language that does not follow the rules of standard grammar and usage. It is sometimes used in casual conversation or in friendly letters. Expressions like *them there* and *I been asking him* are nonstandard English. So are words like *ain't* and *cool*.

Try to be aware of the type of language you use in every situation. Nonstandard English may be acceptable in casual conversation with people you know well. However, in class discussion, in talks, and in most writing, you should use standard English. Whenever you speak or write to someone you don't know well, use standard English. This will help you to make a good impression.

Check It Out Compare these examples of standard and nonstandard English.

Standard	Nonstandard
1. The baby doesn't talk yet.	1. The baby don't talk yet.
2. Those bananas aren't ripe.	2. Them bananas ain't ripe.

3. You never said anything.
4. You and I stand here.
5. I sit in the back.

3. You never said nothing.
4. You and me stand here.
5. I set in the back.

- What is nonstandard about the second sentence in each pair?

Try Your Skill   Choose the sentence in each pair that is written in standard English.

1. There ain't no top to this box.
   There isn't any top to this box.
2. Let's us set down on this bench.
   Let's sit down on this bench.
3. You couldn't see anything but snow.
   You couldn't see nothing but snow.
4. I've seen you somewhere before.
   I seen you somewheres before.

Keep This in Mind

- Standard English is correct in any situation.
- Use standard English in class discussion, in talks, and in most writing.

Now Write   Make each sentence below show standard usage. Choose the correct word from the two shown in parentheses. Write the sentences using the correct word. Label your paper **On Occasion,** and save it in your folder.

1. Harry (don't, doesn't) know where he put them.
2. These strings (are, is) all tangled.
3. Maury and (him, he) will help us.
4. (These, Them) spoons should be washed.
5. Don't eat (no, any) dessert yet, Martha.

Write On!

Using and Misusing Slang

Here's the Idea What would you think if someone said to you, "Hey, *like wow*, you're really *groovy*"? You would probably think the language sounded very odd. However, the words *wow* and *groovy* were once very popular. These words were slang terms in the late fifties and early sixties. They sound strange today because they are no longer commonly used.

Slang is a type of nonstandard English. It is made up of colorful words and phrases that are fashionable for a short time. You probably know many slang terms that are popular today. Some of these terms are very clever. Some express ideas in fresh, new ways. However, even the most clever of these terms should be avoided in most speech and writing. There are two reasons for avoiding slang.

First, slang is not always understood by everyone. It is often known only to certain groups. If you use a slang term, you risk being misunderstood by some readers or listeners.

Second, most slang is temporary. It seldom lasts long enough to become accepted as standard. Therefore, writing that uses slang quickly becomes dated and odd-sounding.

Slang should be used only in casual conversations with friends. It should never be used in compositions, reports, business letters, or talks. However, it may be used to make the dialogue in a story more realistic.

If you are uncertain about whether a word is slang, check it in a dictionary. If a word is slang, it usually will not be included in the dictionary. If it is included, it will be labeled *slang*.

Check It Out   Read the following sentences. The words in italics are examples of slang from the 1960's and 1970's.

1. Though many Presidents were interested in sports, few of them were *jocks* themselves.
2. When the ship struck the pier, the captain did not *freak out*.
3. In class we had a really *heavy rap session* about the future.
4. Andrea and I thought the short story was *far out*.

- Which of the slang terms used above are still popular? Which are not?
- What does this tell you about slang?

Try Your Skill   Rewrite the sentences in **Check It Out.** Change the slang expressions to standard English.

Keep This in Mind

- Current, popular, nonstandard English is known as slang.
- Use slang only in casual conversation with friends or in dialogue in a short story.

Now Write   Find a magazine that is popular with teenagers. Look through this magazine for examples of slang. Write down the examples you find. Compare these with examples found by your classmates. What standard English words or phrases could be used in place of these slang terms? Label your paper **Write On!** and save it in your folder.

Improving Your Sentences

One of a Kind

Writing Good Sentences

Here's the Idea   A sentence is a group of words that states a complete thought. Sentences can state thoughts in many ways. Read the following sentences about fog. Which sentence do you think is more interesting?

Fog doesn't make any noise.   The fog comes on little cat feet.

You probably prefer the sentence on the right, which was written by the poet Carl Sandburg. It's a more interesting sentence because it states the idea in a clear, fresh way. It appeals to your imagination. It has a stronger impact.

Below are other examples of sentences that express ideas in clear, direct, and original ways.

What we have to learn to do, we learn by doing.—ARISTOTLE
You can never plan the future by the past.—EDMUND BURKE
The human heart has hidden treasures.—CHARLOTTE BRONTË
My soul has grown deep like the rivers.—LANGSTON HUGHES

Every sentence makes a point. No matter what point you are making in a sentence, you can make the sentence effective. Keep to one idea. Be clear and direct. Use your senses and imagination to express an idea in an original way.

Check It Out   Read the following sentences.

1. It would be night soon, and I was afraid.
2. The waves pounded the rocky shore.
3. Do you know how to eat with chopsticks?
4. Americans should use less of the world's fuel.
5. Adobe is sun-dried clay used for building.

- Does each sentence express a single complete thought?
- Is each sentence clear and direct?

Try Your Skill Number your paper from 1 to 5. Write a sentence in response to each of the five directions below. Make your sentences direct, lively, and original. Use details from your memory or from your imagination.

1. Describe your family.
2. Explain why you like music.
3. Tell one event from your childhood.
4. Give a definition of a good vacation.
5. Tell how you travel to school each day.

Keep This in Mind

- A sentence is a group of words that expresses a complete thought.
- Every sentence should have a meaning that is clear to the reader.
- A good sentence is clear, direct, and lively.

Now Write Write a sentence that tells something you did recently. Write a sentence that tells what your favorite possession is. Then write a sentence that describes it. Write a sentence that tells why you like your best friend. Finally, write a sentence that explains how to do something.

Read your five sentences. Are they clear and interesting? If not, rewrite them.

On your paper, write the title of this lesson, **One of a Kind.** Copy your sentences and put them into your folder.

Say Something

Avoiding Empty Sentences

Here's the Idea   Sentences that do not tell the reader anything are called **empty sentences.** There are two kinds of empty sentences. The first kind of empty sentence repeats an idea.

> Solving math problems is easy for me because I am good at math.

It is understood that a person who is good at math solves math problems easily. The idea should not be stated twice.

You can improve this kind of empty sentence by making it simpler. You can also improve it by adding more information.

> I have always been good at math.
> Solving math problems has always been easy for me, and I have always enjoyed problems with fractions.

The second kind of empty sentence gives an unsupported opinion. The writer makes a strong statement that captures a reader's attention, but leaves the reader asking "Why?"

> TV commercials should not be aimed at young children.

Such strong statements are empty of meaning unless supported by facts, reasons, or examples. Supporting information may be given in the same sentence or in another sentence.

> TV commercials should not be aimed at young children, who respond to what they watch without thinking.
> TV commercials should not be aimed at young children. Studies show that children respond to what they watch without thinking about it.

Supporting evidence might also be developed in longer pieces of writing, such as paragraphs or compositions.

You must offer readers a reason for an opinion. Otherwise,

your writing will seem empty. Your readers may not agree with your opinion, but they will know why you think as you do.

Check It Out   Read the following empty sentences.

1. This book is boring, and I think it is very dull.
2. All states should have safety inspections for cars.
3. Breakfast cereals contain too much sugar.
4. Many people enjoy tennis because it is an enjoyable game.
5. Reading is important for everyone.

- Which sentences repeat an idea? Which sentences give an unsupported opinion?
- How would you improve these empty sentences?

Try Your Skill   Rewrite each of the empty sentences below.

1. Our refrigerator doesn't work because it is broken.
2. Don got a raise, so he is making more money now.
3. Every family member should help do household chores.
4. The U.S. should give money to support its Olympic athletes.

Keep This in Mind

- There are two kinds of empty sentences. One kind repeats an idea. The other kind states an opinion without supporting it.
- Improve sentences that repeat an idea by making them simpler or by adding more information. Improve sentences with unsupported opinions by including reasons for your opinion.

Now Write   Label your paper *Empty Sentences*. Find or write two examples of each kind of empty sentence. Then improve the sentences by eliminating repetition or by supplying reasons. Write the improved sentences. Keep your paper in your folder.

Part 3

Streamlining

Avoiding Padded Sentences

Here's the Idea   A **padded sentence** contains useless words and phrases. The main idea is buried by unnecessary words. Read these examples of phrases that pad sentences:

on account of the fact that	what I want is
because of the fact that	the point is
due to the fact that	the reason is
what I mean is	the thing is
what I think is	

Often, you can improve a padded sentence by taking out the unnecessary words. Sometimes, you will have to rewrite the sentence completely.

Padded: What I mean is that the store manager was rude.
Improved: The store manager was rude.

Padded: I kept the entire group waiting due to the fact that I couldn't find my money for quite a while.
Improved: I kept the entire group waiting while I looked for my money.

Many groups of words using *who, which,* or *that* are unnecessary in a sentence. When you use them, be sure they add to the meaning of the sentence. Notice how the sentence below is improved when unnecessary words are removed.

Padded   Our car, which is old and pink, attracts attention.
Improved   Our old, pink car attracts attention.

Check It Out   Read these padded sentences.

1. What I think is that the butler did it.
2. I took my shoes off on account of the fact that my feet hurt.

3. My cousin Jackie, who is older, teaches at Longmeadow High School.

- How would you improve each of these padded sentences?

Try Your Skill Improve the padded sentences below. Take out any unnecessary words or phrases or rewrite the entire sentence.

1. It took the letter two weeks to get there on account of the fact that the ZIP code was wrong.

2. My old typewriter is just fine for me due to the fact that I'm used to it.

3. The sandwiches, which were made with tuna salad, tasted good with tomato soup.

4. The reason why I couldn't lock your bicycle is because I lost the key.

5. Sam is doing all the shopping this week and the reason is that he thinks he can cut the food bill.

Keep This in Mind

- Padded sentences have unnecessary words and phrases.
- Omit any words that add nothing to the idea in a sentence. Sometimes you will have to rewrite a sentence completely.

Now Write Label your paper *Padded Sentences*. Find or write four examples of padded sentences. Improve the sentences by removing any unnecessary words and phrases. Rewrite the complete sentence if necessary.

When you have finished, put your paper into your folder.

Part 4

Together Again

Combining Sentences

Here's the Idea   Some sentences that you write contain related ideas. Often you can combine them into one sentence.

Sometimes two sentences contain similar ideas of equal importance. You can combine sentences like these with a comma and the word *and*.

> Jeanne will design the posters. Doug will have them printed.
> Jeanne will design the posters, **and** Doug will have them printed.

Sometimes two sentences state contrasting ideas of equal importance. You can combine sentences like these with a comma and the word *but*.

> Julio wanted pizza. Cora insisted on hamburgers.
> Julio wanted pizza, **but** Cora insisted on hamburgers.

At other times, two sentences state a choice between equally important ideas. You can combine sentences like these with a comma and the word *or*.

> I could buy a gerbil now. I could wait until I have enough money for a snake.
> I could buy a gerbil now, **or** I could wait until I have enough money for a snake.

Check It Out   Read the following sentences.

1. You can use varnish, or you can paint the wood.
2. This knob controls the volume, and that one adjusts the tone.
3. Linda drove in four runs, but we still lost the game.

- Which sentence combines similar ideas?
- Which sentence combines contrasting ideas?
- Which sentence combines equal ideas and offers a choice between them?

Try Your Skill   Combine each pair of sentences. Follow the directions given in parentheses.

1. A lion came down to the river to drink. The gazelles scattered in all directions. (Join with **, and.**)

2. The true camel has two humps. The dromedary has only one. (Join with **, but.**)

3. The countdown went smoothly. The launch was on time. (Join with **, and.**)

4. We could practice every weekday afternoon. We could practice all day on Saturday instead. (Join with **, or.**)

5. Diesel engines use less fuel. Gasoline engines run more smoothly. (Join with **, but.**)

Keep This in Mind

- If two sentences state ideas that are closely related, you can sometimes combine them to make one sentence.
- Use a comma and *and* to join sentences that state similar ideas of equal importance.
- Use a comma and *but* to join sentences that state contrasting ideas of equal importance.
- Use a comma and *or* to join sentences that offer a choice between ideas of equal importance.

Now Write   The following paragraph would be smoother and clearer if some sentences were combined. Rewrite the paragraph. Combine the numbered pairs of sentences with *and* or *but*. Keep your paper in your folder.

1. The weather had been hot for days. The crops were dry. 2. Rain was desperately needed. None came. 3. By evening the crops had withered dangerously. The farmers had given up hope. 4. Fortunately, a breeze began to blow during the night. The town awoke to the sound of rain pattering on its roofs and windowsills.

Part 5

Something Borrowed

Combining Sentence Parts

Here's the Idea   Sometimes only parts of two sentences are closely related. If so, you may be able to combine the parts in one sentence. Any repeated words or ideas can then be dropped.

Some sentence parts state similar ideas of equal importance. Such parts can be combined with *and*.

> The astronauts opened the cargo doors. *The astronauts* released the satellite.
> The astronauts opened the cargo doors **and** released the satellite.

Notice that the repeated words, *the astronauts*, were dropped.

Other sentence parts express contrasting ideas of equal importance. Such parts can usually be joined by *but*.

> We discovered the leak. *We* couldn't stop it.
> We discovered the leak **but** couldn't stop it.

Sometimes sentence parts express a choice between ideas. Such parts can usually be joined by *or*.

> Do you want to go to a movie? *Do you want to go* to a ball game?
> Do you want to go to a movie **or** to a ball game?

Check It Out   Study the following examples.

> 1. Lucy may be a famous singer some day.
>   *Lucy may be a famous* dancer *some day.*
>   Lucy may be a famous singer *or* dancer some day.
> 2. We were tired from the trip.
>   *We were* happy to be home safe.
>   We were tired from the trip *but* happy to be home safe.

3. The engine coughed.
The engine died.
The engine coughed *and* died.

- Which sentence combines similar parts of equal importance?
- Which sentence combines contrasting parts?
- Which sentence combines parts that offer a choice between ideas?

Try Your Skill   Combine each pair of sentences. Follow the directions in parentheses.

1. Tina rowed. Jeff *rowed*. (Join with **and.**)
2. Do you have a pen? *Do you have* a pencil? (Join with **or.**)
3. I dialed the number. *I* held my breath. (Join with **and.**)
4. Our quarterback was eager. *Our quarterback was* inexperienced. (Join with **but.**)
5. Volcanoes release ash. *Volcanoes release* lava. (Join with **and.**)

Keep This in Mind

- Use *and* to combine similar sentence parts of equal importance.
- Use *but* to combine contrasting sentence parts.
- Use *or* to combine sentence parts that offer a choice.

Now Write   Combine the following pairs of sentences. Use *and, but,* or *or.* Decide on your own how to combine the sentences.

1. You can take this bus. You can wait for the express.
2. Are frogs reptiles? Are frogs amphibians?
3. The news startled Carlos. The news also startled his mother.
4. Sarah enjoyed the play. Sarah had to leave early.
5. Sunlight reddened the trees. Sunlight glowed on the lake.

Exploring Paragraphs

Part 1

Togetherness

Defining a Paragraph

Here's the Idea   A **paragraph** is a group of sentences that work together. They develop one main idea. Each sentence in a paragraph says something about the main idea.

See if the sentences in each of these groups work together.

1   Captain Lockwood shifted uneasily in her seat as she landed the jumbo jet. She could see nothing anywhere on this empty land. The trees and rocks were bathed in a strange pink light. Suddenly she gasped, as a sickening odor began to creep into the plane. She cleared her throat. She felt tense. She told her passengers that they had landed on an unknown planet.

2   The mist hung over the lake like a curtain. Sleepy ducks shook themselves awake to prepare for daybreak. The old rowboat skimmed across the smooth, dark surface. A baited hook made circles as it dropped into the water. Quietly, the lone fisherman turned up his collar and settled in for a morning's fishing.

3   The next time you're looking for a healthy, crunchy snack, try sprouting beans. First, combine a few tablespoons of lentils and two cups of water in a quart jar. Second, cover the jar with cheesecloth. Let the beans soak overnight. Rinse and drain the beans twice each day for three days. By the fourth day, your sprouts will be ready to eat. Try them in a sandwich or in a salad.

Check It Out   Look again at the three groups of sentences. The first group of sentences tells a story. The second group describes a scene. The third group explains a process. Are these groups of sentences paragraphs?

- Does each group of sentences develop one idea?
- Does every sentence in each group say something about the main idea?

Try Your Skill Read the groups of sentences below. One of them is a paragraph. Two are not. Number your paper from 1 to 3. For the group that is a paragraph, write the main idea. For each group that is not a paragraph, explain why it is not.

1 Some people always seem to do their best work late in the day. Many old movies are on TV after midnight. These people are called "night people." They often take a long time to wake up in the morning. They get more energy as the day goes on. By evening, they are usually going at full speed.

2 Once there were millions of buffalo roaming free on the Great Plains. Many Indians also lived in that part of the Old West. If you want to see buffalo now, you have to go to a zoo or animal farm. A good zoo has healthy-looking animals. Some zoos are famous for one particular animal.

3 The dog that roams our neighborhood draws a lot of attention. His eyes have a droopy, sad look. His ears are small and pointed. A curly, spotted coat of fur covers his short, stubby body. When this strange-looking creature passes by, everyone stares at him.

Keep This in Mind

- A paragraph is a group of sentences that develop one idea.
- Every sentence in the paragraph should say something about the main idea.

Now Write On your paper, write **Togetherness.** From this lesson, choose one of the groups of sentences that is not a paragraph. Take out any sentences that do not belong. Copy the remaining sentences in the form of a paragraph. You may have to change some sentences slightly. Finally, read the completed paragraph to yourself. Notice how the paragraph now develops one idea.

Keep the paragraph in your folder.

Part 2

All the Same

Recognizing Paragraph Unity

Here's the Idea A paragraph develops one main idea. All the sentences in a paragraph should say something about that main idea. When they do, a paragraph has **unity.**

Read the following paragraph. Notice how all the sentences develop the idea of saving a school.

> Our city must not close Lakeside High School. It is true that enrollment has dropped from 1,745 students to 1,380 in the last five years. However, closing Lakeside would deal a severe blow to our North Side neighborhood. First, Lakeside has never been a problem school. Second, the thirty-year-old building is still in good condition. Most important, this experimental school offers job training programs that few other schools in the city offer. Our students deserve a good education in their own neighborhood. Keep Lakeside open.

Check It Out Now read the following paragraph.

> More than one-fourth of the world's population lives in cities or their surrounding areas. Tokyo, Mexico City, Shanghai, New York, and Buenos Aires are the five most heavily populated city areas in the world. Tokyo, for instance, has more than eleven and a half million people in its city area. New York City, with almost ten million people, is the most heavily populated city area in the United States. All over the world, more and more people are living in or near cities.

- Do all of the sentences say something about one main idea? Does the paragraph have unity?

Try Your Skill Each main idea below is followed by several sentences. Some of the sentences say something about the main idea. Some do not. Copy each main idea on your paper.

Below it, list only those sentences that say something about the main idea.

Main Idea: The trunk of an elephant is strong and useful.

1. An elephant uses its trunk to feel and grasp objects.
2. An elephant is smart and can learn many tricks.
3. Elephants take good care of each other.
4. The trunk of an elephant is about six feet long and weighs about three hundred pounds.
5. An elephant can sleep standing up.
6. An elephant smells, drinks, and feeds itself with its trunk.
7. One of the most famous elephants in this country was named Jumbo.

Main Idea: The United States has received many immigrants throughout its history.

1. Most of the original colonists came from England and Ireland.
2. Many immigrants have had trouble finding jobs.
3. After 1820, most immigrants came from Germany and Italy.
4. An immigrant must pass tests before becoming a citizen.
5. Recently, many immigrants have come from Mexico and the West Indies.
6. Part of a citizenship test is written, and part is spoken.

Keep This in Mind

- Each sentence in a paragraph should say something about the main idea. Then a paragraph has unity.

Now Write Choose a hobby, sport, or activity that interests you. Write the topic you choose. Number your paper from 1 to 5. Then, write five sentences that say something about your topic.

When you have finished, put your paper into your folder.

Part 3

What's the Big Idea?

Using a Topic Sentence

Here's the Idea   Most paragraphs begin with a sentence that states the main idea. This sentence is called the **topic sentence,** and it has two important purposes.

First, it helps you unify your paragraph. A topic sentence helps you, the writer, keep your main idea in mind. Check to make sure that every sentence in a paragraph works with the topic sentence. Omit sentences that do not say something about the main idea.

Second, a topic sentence acts as a guide for your readers. It tells your readers what to expect in the sentences that follow.

Check It Out   Read the paragraph below.

> Is the idea of an iceberg off the coast of Saudi Arabia simply a wild mirage? Some scientists don't think so. They believe that someday icebergs might be towed from the Antarctic to the Red Sea. There the icebergs would be melted for drinking water and irrigation. Tests are being conducted with 125-ton wooden icebergs to see if the idea will work.

- What is the topic sentence?
- What is the main idea of this paragraph?

Try Your Skill   Read the three groups of sentences below. Decide which sentence could be used as the topic sentence for each group. Number your paper from 1 to 3. Copy the topic sentences.

1. (a) Wearing rubber gloves, first remove the old finish with a varnish remover and steel wool.

(b) Then rinse the table carefully and allow it to dry.

(c) A coat of lemon oil applied with a soft rag will provide the final, gleaming touch.

(d) Next, sand the surface smooth with sandpaper.

(e) With a little know-how and a lot of energy, you can transform a dingy, old wooden table into a showpiece.

2. (a) He joined the major leagues in 1948 as a forty-two-year-old rookie for the Cleveland Indians.

(b) Seventeen years later he pitched three shutout innings for Kansas City in his final major league game.

(c) He began playing in the National Negro League, where he pitched 3,000 games and won 300 of them by shutouts.

(d) Satchel Paige was a major league pitcher with an arm of steel.

(e) At an age when most ball players have retired, he pitched two shutouts in his first three games in the major leagues.

3. (a) Wolves share food with each other.

(b) Wolves are now believed to be noble and wise animals.

(c) A destructive wolf may be only ill or hungry.

(d) They are friendly and playful with their own group.

(e) Wolves protect each other.

Keep This in Mind

- A paragraph must have a topic sentence.
- A topic sentence states the main idea of the paragraph.

Now Write   On your paper, write the title of this lesson, **What's the Big Idea?** Choose two topics you would like to write about. You might choose to write about a friend, a pet, or a hobby. Write a topic sentence for each of your topics. Put your work into your folder.

Part 4

Show Your Support

Developing a Paragraph

Here's the Idea   The main idea of a paragraph is introduced in the topic sentence. The main idea should be developed in the sentences that follow. There are three ways to develop the main idea: descriptive details, specific examples, or facts and figures. One way will usually be more suitable than another to develop a particular main idea.

Descriptive details can make a subject come to life for the reader.

> The armored tank of the animal kingdom is the armadillo. This thick-shelled, short-legged mammal is slow-moving and might easily be caught. Because the armadillo has small back teeth, it cannot bite in self-defense. When stopped by an enemy, the armadillo rolls itself into a tight ball. With only its armored shell exposed, the armadillo is safe from attackers.

Specific examples can develop a general statement.

> A special family tradition can make any day a holiday. Each winter after the first big snowfall, the members of my family rush outside to celebrate. For hours we toboggan down the slippery hill at the end of our street. Chilled and weary, we return home to thaw. We wrap our hands tightly around mugs of steaming chocolate. We laugh and recall past winters.

Facts and figures can prove a point or make an idea clear.

> Despite their small size, some insects are able to perform amazing feats. A tiny flea, for instance, is able to jump seven inches high and a distance of thirteen inches. The male cicada, a flylike insect, can produce a noise that can be heard over a distance of one-quarter of a mile. The speed of the great monarch butterfly has been recorded at twenty miles per hour. These tiny insects are small-scale Olympic heroes.

Read the following paragraph.

   Coal will probably be an important fuel in the energy plans of the United States for the next twenty years. Coal represents as much as ninety percent of the total fossil-fuel reserves of the U.S. Yet it supplies less than twenty percent of the nation's energy needs. A proposal has been made to double coal production in the next ten years or so. This increase will help reduce our dependence on foreign energy supplies. It will also give the U.S. time to develop other energy sources.—*Scientific American*

   •   Is the topic sentence developed by descriptive details? Is it developed by examples? Is it developed by facts and figures?

Try Your Skill   Find and write the topic sentence in the following paragraph. Then write *Descriptive Details, Specific Examples,* or *Facts and Figures* to tell how the main idea is developed.

   Many people consider Jim Thorpe to be America's greatest athlete. In the Olympics of 1912, he won the pentathlon and the decathlon. As a major league baseball player in 1919, his batting average was .327. As a professional football player, he consistently kicked a football more than sixty yards. No other athlete has played so well in so many different sports.

Keep This in Mind

   •   The main idea of a paragraph may be developed by using descriptive details, specific examples, or facts and figures.

Now Write   On your paper, write **Show Your Support.** Take out the topic sentences you wrote in the last lesson. Choose one. List three details, examples, or facts and figures that you could use to develop the topic sentence. Save your work.

Part 5

Brand Names

Recognizing Three Kinds of Paragraphs

Here's the Idea When you write, you may want to tell a story. You may want to describe something or someone. You may want to explain something or tell how to do something. For each of these times you would use one of the three main kinds of paragraphs.

A **narrative paragraph** tells a story or tells something that happened. It usually tells the story in the order that it happened.

A **descriptive paragraph** is a picture in words. It appeals to the senses. This kind of paragraph describes something so that you can see, hear, feel, smell, or taste it.

An **explanatory paragraph** explains something. It tells *how* to do something, *why* something happened, or *what* something is. A *how* paragraph explains something step by step. A *why* paragraph gives reasons or facts to support an idea or opinion. A *what* paragraph defines something.

Check It Out Read the paragraph below.

> The afternoon sun was beaming through the sheer white curtains at the window. The delicate leaves of the fern plants rustled faintly as the cat sprang to the window seat. Glossy patches of orange and brown cat fur shone like autumn leaves in the sunshine. With a lazy purr, the cat nestled against the well-worn cushions for a midday snooze.

- Does this paragraph tell a story, describe, or explain? Is the paragraph narrative, descriptive, or explanatory?

Try Your Skill Read these paragraphs. What kind is each? On your paper, write *Narrative, Descriptive,* or *Explanatory.*

1   At last, we were off on our trip to visit Grandma and Grandpa Johnson. First, we stopped for gas. We also had the tire pressure and the oil checked. Then, we checked our map to find the best route. Finally, we headed for the highway to begin the long drive to Detroit.

2   Jogging has many advantages over other sports. Unlike tennis, jogging doesn't require any special equipment, outfit, or court. Unlike baseball or football, jogging does not require a team of players. Unlike a golf game, which can take up to a whole day, jogging can be completed in a short time. Why bother with more complicated sports when jogging is so easy?

3   To fix a broken window, first remove all the broken glass from the frame. Second, remove the old putty and any bits of old wood or paint. When the frame has been cleaned out, paint it. Then, put in the new glass. Finally, put new putty around the window to seal the glass in the frame.

Keep This in Mind

- A narrative paragraph tells a story or tells something that happened.
- A descriptive paragraph describes something or someone.
- An explanatory paragraph explains *how, why*, or *what*.

Now Write   On your paper, write the title of this lesson, **Brand Names.** Read over your topic sentence and notes from **Now Write** in the last two lessons. Which of the three kinds of paragraphs would you use for your topic? Write its name on your paper. Explain why it is the best kind to use for your topic. Save your work in your folder.

Writing a Paragraph

Part 1

Stepping Stones

Writing as a Process

Here's the Idea   Now that you know what a paragraph is, you are ready to start writing a paragraph of your own. Before you begin, however, you should understand a few things about writing. Writing is a process. Whatever you write, you must go through certain steps. These steps are called the **process of writing.**

The first step takes place before you begin to write. It is called **pre-writing.** Pre-writing is all of the planning you do before you write. It includes choosing and narrowing a topic. It also includes gathering and organizing your ideas.

The second step is **writing the first draft.** In this step, you write down your ideas in good order, letting your thoughts flow freely. Don't worry too much about grammar, capitalization, punctuation, or spelling. Just write your ideas down in paragraph form. You will have time later to correct any errors.

The final step in the writing process is **revising.** Now you check to see that your ideas are well organized and make sense. You might take some ideas out, add new ones, or shift sentences around. When you are satisfied with your paragraph, you proofread to make sure that your grammar, capitalization, punctuation, and spelling are correct.

As you work through this chapter, you will use the three steps of the process of writing to write a paragraph. You will see how the process can help you to become a better writer.

Check It Out   Read how one writer writes.

> "I've always been an early riser. I love to get up at sunrise and start writing. In the early morning I can let my thoughts flow on and on, as if I were a river of ideas. Later, I'll go back and revise, of course, but in those early hours I feel as though I could write forever."
>
> —TERRI S. BLAKE

- How does Terri Blake follow the process of writing?

Try Your Skill   Read the list of writing activities below. Decide which part of the process of writing each activity belongs to. Write *Pre-writing, Writing a first draft,* or *Revising.*

1. putting your ideas into sentences for the first time
2. reading a magazine to get ideas for a paragraph
3. checking spelling and punctuation
4. making a list of topics for a paragraph
5. rewriting a sentence so that it makes more sense
6. organizing ideas

Keep This in Mind

- Pre-writing is the planning you do before you write.
- Writing the first draft is writing a rough version of your paragraph.
- Revising is improving what you have written.

Now Write   One of the best ways to practice writing is to keep a journal. A journal is a notebook in which you write down your thoughts, feelings, and ideas about anything that interests you.

Keeping a journal can also help you come up with ideas to write about. If you read a good book, write about it in your journal. If something interesting or exciting happens to you, put it in your journal. Try to write something in your journal every day.

Begin your journal today. Take out some paper and write about something funny or frightening that happened to you recently. Label your paper *Journal.* When you get a notebook to use as your journal, add this paper to it.

Part 2

A Matter of Choice

Pre-Writing: Choosing a Subject

Here's the Idea   Often your teacher will give you a specific topic to write about. Sometimes, however, you will be given the chance to choose your own topic. Choosing a good topic requires careful thought. A good topic will interest both you and your readers. As you think about a topic for a paragraph, ask yourself some questions like these:

What do I know about?
What would I like to learn more about?
What interesting things have I read about or experienced?
What is happening around me that I could see and describe?

The answers to these questions might give you ideas for some paragraph topics.

You may also have a number of possible topics in your journal. Read over the thoughts, feelings, and experiences you have written down there. You might be surprised at how many good topics you will find.

Reading books, magazines, and newspapers is another good way to find interesting topics. If you read something that interests you, make a note about it in your journal. You may even want to clip out interesting articles and paste them in your notebook.

Brainstorming can help you to find topics to write about, too. When you brainstorm, you start with one general idea. Then you write down everything that comes to mind about that idea. You can brainstorm alone or with others.

Check It Out   Following is an example of some notes one student made while brainstorming. Notice the way one general idea can lead to several topic ideas.

A day at the zoo

Jim and I went to the zoo.

The Zoo (main idea)

The monkey house
The seal pond
The lion house

My Aunt Sarah is a zookeeper.
↓
She takes care of the children's zoo.

How zoos help to protect wildlife
↓
Caring for baby animals at the zoo

- What topic ideas can you find in the notes?
- What other ideas about the zoo can you add?

Try Your Skill   Below are six general topics. Choose one and do some brainstorming about it. Write down everything that comes to your mind. Then try to find several topic ideas in your notes. Save these ideas in your folder.

basketball	cars	museums
music	summer	outer space

Keep This in Mind

- A good topic will interest you and your readers.
- Use different methods to find a topic. These include journal-writing, reading, and brainstorming.

Now Write   Develop a list of topics for a paragraph. Try out the different methods you have learned about in this lesson. Save the list in your folder.

Part 3

Straight and Narrow

Pre-Writing: Narrowing a Topic

Here's the Idea Sometimes the subject you want to write about is too general or too broad to be covered in one paragraph. Telling everything you know about sports, for instance, requires more than one paragraph. You need to narrow the subject so that you can write a lively, detailed paragraph.

One good way to narrow a subject is to ask questions about it. Ask questions like *who? what? when? where? why?* and *how?* Then use the answers to develop a specific topic. For example, you could narrow the subject "sports" like this:

Who?	Aztec Indians
What?	invented basketball
When?	16th century
Where?	Mexico
Why?	to amuse spectators
How?	put ball through stone ring

Now you have narrowed the general subject "sports" to the specific topic "the origin of basketball." You can use this topic to write a detailed and interesting paragraph like this one:

> The game of basketball is more than four hundred years old. A form of the game was first played by the Aztec Indians in Mexico. The object of the game was to put a solid rubber ball through a stone ring. While this sounds very much like modern basketball, there was one important difference. The Aztecs often chopped off the head of the captain of the losing team!

You need not answer all of these questions every time you narrow a topic. Some questions will not always apply. However, answer as many as you can. Your writing will become livelier and more interesting.

Check It Out See how the general subject "caves" has been narrowed.

Who?	Carla Lombardo
What?	explored Mammoth Cave
When?	July, 1990
Where?	Mammoth Cave National Park, Kentucky
Why?	wanted to see a big cave
How?	took a walk by herself
Narrowed Topic	Carla Lombardo's walk alone through Mammoth Cave last July

• Do you see how asking questions about a general subject can help you to narrow it?

Try Your Skill These subjects are too general for one paragraph. Choose two and write them on your paper. Ask *who? what? when? where? why?* and *how?* about each subject. Use the answers you get to write a narrowed topic for each general subject.

a difficult choice	boats	hobbies	flying saucers
losing something	movies	sports	feeling scared

Keep This in Mind

• Narrow a general subject by asking *who? what? when? where? why?* and *how?* questions.
• Choose a topic that you can cover in a paragraph.

Now Write In this section you will be writing a paragraph. You will complete one step of the process in each lesson.

In the last lesson, **A Matter of Choice,** you developed a list of ideas for a paragraph. Choose one idea that you would like to write about. Ask questions to narrow your subject. When you have a narrowed topic, write it down and keep it in your folder.

Part 4

Direct Contact

Pre-Writing: Writing a Topic Sentence

Here's the Idea You have learned that a topic sentence introduces the main idea of a paragraph. It tells the reader what the paragraph is about. A topic sentence should also be interesting. It should make the reader want to read the rest of the paragraph. To write good topic sentences, follow these two guidelines.

First, make your topic sentence **direct and interesting.** A direct statement is more likely to be interesting and to hold your reader's attention. Introduce the main idea clearly right away. Avoid extra words that introduce you instead of the topic. For example, do not write a topic sentence that says, "I'm going to write a paragraph about how to fix a flat tire on a bicycle." Instead, write a direct statement such as "Here's a timesaving method for fixing flats on your bicycle." To add interest, you might use humor or an unusual twist, as in "Here's how to get extra mileage out of your bicycle tires."

Second, make your topic sentences **informative.** An informative topic sentence will tell the reader exactly what your paragraph is about. Avoid sentences such as "Everyone likes to ride bicycles." This sentence says nothing about fixing a flat tire. "Fixing flats can be quick and easy when you know the cyclist's secret" informs the reader about the topic.

Check It Out Read the topic sentences below.

1. California is called the grape capital of the United States.
2. The Wright Brothers showed people how to fly.
3. The North Pole is sitting on top of the world.
4. Many ancient cities had walls around them for protection against enemies.

- Do these topic sentences attract your attention? Are they direct and interesting? Are they informative?
- Do these topic sentences avoid extra words? Which topic sentences use unusual twists?

Try Your Skill   Here are three poorly written topic sentences. Decide what the topic is in each sentence. Rewrite each of these sentences. Make each sentence direct, interesting, and informative.

1. In this paragraph I'm going to tell you about my first trip to Mars.
2. I guess if I stretch my brain I can remember what happened the night I learned to swim.
3. What I really want to write about in this paragraph is what real friendship is.

Keep This in Mind

- A topic sentence should catch the reader's attention. It should be direct, interesting, and informative.
- Avoid extra words that introduce you instead of your topic.

Now Write   Think about the narrowed topic you developed in the last lesson, **Straight and Narrow.** Write a topic sentence for your subject. Be sure your topic sentence is direct, interesting, and informative. Save your topic sentence in your folder.

Part 5

Round Up

Pre-Writing: Developing a Paragraph

Here's the Idea   A topic sentence tells the reader what your paragraph is going to be about. The rest of the sentences in the paragraph add details. These details may include descriptive details, examples, and facts and figures. The type of detail depends on the kind of paragraph you are writing. How can you find the details you need to write your paragraph?

One way to gather information is through **personal observation.** Personal observation is helpful whenever you want to describe something or someone. You can use your senses of sight, hearing, taste, smell, and touch to gather details.

Another way to gather information is by **brainstorming.** If you were writing a paragraph about your hobby, you might brainstorm on that subject. The ideas you jot down could become the details that would develop your paragraph.

A third way to find details for your paragraph is by doing **research** in a library. There you will find encyclopedias, newspapers, magazines, books, and other sources. You can look up the facts and figures you need to explain your main idea.

After you have listed your details, make sure each detail supports your topic. Take out any details that do not.

Check It Out   Read the following pre-writing notes for a paragraph about two friends and an old house.

George and I played in the house

windows boarded up

house at the corner of Elm Street and 4th Avenue

large trees around the house

the wind made weird noises in the house

George and I thought the house was haunted

we would dare each other to go in

70

trees provide shade

old empty houses are scary places

no one lived in it

- What kinds of information can you find in these notes? Are there descriptive details? Are there facts and figures?
- What idea was taken out? Why?

Try Your Skill   Here are three topic sentences. What kind of information would you use to develop each paragraph? How would you gather this information? Write *Descriptive Details, Examples,* or *Facts and Figures* to tell what kind of information you would use. Then write *Personal Observation, Brainstorming,* or *Library Research* to explain how you would find the information. You might use more than one method to find information for some paragraphs.

1. The sun was a blazing orange as it sank behind the hill.
2. Do you know which baseball players have the highest lifetime batting averages?
3. My favorite pastime is working with our personal computer.

Keep This in Mind

- Gather details for your paragraphs through personal observation, brainstorming, and library research.
- The kind of details you look for will depend on what your paragraph is about.

Now Write   Look again at the topic you chose and the topic sentence you wrote. Decide what kind of details you need to develop your paragraph. Use personal observation, brainstorming, or library research to gather your details. Save your prewriting notes in your folder.

Part 6

Let's Get Organized

Pre-Writing: Organizing a Paragraph

Here's the Idea   Once you have gathered information to develop your paragraph, you will need to organize that information. You have to decide the order in which you want to present your ideas to your reader.

One way to organize details is to arrange them in the order that they happened or should happen. This is called **chronological order.** You can use chronological order when you are telling a story. You can also use it when explaining how to do something or how something works.

Another way to organize details is to arrange them in the order that you want the viewer to notice them. This is called **spatial order.** Spatial order is helpful when you are writing a description. It helps you to paint an accurate word picture for your readers.

A third way to organize details is to arrange them in the **order of their importance.** You could start with the least important idea and move toward the most important. You could also reverse that order. Use this method of organization when some of the ideas in your paragraph are more important than others.

A fourth way to organize details is to arrange them from **general to specific.** Start out with the most general details and work toward the most specific. This method of organization can help you to define unfamiliar objects and ideas for your readers.

Check It Out   Read the following poorly organized paragraph on how to make a duck decoy.

> Duck decoys are painted wooden models of ducks. A decoy should float on water just like a real duck. Using a carving knife

with a heavy handle, carve the features of the head, neck, and tail. Use small glass beads for eyes. Use a lightweight wood such as pine or spruce. To make a duck decoy, you need a large block of wood, a carving knife, lots of sandpaper, and oil paints. After sanding, paint the duck decoy with oil paints. After carving the basic shape of the duck, you will have to sand it smooth.

· What kind of order should be used in this paragraph?
· How could you organize the ideas so that they make sense?

Try Your Skill   Put the following pre-writing notes in chronological order.

Sharon and I like to try new recipes
First we mixed ingredients, put them in pot on the stove
Tried to make a fancy chocolate pudding once
Just after pudding began cooking, Sharon knocked milk off counter onto floor
In the future, Sharon and I will be more careful
While cleaning up the milk, the pot boiled over
We took sponges, cleaned up milk
Pudding spattered all over walls and stove

Keep This in Mind

· The details in a paragraph can be arranged in chronological order, spatial order, the order of their importance, or general to specific order.
· Choose the type of organization that best fits the kind of paragraph you are writing.

Now Write   Organize the details you gathered in the last lesson, **Round Up.** Use one of the four methods of organization you learned in this lesson. Save your organized notes in your folder.

Part 7

Blazing the Trail

Writing the First Draft

Here's the Idea   At this point in the process of writing, you have a topic sentence and a set of organized pre-writing notes. Now you are ready to begin the second step—writing the first draft.

This draft is your first chance to write your ideas in paragraph form. As you write, remember that writing is a process of discovery. In your first draft you are exploring to see how well your ideas work and how well you can express them.

As you write, you may decide to add some new ideas. You might take out some others that don't really develop your topic. You could change the order of the ideas in your paragraph if that becomes necessary. You might also decide to rewrite your topic sentence. Keep in mind that this draft is just your first try at writing your paragraph. You may write several drafts before your paragraph says just what you want it to.

As you write your first draft, don't be concerned about grammar, capitalization, punctuation, and spelling. You can correct your errors later. Skip lines as you write so you will have room for these corrections and for any additional ideas you may want to add.

Check It Out   Read the first draft below. Compare it with the pre-writing notes for this paragraph in **Check It Out** on page 70. Remember, this is only a rough draft. More changes will be made during revision.

> At the corner of Elm Street and 4th Avenue was a house. My friend George and me used to play in it when we were little. The house had boarded up windows and old brick walls. There were a

lot of trees around it. On bad days, the wind would rush through the house. George and me would dare each other to go in. We'd give all kinds of excuses not to go in.

- Are there any ideas in this paragraph that were not part of the pre-writing notes?
- Are there any ideas that have been left out?

Try Your Skill   In the **Try Your Skill** section of the last lesson, you organized notes for a story about a cooking accident. Now, use your organized notes to write a first draft of the paragraph. Compare your rough draft with those of your classmates.

Keep This in Mind

- Writing a first draft is a process of discovery. Don't be afraid to make changes as you write.
- Use your organized pre-writing notes as a writing plan.
- Don't worry about grammar, capitalization, punctuation, and spelling in your first draft.

Now Write   Take out your topic sentence and the notes you organized in the last lesson. Use them to guide you as you write the first draft of your paragraph. Save your first draft in your folder.

Part 8

Stop Sign

The First Draft: Ending a Paragraph

Here's the Idea   At the end of a paragraph, you want to sum up the main idea you have developed. You should also put a little interest into the last sentence.

A good ending works well with the other sentences in a paragraph. It ties everything together. It should not add any new information. For instance, you would not end a paragraph about inventions that gave people light by writing something about the life of Thomas Edison.

A good ending is also interesting. Try using humor, a catchy way of saying something, or an interesting phrase that ties everything together. If you can do this, your paragraph will be much stronger. For example, you might end the paragraph about inventions by saying, "All of these inventions have brightened people's lives."

Check It Out   Read the paragraph below.

> Why did dinosaurs disappear from the earth? Some scientists think that dinosaurs died because of disease or because the climate became too cold for them. Scientists also blame a change in plants, the food of some dinosaurs. Others suggest that the development of mammals threatened the dinosaurs. Sixty-five million years ago the last dinosaurs died out, but today their disappearance is still a mystery.

- Does this paragraph have an ending?
- Does the ending work with the rest of the paragraph?
- Does the ending sum up the main idea?
- Is the ending interesting?

Try Your Skill   Below are two paragraphs with poorly written endings. Rewrite each ending so that it works well with the rest of the paragraph. Try to make each ending sum up the main idea in an interesting way.

1   Niagara Falls is one of the greatest shows on earth. The water roars over the rocky ledge, plunging 167 feet below. About 2,000 tons of water a minute pour into the rocky gorge. From the gorge, the water explodes upward in a swirling curtain of spray. The United States and Canada use the falls for hydroelectric power.

2   Where would we be without wood? For thousands of years people have used it to fuel fires for heating, cooking, and keeping wild animals at bay. We use it for building homes, for furniture, and tools. Most of the paper we use comes from pulpwood. Today, many things are made of plastic.

Keep This in Mind

- A paragraph should have an ending.
- A good ending works well with the rest of the paragraph and doesn't add any new ideas.
- A good ending sums up the main idea of a paragraph.
- A good ending is interesting.

Now Write   Review what you have written in your first draft. Then write an ending that works well with the rest of the paragraph. Use the ending to sum up the idea of the paragraph. Make your ending interesting. Save your paper in your folder.

Part 9

Famous Last Words

Revising Your Paragraph

Here's the Idea   The third and final step of the writing process is revising. When you revise, you take a fresh look at what you have written. You make changes so that your writing is the best it can be.

At this point, you will have to work very carefully and thoughtfully. First, check your ideas. Be sure your paragraph has a good topic sentence. See that all of your details help to develop the main idea of your paragraph. Are there any unrelated details? Could you add any details that would improve your paragraph?

Next, check the order of your details. Have you chosen a method of organization that suits the kind of paragraph you are writing?

Now look at the ending sentence of your paragraph. Is the ending interesting? Does it work well with the rest of the paragraph? Does it sum up the main idea of your paragraph?

Finally, check the language you have used. Is it direct, lively, and interesting? Try reading aloud what you have written. Sometimes your ears will catch what your eyes miss.

After revising your ideas, your organization, and your language, proofread your work. Be sure you have used correct grammar, capitalization, punctuation, and spelling. Use a dictionary and the Handbook sections of this book to help you proofread your paragraph.

Check It Out   Read the following paragraph. Notice how the author has revised it.

- What are some specific things the writer has done to make this paragraph better?

¶ *When I was young, I had my own personal haunted house.*

an old, empty mansion

~~At~~ the corner of Elm Street and Fourth Avenue was ~~a house~~.

that

My friend George and ~~me~~ used to play in it ~~when we were little~~.

its windows *long ago;* *its were crumbling with age.*

The house had ~~boarded up windows and old~~ brick walls. ~~There~~

The mansion was surrounded by tall oak trees *stormy winter*

~~were a lot of trees around it.~~ On bad days, the wind would rush

loose floorboards and shutters with an eerie, wailing sound *enter the house.*

through the house. George and ~~me~~ would dare each other to go

invent *I* *avoid going* *The house wasn't*

~~in~~. We'd ~~give~~ all kinds of excuses ~~not to~~ go in. *really haunted, but it will always be one of my favorite childhood memories.*

Try Your Skill   Read the following sentences. Proofread each one for errors in grammar, spelling, punctuation, and capitalization.

1. Black bear's hibarnat every Winter.
2. juan leeped from the truck to the grownd.
3. When you are tired its hard to get up and jog.
4. Put on these Ear muffs on your head.
5. I seen mr. Roberts run toward the gym.

Keep This in Mind

- Revising is the final step in the process of writing.
- Revise your first draft to improve your ideas, organization, and word choice.
- Proofread to find and correct errors in grammar, capitalization, punctuation, and spelling.

Now Write   Use what you have learned in this lesson about revising to revise the first draft of your paragraph. When you are satisfied with your paragraph, write it in its final form. Make your work as neat as possible. Proofread the paragraph, reading it aloud one last time. Save your paragraph.

The Process of Writing

The Process of Writing

From this point on you will be learning and practicing the skills of writing. You will be writing about what is important to you. You will also be practicing different kinds of writing.

There will be a great deal of variety in your writing experiences. Whenever you write, however, there will be something that remains the same: the process of writing. You will always work your way through the three stages of pre-writing, writing the first draft, and revising.

On these six pages you can review the process of writing from beginning to end. First, read about each step in the process. Then look at the example that shows how one person followed each step.

Pre-Writing   Have you ever begun a project without taking the time to prepare for it? If you have, you know that the confusion that results can take up more time than the planning would have. The same thing is true for writing. If you pay attention to the pre-writing stage, you will find that the rest of the writing process goes much more smoothly.

Before you write, you need to choose a subject. Brainstorming, journal writing, and reading are all ways to discover interesting subjects to write about. When you have chosen a subject, narrow it. Make it specific enough so that you can handle it in a given length.

Next, you must gather details to develop your topic. These details may include descriptive details, examples, or facts and figures. You can gather these details through brainstorming, personal observation, and library research.

When you have gathered your details, organize them. First, select the details you want to include when you write. Be sure to select only the details that support your topic. Then arrange them in an order that suits the type of writing you are doing. Choose chronological order, spatial order, order of importance, or general to specific order.

Look at the pre-writing notes below. Notice that the student listed several possible topics before choosing one. Notice, too, how the student listed many details to develop the topic. These details will be very helpful when the student writes a first draft.

Pre-Writing Notes

u list
sible
opics
and
oose
one.

u list
tails,
oose
those
want
lude,
and
anize
them.

topics

sunset at the lake

downtown at Christmas

monkey house at zoo

the county fair

school dance

details

① smells of peanuts, popcorn   ② hot dogs

⑤ sword swallower   ③ cotton candy

⑥ two-headed calf   side shows

exhibits of crafts   ⑧ ferris wheel

vegetables, jams, cakes   ⑦ roller coaster

games of chance   loud music

pie-eating contest   ④ dusty ground

Writing the First Draft   At this point in the process of writing, you are ready to write. Simply put your pencil to paper and begin writing your ideas in sentence form. Don't worry about grammar, capitalization, punctuation, or spelling at this point.

Don't try to make anything perfect at this stage. Let whatever happens, happen. You will have time later to revise your writing. Skip lines as you write so you will have space to make corrections.

Look at the first draft below. You will probably find some mistakes. You may also think that some sentences could be worded better. That's to be expected. Remember, this is just a first draft.

First Draft

You write a paragraph about your topic.

We passed through the entrance gate to the county fair. The delicious smell of roasting peanuts, hot dogs, and cotton candy mixed with the dust kicked up by our shoes. A man called us over to see the amazing sword swallower and the incredible two-headed calf. The huge roller coaster looked dangerous and exciting as it swung around its tracks. High above, the brave passengers on the ferris wheel looked down at us. Joey and I couldn't decide what to do first.

Revising   At this stage of the process you have to check what you have written. Your goal is to improve your writing. Here are some questions you should ask yourself about your first draft.

1. Have I written an interesting, direct, and informative topic sentence?
2. Have I included enough details to develop my topic thoroughly?
3. Have I organized my details to suit the type of writing I am doing?
4. Have I used lively, vivid language?
5. Have I written a strong ending?

As you answer these questions, you will discover how your first draft can be improved.

Proofreading   The last stage of revising is called proofreading. Read your draft carefully. Find and correct any errors in grammar, capitalization, punctuation, and spelling. Use a dictionary and the Handbook sections of this book to help you to check your work.

As you correct your first draft, use these proofreading marks.

Proofreading Symbols

Symbol	Meaning	Example
∧	add	would *have* gone
≡	capitalize	United states
/	make lower case	our club President
∼	reverse	thier
ℐ	take out	finished the the race
¶	make new paragraph	....be over. New ideas
⊙	period	....and stop Before we
∧	add comma	Red, blue and green are

Notice how the first draft below has been revised. Pay special attention to the proofreading marks the writer used to make corrections. How has the writer improved the first draft?

Revision

greeted us as
We passed through the entrance gate to the county fair. The ~~delicious~~ smell of roasting peanuts, hot dogs, and ~~cotton candy~~ ~~mixed with the dust kicked up by our shoes.~~ A *red-shirted* man *to our right* called us over to see the amazing sword swallower and the incredible two-headed calf. *To our left,* The huge roller coaster ~~looked~~ *swung around* dangerous *by* ~~and exciting as it swung around~~ *in* its tracks. High above, the ~~brave~~ passengers on the *double* ferris wheel ~~looked down~~ *waved* at us. Joey and I ~~couldn't~~ *stood in the middle of the* ~~decide what to do first.~~ crowd. *We didn't know where to begin.*

Making the Final Copy   When you are satisfied that your writing is clear and correct, make a final copy. Write carefully. Make your work as neat as possible.

When you have finished your final copy, proofread your work one last time. If you discover a mistake, correct it neatly.

Final Copy

> The smell of *roasting* peanuts and hot dogs greeted us as we passed through the entrance gate to the county fair. A red-shirted man to our right called us over to see the amazing sword swallower and the incredible two-headed calf. To our left, the huge roller coaster swung around dangerously in its tracks. High above, the passengers on the double Ferris wheel waved at us. Joey and I stood in the middle of the crowd. We didn't know where to begin.

You can learn to write only by writing. Whenever you write, follow all of the steps in the process of writing. Each time you write you will be learning something about writing, and about yourself.

The Narrative Paragraph

Part 1

In Detail

Pre-Writing: Developing a Narrative

Here's the Idea   You have learned what a paragraph is and how to write one. Now you will be learning to write different kinds of paragraphs.

Keep in mind that no matter what kind of paragraph you write, the three steps that make up the process of writing will always remain the same. What will change are the choices you make during each step. You want to make the right choices for the kind of paragraph you are writing. In this lesson you will learn about some of the choices you might make as you write a narrative paragraph.

A narrative paragraph tells a story. When you write about what you did during your summer vacation or about what happened in class one day, you are writing a narrative. A narrative can also be a made-up story, such as an imaginary adventure. When you look for a subject for your narrative paragraph, try to choose an interesting or exciting event. Narrow the subject so that it can be covered in one paragraph.

Once you have chosen a subject, you must gather supporting ideas to develop your story. The best way to develop a narrative paragraph is to use specific details. These should be vivid, interesting details that will make the story seem real to your readers.

You can find specific details to develop your story by asking questions such as *who? what? where? when? why?* and *how?* about the story. The answers you get will give you the specific details you need to write a good narrative paragraph.

Check It Out   Read this narrative about a frightening fall.

On Tuesday afternoon my sister Rosa and I had a frightening fall. We were riding the self-service elevator to our apartment on the sixth floor. Between the fourth and fifth floors, the elevator suddenly hesitated, and then stopped. The next moment it began to fall rapidly. Rosa quickly punched the emergency button. The elevator made a screeching sound and came to a stop just above the first floor. We were dizzy and frightened, but we were safe.

- Is this narrative developed by details?
- Does this narrative show *who? what? where? when? why?* and *how?*

Try Your Skill   Choose one of the topics below and narrow it so that it can be covered well in one paragraph. Ask the questions *who? what? when? where? why?* and *how?* to gather specific details about the topic. List as many details as you can.

a funny incident at home
a concert, dance, or sports event
an imaginary story

Keep This in Mind

- Develop narrative paragraphs by using specific details.
- To gather specific details, answer the questions *who? what? where? when? why?* and *how?* about your topic.

Now Write   Choose one of the topics you did not use in **Try Your Skill.** Narrow the topic to a story you can tell in one paragraph. Gather lively, specific details for your story by asking the questions *who? what? when? where? why?* and *how?* Save your pre-writing notes in your folder.

Part 2

Time Marches On

Pre-Writing: Using Chronological Order

Here's the Idea Once you have gathered details for your narrative paragraph, you must decide how to organize those details. Remember, whether you are writing about a real or an imaginary event, you are telling a story. The best way to tell a story is to arrange the events in the order that they took place. This is called **chronological order.** Chronological means "arranged in the order of time."

Use a natural time order to organize the events in your narrative. Tell what happened first, what happened second, and so on. This type of order helps the reader follow the events and understand your story.

Look at this narrative paragraph. Notice that the events are told in the order that they happened.

> The dog stayed on the small hill until he saw Joy coming across the street toward him. I opened the window and could hear her faintly calling, "Good dog, here's some food. Have some food." As she began to cross the street, he leaped off the hill. He bounded through and over the snow into the darkened park. Joy waited for a few minutes. She called to the dog and extended her hand. Finally she emptied the food onto the top of the hill. Then she turned and walked back to the building.   —PAUL WILKES

Check It Out Read this imaginary narrative.

> The morning of the sled-dog race, Debbie and her brother Mark were up before the sun had lightened the cold New England sky to finish the chores around the family kennels. They packed their racing equipment in the farm truck—the harnesses made of white bands with each dog's name stitched in red, the

hitching lines, water pans, and the medicine kit. Mark tied the light ashwood racing sled on top, where it sat like a strange wild bird. The team of five strong husky dogs was lifted into individual boxes built into the truck. When everything was ready, Mark took the wheel, and Debbie hoisted herself into the seat beside him. —VICTORIA FURMAN

- Are the events of this narrative arranged in chronological order? How do you know?

Try Your Skill   Below are two lists of events for narrative paragraphs. The lists are not in chronological order. On your paper, write the events in chronological order.

1. (a) I was given an X-ray.
   (b) The ambulance came and took me to a hospital.
   (c) I broke my arm skating.
   (d) Friends wrote on my cast.
   (e) My arm was put in a cast.
2. (a) The vase rolled off the edge of the table.
   (b) Ellen's little brother bumped into a table.
   (c) An expensive vase toppled over on its side.
   (d) Ellen dove toward the table and caught the vase in one hand.

Keep This in Mind

- In a narrative paragraph, use chronological order to organize events.

Now Write   Look at the pre-writing notes you gathered in the last lesson, **In Detail.** Organize your notes in chronological order. Save your organized notes in your folder.

Part 3

Who's Talking Here?

Pre-Writing: Choosing a Point of View

Here's the Idea   As you are developing your narrative paragraph, you must choose a point of view. **Point of view** means the
eyes and mind through which something is written. You can
use a first-person point of view or a third-person point of view.

When you use the **first-person point of view,** you use the first-
person pronoun *I. I* is the narrator, the person telling the story.
I cannot tell what anyone else in the story is thinking or feeling.
I can tell only what he or she can see.

When you use the **third-person point of view,** you often use the
pronouns *he* and *she*. The narrator is not a character in the
story, but the narrator can see and hear everything.

A writer usually uses the first-person point of view to tell
about something he or she did. The third-person point of view
is often used to tell about things that happened to other
people. The first-person point of view is more personal than
the third-person. The third-person, however, lets the narrator
tell more about the characters. Whichever point of view you
use, stay with it throughout your paragraph. Don't switch back
and forth from one point of view to the other.

Check It Out   Read the following two paragraphs.

1   One day, a high summer flood washed him out of the burrow
where he lived with his father and mother, and carried him,
kicking and clucking, down a roadside ditch. He found a little
wisp of grass floating there, and clung to it till he lost his senses.
When he revived, he was lying in the hot sun on the middle of a
garden path, very draggled indeed, and a small boy was saying,
"Here's a dead mongoose. Let's have a funeral."

—RUDYARD KIPLING

94

2 My kid sister Cheryl and I always bragged about our Sioux grandpa, Joe Iron Shell. Our friends, who had always lived in the city and only knew about Indians from movies and TV, were impressed by our stories. Maybe we exaggerated and made Grandpa and the reservation sound glamorous, but when we'd return home to Iowa after our yearly summer visit to Grandpa, we always had some exciting tale to tell.

—VIRGINIA DRIVING HAWK SNEVE

- Which of these paragraphs uses a first-person point of view? Which uses third-person? How do you know?

Try Your Skill Below are four sentences. Use these sentences to write two paragraphs. For the first paragraph, fill in the blanks with pronouns for the first-person point of view. For the second paragraph, use the third-person point of view.

1. _____ climbed upon the horse's back.
2. Immediately, the horse took off at a gallop, before _____ could get _____ feet in the stirrups.
3. _____ hung on to the reins tightly and shouted, "Whoa!"
4. The horse stopped suddenly, throwing _____ over its head.

Keep This in Mind

- Point of view shows through whose eyes a story is told.
- With the first-person point of view, the first-person pronoun *I* is used. *I* tells the story.
- With the third-person point of view, third-person pronouns, such as *he* or *she*, are used. The narrator is not part of the story.

Now Write Look at the pre-writing notes you have organized for your narrative paragraph. Decide whether you want to use the first-person point of view or the third-person point of view to tell your story. Write down your choice and save it.

Part 4

Telling Time

Writing the First Draft

Here's the Idea   At this stage of the process of writing, you are ready to begin writing the first draft of your narrative paragraph. Now you will write your ideas in paragraph form for the first time.

Remember that you are telling a story. If you tell a story as it happened, you need special words and phrases to help you show chronological order. These are called **transitional words and phrases.**

Good transitions help make your writing clear. They tell your readers *what* is happening *when*. The list below shows some common transitional words and phrases. Use them whenever you need a transition in your narrative paragraph.

first	now	at the beginning	before
then	soon	in the middle	after
next	later	at the end	by the time
finally	when	at last	at the same time

Sometimes you can use very specific transitional phrases, such as *after a few minutes*, *early this morning*, or *six hours later*. These specific transitional phrases will tell your reader more than a simple *then* or *next*.

As you write your first draft, try to use a variety of transitional words and phrases to show the order of time clearly. Experiment with different types of transitions to find which ones work best in your paragraph.

Check It Out   Notice the transitional words as you read this narrative paragraph.

> As the ocean liner entered the harbor, the passengers crowded against the rails. Soon, three tugboats arrived to escort the liner to its berth alongside the pier. When the tugs were in position,

the liner's captain silenced his ship's engines. Slowly, the tugs nudged the liner toward the pier. At the same time, the passengers began preparing to leave the ship. At last their voyage was over.

- Find the transitions. Do they help make the story clear?
- Do the transitional words and phrases help to show time order?

Try Your Skill   Read the paragraph below. Then re-write the paragraph, adding transitional words to show chronological order.

We hiked up into the White Mountains. We set up camp in a clearing near a brook. We cooked supper over the open fire. We sat around the campfire talking. We went to sleep. We got up, broke camp, and moved on.

Keep This in Mind

- Transitional words and phrases help to make a narrative clear.
- In a narrative paragraph, include transitions to show chronological order.

Now Write   Write the first draft of your narrative paragraph. Use transitional words and phrases to show chronological order. Don't worry about grammar, capitalization, punctuation, and spelling. You will revise your paragraph later. For now, just write your ideas as clearly as you can in paragraph form. Save your first draft in your folder.

Part 5

Wrap It Up

Revising Your Narrative Paragraph

Here's the Idea   The first draft of your narrative paragraph is finished. Now you can begin the final step in the process of writing—revising. This is your chance to improve your narrative. Here are some questions you should ask yourself about your first draft.

1. Have I written a good topic sentence?
2. Are my details specific? Have I arranged them in chronological order?
3. Have I used one point of view throughout my story?
4. Did I include good transitional words to show time order?

As you revise your story, try to make it as lively and interesting as you can. One way to make your paragraph come to life is by choosing your words carefully. This means replacing weak and general verbs with strong, specific verbs.

A verb is a word that tells what *happened* or what *is*. Some verbs are strong and show action, like *scream* or *whisper*. Other verbs are weak. These are state-of-being verbs like *is*, *seem*, and *become*. Always try to use strong, active verbs. It is better to say "Alice swims," than to say "Alice is a swimmer."

It is also important to use specific rather than general verbs. For example, think of all the ways to say *speak* that are more interesting and specific. An angry person might *shout, cry, yell,* or *rave*. A talkative person might *mumble, chatter, gab,* or *babble*.

Check It Out   Notice the verbs in this paragraph.

Peggy *slapped* the ball away from the opposing team's guard. The ball *bounced* toward the edge of the court, but Peggy *lunged* for it and *grabbed* it just before it went out of bounds. Then she *whirled* around and *flipped* the ball up toward the basket. As the ball *swished* cleanly through the hoop, the buzzer *squawked*, ending the game. Peggy's last-second shot had given her team the victory.

- How do the verbs in italics make this narrative paragraph come alive?

Try Your Skill   Improve the following paragraph by replacing the verbs in italics with stronger and more specific verbs.

The cab *came* to a halt. Robert *got* out of the cab and *went* to the curb. He *moved* through the crowd of people and *walked* up the steps of the bus station. The cab driver *put* her head out the window of the cab and angrily *asked* for her fare. "Wait a moment," *said* Robert. "I *will be* right back."

Keep This in Mind

- Revise your narrative paragraph to make it livelier and more interesting.
- Include enough specific details to tell the story well.
- Use clear chronological order and good transitions.
- Replace weak, general verbs with strong, specific ones.
- Use the same point of view throughout the story.

Now Write   Using the guidelines in this lesson, revise your first draft. Be sure to add strong, specific verbs. Remember to proofread your paragraph. When you are pleased with your narrative, make a final copy. Proofread it one last time. Save your completed narrative paragraph in your folder.

The Descriptive Paragraph

Part 1

Painting with Words

Pre-Writing: Gathering Sensory Details

Here's the Idea   A descriptive paragraph paints a picture with words. Your reason for writing a descriptive paragraph is to describe a person, place, or thing as clearly as you can. You want your reader to know your subject as well as you do.

The best way to develop your descriptive paragraph is by using sensory details. Sensory details tell about things that can be *seen, heard, felt, smelled,* or *tasted.* You can gather sensory details for your descriptive paragraph through personal observation.

Suppose you want to describe a carnival. As you walk around the carnival, you would make some pre-writing notes about it. What do you *see?* What does the carnival *sound* like? Can you *smell* the popcorn and hot dogs? How does the cotton candy *feel* in your mouth? What does the ice cream *taste* like? These kinds of details will help your readers to imagine that they are right there at the carnival with you.

You can also gather sensory details from your memory. Picture in your mind the person, place, or thing you are describing. Write down as many sensory details as you can remember.

Check It Out   Read the following descriptive paragraph.

We had been lost for two days in the desert. Now we were beginning to wonder if we would ever be rescued. A sandstorm blew past us, like thousands of tiny needles. It stung our tender, burned faces and left us choking. We sat down and drank the last few drops of water from my canteen. Despite its metallic taste, the water cooled our parched throats. Miles away, we could see the faint, green shapes of mountains, shimmering in the heat.

We were too weak, however, to hike that far. Then, quite suddenly, we heard a chopping sound cutting through the air. A helicopter had spotted us and was preparing to land. We were saved!

- What sensory details can you find in this paragraph?
- How do these details help you to share the writer's experience?

Try Your Skill   Think about a person you know very well. Imagine you have to write a paragraph describing that person. Make a list of sensory details you could use in your paragraph. Write down as many details as you can recall. Save your list.

Keep This in Mind

- Develop your descriptive paragraph with sensory details.
- Gather sensory details through personal observation or from memory.

Now Write   Choose a place you would like to describe. It might be a room in your house, a vacant lot, or a stretch of woods. Go to the place you've chosen or imagine it in your mind. Write down as many sensory details as you can. Save your pre-writing notes in your folder.

Part 2

Looking into Space

Pre-Writing: Using Spatial Order

Here's the Idea   Sensory details can bring a description to life for your readers. Unless these details are arranged properly, however, your readers may get a different picture than you want them to.

In your narrative paragraph you organized your details according to the order in which they happened. In your descriptive paragraph you will organize your details in the order that you want your readers to notice them. This is called **spatial order.** Start with the detail that you want your readers to notice first. This might be the most obvious detail about the person, place, or thing you are describing. It might also be the detail that made the biggest impression on you. Then add the other details in an order that shows how they are related to the first detail. For example, you might describe your subject from top to bottom, left to right, front to back, or near to far. These are all ways of using spatial order.

Suppose the subject of your description is an old apartment building. If the television antenna on the roof catches your eye first, you can start your description with that detail. Then you could describe the building from top to bottom. You might move from the roof to the wash hanging from the fourth floor fire escape. At this point you would add the detail about the noise the wash made as it flapped in the breeze. Next, you could describe the woman talking from an open window on the third floor. Then you could tell about flowerpots on the second floor ledge. Finally, you might describe the windows of the drug store on the ground floor. By organizing your sensory details in spatial order, you can lead your readers from one detail to the next.

Check It Out   Read the following description.

Three identical creatures stood in front of the doorway of the spacecraft. From behind them, a greenish light shone, creating frightening shadows. The creatures' heads were huge and covered with transparent pale orange skin. Their small, childlike bodies were clothed in shiny yellow suits. On their feet, the creatures wore slick green boots. As they squeaked a greeting, they took a step toward us.

- How does this description use spatial order?

Try Your Skill   Take out the list of sensory details you made in **Try Your Skill** in the last lesson. Organize these details into the order you would want your readers to notice them. Save your notes.

Keep This in Mind

- Use spatial order to organize the sensory details of your descriptive paragraph.
- Arrange your details in the order you want your readers to notice them.

Now Write   Take out your pre-writing notes from the last lesson, **Painting with Words.** Arrange your details in the order that you want your readers to notice them. You might experiment with a few different arrangements until you find the order that works best for your subject. Save your organized details in your folder.

Part 3

Picture This

Writing the First Draft

Here's the Idea   As you gathered and organized details for your descriptive paragraph, you were trying to create a word picture for your readers. Now you are ready to paint that picture. You are ready to write your first draft.

As you write, keep the person, place, or thing you are describing clear in your mind. If you can picture your subject clearly, you should be able to describe it clearly. To help make the order of your descriptive paragraph clear, include good transitions. In a descriptive paragraph, these are words and phrases that tell *where*. Transitional words and phrases can help you to show how all the parts of your subject are related to each other.

Here are some examples of transitional words and phrases that can help you to keep your description clear.

in	ahead of	down	to the right
on	outside	by	back and forth
above	downstairs	front	at the end of
under	upstairs	north	side by side
behind	close to	east	in back of
near	between	toward	next to
up	beneath	among	facing
over	beside	to the left of	against
below	alongside	in the center	at the top of
onto	high	in the corner	around
inside	low	on the edge	throughout

Check It Out   Read this description of a person eating an orange.

The orange lay atop the other pieces of fruit in the basket. I picked it up and cupped it in my hand. Its outer surface, the peel, felt rough and grainy. I tore through the peel into the smooth, white, inner covering. Inside the white layer, the orange was divided into ten, crescent-shaped sections. Each section was covered by a thin skin. I split open a section and was sprayed by the juice within. I popped the sweet tidbit into my mouth, thoroughly enjoying my snack.

- How does this descriptive paragraph use transitional words to show spatial order?

Try Your Skill Look at the pre-writing notes you organized in **Try Your Skill** on page 105. Add location words to show how the parts of your subject are related to each other.

Keep This in Mind

- In a descriptive paragraph, use transitional words and phrases that tell *where*.

Now Write Write the first draft of your descriptive paragraph. Experiment as you write until your paragraph says just what you want it to. Use transitional words to make your description as clear to your readers as it is to you.

Don't worry about grammar, capitalization, punctuation, and spelling at this time. You will revise your first draft later. Save your first draft in your folder.

Part 4

How Tall?

Revising Your Descriptive Paragraph

Here's the Idea   As you revise your descriptive paragraph, you will be making changes to make your word picture clearer and more interesting. Here are some questions to ask yourself.

1. Have I written a good topic sentence?
2. Have I included enough sensory details to develop my description?
3. Are my details arranged in the order in which I want the reader to notice them?
4. Have I used transitional words and phrases that tell *where,* to make my description clear?
5. Have I used strong, specific verbs?

Another way to make your description clear and interesting is to use vivid adjectives. An adjective is a word that describes someone or something. Choose your adjectives carefully. If you were describing a tree, for instance, you might use the adjective *tall.* However, you could also describe the tree as *lofty, high, towering, gigantic, soaring,* or *sky-high.* One of these adjectives will describe the tree better than the others. Always try to choose the most vivid adjective to make your description clear and interesting.

Be careful not to use too many adjectives. A long string of adjectives will make your writing too wordy. For example, it is not necessary to say "the spiny, prickly, sharp cactus needles." Just choose the adjective that best describes the needles.

After you have revised your ideas, organization, and word choice, proofread your paragraph. Correct any errors in grammar, capitalization, punctuation, and spelling.

Check It Out   Now read this description of a ghost town.

Carol drove north down the dusty road leading to the old Nevada mining town. She found herself standing in front of a rundown wooden building. The blistered front door was hanging by one hinge. Directly above the door hung a peeling sign. The faded letters spelled "Virginia City General Store." Carol imagined how exciting it would have been to have lived a hundred years ago in this famous frontier town.

· What adjectives are used in this paragraph? How do they make the description more interesting?

Try Your Skill   Add vivid adjectives to make this paragraph livelier and more interesting. Don't use too many adjectives.

Inspector Parker seated himself in the chair beside the window. He surveyed the room. Obviously, the victim had been a collector of antiques. The far wall was covered with paintings. A sword hung above the doorway. Every table and shelf had a collection of statues upon it. A musket, which had obviously not been fired in many years, rested against the fireplace.

Keep This in Mind

· Include strong sensory details in your description.
· Use spatial order to organize your details.
· Make the order of your details clear by using transitional words and phrases that tell *where*.
· Use vivid adjectives and strong, specific verbs.

Now Write   Use the guidelines in this lesson to revise your first draft. Be sure to add vivid adjectives to your description. Remember to proofread your paper. When you are satisfied that your work is the best it can be, make a final copy. Proofread your descriptive paragraph. Save it in your folder.

The Explanatory Paragraph

Telling *How*

Part 1

How It's Done

Pre-Writing: Explaining a Process

Here's the Idea A paragraph that explains something is an **explanatory paragraph.** When it explains how something is done or how something happens, it is an explanatory *how* paragraph.

There are two kinds of explanatory *how* paragraphs. One kind explains *how to do something.* In this kind of paragraph, you might explain how to change a bicycle tire, how to make bread, or how to plant tulips.

You can also write an explanatory *how* paragraph to explain *how something happens* or *how something works.* For example, you could write about how water turns to ice, or how the heart pumps blood. No matter what kind of topic you choose, be sure that you understand the subject well yourself. Also be sure that you can explain the subject fully in one paragraph.

Now you must gather your supporting details. Whether you write about how to do something or how something happens or works, you are explaining a process. A process is made up of a series of steps. Each step in the process is important. Be sure to include all of the steps when you gather details for your pre-writing notes. Present each step simply and clearly.

Check It Out Read the following pre-writing notes. They are for a paragraph explaining how to grow an avocado plant.

> remove pit from avocado—wash thoroughly
> support pit with toothpicks in glass of water
> put glass in sunny window
> when roots develop, plant pit in pot filled with soil
> plant pit halfway in soil, root end down
> place plant in sunny spot
> water twice a week

- Do you see that these notes include all the steps necessary to grow an avocado plant?

Try Your Skill   A six-year-old child gave the following explanation of how to make stew. Could you follow the steps?

Corn Beef Stew

First you have to get in the wagon and drive downtown. Then you buy:

The tall French-Italian bread
The butter
The paper towels

Then you get in the wagon and drive back home.

Then take everything out and put it away. Put the bag between the cat food—but fold it up.

Cook it in the stove in your pan. Look in the window all the time to see if it's done.

Then say a prayer and eat.

Serves for a pretty long time if there's only 3 people. (Eat out in between.)
                                                        —*Smashed Potatoes*

- List at least five errors in these directions.

Keep This in Mind

- An explanatory *how* paragraph explains how to do something or how something happens or works.
- An explanatory *how* paragraph should include all the steps of the process being explained.
- Each step in the process should be explained simply and clearly.

Now Write   Think of a simple process that you would like to explain. Be sure you can explain it fully in one paragraph. Make notes about the process. Don't leave out any steps. Save your list in your folder.

Part 2

From Beginning to End

Pre-Writing: Using Step-by-Step Order

Here's the Idea   The pre-writing notes that you made for your explanatory *how* paragraph include all the steps of a process. To make your explanation clear to your reader, these steps should be presented in chronological, or **step-by-step,** order. This is the order in which a process takes place or should be completed.

As you arrange your notes in step-by-step order, make sure you do not leave a step out or put it in the wrong place. Either error could confuse your readers. For example, suppose you were explaining how to build a kite. What would happen if you forgot to tell your readers what materials they need? What would they do if you told them how to attach the paper *before* you told them how to build the frame?

Begin organizing your notes by listing the first step in the process you are explaining. Then list the rest of the steps in the natural time order of the process.

Check It Out   Read the following paragraph.

> You can make your own jigsaw puzzle. First, select a large magazine picture and a sheet of heavy cardboard of equal size. Next, spread paste evenly on the back of the picture and on one side of the cardboard. When the paste has dried for a few minutes, lay the picture on the cardboard. Then use the sides of your hands to smooth out the wrinkles from the center of the picture outward. After the paste is completely dry, use a pair of sharp scissors to cut the mounted picture into odd-shaped pieces.

- What process is explained in this paragraph?
- Are all steps in this process presented in the order that they should be done?

Try Your Skill   Read the following pre-writing notes. They are for a paragraph that explains how to change a flat bicycle tire. Organize them into step-by-step order.

Changing a Flat Bicycle Tire

put your tools back into their case
tighten the loose bolts
remove flat tire from wheel
fill new tire with air, and ride away
loosen bolts holding wheel to bicycle
remove wheel
put new tire on the wheel
take out necessary tools
put new tire and wheel back on bicycle

Keep This in Mind

- In an explanatory *how* paragraph, explain the process step-by-step.
- Organize the steps of the process in the order that they take place or should be done.

Now Write   Organize the pre-writing notes you gathered in the last lesson, **How It's Done.** Put them into step-by-step order. When you have organized your notes, check to see that you haven't left out any steps. Save your organized notes in your folder.

Part 3

Stepping Out

Writing the First Draft

Here's the Idea   You can't build a model rocket, a tree-house, or a bookcase without a plan. You need a plan to write a paragraph, too. The notes that you organized for your explanatory paragraph are a plan you can follow as you write your first draft.

Start your paragraph with a strong topic sentence that tells the reader what process you are explaining. Then use your prewriting notes to write your explanation. Be sure to explain each step simply and clearly.

One way you can make your explanation clear is by using transitions. Transitions help show your reader *when* each step in the process takes place or should be done. Transitions can also show your readers how the steps are related to each other.

Here is a list of transitional words and phrases. Use these words and phrases and others like them as you write your first draft.

first	then	at first
second	now	to start with
third	when	after that
fourth	while	at the same time
next	until	the next step
last	finally	at last

Check It Out   Read the paragraph below.

The next time you are bothered by hiccups, try this unusual cure. First, fill a glass with water. Next, bend over the sink, holding the glass. Then lean forward, placing your lips against the farthest rim of the glass. Finally, tilt the glass away from you, and drink as much water as you can. When you fnish your backwards drink, your hiccups will be gone.

- Which transitional words and phrases in this explanatory *how* paragraph help show step-by-step order?

Try Your Skill   Read the following paragraph. Add transitional words and phrases to make the step-by-step order logical and clear. Use as many transitional words as possible.

Pitching a tent is easy when you follow a few simple steps. _____ take the tent and all the stakes and poles out of the carrying case. Lay all the equipment on the ground. _____ open up the tent so it is spread out flat. _____ put each stake by each stake holder on the tent. When each stake has been placed by its holder, nail the stakes into the ground. _____ take the tent poles, put them inside the tent, and stand them upright where they belong. _____ tie the strings which are on top of the tent to the proper stakes. Your tent is ready to use.

Keep This in Mind

- In an explanatory *how* paragraph, use transitional words and phrases to show step-by-step order.

Now Write   Using your organized pre-writing notes from the last lesson, write the first draft of your explanatory *how* paragraph. Remember to explain each step simply and clearly. Use transitional words and phrases to show step-by-step order. Save your first draft in your folder.

Part 4

Step Back

Revising Your Explanatory *How* Paragraph

Here's the Idea In an explanatory *how* paragraph, your purpose is to explain a process as simply and as clearly as you can. You want your readers to understand the process as well as you understand it. As you read over the first draft of your explanatory paragraph, ask yourself if you have achieved these goals. Use these questions to help you to revise your first draft.

1. Does my topic sentence tell the reader what process I am going to explain? Is it direct and interesting?
2. Have I included all the steps of the process?
3. Have I explained each step simply and clearly?
4. Have I arranged the steps in the order that they take place or should be done?
5. Have I used transitional words and phrases to show step-by-step order?

You may find it helpful to have someone else read the first draft of your explanatory *how* paragraph. Ask a classmate to read your paragraph and to tell you whether or not you have written a good explanation. He or she could use the questions in this lesson to see how good your paragraph is. Use your classmate's opinions to help you revise your paragraph.

When you have reviewed your ideas, be sure to proofread your paragraph. Correct any errors in grammar, capitalization, punctuation, and spelling.

Check It Out Read the following explanatory *how* paragraph.

> This paragraph is going to be about how trout develop. When the trout hatch, they are called fry. But first the trout are in eggs.

Then they hatch. After they hatch, the trout get their food from a yolk sac. The sac is attached to their bodies. In the eggs, trout feed on egg yolk. In three months, the yolk in the sac is gone. Then the trout have to hunt for food. All of this is after they hatch. The trout become adults in two to five years. And that is how trout develop.

- Is this a good explanatory *how* paragraph? Explain your answer.

Try Your Skill   Use the guidelines in this lesson to revise the paragraph in **Check It Out.** Make the paragraph as clear as possible. Compare your revised paragraph with those of your classmates.

Keep This in Mind

- Revise your explanatory *how* paragraph so that it is clear and simple. The reader should be able to understand the process you are explaining as well as you do.
- Include all the steps in the process. Explain each step simply and clearly.
- Arrange the steps in step-by-step order. Use transitional words and phrases to show this order.

Now Write   Using the guidelines in this lesson, revise the first draft of your explanatory *how* paragraph. When you are satisfied that your paragraph is the best it can be, proofread it one last time. Make a final copy of your paragraph and save it in your folder.

The Explanatory Paragraph

Telling *Why*

Part 1 **Present Your Case**
Pre-Writing: Developing an Opinion

Part 2 **It's Important to You!**
Pre-Writing: Organizing an Opinion

Part 3 **First of All**
Writing the First Draft

Part 4 **The Defense Rests**
Revising Your Explanatory *Why* Paragraph

Present Your Case

Pre-Writing: Developing an Opinion

Here's the Idea An explanatory paragraph can explain *how*. An explanatory paragraph can also explain *why*. Such a paragraph is called an explanatory *why* paragraph. The purpose of an explanatory *why* paragraph is to present an opinion in writing.

It is only natural to have strong feelings about the things that happen in your life. That's why subjects for explanatory *why* paragraphs are not hard to find. Ask yourself what you feel strongly about. When you watch the news or read a newspaper, which stories make you feel angry? Which make you feel good? Why? How do you feel about school, your neighborhood, and your town? Your answers to these questions are opinions that you can develop in your writing.

Whenever you set out to explain *why*, your first step is to make your opinion clear in your own mind. You can do this by writing a sentence that states your opinion clearly and directly. This statement of opinion can become the topic sentence of your explanatory *why* paragraph. Here are some typical statements of opinion.

1. Everyone should recycle cans and bottles.
2. All students should learn how to use the library.
3. Watching television can be educational.

Once you have your opinion clearly in mind, you need to make your reader understand why you feel the way you do. To do this, you must list specific reasons and facts that you can use to develop and support your opinion. Your reasons should be logical and clear. Your facts must be accurate.

Check It Out Read these pre-writing notes.

Opinion: Everyone should recycle cans and bottles.

Reasons/Facts: Recycling cans and bottles will lower the cost of canned and bottled goods as much as 20% in some cases.

Recycling cans and bottles could lead to much less litter in our environment.

Recycling saves energy and materials.

- Is the opinion stated clearly and directly?
- Do the reasons support the opinion well? Explain your answer.

Try Your Skill Below are three opinions that could be developed in explanatory *why* paragraphs. Choose one opinion and list some logical reasons and facts to support it.

1. All national holidays should be celebrated on Mondays.
2. A good breakfast is important for your health.
3. All students should be taught computer skills.

Keep This in Mind

- In an explanatory *why* paragraph, you present and support an opinion.
- Suport your opinion with logical reasons and accurate facts.

Now Write Think of some issues you feel strongly about. What are your opinons about these issues? You might consider your feelings about something that is happening in your school or community. You might also consider your feelings about some current event. Choose one opinion that you would like to write about. Write a sentence that states your opinion clearly and directly. Then list all of the reasons and facts you can think of to support your topic. Be sure your reasons are logical and your facts accurate. Save your pre-writing notes in your folder.

Part 2

It's Important to You!

Pre-Writing: Organizing an Opinion

Here's the Idea After you have developed a list of supporting reasons and facts for your opinion, you must decide how to present them in your paragraph. You want to organize your reasons and facts in a way that will have the greatest impact on your readers.

One way to organize your details is to save your strongest reasons for the end of your paragraph. This method of organization is called **least important to most important idea.** When you organize your ideas this way, you leave the strongest reason fresh in your reader's mind.

Here are three reasons why telephone lines should be placed underground.

1. There would be no poles and wires to clutter the landscape.

2. It would be cheaper to maintain underground lines because they would not be exposed to the weather.

3. Since lines could not be harmed by bad weather, people would be able to make emergency calls during storms.

The first reason is a good one. It probably isn't as important to people as saving money, however. The last reason is the most important since it affects people's safety. These reasons have been listed in order, from the least important to the most important.

Check It Out Read the following paragraph.

People should travel in car pools. First, using fewer cars helps to solve parking problems. More important, fewer people driving means less energy used. Most important, sharing rides is a way of reducing pollution. Our nation's energy crisis and pollution problems would be greatly reduced if more people shared rides.

- Is the opinion supported with good reasons and accurate facts?
- Are the reasons presented in the order of their importance, from the least important idea to the most important?

Try Your Skill   Here is a set of pre-writing notes for an explanatory *why* paragraph. Read the opinion. Then organize the supporting reasons from the least important idea to the most important. Compare your list with those of your classmates.

Opinion: Everyone should exercise regularly.

Reasons: 1. Regular exercise can help you to relax.
2. Doctors believe that regular exercise can improve your health.
3. Exercise is fun for the whole family.

Keep This in Mind

- Organize your explanatory *why* paragraph from the least important idea to the most important.

Now Write   Organize the list of reasons and facts you wrote in **Present Your Case.** Begin with the least important idea and work toward the most important. Save your organized notes in your folder.

Part 3

First of All

Writing the First Draft

Here's the Idea As you write the first draft of your explanatory *why* paragraph, remember that you should state your opinion clearly. Also make sure that you support your opinion with convincing reasons and facts.

Present your opinion in the topic sentence. Write a clear, direct sentence that tells your readers how you feel about your subject. Do not, however, use the first-person pronouns *I* or *my* in your topic sentence. Do not write "*I believe* that motorcycles are dangerous," or "*In my opinion*, motorcycles are dangerous." Your readers already know that you are presenting your opinion. It is better to say "Motorcycles are dangerous."

In the body of your paragraph, present your reasons and facts in the order of their importance. One way to make this order clear is to use transitional words and phrases.

There are two kinds of transitional words and phrases that can help you write your *why* paragraph. One kind helps you to state reasons and facts. The other kind helps you to put those reasons and facts in the order of their importance.

To State Reasons or Facts:	because, so, since, therefore, as a result, if (something) . . . then (something)
To Make Order of Importance Clear:	the first reason, second, more important, most important, finally

After you have finished the body of your paragraph, end your explanation with a strong sentence that sums up your opinion and your reasons.

Check It Out Read the following paragraph.

Television can be educational. First of all, children can learn skills such as math and reading at home as a result of watching educational programs. Second, if students watch and discuss good programs, they can learn to choose TV programs more wisely. Finally, by taking viewers back through history, or on adventures around the world, TV expands their knowledge. Opportunities for knowledge are as close as the nearest television set.

- Does the topic sentence state an opinion clearly?
- What transitional words and phrases show the reasons? Which show their order of importance?
- Does the ending sentence sum up the writer's opinions?

Try Your Skill   Add transitional words and phrases to the following explanatory *why* paragraph.

Everyone should be required to walk his or her dog on a leash. _____ if the dog is kept on a leash, it cannot run loose and damage other people's property. _____ dogs run loose, they can dig up lawns, knock over garbage cans, and destroy other property. _____, dogs should be kept on a leash to protect them from traffic. _____ they wander into the street, they could be hit by a car. _____, dogs should be kept on a leash _____ that they don't bite or harm people. When everyone walks his or her dog on a leash, we can be sure that property, dogs, and people will all be safe.

Keep This in Mind

- In an explanatory *why* paragraph, state your opinion in the topic sentence.
- Use transitional words and phrases.
- Sum up your opinion in your ending sentence.

Now Write   Using your notes from **It's Important to You!,** write the first draft of your explanatory *why* paragraph. Use transitional words and phrases to present reasons and facts and to show their order of importance. Save your work.

Part 4

The Defense Rests

Revising Your Explanatory *Why* Paragraph

Here's the Idea   When you revise the first draft of your explanatory *why* paragraph, try to make your opinion clearer and your reasons more convincing to your readers. Here is a list of questions to ask yourself as you revise.

1. Does my topic sentence state my opinion clearly and directly?

2. Have I included logical reasons and accurate facts to support my opinion?

3. Have I arranged my reasons from the least important idea to the most important?

4. Have I included transitional words and phrases to present my reasons and to make the order of their importance clear?

5. Does my ending sentence sum up my opinion and my reasons?

Remember to proofread your paragraph. Correct any errors in grammar, capitalization, punctuation, and spelling.

Check It Out   Read the following first draft.

In my opinion, everyone should participate in some kind of competitive sport. Competitive sports, like baseball and basketball, are good for your body. They keep you healthy. I also think that competitive sports are good for your mind. Competitive sports are fun and exciting, too. There is nothing like scoring the winning goal in a soccer game, or crossing the finish line in a race. I just think everyone should participate in competitive sports.

- How could the topic sentence of this paragraph be improved?

- Could the reasons be better organized? How?
- Could any of the ideas be more fully developed?
- Does the ending sentence sum up the ideas in this paragraph?

Try Your Skill   Revise the paragraph in **Check It Out.** Use the questions in **Here's the Idea** to guide your revision.

Keep This in Mind

- In an explanatory *why* paragraph, state your opinion clearly and directly in your topic sentence.
- Use logical reasons and accurate facts to support your opinion.
- Use transitional words and phrases to state your reasons and facts and to show the order of their importance.
- Write a concluding sentence that sums up your opinion and reasons.

Now Write   Revise your first draft. Follow the guidelines in this lesson. Try to make your opinion clearer and your reasons more convincing. Be sure to proofread your paragraph. When you have finished revising your work, make a final copy. Proofread it one last time. Save your paragraph in your folder.

The Explanatory Paragraph

Telling *What*

Part 1

Please Explain

Pre-Writing: Learning About Definitions

Here's the Idea In many everyday situations, you may be asked to explain what something is. In your classes you may be asked to explain a *banjo,* a *simile,* or *gravity.* You can explain objects and ideas clearly by learning to write an explanatory *what* paragraph.

An explanatory *what* paragraph is a definition of something. The subject may be a real thing, such as a blast furnace or a three-stage rocket. The subject may also be an idea, such as democracy or friendship.

A good definition does three things. First, it presents the subject, the object or idea to be defined. Then, it puts the subject into the general class to which it belongs. Finally, it shows the particular characteristics of the subject. That is, it shows how the subject is different from all the other members of its class.

For example, imagine that you want to define *collie.* First, you would write that a collie is a dog. That puts the subject in its general class. Now you must tell how a collie is different from other dogs. You could write that a collie is a large dog. That's a start. It shows how collies are different from beagles, dachshunds, and other small dogs. However, because there are many other big dogs besides collies, you might add that collies have long hair. Still, there are many other large dogs with long hair. You could add that collies have long, narrow heads. However, an Irish setter is also a large dog with long hair and a long head. You add that collies were originally bred in Scotland for herding sheep. Now you have a specific definition:

> A collie is a large, long-haired dog originally bred in Scotland for herding sheep.

Check It Out   Read the following explanation of a tornado.

A tornado is a violent windstorm. It can be recognized by its dark, funnel-shaped cloud. Tornados strike most often in the south and central parts of the United States. Tornados usually occur in late spring. They are formed when a mass of cold air forces warm, moist air to rise rapidly. As the warm air rises, a revolving motion begins, with winds swirling up to 500 miles per hour. The revolving motion is the basis for the name *tornado*, a Spanish word meaning "twister."

- What is the subject of this definition?
- To what general class does the subject belong?
- What are some particular characteristics of the subject?

Try Your Skill   Look at each item below. Write the general class to which it belongs. Then choose three of the items and write the specific characteristics of each. Look up any unfamiliar words in a dictionary.

1. apple	4. Earth	7. monarchy	10. condor
2. saxaphone	5. daffodil	8. station wagon	11. polio
3. kayak	6. DC-10	9. soccer	12. beach

Keep This in Mind

- An explanatory *what* paragraph explains what something is.
- A good definition puts a subject into its general class. Then it gives the particular characteristics of the subject.

Now Write   Divide a piece of paper into two columns. Label one column *Real Objects* and the other *Ideas*. In each column, list at least five possible subjects for an explanatory *what* paragraph. Save your list in your folder.

Part 2

Be Particular

Pre-Writing: Developing a Definition

Here's the Idea   There are many subjects you may choose to define in an explanatory *what* paragraph. You may define real objects, such as Latex paint, chow mein, sagebrush, or a diesel engine. You may also define ideas or terms, such as friendship, freedom, inflation, or progress.

The subject you choose should be defined in the topic sentence of your paragraph. The rest of the paragraph should develop the definition as fully as possible. The best way to develop a definition is with specific details or facts and figures.

You may develop some definitions in a detailed, factual way. If you define *diesel*, for example, you will probably use facts and figures to develop your explanation. A dictionary or an encyclopedia can help you to gather complete and accurate details for your pre-writing notes.

Sometimes, you may develop a definition in a detailed, but more personal, way. For instance, if you define friendship, your pre-writing notes will almost certainly include specific details from your own experience.

When your pre-writing notes are complete, organize them. A definition is usually organized from the general to the specific. That is, a definition begins with a general statement about the subject, such as "A tangerine is a small, orange citrus fruit similar to an orange." Then the definition continues with specific details that further define the subject.

Check It Out   Read the following definition of a family.

A family is a group of closely-related people who share life together. Members of a family stand by each other in any situation. When my best friend moved away, my family shared my sadness. When I won first prize at a craft fair, my family celebrated with me. My family always supports me. I am happy to be a member of the Graleno family.

- Does this paragraph develop the definition given in the topic sentence? Is the paragraph developed by specific details or facts and figures?

Try Your Skill   Look at the lists of objects and ideas below. Choose one word from each column. Make some pre-writing notes about each word for an explanatory *what* paragraph. Gather facts and figures from an encyclopedia or dictionary to help you define the object you choose. Use details from your own experience to define the idea.

Objects	Ideas
a helicopter	home
a rose	courage
ice cream	loneliness
an apple	a friend

Keep This in Mind

- Define the subject of your explanatory *what* paragraph in the topic sentence.
- Develop your explanatory *what* paragraph with specific details or facts and figures.

Now Write   Look at the different lists of pre-writing notes that you have made for the last two lessons. Choose one subject and make some pre-writing notes about it for an explanatory *what* paragraph. Be sure to develop your subject with either specific details or facts and figures. Organize your notes from the general to the specific. Save your pre-writing notes in your folder.

Part 3

Put It in Writing

Writing the First Draft

Here's the Idea   Once you have organized your pre-writing notes, you are ready to write the first draft of your explanatory *what* paragraph.

The first thing you must do is define your subject. You do this in the topic sentence of your paragraph. Make sure your definition includes the general class that the subject belongs to. The definition should also tell a little about how the subject is different from the other members of its class. "A canoe floats on water" is not a good definition. A better topic sentence would be "A canoe is a small, narrow boat that is propelled through the water by a person with a paddle."

After you have defined your subject, you must develop that definition with the details you have gathered and organized. Be sure to include enough details to fully develop your paragraph.

Finally, write a good ending sentence for your paragraph. A good ending will be lively and interesting, leaving your readers with some detail that will remain in their thoughts. Your readers will be more likely to remember your paragraph if you have written a good ending sentence.

Check It Out   Read this explanatory *what* paragraph.

> A gauntlet is a heavy, metal-plated glove once worn by knights during the middle ages. In those days, knights wore armor to protect themselves during combat. The gauntlet was designed to protect their hands. Most gauntlets were made by bolting metal plates onto a leather glove. This allowed the knight to move his fingers freely. When one knight wished to do battle with another, he would throw one of his gauntlets to the ground. In this way, he challenged his enemy to a fight.

- Is the subject of this explanatory *what* paragraph clearly defined in the topic sentence?
- What details develop the subject in the body of the paragraph?
- Is there an interesting ending to this paragraph?

Try Your Skill   Choose one of the subjects you developed details for in the **Try Your Skill** of the last lesson, **Be Particular.** Write a topic sentence that clearly and completely defines that subject. Pay attention to the guidelines given in this lesson.

Keep This in Mind

- In an explanatory *what* paragraph, define your subject clearly and completely in your topic sentence.
- Use details to develop your definition in the body of your paragraph.
- Write a lively, interesting ending sentence for your paragraph.

Now Write   Write the first draft of your explanatory *what* paragraph. Follow the guidelines in this lesson. Save your first draft in your folder.

Part 4

Another Look

Revising Your Explanatory *What* Paragraph

Here's the Idea   The last step in writing an explanatory *what* paragraph is revising. At this point, take time to carefully read over your first draft. Ask yourself these questions as you revise your paragraph.

1. Does my topic sentence present and define my subject?
2. Have I defined my subject clearly and completely?
3. Have I included enough details to develop my definition?
4. Are my details organized from general to specific?
5. Have I written a strong, interesting ending?

When you are satisfied that you have written a good definition, proofread your paragraph. Find and correct any errors in grammar, capitalization, punctuation, and spelling.

Check It Out   Read this explanatory *what* paragraph.

An air conditioner makes cold air. It is a big metal box that you put in your window. When you turn it on, it takes in hot air from outside and blows it through some pipes. Inside the pipes, the air gets cold. Then it comes out. We have an air conditioner in our house.

- How would you improve the definition in the topic sentence?
- Are the details organized from general to specific? How might you change them?
- Does the paragraph have a good ending sentence? How could you improve it?

Try Your Skill   Here are some poorly written topic sentences for explanatory *what* paragraphs. Revise these sentences so that they clearly and directly define their subjects. Use a dictionary or an encyclopedia if you need more information to write a good topic sentence.

1. A quarterback plays on a football team.
2. A python is a long snake.
3. A piano is a big, black instrument with lots of keys.
4. A BMX is a bicycle.
5. A frog is an animal that is green.

Keep This in Mind

- In an explanatory *what* paragraph, define your subject clearly and directly in your topic sentence.
- Develop your definition with enough details to make it complete.
- Organize your details from the general to the specific.
- Write a strong, interesting ending.

Now Write Revise your explanatory *what* paragraph. Follow the guidelines in this lesson. When you feel that your definition is clear and complete, make a final copy. Proofread the final copy one last time. Save your paragraph in your folder.

Exploring Compositions

Part 1

Going to Great Lengths

Learning About Compositions

Here's the Idea   What happens when you need to say more about your subject than is possible in one paragraph? When you have a subject that cannot be covered in one paragraph, you need to write a composition.

A **composition** is a group of paragraphs that tell about one main idea. Like a paragraph, a composition may be narrative, descriptive, or explanatory. A composition has three parts: an introduction, a body, and a conclusion.

The **introduction** is a paragraph that tells what a composition is about. The introduction to a composition is like the topic sentence of a paragraph.

The **body** of a composition is the part that develops the main idea. In a narrative, the body presents the events that tell the story. In a description, the body contains the details that make up a word picture. In an explanatory composition, the body presents steps in a process, reasons, or facts.

A composition ends with a **conclusion**. Sometimes the conclusion is a paragraph that summarizes the story, description, or explanation. The conclusion can also be a paragraph that clearly signals an ending to the idea you have developed.

Check It Out   Read the composition below.

My Special Day

Shortly after Thanksgiving, the downtown area begins to undergo a great change. Wreaths, ribbons, and sparkling lights appear. The sights and sounds of the holiday season are everywhere. At this time of year, my favorite adventure is a day of shopping.

The adventure begins when the subway train hisses to a stop. The doors open, spilling crowds of people into the dark underground station. Eager shoppers climb the stairs to the street.

Snow is falling softly. The air is cold. The crowd scatters.

All day long, we parade past store windows with holiday displays. In one window an electric train chugs around a mountain of gifts. In another window shiny copper skillets and kettles are displayed. My favorite window holds fancy cakes, cookies, and candies decorated for the holidays.

In the square, a red-cheeked Santa Claus stands next to a black iron kettle. He nods a greeting to passers-by as he clangs his big bell. Across the square, children are singing carols.

At dusk, the lights on the huge fir trees in the park are turned on. The lights shine brightly through the lightly falling snow. We cross through the park as we head home. My arms are full of packages. My mind is full of my holiday in the city.

- Which part of this composition is the introduction? Which is the body? Which is the conclusion?

Try Your Skill   Write the name of the part of a composition to which this paragraph belongs. Write your reasons.

Her next task was to reach the zoo before David did. Pam raced up the street toward the taxi stand. Jumping into the lead cab, she shouted, "The zoo, driver, and quickly!" Five minutes later, they pulled up at the main entrance. Pam caught sight of David just as he was entering the main gate.

Keep This in Mind

- A composition is a group of paragraphs that tell about one main idea.
- A composition has three parts: an introduction, a body, and a conclusion.

Now Write   Write a paragraph that explains what a composition is. Define the term *composition* in your topic sentence. Tell how many parts a composition has. Tell what each part does. Make sure your paragraph has a good topic sentence and a good ending sentence. Save your paragraph in your folder.

Part 2

Bright Ideas

Pre-Writing: Choosing a Topic

Here's the Idea   You can't begin a painting without knowing what you want to paint. In the same way, you can't begin a composition without first choosing a topic. Choose a topic that interests you and that you know something about. Be sure to choose a topic that you can cover thoroughly in four or five paragraphs.

There are many ways to find topics for compositions. One good place to look is in your journal. There you are likely to find topics that are too detailed to be covered in one paragraph. As you read books, magazines, and newspapers, keep your eyes open for possible composition ideas. You might also discuss possible topics with your classmates. Finally, do some brainstorming. Keep a list of all the different composition ideas you find. Refer to this list whenever you need a topic for a composition.

When you choose a topic, you must be sure that it is narrow enough for a composition. Although a composition is longer than a paragraph, some subjects are still too broad and general to be covered thoroughly in a few paragraphs. You can narrow your topic by asking questions about it such as *who? what? where? when? how?* and *why?* The answers to these questions will give you specific details about your topic. For example, the subject "an embarrassing incident" is too broad and general for a composition. By asking questions, you can narrow it to one, specific main idea such as "The school play last spring when I tripped on stage and ripped my costume."

Check It Out   Here is an example that shows how a general topic can be narrowed by asking questions about it.

144

General subject:	A summer vacation
Who?	Sandra and I
What?	train trip
Where?	across Canada, from Quebec to Vancouver
When?	last summer
How?	by train
Why?	to see Canada and to enjoy traveling by train for a week
Specific topic:	My train trip across Canada with Sandra last summer

- Do you see why the specific topic is better for a composition than the general subject?

Try Your Skill   The subjects below are too general for a composition. Choose one subject and ask *who? what? where? when? how?* and *why?* about it. Write your answers on a piece of paper. Then develop a narrow topic from the answers you have written.

a funny story   a party
baseball   cooking
old houses   a wonderful gift

Keep This in Mind

- Choose a topic that interests you and that you know something about.
- Narrow your topic so that it is specific enough to be covered well in a composition.

Now Write   Choose a subject that you would like to write about in a composition. Narrow your subject by asking *who? what? where? when? how?* and *why?* about it. Use your answer to develop a narrow, specific topic. Save your topic in your folder.

Part 3

Collect Your Thoughts

Pre-Writing: Organizing Ideas

Here's the Idea   Now that you have chosen a topic and narrowed it, you must gather ideas for your composition. These ideas may include descriptive details, specific examples, and facts and figures. You might gather these ideas through brainstorming, through research in a library, or from your own experience. Write down these pre-writing ideas.

Before you actually begin writing the first draft of your composition, you must organize your ideas. Read over your pre-writing notes. Which notes seem to be about the same main ideas? Group your pre-writing notes around two or three main ideas. Each group of notes will become a paragraph in the body of your composition.

Next, organize your main ideas and the details grouped around them. Decide which main idea you want to present first. Then decide in what order you will present the details grouped around that main idea. Use chronological order, spatial order, the order of importance, or general to specific order to organize the main ideas and details in your composition.

Check It Out   Look at these pre-writing notes for a composition about satellites.

Russians launch first satellite, Sputnik I, in 1957
defense: satellites used to warn against nuclear missile attacks
most satellites used for communication
more than 3,000 satellites now in orbit
satellites send information to antennas on earth
satellites send radio, telephone, television signals
Explorer I—launched in 1958—first U.S. satellite
weather satellites help show storms
signals beamed into space from antenna, bounced off satellites, and sent to another antenna on earth

- These notes could be grouped under three main headings: History, Uses, and How Satellites Work. What notes would fit under each main heading?
- Do you see how each group of notes could be developed into a paragraph?

Try Your Skill   Read the following notes for a composition about a day at the circus. Group these notes around two main ideas. Tell what the main ideas are.

the tight-rope walker
    crossed a thin wire
saw the dancing dogs
    perform tricks

saw prancing horses
saw the elephants on
    parade
clowns made us laugh
the lion tamer was very brave

Keep This in Mind

- Gather ideas for your topic through brainstorming, through library research, or from personal experience.
- Organize your pre-writing notes by grouping them around several main ideas. Each group will become a paragraph in your composition.

Now Write   Make some pre-writing notes for the topic you chose in the last lesson, **Bright Ideas.** Group your notes around two or three main ideas. Save your organized notes in your folder.

Part 4

Words in Orbit

Writing the First Draft

Here's the Idea Now that you have a set of organized notes, you can begin writing the first draft of your composition. As you write the first draft, make sure each part of your composition fulfills its purpose.

Your first paragraph, or **introduction,** has two purposes. First, it must be interesting enough to capture the reader's attention. Second, it must let your readers know exactly what you are writing about. Make sure you state your topic clearly.

The **body** of your composition contains paragraphs that develop your topic. Each group of ideas from your pre-writing notes will become a paragraph in the body of your composition. Each paragraph should have a topic sentence that states the main idea of the paragraph. The paragraphs and the ideas within them should also be in logical order. You may use chronological order, spatial order, order of importance, or general to specific order to arrange your ideas. Use transitional words and phrases between paragraphs and within paragraphs to make your ideas flow naturally.

The **conclusion** is the paragraph that ends your composition. The conclusion may be a summary of your ideas. It may be a general statement about your story, description, or explanation. The conclusion should signal an end to your composition. Don't introduce any new ideas in your conclusion.

Check It Out Read this first draft. Remember, this is just a rough draft. It will be revised later.

> I want to write about how satellites in space have become very important. The first american satellite was Explorer I. It was launched in 1958. Ever since 1957, when the Russians put Sputnik I in orbit, satellites have been helping people. There have

been more than 3,000 satellites put in space. Most early satellites were primitive.

Defense satellites are used to warn about an attack by nuclear missiles. Communications satellites are used to send radio and TV signals. They send telephone calls across long distances. Weather satellites show storms. Some satellites help ships and planes find their way.

The information from satellites is picked up on earth by big antennas. Radio, television and telephone signals are beamed up to a satellite. They bounce off the satellite's antenna, and land back on earth 10,000 miles away. This happens fast. Some satellites have cameras and sensors to study things.

As more satellites get put into space, they will help people more and more. Satellites are an important part of our future. Someday we will send satellites to another galaxy.

- Do you see how each group of pre-writing notes on page 146 has become a paragraph in this composition?
- Has the writer added any ideas that weren't in the pre-writing notes? Have any ideas been taken out?

Try Your Skill Reread the first draft on satellites. How would you change it to make it better? Discuss your ideas with your classmates.

Keep This in Mind

- Your first draft should have an introduction, a body, and a conclusion.
- Organize the paragraphs and the ideas within them logically.

Now Write Use your organized notes to write the first draft of your composition. Make sure you have an introduction, a body, and a conclusion. Make sure the ideas are organized logically. Save your first draft in your folder.

Part 5

Second Thoughts

Revising Your Composition

Here's the Idea The word *revising* comes from a Latin word meaning "to look at again." This is what you must do now with your first draft. Revising gives you a chance to improve your ideas, your organization, and your word choice. This is also the time to correct any mistakes you find in grammar, capitalization, punctuation, and spelling. The purpose of revising is to make your writing the best it can be.

Here are some questions you should ask when you revise.

1. Do I have enough details to develop my topic completely?
2. Are there any unrelated details that should be taken out?
3. Have I organized my details around two or three main ideas?
4. Will my introductory paragraph capture the reader's attention? Does it tell the reader what my composition is about?
5. Does each paragraph in the body tell about one main idea?
6. Have I arranged my paragraph and the ideas within them logically?
7. Have I used transitional words and phrases to lead the reader from one idea to the next?
8. Have I used strong and specific verbs? Have I used vivid adjectives?
9. Have I written a good conclusion that sums up my ideas?

Check It Out Notice how these paragraphs from the first draft of the composition on satellites have been revised.

- How have these paragraphs been improved through revision?

~~I want to write about how~~ satellites in space have become

very important ∧ *to life on earth.* ⟨The first american satellite ~~was~~ Explorer I ∧ It

was launched in 1958.⟩ Ever since 1957, when the Russians ∧put *launched*

Sputnik I in ∧orbit, *c to* satellites have ∧been ~~helping people.~~ *become necessary parts of our* ~~There~~

~~have been~~ more than 3,000 satellites put in ∧space. *c to* ~~Most early~~ *c have been rocketed*

~~satellites weren't too advanced.~~ *Since then,*

¶ *Satellites have many uses.*

∧Defense satellites ~~are used to~~ warn ∧about an attack by nu- *can* *us*

clear missiles. Communications satellites ∧are ~~used to send~~ radio *can transmit*

and TV signals ∧ ~~They~~ send telephone calls across long dis- *and*

tances. Weather satellites ∧~~show~~ storms ∧, *can predict* *c such as hurricanes and blizzards.*

Some satellites ∧help ships and planes ∧~~find their way.~~ *can even* *to navigate toward their destinations.*

Try Your Skill   Use the guidelines in this lesson to revise the last two paragraphs of the composition about satellites on page 149. Use proofreading symbols (page 85) as you revise. Compare your revision with those of your classmates.

Keep This in Mind

- Revise your composition to improve your ideas, your organization, and your word choice.
- Proofread your composition to find and correct errors in grammar, capitalization, punctuation, and spelling.

Now Write   Revise your composition, using the guidelines presented in this lesson. Ask yourself the questions in **Here's the Idea** as you revise. Save your revised composition.

Part 6

The Finished Product

Making a Final Copy

Here's the Idea   After you revise your composition, you still have one last task to complete. Now you must write your final copy. This is the only copy of your work that your readers will see. It should be as neat, clean, and free of errors as you can make it.

Write your final copy on clean, white, lined paper. Use pen, not pencil. In the upper right-hand corner of your paper, write your name, the subject, and the date. On the second line of your paper, write the title of your composition. Center the title.

Copy each line of your composition carefully. Leave at least one inch on the right and left sides of your paper. Leave at least one line blank at the bottom of your paper. Write on only one side of a sheet of paper. If you need more than one sheet, number every sheet after the first one. Write the number of each page at the very top in the center.

When you are done, proofread your final copy one last time. Neatly correct any errors that you find. If you have to cross out more than three or four errors on a page, write that page again.

Check It Out   Look at the beginning of the final copy of the satellite composition.

- Does this final copy follow the guidelines for proper form given in this lesson?

Tyrone Marpe
English
November 21, 1990

Helping Hands in Space

Satellites in space have become very important to life on earth. Ever since 1957, when the Russians launched *Sputnik I* into orbit, satellites have become necessary parts of our lives. The first American satellite, *Explorer I*, was launched in 1958. Since then, more than 3,000 satellites have been rocketed into space.

Try Your Skill   Write the answers to these questions about the final copy of a composition.

1. What kind of paper should you use?
2. What three pieces of information are written at the top of the first page?
3. Where do you write the title?
4. How much space do you leave on the right and left sides of your paper?
5. If you use more than one sheet of paper, how should you number the following pages?
6. How should errors be corrected?

Keep This in Mind

- The final copy of your composition should be clear, neat, and free of errors.

Now Write   Use the guidelines in this lesson to write a final copy of your composition. Be sure it is neat, clean, and free of errors. Save your final copy in your folder.

Part 7

A Reminder

Guidelines for Writing a Composition

In the next few sections of this book, you will be writing many different kinds of compositions. Whatever type of composition you write, however, the process of writing will remain the same. Here is a checklist of the steps to follow when you write a composition. Refer to these guidelines often as you write your compositions.

Guidelines for Writing a Composition

Pre-Writing

- Choose a topic that interests you and that you know something about. Narrow the topic so that you can cover it well in the assigned length of your composition.
- Gather details to develop your topic.
- Group similar details around two or three main ideas.
- Organize your details into an order that suits the type of composition you are writing.

Writing the First Draft

- Begin your composition with an interesting introductory paragraph that tells your reader what your composition is about.
- After your introduction, present the body of your composition. Use your organized details to develop your topic. Each group of details will become a paragraph in the body of your composition.
- Use transitional words and phrases to lead your readers from one idea to the next.

- Add, take out, and reorganize your ideas if you need to.
- Finish your composition with a concluding paragraph that sums up your ideas.
- Add an interesting title to your composition.

Revising

- Be sure your composition has an introduction, a body, and a conclusion.
- Check to see that you have included enough details to develop your topic.
- Organize the paragraphs and the ideas within them logically.
- Be sure the topic sentence of each paragraph presents the main idea of that paragraph.
- Use effective transitional words to make your ideas flow smoothly.
- Make sure you have used vivid language.
- Proofread to find and correct errors in grammar, capitalization, punctuation, and spelling.

Final Copy

- Rewrite your composition neatly in ink on white, lined paper.
- Write your name, subject, and the date in the upper right-hand corner of your paper.
- Write the title on the second line in the center.
- Proofread your final copy one last time. Neatly correct any errors you find.

The Narrative Composition

Part 1 **Elementary!**
Pre-Writing: Planning a Story

Part 2 **Where the Action Is**
Pre-Writing: Plotting a Story

Part 3 **What Do You Know?**
Pre-Writing: Choosing a Point of View

Part 4 **Write Away**
Writing the First Draft

Part 5 **What Do You Say?**
The First Draft: Dialogue

Part 6 **Moving On**
The First Draft: Transitions

Part 7 **The Final Event**
Revising Your Narrative Composition

Part 1

Elementary!

Pre-Writing: Planning a Story

Here's the Idea   When you write a narrative composition, you are telling a story. Some narratives tell real stories. Others tell stories invented by the writer.

Whether your story is real or imaginary, it should have a point. It should not be just a series of events. A narrative should tell the reader something special about the way people think, feel, and act.

Every narrative must have a setting, some characters, a plot, a conflict, and an ending.

The **setting** tells where and when the story takes place. Your setting could be a summer camp in the mountains, another planet, or a traveling carnival. The time may be the past, the present, or the future. Use specific details to describe your setting. That way your readers will get a clear picture of where your story takes place.

The **characters** are whoever takes part in the story. Characters can be people or animals. Describe your characters carefully to the reader. Let the characters tell something about themselves. For instance, instead of saying "Annie was very kind," you might *show* that she was kind. "When the skiers returned from the frigid slopes, Annie made hot chocolate and built a roaring fire."

A narrative must also have a **plot.** The plot is all of the events that tell the story. At the center of these events is a **conflict.** The conflict is some problem that a character struggles with. A character might struggle with a personal problem or with another character. A character might also struggle with the forces of nature. It is the conflict that gives meaning to a story.

Check It Out Look at these pre-writing notes.

Setting: dusk, along a big bend of Alice Creek
Characters: my friend Jim and I
Plot: Jim and I are fishing
I catch a huge muskie and try to reel it in
Conflict: me against the big muskie

- Do these pre-writing notes include all of the elements of a narrative composition?

Try Your Skill Alone or with a writing partner, develop a plan for an imaginary story. What will the story be about? Where and when will the story take place? Who will the characters be? What will the conflict be? Make some pre-writing notes about your story.

Keep This in Mind

- A narrative composition tells a story that has a point.
- A narrative should have a setting, characters, a plot, and a conflict.

Now Write Begin thinking about some stories you would like to tell. As ideas come to you, write them down in your journal. Label the page *Story Bank*. Include ideas for both real and imaginary stories. Remember, a good story will tell about characters who face a conflict. Save your story bank in your folder.

Part 2

Where the Action Is

Pre-Writing: Plotting a Story

Here's the Idea Once you have an idea for a narrativ
composition, you must plot your story. The plot, you remem
ber, is all of the events that tell the story.

If you are going to tell a real story, make notes abou
everything that happened. Try to remember specific detail
about each event in the story. Write down names, date
places, and times. Try to recall sensory details as well. Mak
sure that these details are accurate. Include the same types o
details when you plot an imaginary story. The only differenc
is that the events and details in an imaginary story are made u

As you plot your story, make sure that the events are ar
ranged in chronological order. This will make it easy for th
reader to follow the action of the story.

Check It Out Notice how the writer has plotted this stor
about catching a fish.

1. Jim and I at a big bend in Alice Creek
   –dusk, cool
   –Saturday in September.
2. Old-timers tell story about a huge muskie. Lives in this par
of the creek.
3. We start fishing for the muskie.
4. I work my way upstream to a pool of deep water.
5. I feel a great tug on my fishing rod—the muskie!
6. I battle with the muskie against the current.
   –my feet slipping on wet rocks.
   –fish pulls my line under a log
   –I call to Jim to bring a net.
7. Just as Jim nets the fish, my line breaks. Fish ends up in ne

₣ ⟵⑧ We are impressed with strength of muskie. We decide to let him go. He swims off into the twilight.

- Are these notes in chronological order?
- Has the writer included specific details in these notes?
- Do you see how the writer grouped these notes into paragraphs?

Try Your Skill   Here are some pre-writing notes for a story about a baseball game. Arrange them in chronological order.

Andy came up to bat
fans and players rushed onto the field
our team playing for the league championship against the Tigers
score tied in the bottom of the last inning
we carried Andy off the field on our shoulders
shared Andy's pride and the team's joy at the victory
Andy hit the first pitch over the left field fence—a home run

Keep This in Mind

- The plot is all of the events that tell a story.
- Plot your narrative by arranging the events in chronological order.

Now Write   In the last lesson, **Elementary!**, you made a list of possible stories to tell. Now choose the one you like best and make some pre-writing notes about it. First, decide on the setting, characters, plot, and conflict. Then, plot your narrative by listing the events that tell the story. Include specific and sensory details. Finally, arrange the events in chronological order. Save your pre-writing notes in your folder.

Part 3

What Do You Know?

Pre-Writing: Choosing a Point of View

Here's the Idea Before you can begin writing your narrative composition, you must choose a narrator. The narrator is the person who tells the story. Your choice of a narrator will depend on your choice of a point of view.

In the **first-person point of view,** the story is told by one of the characters. This character is identified by the pronoun *I*. The reader knows only what this character knows. The first-person point of view is a good choice for a story in which you are one of the characters.

In the **third-person point of view,** the narrator is not a character in the story. The narrator stands outside the story. He or she reports on the actions of the characters. This point of view uses the pronouns *he* and *she*.

There are two types of third-person point of view—limited and omniscient (om • ni′ • shunt). In the **third-person limited** point of view, the narrator tells only what he or she sees. The narrator never gives an opinion about what is happening in the story. The readers never find out what the characters are thinking or feeling unless the characters themselves say so.

In the **third-person omniscient** point of view, the narrator knows everything that is happening in the story. The narrator also knows what each character in the story is thinking and feeling. *Omniscient* means "knowing of all things." This point of view allows the writer to choose which details to bring out and which to keep hidden.

Check It Out Read these two paragraphs.

1. I watched nervously as Marion came to bat. On the first pitch, she hit a double to center field. Both runners scrambled around the bases and scored. The excitement brought me to my feet cheering. I saw Marion smile as she stood on second base.

2. Marion hit a double to center field. Both runners scrambled around the bases and scored. In the stands, the fans from Bedford High jumped up and cheered wildly. On the field, Marion smiled as she dusted off her uniform.

- What is the point of view of each paragraph? How do you know?

Try Your Skill   Number your paper from 1 to 5. Identify the point of view of each sentence. Write *First Person* or *Third Person*.

1. Later in the morning I tried to telephone Carol.
2. Carol was in the shower when the phone started ringing.
3. Jan wished that Carol would hurry up and answer.
4. When the phone had rung for the tenth time, I groaned and hung up.
5. When Carol picked up the phone and found no one there, she slammed down the receiver.

Keep This in Mind

- In the first-person point of view, the reader knows only what the narrator, *I*, knows.
- In the third-person limited point of view, the narrator tells everything he or she can see and hear. The narrator knows nothing about what the characters think or feel.
- In the third-person omniscient point of view, the narrator knows everything about the characters. He or she knows their thoughts, feelings, and actions.

Now Write   Read the pre-writing notes you have made. Decide which point of view would best suit your story. Write down your decision alongside your pre-writing notes. Save your notes in your folder.

Part 4

Write Away

Writing the First Draft

Here's the Idea   You have planned and organized your narrative composition. Now you are ready to begin writing the first draft. Like any composition, a narrative has an introduction, a body, and a conclusion.

The **introduction** sets the scene and introduces the characters. Write an introduction that will capture the reader's interest. Use strong sensory details to tell *where* and *when* the story is taking place. Use specific details to describe your characters.

The **body** of your narrative composition develops the plot. This is where you describe the events that tell your story. This is also where you introduce the conflict. The conflict should develop naturally from the plot. Don't just tell the reader that a character has a problem. Let the events that tell your story show the conflict in action.

In the **conclusion,** the conflict is settled, and the story is brought to a close. The conclusion should follow naturally from what has gone before. A shy character shouldn't suddenly become bold. If you have been telling a story that takes place in the future, don't shift to the present. If you have been using third-person point of view, stay with it.

Check It Out   Read the following introduction to a narrative composition.

> Alice Creek was a swift, roaring torrent at the narrow bend where Jim and I had camped. Here and there a fallen tree jutted out into the water. A jumble of boulders lined the banks. Old-timers had told us about a huge muskie that was lurking in this part of the stream. That Saturday, in the cold, gray dusk of late September, we had come to look for the famous fish.

- Does the introduction use sensory details to set the scene? What are they?
- Does the introduction introduce the main characters?
- Does this introduction capture your interest? How?

In the following paragraph from the body of a narrative composition, the narrator tells about the conflict. Rewrite the paragraph. Do not simply *tell* the reader what the main character's problem is. Use action to *show* the conflict.

> Jenny stood at the edge of the diving board. Her teammates stood around and watched. Jenny was afraid. She knew that if she didn't jump, her teammates would be disappointed. They urged her on. She looked at the water below. Her fear returned. She made her decision.

Keep This in Mind

- The introduction of a narrative sets the scene and introduces the main characters.
- The body of a narrative presents the plot and develops the conflict.
- The conclusion of a narrative settles the conflict and brings the story to a close.

Now Write   Begin writing the first draft of your narrative composition. For now, just write the introduction. Be sure to use specific details as you set the scene and introduce your characters. Make your introduction interesting. Save your introduction in your folder.

Part 5

What Do You Say?

The First Draft: Dialogue

Here's the Idea   A **dialogue** is a conversation between two or more characters. Sometimes you may want to use dialogue to add life and interest to a narrative composition.

First of all, dialogue can help you tell your story. Instead of *you* telling the readers what happened, a *character* can do it for you through dialogue. If one character says to another, "After I finished dinner, there was a loud knock on the door," that character is helping the writer to move the story along.

Second, dialogue can be a clue to a character's personality. *What* a character says and *how* a character says it can tell a great deal about that person. A character who has nothing but bad things to say about people, or who is always yelling at other characters, is probably a cruel or troubled person.

Dialogue always includes words that tell the reader who is speaking. These words are called **dialogue tags.** Some examples are *she said* and *Carlos said*. Dialogue tags may tell the reader not only *who* is speaking but also *how* that character is speaking. If a character is trying to keep his conversation private, you might say *he whispered*. If a character is angry, you might say *she yelled*. Pay attention to the situation your characters are in. Write a dialogue tag to suit that situation.

Always start a new paragraph when a different speaker talks. Put quotation marks around the speaker's exact words. Look at Handbook Section 17 on pages 581–584 for more information about writing dialogue correctly.

Check It Out   Read the following dialogue.

> "I'm going to go upstream and see if I can hook that muskie," I said.
>
> "Are you kidding?" laughed Jim. "Those old-timers are probably lying about that fish. They're just making fun of us."

"I'm going anyhow," I said. I grabbed my fishing rod and began walking up the rocky bank.

"You'll be sorry!" Jim called out.

- How does the dialogue help tell the story?
- What does the dialogue tell you about the characters?
- Does the dialogue suit the characters?
- Has the writer used good dialogue tags?

Try Your Skill   Rewrite this paragraph using dialogue. Use dialogue tags that suit the speakers' situations.

Beth told her brother that he had ruined her drawing pens. Her brother said he had needed to use them, so he did. Beth was angry. She told Paul he had no right to borrow her art supplies without her permission. Paul told her that drawing pens weren't important and that she could easily replace them. Paul laughed and told Beth he was going to his baseball game. Beth told him he would have to replace her pens. Paul stopped laughing. He asked Beth to be fair. Beth said she was being fair. Finally, Paul agreed to replace the pens. Beth also made him promise to ask her permission before he borrowed anything of hers again.

Keep This in Mind

- Dialogue is conversation between characters.
- Dialogue can show what a character is like. It can also help to move the story along.
- Dialogue tags tell the reader who is speaking and, often, how they are speaking.

Now Write   Continue writing the first draft of your narrative composition. Include dialogue that will help you tell your story. The dialogue should also tell the reader what your characters are like. Use dialogue tags that suit the situation your characters are in. Save your first draft in your folder.

Part 6

Moving On

The First Draft: Transitions

Here's the Idea The events of a narrative are usually told in chronological order. To make the order clear, you need good transitions. You know that when you write a narrative paragraph, transitions are important between sentences. It is also important to use transitions between paragraphs. Transitions will help your story to flow smoothly from one paragraph to the next. They can also help show how much time has passed between events. Some examples of transitional words and phrases you can use to link paragraphs are *two years later, last week, moments later,* and *yesterday.*

Check It Out Read the body and conclusion of the story about the two fishermen.

> I climbed over the boulders and fallen trees. Finally, I spotted a deep pool away from the main flow of the current. I waded into the pool and cast out my line.
>
> Moments later, I felt a heavy tug on my line. Then I saw him, a huge, silver-gray fish swimming upstream with my hook in his mouth. I had never seen a muskie that big. He yanked hard at my line, almost jerking the fishing pole from my hands. I felt my feet begin to slip on the rocky creek bottom. The muskie was trying to pull my line under a log halfway across the stream. He was not only huge, he was also clever.
>
> "Jim!" I shouted. "Get over here quick and bring a net!"
>
> I saw Jim pick up the big net and dash out into the water. The muskie continued to fight. I lost my balance on the slippery rocks and crashed into the water. The heavy tension on my fishing line meant that it would soon break. Just then my line snapped. Jim reached down and scooped up the thrashing muskie. He could hardly lift it.

After a few moments rest, we brought the fish up to the bank and inspected it. My hook was not the only one that this muskie had felt. We could see the scars from the muskie's other battles. Jim and I knew that we could not keep such a noble, old warrior. I removed the hook from his mouth, and we turned him loose. Then, with one last defiant slap of his tail, he swam off into the twilight.

- What transitional words and phrases were used between paragraphs? within paragraphs?

Try Your Skill   Rewrite this paragraph, using transitional words and phrases to make the paragraph flow more smoothly.

I got on the bus at Pembroke station. I thought I would take a nap during the long ride to Westville. The bus hit a guardrail and skidded to a halt. I woke up. I wondered what had caused the accident. The bus driver said that one of the front tires had blown out.

Keep This in Mind

- Use transitional words and phrases to show time order within paragraphs and between paragraphs.

Now Write   Finish writing the first draft of your narrative composition. Be sure to use transitional words and phrases that show time order. Write a conclusion that settles the conflict and brings the story to a close. Save your first draft in your folder.

Part 7

The Final Event

Revising Your Narrative Composition

Here's the Idea   When the famous writer Ernest Hemingway wrote a story, he sometimes revised it five or more times before he allowed it to be published. Hemingway knew something that all experienced writers know. He knew that revision is important to good writing.

Read over your story carefully. How can you make it better? Here are some questions to ask yourself as you revise.

1. Does my introduction set the scene and introduce the characters?

2. Have I used enough events and details to tell my story well?

3. Have I arranged the events in chronological order?

4. Have I developed the conflict in the body?

5. Have I used the same point of view throughout my story?

6. Have I included dialogue that helps tell my story and tells about my characters? Have I written it correctly?

7. Have I used transitional words and phrases within paragraphs and between paragraphs?

8. Does my conclusion solve the conflict and bring my story to a satisfactory close?

When you are satisfied with the ideas and organization of your narrative, proofread it. Correct any errors in grammar, capitalization, punctuation, and spelling. Be especially careful when you proofread dialogue. Refer to the Handbook, pages 581–584, for the correct form for dialogue.

Check It Out   Read these paragraphs from a narrative.

It was all these sounds that distracted me. When I heard a new high-pitched buzzing added to them, I didn't really think about it.

Just about the time that I realized what it was, Buzz heard it and yelled "Rattler," and the snake struck. I felt a dull thud against my boot, and I looked down and saw a thin stream of yellowish liquid running down the leather. At the same moment I saw a coiled Timber Rattlesnake. I had almost stepped on it!

Buzz was yelling to me, and I guess I panicked. In a dream, I watched myself raise the snake stick and bring it down right on the snake's neck. It didn't even twitch. In a second or two, Buzz was beside me.

The first thing he did was to look at my leg. "You're sure it didn't touch your leg?" he asked me. I was so scared I could only point to the wet spot on my boot and the two small fang marks in the leather. Once he saw that I was all right, he exploded. "Don't you look where you're going? Didn't you hear it? You almost stepped on that snake, and now you've killed it."

—BARBARA BRENNER

- What are some of the things that make this a good narrative? Why?

Try Your Skill   Proofread the following dialogue. Correct any errors that you find. See pages 581–584 in the Handbook for help.

I think you should tie that horse down, said Willard."
"I'm not going to do it, she said." Chestnut doesn't like being tied to a post." Besides, I'll be back in a minute
"You'll have to take the responsibility for what happens then", said Willard.

Keep This in Mind

- Revise your narrative composition until the story it tells is as good as you can make it.

Now Write   Revise your narrative composition. Follow the guidelines in this lesson. When you are pleased with your story, make a final copy. Save your final copy in your folder.

The Descriptive Composition

Part 1

Sensational!

Pre-Writing: Using Sensory Details

Here's the Idea A descriptive composition paints a picture with words. It might describe a scene, such as a park in the city. It might describe a thing, such as a cab. It might also describe a person, such as a clown.

Begin planning your word picture by choosing and narrowing a subject. Next, begin gathering sensory details by observing your subject in person or by working from memory. Then list as many sensory details as you can. Ask yourself how your subject looks, sounds, smells, tastes, and feels.

When you finish making your notes, read them over carefully. Cross out any details that will not help you to describe your subject. Then organize your notes in spatial order. Group your details around two or three main ideas. Each of these idea groups will become a paragraph in your composition.

Next, put your main ideas and the details grouped around them into a logical order. You will probably want to use spatial order to show how all the parts of your subject are related.

Check It Out Look at these pre-writing notes.

Topic: Grandma Sarah's apartment

Grandma Sarah and the sea
    lives in New Bedford, near harbor—busy
    fishing boats—treasures from Grandfather's sailing days

bedroom
    four-poster bed, maple, (center),—Chinese clock (red dragons)—oval mirror—sea chests, leather, wood, brass—smells of fresh-washed linen, lavender

favorite corner
    window facing sea—colorful seashells—when the window is open, smell of salt and sea—muffled clang of harbor buoy—comfortable rocking chair

Popeye, the talking parrot
    has a perch near the rocking chair—pale green parrot—loud
    squawks—"You old sea dog!"

- What senses have been used to gather the details in these pre-writing notes?
- What main ideas have the details been clustered around? How have these idea clusters been organized?

Try Your Skill   Below are some pre-writing notes for a descriptive composition about a pizza parlor. Along with the notes are three main ideas. Decide which notes belong with which main idea. Cluster the notes around that main idea.

Main Ideas:	Regina's Pizzeria (outside)	Regina's Pizzeria (inside)	Regina's is the best pizza
Details:	small, old building red and white checked placemats neon sign mushrooms, pepperoni		10 wooden tables crispy crust refrigerator for soda oldies jukebox long lines creamy cheese

Keep This in Mind

- Gather sensory details to develop your description.
- Group your details around several main ideas.
- Use spatial order to organize your composition.

Now Write   Make a list of some people, places, and things that you would like to describe. Choose the one that interests you the most. Use your senses to gather details about your subject. Group your details around several main ideas. Then, organize your main ideas and details in the order you want your reader to notice them.

Part 2

A Clear Picture

Writing the First Draft

Here's the Idea   After you have planned your description, you are ready to begin writing the first draft. Keep in mind the person, place, or thing you are describing.

Begin your first draft with an introduction. The **introduction** usually describes the setting of your subject. This paragraph should be interesting enough to make the reader want to continue reading. The introduction must also tell the reader about the person, place, or thing being described.

The paragraphs that follow the introduction are the **body.** In the body, present the sensory details that develop the description. Remember, each group of ideas you created during prewriting will be a paragraph in your composition.

The final paragraph of a descriptive composition is the **conclusion.** The conclusion sums up the description and brings the composition to a close.

As you write your first draft, use transitional words and phrases to make the order of details in your description clear. Here are some examples of transitional words and phrases that show *where* things are in your description: *behind, in front, near, in the distance, to the left,* and *to the right.*

Check It Out   Read the introduction and body of the first draft of this description. Remember that these paragraphs will be improved during revision.

> Grandma Sarah loves the sea. Her second-floor apartment is at the New Bedford harbor. She watches the fishing boats. The apartment has lots of things from the sea. And from my grandfather's sailing voyages.
>
> In the center of the bedroom is a maple bed. On the table is a chinese clock with red dragons. On the wall is an oval mirror. On

the opposite wall are two wooden sea chests. They are scratched and worn. They are filled with letters and things from Grandfather.

In the corner is my grandmother's favorite place. In this corner, there is a window facing the sea. The windowsill has colorful seashells on it. In the mornings, Grandma Sarah opens the window, and the breeze smells like the sea. She sits near the window. She sees the boats. She listens to the harbor buoy.

Near the door sits a pale green parrot named Popeye. Popeye squawks, "Come aboard, mate! You old sea dog!"

- Does the introduction set the scene?
- What sensory details are used in these paragraphs?
- What transitional words and phrases are used?

Try Your Skill Below is an introductory paragraph for a descriptive composition. Rewrite this introduction. Make it interesting. Use your imagination to add sensory details.

Our school gym is a big place. It has two or three doors on its ends and lines painted on the floor. The ceiling is high. It's a great place to see a basketball game. There have been lots of basketball games played in this place.

Keep This in Mind

- In a descriptive composition, the introduction presents the subject. The body contains sensory details that develop the description. The conclusion sums up the description.
- Transitional words and phrases that tell *where* help make the order clear.

Now Write Begin writing the first draft of your descriptive composition. Follow the guidelines in this lesson. For now, just write the introduction and the body. Save your work.

Part 3

Once More, with Feeling

The First Draft: Ending a Description

Here's the Idea   The conclusion is the final paragraph of your descriptive composition. These are the last words of your description that your reader will see. Don't shortchange the reader with a hasty, dull ending. Take the time to write a strong, clear conclusion.

First, read over the topic sentences for each of the paragraphs in your composition. These are the ideas that you used to develop your subject. Try to pull these ideas together so that they sum up the main idea of your composition. Try to present that main idea in a different way. Don't just copy the same words and phrases.

Second, ask yourself why you are telling the reader about your topic. Why is it interesting and important to you? Share your feelings about your subject with the reader. When you do that, the reader will feel closer to your subject. You will have made your subject something special.

Be sure your conclusion follows naturally from what has come before it. If your subject was humorous, end on a light or humorous note. If you have described a scene that is quiet and peaceful, give your conclusion a quiet and peaceful feeling.

Check It Out   Review the descriptive composition shown in the last lesson. Notice how the description is organized. Then read the conclusion below.

> I like to visit Grandma Sarah. We sit together in her special room. We laugh at the noisy Popeye. We talk of the past and places far away. Best of all, we watch the sea that she has always loved.

- Does the conclusion summarize the ideas of the composition?
- Does the conclusion follow naturally from the paragraphs that come before it?
- Does the writer share any feelings about the subject in the conclusion?

Try Your Skill   Look at the pre-writing notes about Regina's Pizzeria on page 175. Imagine you have used these notes to write a descriptive composition. How would you end your composition? Write an ending paragraph for such a composition. Use your imagination to create any additional details that you need. Be sure your conclusion presents your feelings about the subject.

Keep This in Mind

- In the conclusion, sum up the ideas in your composition.
- Be sure your conclusion follows naturally from what has come before it.
- Use the conclusion to tell the reader how you feel about your subject.

Now Write   Write a conclusion for your descriptive composition. Pull together the ideas in the body of your composition so that they summarize the main idea. Share your feelings about your subject. Save your first draft in your folder.

Part 4

Finishing Touches

Revising Your Descriptive Composition

Here's the Idea   Have you ever seen a photograph that was out of focus? The picture is blurred. The subject of the photograph is fuzzy. It's hard to tell what the picture is about.

The first draft of your descriptive composition may be blurred and fuzzy, too. You need to bring it into focus, to make the picture sharp and clear. Revising your composition can help you to do this. Here are some questions to ask yourself as you revise your first draft.

1. Have I included enough strong sensory details to develop my description?

2. Have I organized my details in the order that I want my readers to notice them?

3. Have I used transitional words and phrases to make the order of my details clear?

4. Will my introduction capture a reader's attention? Does it tell the main idea of the composition?

5. Does each paragraph in the body of my composition have a topic sentence that presents the main idea of that paragraph?

6. Does my conclusion sum up the ideas in my composition? Does it follow naturally from the rest of my description? Does it tell the reader how I feel about my subject?

When you have revised your ideas and your organization, proofread your composition. Correct any errors in grammar, capitalization, punctuation, and spelling.

Check It Out   Notice how these paragraphs from the composition about Grandma Sarah have been revised.

- What kinds of revisions has the writer made? How have the changes improved the description?

Grandma Sarah ~~lives by~~ *has always loved* the sea. ~~Her~~ *From* second-floor apartment *that overlooks*
my grandmother can *in the busy port.*
is at the New Bedford harbor, ~~She watches~~ the fishing boats. The
itself is filled with reminders of *of the long ago days of*
apartment ~~has lots of things from~~ the sea. And from my grand-

father's sailing voyages.
Against the wall *tall* *four-poster* *sits*
^ In the center of the bedroom is a *maple* bed. On the table is a
painted *from England.*
chinese clock with red dragons. On the wall is an oval mirror. On
Against *stand* *by the door hangs* *from India.*
the opposite wall are two wooden sea chests. They are scratched
now, but *souvenirs sent home by*
and worn. They are filled with letters and things from Grand-

father.
far *of the room* *small alcove,*
In the corner is my grandmother's favorite place. In this
is lined with
~~corner,~~ there is a window facing the sea. The windowsill has

colorful seashells ~~on it.~~ In the mornings, Grandma Sarah opens
of salt and
the window, and the breeze smells like the sea. She sits near the
watching *and* *ing* *muffled clang of the*
window. She sees the boats. She listens to the harbor buoy.

Try Your Skill   Revise the last paragraph of the body of the
composition about Grandma Sarah. This paragraph is on page
177. Use your imagination to add details. Make this paragraph
as interesting as the revised paragraph in **Check It Out** above.

Keep This in Mind

- Revise your description so that the picture it presents is sharp and clear.

Now Write   Use the guidelines in this lesson to revise your
descriptive composition. When you are satisfied with your
composition, give it a title. Then make a final copy. Proofread
your composition one last time.

The Explanatory Composition

Telling *How*

Part 1

How's That?

Pre-Writing: Planning an Explanation

Here's the Idea   Do you know how to fly a model airplane, make a pie, or build a tree house? Do you know how tad-poles become frogs, or how the space shuttle is carried into orbit? Any process that you understand well can become the subject of an explanatory *how* composition. An explanatory *how* composition explains how to do something or how something works or happens.

When you are looking for a subject for an explanatory *how* composition, choose a process that you know about. Think about hobbies, sports, or any area of study that interests you. Be sure the process you choose can be explained well in the assigned length of your composition.

Once you have chosen a topic, you must gather the details you will need to make your explanation complete. In an explanatory *how* composition, the details you need are all of the steps involved in the process you are explaining. Be sure your list of details is complete. If you leave out any important steps, your readers may not be able to understand your explanation.

As you make your pre-writing notes, write down each step as simply and clearly as you can. You want your readers to understand your subject as well as you do.

Check It Out   Read these pre-writing notes about a once-popular craft called tie-dying.

How To Tie-Dye a T-Shirt

1. Collect materials.
     plain, light T-shirt, string or rubber bands,
     stick, bucket, salt, dye, rubber gloves
2. Prepare T-shirt.
     wash, fold, twist, tie

3. Dye T-shirt.

    mix solution, soak shirt, hang to dry

- Do these notes list all of the important steps involved in this process?

Try Your Skill   Here is a process that is not very clear. In these pre-writing notes, the writer has left out some important steps and ingredients. On a piece of paper, write down the missing information.

How To Make Lemonade

1. Things you need:	–lemons
	–water
	–ice
2. Getting ready:	–slice lemons in half
	–measure out 1 quart water
3. Making the lemonade:	–squeeze lemons into water
	–add pre-measured sugar
	–stir and serve

Keep This in Mind

- An explanatory *how* composition explains a process. The composition may explain how to do something. It may also explain how something happens or works.
- The details that develop an explanatory *how* composition include the steps that make up a process. Be sure to include *all* of the important steps.
- Explain each step simply and clearly.

Now Write   Select a topic for your explanatory *how* composition. Choose a process that you know about and are interested in. For your pre-writing notes, make a list of all of the important steps in the process. Save your notes in your folder.

Part 2

Step It Up

Pre-Writing: Using Step-by-Step Order

Here's the Idea   Every process has its own order. That is, the steps that make up a process must happen in a certain order. Otherwise, the process won't work properly. The process of writing is a good example. You know that you must complete the first step, pre-writing, before you complete the second step, writing the first draft. You must write the first draft before you can complete the third step, revising. The order in which the steps of a process are performed or happen is called **step-by-step order.**

Organizing details in step-by-step order is very important. If any step is missing or out of order, your readers will not be able to follow your explanation. Suppose you were explaining how to make a pizza. How would the pizza taste if you forgot to tell your readers to add the spices? What kind of mess would your readers wind up with if you told them to put the cheese in the pan *before* the crust?

Begin organizing your notes by finding two or three main ideas among them. These main ideas might be the most important steps in the process. Group the rest of your details around whichever main idea they help to explain. Each idea group will become a paragraph in your composition. Finally, arrange your main ideas and their details into step-by-step order.

Check It Out   Look at these pre-writing notes for a composition about how coral reefs are formed.

1. **what coral is**—a kind of tiny sea creature
2. **conditions needed for coral reef growth**—lots of sunlight; shallow, warm saltwater; no mud or sediment in the water
3. **how reef forms**—living coral settle down on rocks or other hard surfaces

4. coral use lime from their bodies to attach themselves to rocks
5. lime hardens, creates a natural armor for the living coral
6. when coral die, hard lime skeleton remains—more living coral attach themselves to the skeleton
7. after hundreds of years, the coral have built their colonies into the enormous structures we call reefs

- Are these notes organized in step-by-step order? Is each step explained simply and clearly?
- What three main ideas are these notes grouped around? Do you see how each group of details could become a paragraph in a composition about coral reefs?

Try Your Skill   Here are some jumbled notes for a composition on how to make stilts. List the steps below in the correct step-by-step order. Add any details you think might be necessary. Keep your work in your folder.

wipe off excess stain

attach footholds with screws

measure boards for footholds two feet from one end

sand completed stilts

after measuring, saw cube of wood diagonally to make two footholds

brush stain on sanded stilts

get two long wooden boards and a cube of wood

Keep This in Mind

- Use step-by-step order to organize the details in your explanatory *how* composition.

Now Write   Take out the pre-writing notes you made in the last lesson, **How's That?** Organize them into step-by-step order. Check your notes carefully to be sure that you haven't left out any steps. Save your organized notes in your folder.

Part 3

Time After Time

Writing the First Draft

Here's the Idea   When you write an explanatory *how* composition, your goal is to present a process simply and clearly. To help you to achieve that goal, you organized your pre-writing notes into step-by-step order. To be sure your explanation is clear, however, you must go one step further. As you write your first draft, you must include strong transitions. Transitions will make the order of your details clear to your reader.

Transitions help to show the order of details within a paragraph. They can also help to link one paragraph to another. Think of them as stepping stones that let the reader cross from one idea to another.

Here is a list of transitions you can use in your *how* composition. These words and phrases will help you tell your readers *when* to do something or *when* something happens.

first	to begin with	before	now
second	the first step	to start	during this time
third	the next step	when	at the same time
next	after that	finally	as soon as
then	at last	last	afterwards

Check It Out   Read the body of an explanatory *how* composition about tie-dyeing.

First of all, you will need a few things to get started. Find a plain T-shirt that is white or light-colored. Also collect some string or rubber bands, a stick, a bucket, and salt. You need to buy a package of colored dye and a pair of rubber gloves to protect your hands.

Next, wash the T-shirt. Then fold or twist several bunches of the material. Tie the string or elastics around those areas that you want to be free of dye. These folds and twists will create the final patterns on your shirt.

Now you are ready to dye the shirt. Before you begin, put on the rubber gloves. Then mix the dye, water, and salt in the bucket, following the package instructions. Next, dampen the T-shirt. Then dip the parts of the T-shirt to be dyed into the dye solution. Use the stick to stir the solution often. Keep checking the color of the shirt. Remove it when it is the shade you want and hang it up to dry. Be sure to place plenty of newspaper under the drying T-shirt.

- What transitional words and phrases has the writer used within paragraphs? between paragraphs?

Try Your Skill Look at the work you did in **Try Your Skill** in the last lesson, **Step It Up.** Reread the steps in the process of making stilts. What transitional words and phrases would make the order clear? On your paper, rewrite each step, adding transitions.

Keep This in Mind

- In an explanatory *how* composition, include transitions to help make step-by-step order clear.
- Use transitional words and phrases within paragraphs and between paragraphs.

Now Write Write the first draft of your explanatory *how* composition. Remember, your composition needs an introduction, a body, and a conclusion. Write an interesting and informative introduction for your composition. Develop the explanation of your process in the body. Let each group of ideas from your pre-writing notes become a paragraph in the body. Follow the guidelines in this lesson about using transitional words and phrases. Your concluding paragraph might be the final step in the process. It could also be a summary of the process. Save your first draft in your folder.

Part 4

The Final Step

Revising Your Explanation

Here's the Idea   A house was once put up by a builder who had trouble understanding the architect's badly written directions. When the house was completed, it was facing the wrong direction. If the architect had revised his directions and made them clear, complete, and correct, a terrible mistake could have been avoided.

When you revise your explanatory *how* composition, be sure that you have explained the process clearly, completely, and correctly. Remember, you want your readers to understand the process as well as you do.

Here are some questions you should ask yourself as you revise your explanatory *how* composition.

1. Does my introduction tell the reader what my composition is about? Did I write a strong topic sentence for my introductory paragraph?

2. Did I include *all* of the steps in the process I explained?

3. Have I arranged my details in step-by-step order?

4. Does each paragraph in the body of my composition begin with a topic sentence?

5. Have I used transitional words and phrases that show the order of my details?

Be sure to proofread your composition. Find and correct any errors in grammar, capitalization, punctuation, and spelling.

Check It Out   Read the following paragraph from a composition about roller skating.

You have to learn to roller skate. You have to be prepared to fall down a lot before you can skate well. Use the toe stop at the front of the skate to stop yourself. Tie the laces up tight. You want your feet to fit snuggly into the shoes. Then, start skating with your legs pretty close together. Don't try any fancy turns, yet. First, pick a flat, hard surface to skate on, such as a paved driveway or playground. Don't try any hills.

- Does this paragraph have a good topic sentence? How would you improve it?
- Are the details arranged in logical order? How would you arrange them?
- What else would you do to improve this explanation?

Try Your Skill   Revise the following paragraph from a composition about how to make party salads. Be sure to use step-by-step order. Make the explanation clear.

This is how to make Waldorf Salad. You will need celery, apples, and grapes. Pour mayonnaise over the salad and mix it all together. Take the chopped up celery and apple pieces and put them in a bowl. Chop the celery, apple, and walnuts. Finally, sprinkle the chopped walnuts over the top of the salad. Put the grapes in, too.

Keep This in Mind

- Be sure your explanatory *how* composition is clear, complete, and correct.
- Arrange your details in step-by-step order.
- Use transitional words and phrases to show the order of details.

Now Write   Revise your composition according to the guidelines in this lesson. When you have finished revising your composition, make a final copy. Proofread it one last time and neatly correct any errors you find. Save your composition in your folder.

The Explanatory Composition
Telling *Why*

Part 1

Viewpoints

Pre-Writing: Developing an Opinion

Here's the Idea   Most people have strong opinions about many subjects. You have opinions, too. You can state an opinion in an explanatory *why* composition. You may want to explain why something is so or why you think something should be changed. Whatever your opinion is, you want to make it clear to your readers. You want them to understand why you feel the way you do.

As you search for a subject for your explanatory *why* composition, think about the things that affect your life. Think about your school, your neighborhood, your city, your country. What issues do you feel strongly about? What would you change?

Before you can present your opinion to your readers, you must be sure that it is clear in your own mind. Write a sentence that states your opinion. Make this sentence clear and direct. When you are ready to write your first draft, this sentence can become the topic sentence of your introductory paragraph.

Gather specific reasons and facts to support your opinion. You may want to use an encyclopedia or other reference work to help you gather material. Be sure your reasons are clear and logical and your facts accurate.

Check It Out   Here are some pre-writing notes for an explanatory *why* composition.

Opinion: Everyone should learn how to swim.
Support: 1. Swimming is a good way to cool off in the summer.
            2. Swimming is good exercise.
              –strengthens heart and lungs
              –improves circulation of blood
              –develops strong muscles in chest, arms, and legs

3. Swimming lets you safely enjoy a number of water sports.
   –boating
   –water-skiing
   –fishing
4. Knowing how to swim can save lives.

- Is the writer's opinion stated clearly?
- Do these notes support the opinion well? Explain your answer.

Try Your Skill   Read the following paragraph from an explanatory *why* composition. On a piece of paper, write down the writer's opinion. Then make a list of the reasons and facts the writer used to support the opinion.

Everyone should finish high school. Statistics show that high school graduates are more successful than non-graduates in many ways. First of all, high school graduates find it much easier to get jobs than non-graduates do. In addition, high school graduates working at the same jobs as non-graduates get promoted much faster. Most importantly, graduates, on the average, earn much more money than people who do not finish high school.

Keep This in Mind

- An explanatory *why* composition presents an opinion in writing.
- State your opinion clearly and directly.
- Gather specific reasons and facts to support your opinion. Be sure your reasons are clear and logical and your facts accurate.

Now Write   Choose and narrow a topic for your explanatory *why* composition. Write a sentence that states your opinion. Then gather as many supporting reasons and facts as you can to support your opinion. You may want to use an encyclopedia or other reference work. Save your work in your folder.

Part 2

Last, but Not Least

Pre-Writing: Organizing Your Reasons

Here's the Idea   When a lawyer presents a case to a jury, she or he often saves the most important evidence for the end of the presentation. In this way, the jury is left with the most convincing evidence fresh in their minds.

You can organize the details for your explanatory *why* paragraph in the same way. You can do this by arranging your notes so that the most important reason is presented last. This type of organization is called *least important to most important idea,* or more simply, the **order of importance.**

When you are ready to organize your notes, read them over carefully. Look for two or three main ideas among them. These main ideas will be the major reasons you are going to use to support your opinion. Then look at the rest of your details. To which main idea does each detail belong? Group all of the details around your main ideas.

Once you have grouped your ideas, find the reason you think is the least important. This reason, along with its details, will be the first one you present. Follow this reason with your other ideas. Make sure you end with the most important one.

Check It Out   Look back to the last lesson. Notice the opinion in **Check It Out.**

• Is the supporting evidence for the opinion listed in order of importance? Explain your answer.

Try Your Skill   Read the following paragraphs. They are from the body of a composition about requiring deposits for soft drink bottles. Rearrange the paragraphs so that they are presented from the least important to the most important idea.

Requiring deposits would also save energy. Glass bottles are made mostly by melting sand, soda, and lime. Since the heating furnaces must be at temperatures of about 3000° F. (1649° C), the process of making glass bottles requires huge amounts of energy. There are more than a hundred bottling plants located in thirty states. These plants produce about forty billion bottles a year. By recycling returnable bottles, we could save much energy.

In addition to saving money and energy, requiring bottle deposits would help our environment. Two billion tons of solid wastes pollute the environment each year. A large part of the pollution we see is the litter of bottles. Sidewalks and roadsides, especially in cities, are spoiled by litter.

Requiring a deposit would save money. Since returnable bottles can be recycled, the costs of making bottles would be less. As a result, beverages themselves would cost less. Because of the deposit, people would return empty bottles. This would also lower the cost of cleaning up litter everywhere.

Keep This in Mind

- Organize the supporting reasons and facts in an explanatory *why* composition according to the order of their importance. Start with the least important reason or fact and end with the most important.

Now Write Organize your pre-writing notes for your explanatory *why* composition. First, group your details around several main ideas. Then organize your main ideas and details in the order of their importance. Save your organized notes in your folder.

Part 3

On Your Mark

Writing the First Draft

Here's the Idea You have spent a lot of time developing an opinion and reasons to support it. Now you are ready to put your opinion in writing.

In the **introduction,** make sure you include a sentence that states your opinion. You could use the sentence you wrote for your pre-writing notes.

In the **body** of your composition, present the reasons that support your opinion. Develop each important reason in a separate paragraph. Be sure that your reasons are presented in the order of their importance.

In the **conclusion**, sum up your opinion and your reasons. This paragraph gives you one more chance to present your views and convince your readers.

As you write your first draft, there are two kinds of transitions that can help you to present your ideas. One kind helps you to present reasons or facts in the order of their importance. It includes such transitional words and phrases as *the first reason, second, most important,* and *finally.*

The other kind of transition helps you to state your reasons or facts. It includes such transitional words and phrases as *because, so, since, therefore,* and *as a result.*

Check It Out Read this composition about swimming.

> Everyone should learn how to swim. Most people think of swimming as simply a way to cool off during the heat of summer. But swimming has more important benefits.
>
> First of all, swimming is one of the best exercises you can do for your body. It strengthens the action of your heart and aids the circulation of your blood. It also helps you build strong muscles.

An even more important reason to learn how to swim is water safety. Many of us enjoy boating, fishing, or water-skiing. Yet, thousands of people drown each year while participating in these activities because they don't know how to swim.

Most importantly, knowing how to swim can save lives. Just last month, a 13-year-old boy saved his brother from drowning in Miner Lake when their canoe capsized. That is just one example of how swimmers have saved lives.

Swimming is more than simple fun. Knowing how to swim will keep you in good health, let you participate safely in water sports, and may even save someone's life.

- Does the introduction state the opinion clearly and directly?
- What transitions help to present the supporting reasons in the order of their importance?
- Does the conclusion sum up the opinion and reasons?

Try Your Skill   Write the transitional words and phrases you find in **Check It Out.**

Keep This in Mind

- State your opinion in your introduction.
- Use transitional words and phrases to present your reasons and facts and to show the order of their importance.
- Sum up your opinion and reasons in your conclusion.

Now Write   Write the first draft of your explanatory *why* composition. Follow the guidelines in this lesson. Save your first draft in your folder.

Part 4

Close-Out

Revising Your Explanation

Here's the Idea   When you have been working on a composition for a long time, it is often helpful to get away from it. After you have finished the first draft of your explanatory *why* composition, put it away for a day. Then, carefully reread what you have written. You will find that it is much easier now to see where your composition needs to be revised.

As you reread your first draft, keep in mind that you want your opinion to be clearly stated. You also want to give good, logical reasons to support it. Here are some questions to ask yourself as you revise your explanatory *why* composition.

1. Have I written a sentence in the introduction that states my opinion simply and directly?

2. Have I used specific reasons and accurate facts to support my opinion?

3. Have I arranged my ideas in the order of their importance, from the least important to the most important?

4. Have I used transitional words and phrases that show the order of my ideas?

5. Have I used transitional words and phrases that help to present my reasons and facts?

6. Does my conclusion sum up my opinion and the reasons that support it?

When you have revised your ideas and checked your organization, proofread your composition. Correct any errors in grammar, capitalization, punctuation, and spelling.

Check It Out   Look back at **Try Your Skill** in Part 2, **Last, but Not Least.** There you were presented with paragraphs from the body of a composition about requiring deposits on bottles. Now read the revised conclusion to that composition.

- Does this revised conclusion sum up the ideas?
- What kinds of changes has the writer made?

Try Your Skill How could you make the following paragraph better? Use the guidelines in this lesson to help you. Compare your revision with those of your classmates.

> It is my opinion that they should build a new dam on the Blue River. Last year the river flooded twice. It wrecked everything. I know two people drowned and it ruined crops. That was expensive. Besides, it would be nice to dam the river. You could make a lake behind the dam. You could go swimming and sailing. I don't know anyone who wouldn't like to have a dam on the river. Think of the fun you could have.

Keep This in Mind

- State your opinion clearly and directly.
- Arrange your supporting reasons and facts in the order of their importance.
- Include transitions to show the order of your ideas and to help you to present them clearly.
- Write a conclusion that summarizes your opinions and your supporting ideas.

Now Write Following the guidelines in this lesson, revise your explanatory *why* composition. When you are satisfied with your revised composition, make a final copy. Proofread it one last time. Correct any errors you find. Save your work.

Writing a Report

Part 1

In-Depth

Writing a Report

Here's the Idea   In the last four chapters, you have been learning to write different types of compositions. You have told stories, described persons, places, and things, and explained *how* and *why*. Now you are going to learn how to write a special type of composition called a report. A **report** is a composition that presents in-depth information about a topic.

Most compositions include your opinions about a topic. A report, however, deals only with facts. A fact is a statement that can be proven true. You gather facts from outside sources. These outside sources usually include books, encyclopedias, magazines, and newspapers. You use the information you gather to develop your topic.

You may be assigned a specific report topic, or you may be asked to choose one yourself. Be sure to choose a topic that is not too general. You must be able to present your information thoroughly in the assigned length of your report. For example, suppose you wanted to write a report about baseball. Topics such as "The History of Baseball" and "The Life of Babe Ruth" would be much too general for a short report. You could, however, write about "The Day Jackie Robinson Broke the Color Barrier" or "How the Minors Differ from the Majors."

It is not hard to narrow a subject in this way. Once you have a general subject in mind, begin reading about it. As you read, you may run across specific aspects of your subject that will be narrow enough to be topics for your report.

Check It Out   Read the following paragraphs.

> One of the most famous leaders in India's history was Mohandas K. Gandhi. Gandhi was educated in Britain. He then became a lawyer in South Africa and helped Indians who lived there.

During World War I, Gandhi returned to India. He tried to help the poor people of India. He led a simple life, following the ways of the Hindu faith. Millions of Indians looked up to him as a holy man, or *mahatma*. During the 1920's and 1930's, Gandhi led the Indian people in strikes, fasts, and protest marches against their British rulers.

In 1948, India was finally made an independent country by the British. Gandhi, more than any other person in Indian history, was responsible for this.

- Is this composition a report? Explain your answer.
- What facts can you find in these paragraphs? Has the writer included any personal opinions?

Try Your Skill   Tell whether each of the topics below would be a good topic for a short report. Give reasons why.

1. American presidents
2. George Washington at Valley Forge
3. why I like ice cream
4. the invention of ice cream
5. circus clowns at work
6. my trip to the circus

Keep This in Mind

- A report is written with information gathered from outside sources.
- A report is based on facts, not the writer's feelings or opinions.

Now Write   Choose a topic for a report. First, find a general subject you are interested in. You might want to use a subject you have studied in another class. Then do some reading about your subject.

As you read, find some specific aspects of your subject that would make good report topics. Choose one of these ideas. Remember, your topic should be narrow enough to be covered well in a short report. Save your topic in your folder.

Part 2

Digging for Details

Gathering Information

Here's the Idea   Once you have chosen a topic for your report, you must find some good sources of information about it. Books, encyclopedias, magazines, and newspapers are all good sources. All of them are available in your school and community libraries.

As you read about your topic, copy down the important facts you will include in your report. The best way to do this is on note cards. Follow these guidelines when making note cards for a report.

1. Use a separate 3″ × 5″ note card for each fact or idea.

2. Write down exactly where the fact or idea came from. Write the name of the source and the page number where you found the information.

3. Make sure you take notes in your own words. **Do not copy sentences directly from your source.** Using another writer's work word for word is not acceptable.

4. Make a *source card* for each source you use. On this card, write down the following information for each type of source. You will need this information when you list your sources in Part 6.

Book:	author, title, publisher, date published
Magazine:	author of article (if there is one), title of article, name of magazine, date published, page number of article
Encyclopedia:	author of article (if there is one), title of article, name of encyclopedia, volume number, page number of article, date published
Newspaper:	author of article (if there is one); title of article; name of newspaper; date published; section, page, and column number of article

Check It Out   Read this note card.

> *In 1836, Henry B. Clarke built*
> *a beautiful house at the*
> *corner of Michigan Avenue*
> *and Sixteenth Street.*
>
> *Chicago, Growth of a Metropolis*

- Does the note card include one important fact or idea?
- Does the note card list the source of the information?

Try Your Skill   Make two or three note cards. Use information from the following paragraph. It is from the same book that was used in **Check It Out.**

Overland travel was always uncomfortable. Indeed, in spring and fall roads were impassable. One solution that brought some relief in the 1840's were "plank roads". They were simple boards nailed to long timbers. In 1848, 200 wagons a day rumbled into town, most choosing to pay tolls for the privilege of using these improved roads.

Keep This in Mind

- As you read about your topic, take notes in your own words on note cards. Include the name of the source and the page number.
- Make a source card for each source you use.

Now Write   Go to the library and find two or three good sources for your topic. Follow the guidelines in this lesson as you make note cards about the important ideas you find in your sources. Make source cards, too. Save your cards.

Part 3

Divide and Conquer

Organizing Your Notes

Here's the Idea   Once you have gathered all the information you need for your report, you must organize it. If you take the time to organize your notes clearly and logically, you will have a good plan for writing the first draft of your report.

Begin organizing your information by reading your note cards. You will find that some of the notes relate to one specific main idea. Other notes relate to a different main idea. Separate the cards into piles. Each pile should develop one main idea.

Suppose you are writing about how minor league baseball differs from major league baseball. You might find that your notes tell about three main ideas: the players, the games, and the players' lifestyles. You would separate your note cards into three piles that match these three main ideas. Each main idea will become a paragraph in your report.

Once you have grouped your note cards into piles, arrange the piles into the order you will write about them. Then, on a piece of paper, write a sentence that describes the main idea of each pile. These sentences can become topic sentences when you write your report. Underneath each sentence, write down the facts from the note cards that develop the idea. Arrange these facts in the order that you want to present them. Now you have a plan for writing the first draft of your report.

Check It Out   Read this plan for a report about volcanoes.

1. **The planet Earth is made up of different layers.**
   - center of earth is hot mass of liquid metals
   - next comes mantle (thick, semi-liquid layer)
2. **The surface is covered with solid materials called plates.**
   - plates make up continents and ocean floors
   - plates move around on top of mantle

3. The plates rub against each other causing friction and heat.
- heat builds up beneath surface
- liquid rock and gases expand, force their way through cracks in plates
- hot materials become volcano

- Do you see how each sentence describes a main idea?
- Do you see how each group of ideas can become a paragraph in the report?

Try Your Skill   Below are two main ideas for a report about the homes of early American pioneers. Group the facts below them with the main ideas they belong to.

A. How the houses were made   B. How the houses were furnished

1. building materials—stone, logs, sod
2. kitchens—stone hearth, tables and chairs
3. quilts covered beds (also animal skins)
4. log walls, sealed with clay and pitch (called "chinking")
5. door hinges made of leather
6. some had no beds—just buffalo robes on the floor

Keep This in Mind

- Organize your note cards into piles. Each pile of cards should relate to one main idea.
- Each main idea will become a paragraph.
- Arrange the main ideas and facts in the order you will write about them.

Now Write   Make a writing plan for your report. Separate your note cards into piles. Each pile should cover one main idea. Organize the piles and the facts within them in the order you will write about them. Finally, write a sentence that describes each main idea. Save your writing plan in your folder.

Part 4

It's a Start

Writing the First Draft

Here's the Idea   Once you have created a writing plan, you are ready to begin writing the first draft of your report.

The first paragraph of your report is the **introduction.** The introduction has two purposes. First, the introduction presents your subject. Second, the introduction captures the attention of your reader. It tells the reader what your report is about. Don't begin by saying "I am going to write about . . ." or "My report is about . . ." Instead, begin with a sentence that is both interesting and informative. You might want to present some general facts from your note cards in your introduction.

The next section of your report is the **body.** The body is made up of several paragraphs. Each paragraph develops one main idea. Each paragraph in the body should begin with a strong topic sentence that introduces the main idea of the paragraph. Remember, you can use the sentences you wrote when you organized your notes as the basis for your topic sentences. Then use the facts you arranged under each sentence to develop the paragraph.

The last paragraph of your report is the **conclusion.** The conclusion should summarize the important information in your report.

Check It Out   Read the following introductory paragraph from a report on the causes of volcanoes.

> A volcano is one of the most fascinating and mysterious forces in nature. Often without warning, an entire mountain will explode. Hot ash and flaming lava shoot up from deep inside the earth. Some of these explosions have been so powerful, they have actually affected the climate of the earth. What causes these awesome displays of nature's power?

- Does the introduction present the subject of the paper? What is the subject?
- Is this introduction interesting and informative? Explain your answer.

Try Your Skill   Go back to **Try Your Skill** in the previous lesson, **Divide and Conquer.** Choose one of the two main ideas. Use the main idea and the facts you grouped around it to write a paragraph from the body of a report on early American houses. Be sure the paragraph has a strong topic sentence.

Keep This in Mind

- The introduction of a report tells what the report is about in an interesting and informative way.
- The body develops the topic with facts gathered from outside sources.
- The conclusion sums up the important information in the report.

Now Write   Write the first draft of your report. Use the writing plan you developed in the last lesson to guide you. Be sure your report has an introduction, a body, and a conclusion. Save your first draft in your folder.

Part 5

Another Look

Revising Your Report

Here's the Idea When you have finished the first draft of your report, you must revise it. Take time to read your report and think about it carefully. Use the revision guidelines on page 154 to help you revise. Here are some other questions to ask yourself as you revise your report.

1. Is my introduction interesting? Is it informative?
2. Do I have enough facts to develop my topic thoroughly?
3. Are my facts accurate? Are they clearly stated?
4. Is each paragraph in the body of my report about one idea? Do all the facts in a paragraph tell about that one idea?
5. Does my conclusion summarize the important information in my report?

Step 3 is especially important when you revise your report. Make sure that all of your facts are correctly and clearly stated. Check the accuracy of dates and figures. Be sure you have correctly spelled any names and special words that you have used in your report. Go back to your sources if you are unsure about any of your information.

Be sure to proofread your report. Look for errors in grammar, capitalization, punctuation, and spelling.

After you have revised your report, make a final copy of it. Proofread it one last time, reading it aloud to catch any mistakes your eyes might have missed. Neatly correct any errors you find.

Check It Out Look at this revised paragraph from the body of the report on volcanoes.

- How has the writer improved this paragraph?

The top of the earth is not solid. It is covered with plates.
[surface]
[actually] [twenty different]
Plates are continents. Plates are also ocean floors. These plates
[make up the earth's]
do not sit still. They move around on top of the mantle. Sien-
[These] [and] [often slide]
tists have discovered that the south american plate moves four
[remain] [as much as]
or five inches in a year.
[one]

Try Your Skill   Revise the following paragraph. Rewrite any sentences that do not make sense. Change the order of the sentences wherever necessary. Find and correct any errors in grammar, capitalization, punctuation, and spelling.

Vikings were led by Leif Ericson. They probably came to north america in about 1000 A.D. There are old pieces of pottery in Main and in Canada. These may have come from early Viking explorers. Scientists have old viking writings that tell about a land across the oshean. It might be north america.

Keep This in Mind

· Revise a report as you would any other composition. Try to improve the ideas, organization, and word choice. Proofread for errors in grammar, capitalization, punctuation, and spelling.

Now Write   Use the guidelines in this lesson to revise the first draft of your report. Check your facts for accuracy. After revising your report, copy it neatly in its final form. Proofread it one last time. Save your report in your folder.

Part 6

Name the Source

Preparing a Bibliography

Here's the Idea   Because the information in a report comes from outside sources, you must tell your readers where you got your facts. On a separate page at the end of your report, make a list of the sources that you used to write your report. This list is called a **bibliography.**

As you prepare your bibliography, use the source cards that you made during pre-writing. First arrange the cards in alphabetical order, according to the author's last name. If no author is mentioned, use the first main word of the title.

When your cards are in order, you are ready to write your bibliography. Each source has its own special form. Here are the correct forms to use.

Book:	Leaky, Richard E. *Origins.* Dutton, 1978.
Encyclopedia:	Fisher, H. Dean. "Dolphins." *The World Book Encyclopedia.* Volume 5, pp. 246–246d, 1984.
Magazine:	Hayashida, Tsuneo. "The Japanese Crane, Bird of Happiness." *National Geographic.* October 1983, pp. 542–556.
Newspaper:	Rowley, Gordon E. "Escape to Alcatraz: The Rock's a Nice Place to Visit, but Who'd Want to Live There?" *Chicago Tribune,* 19 February 1984, Sec. 12, p. 3. Cols. 1–5.

Check It Out   Look at the bibliography below.

Bibliography

"Chicago." *The World Book Encyclopedia.* Volume 6, p. 135, 1967.

Mayer, Harold and Richard Wade. *Chicago, Growth of a Metropolis.* University of Chicago Press, 1969.

"The New Chicago." *Holiday.* March, 1967, pp. 71–74.

Dedmon, Emmet. "Fabulous Chicago," *Chicago Tribune,* 13 December 1981, Sec. 3, p. 4, Col. 1.

- Are all of the entries in correct alphabetical order?
- Is the information in each entry arranged in the correct order?
- Does each entry contain all the required information?

Try Your Skill   Make a sample bibliography using these sources. Use the examples in this lesson to guide you.

   1. A book titled *Leonardo Da Vinci,* by Hugh Fraser, published by Macmillan in 1962.

   2. An article titled "Da Vinci, Leonardo," in *The World Book Encyclopedia,* pages 39–41, Volume 5, 1984.

   3. An article titled "When Leonardo Da Vinci Came to Town," in *Time Magazine,* 15 October 1982, pages 71–75.

   4. An article titled "A New Look at Leonardo," in *The Springfield Daily News,* Section C. Page 2, Column 1, 5 May 1980.

Keep This in Mind

- The last page of your report should be a bibliography.
- Each kind of source has its own special form in a bibliography.

Now Write   Make a bibliography for your report. Use your source cards to help you. Follow the correct form for each kind of source as shown in this lesson. Put this page at the end of your report. Save your completed report in your folder.

Clear Thinking

Fact-Finding Mission

Facts and Opinions

Here's the Idea   Your mind is like a computer. In it you have stored thousands and thousands of ideas. These ideas may be facts or opinions.

Facts are ideas that can be proved true. They tell about people, things, and events. The following are facts:

1. Many television shows are written by more than one person.
2. President Lincoln signed the Emancipation Proclamation.
3. Vampire bats have sharp, V-shaped teeth.

Facts can be proved in three different ways:

1. Some facts can be proved through observation. You can prove them by using your senses of sight, smell, hearing, taste, and touch. For example, you can use your sense of sight to prove the first fact listed above. All you have to do is watch the credits that follow most television shows.

2. Some facts can be proved by asking an expert. This is someone who has special knowledge, training, or experience. You can prove the second fact by asking a history teacher.

3. Some facts can be proved by checking a reliable written source. A **reliable source** is one you can count on to give you accurate information. You can prove the third fact listed above by reading about vampire bats in an encyclopedia.

Opinions are very different from facts because they cannot be proved true. The following statements are opinions:

1. Everyone should learn to ice skate.
2. Pandas are beautiful and funny.

These statements tell how some people feel about things. Other people might feel differently. That is why these statements can't be proved.

Opinions often contain certain words that express feelings:

should	beautiful	wrong	marvelous	nice	good
must	ought to	great	terrible	right	bad

Check It Out Read the following statements.

1. The largest bird in the world is the African ostrich.
2. Campers ought to learn first aid.
3. The month of July was named after Julius Caesar.
4. Cats make really nice pets.

- Which statements are facts? Which are opinions?

Try Your Skill Read each pair of statements. Tell which is the fact and which is the opinion. Explain your answers.

1. The Stutz Bearcat was America's first sports car.
   The Stutz Bearcat was beautiful.
2. Matthew Henson was a great hero.
   Matthew Henson was the first black explorer to reach the North Pole.
3. Everyone ought to read *The Pigman*, by Paul Zindel.
   The Pigman is about two young people, John and Lorraine, and their friend, Mr. Pignati.

Keep This in Mind

- A fact is a statement that can be proved true.
- Facts can be proved by making observations, asking an expert, or checking a written source.
- An opinion cannot be proved true.

Now Write Choose two television shows. Write an opinion about each of these shows. Then write a fact about each show. Compare your statements with those of your classmates. How can you tell which is fact and which is opinion? Label your paper **Fact-Finding Mission.** Save it in your folder.

Part 2

A Matter of Opinion

Supporting Opinions

Here's the Idea   Opinions are not facts and cannot be proved true. However, some opinions are better than others. This is because some opinions can be supported by facts. Think about the following opinion:

> People should learn how to do simple auto repairs.

This is a sensible opinion because it can be supported by facts, including the following:

> Most people depend upon cars for transportation.
> Most cars have mechanical problems from time to time.
> Doing auto repairs yourself saves money.

Whenever you speak or write an opinion, back it up with facts. These facts should tell *why* the opinion should be believed. Whenever you read or hear an opinion, be alert for the facts used to back it up. Remember that the more facts there are to support an opinion, the more sensible the opinion is.

Check It Out   Read the following paragraph.

> Renetta told us that her father was a wonderful painter. She said that he had won an art contest at the Uptown Community Center. She showed us a photograph of one of her father's paintings. She also said that her father was offered a job as a sign painter by a company that does outdoor advertising.

- What opinion did Renetta express?
- What facts does she use to support her opinion?
- Are these facts convincing?

Try Your Skill   Read the following dialogue. Which statement is a fact? Which statements are opinions? Are the speak-

220

ers arguing about a matter of fact or a matter of opinion? How do you know?

Erin: Well, that sure was a boring movie!

Ramon: I didn't think so!

Erin: Sure it was. Half the time the actors just drove around in flashy cars.

Ramon: Yeah, those cars were great!

Erin: Movies that star people are a lot more interesting.

Keep This in Mind

- Sensible opinions are ones that are supported by facts.
- Facts used to support an opinion should tell *why* the opinion should be believed.

Now Write Choose one of the following topics or one of your own. Write an opinion about it.

a popular song
movies
clothes or fashions
a book you have read
a hobby you enjoy

Use the opinion as the topic sentence of a paragraph. Follow the opinion with several facts that support it. Title your paper **A Matter of Opinion.** Place it in your folder.

Using
the Library

A Good Place To Visit

Using the Library

Here's the Idea A library can help you in two ways. It's a good place to find an interesting book to read. It's also a good place to find information.

Library books are divided into two groups, **fiction** and **non-fiction.** Fiction books are on their own shelves. They are arranged alphabetically according to the author's last name. The book *Old Yeller,* written by Fred Gipson, would be shelved under **G.**

Nonfiction books are arranged by their subjects. Most libraries use the **Dewey Decimal System.** This system puts nonfiction books into ten major categories, or classes. Each category has its own range of numbers. Each nonfiction book is assigned a number within one of the categories.

000–099	General Works	(encyclopedias, almanacs)
100–199	Philosophy	(ethics, psychology, occult)
200–299	Religion	(the Bible, mythology)
300–399	Social Science	(economics, law, education, government)
400–499	Language	(languages, grammars, dictionaries)
500–599	Science	(math, biology, astronomy)
600–699	Useful Arts	(cooking, sewing, carpentry, television, business)
700–799	Fine Arts	(music, sports, painting, dance)
800–899	Literature	(poetry, plays)
900–999	History	(biography, travel, geography)

On the spine of each nonfiction book is its **call number.** This number is the Dewey Decimal number and other information.

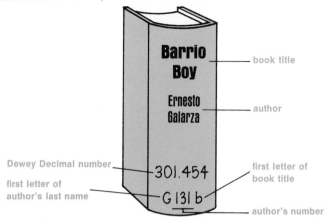

Barrio Boy
Ernesto Galarza

book title
author

Dewey Decimal number — 301.454
first letter of author's last name — G 131 b
first letter of book title
author's number

Check It Out Look at the spines of the books represented below.

True Tales of Bold Escapes
Theodore Roscoe
904 R719t

The City Rose
Ruth White Miller

Nina Baker
Ten American Cities Then and Now
917.3 B175t

Fireweed
Jill Paton Walsh

William Hopke
The Encyclopedia of Careers and Vocational Guidance
R 371.42 En 19 1975

Racing Cars
Raymond Francis Yates
629.1 Y27s

In Nueva York
Nicholasa Mohr

The Columbia Encylopedia
R 031 C723 1963

- How can you tell which books are fiction and which are nonfiction?
- How can you tell what the general Dewey Decimal category of each nonfiction book is?
- How can the call numbers and authors' names on the spines help you find these books?

Try Your Skill   On your paper, make two columns, one for fiction and one for nonfiction. Then, list the books in the appropriate group. Be prepared to explain where they would appear on the shelves.

1. *The Legend of Dr. J.*, Marty Bell 796.32309Er93zB
2. *Light a Single Candle*, Beverly Butler
3. *Five Were Missing*, Lois Duncan
4. *The Jazz Book,* Joachim Berendt, 785.42BER
5. *Black Like Me,* John Howard Griffin, 326G875b
6. *The Great Gilly Hopkins*, Katherine Paterson

Keep This in Mind

- Library books are divided into two groups, fiction and nonfiction.
- Fiction books are filed alphabetically by the author's last name.
- Nonfiction books are classified in ten major categories. Each nonfiction book has its own call number to show where it can be found on the shelves.

Now Write   If you have a favorite author, write his or her name on your paper. If not, find the name of an author. You may want to ask your teacher or a librarian for some help. Write the author's name on your paper.

Next, think of a subject you're interested in. It might be a place, a career, or a hobby. Write it on your paper.

Use your school or public library to find books by the author you have chosen and on the subject you have chosen. Try to find at least three fiction books and three nonfiction books. Write their titles on your paper.

Label your paper **A Good Place To Visit** and put it into your folder.

Card Tricks

Using the Card Catalog

Here's the Idea   The card catalog in the library can help you locate the books you want. You will find every book in the library listed there at least three times.

Every book is recorded on an **author card,** a **title card,** and at least one **subject card.** For a nonfiction book, all the cards give the call number in the upper left corner. The same number appears on the spine of the book. The number determines where the book is located on the library shelves.

All three cards contain the same information, although the information is arranged differently on each card. All three cards tell the publisher, the date of publication, and the number of pages in the book. A notation tells whether the book has illustrations. Sometimes, there is a short description of the book or mention of other books on the same topic.

On an **author card,** the author's name is at the top. The author's name is written with the last name first. Author cards are arranged alphabetically by the author's last name.

Author
Card

> 791.45013   **Winn, Marie**
> WIN
>   The plug-in drug, by Marie Winn.
> New York: Viking Press, 1977.
>   xii, 231 p.: ill.; 22 cm.
>   Includes bibliographical references
> and index.
>
>   O

On a **title card,** the title comes first. Title cards are alpha-betized according to the first word of the title. If *A, An,* or *The* is the first word in a title, look for the title card under the first letter of the second word in the title. The title card for *The Plug-in Drug* would be filed under *P.*

Title
Card

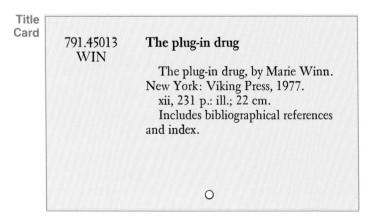

791.45013   **The plug-in drug**
WIN

      The plug-in drug, by Marie Winn.
New York: Viking Press, 1977.
      xii, 231 p.: ill.; 22 cm.
      Includes bibliographical references and index.

On a **subject card,** the subject is at the top. In the card catalog, the subject card is filed alphabetically by the first word of the subject. The subject may be written in capital letters or in red.

Subject
Card

791.45013   **TELEVISION AND CHILDREN**
WIN

      The plug-in drug, by Marie Winn.
New York: Viking Press, 1977.
      xii, 231 p.: ill.; 22 cm.
      Includes bibliographical references and index.

Check It Out Look at the three sample cards shown. Answer the following questions.

- Under what letter of the alphabet would each card be filed?
- Where could you look for more books by Marie Winn?
- Where would you find more books on television?

Try Your Skill Here are the title, author, and call number for a book about television. On your paper, draw three rectangles to represent file cards. Use the information below to make an author card, a title card, and a subject card.

About Television, by Martin Mayer, 338.5544M452a

Keep This in Mind

- Every book in a library is listed in the card catalog on three different cards—author, title, and subject.
- Each card records the call number, the author, the title, and other important information about the book.

Now Write On your paper, write the title of this lesson, **Card Tricks.** Draw three rectangles to represent file cards. Think of a job that interests you. For example, it might be related to medicine, cars, art, or sports.

In the library, go to the card catalog and find a subject card, an author card, and a title card for books related to your job. Copy the information from the cards onto your paper. Keep your work in your folder.

Part 3

It's All There

Using an Encyclopedia

Here's the Idea   One of the most useful sources of general information is an **encyclopedia.** An encyclopedia is a set of numbered volumes containing articles on many subjects. The articles are arranged alphabetically by subject, from the first volume through the last. On the spine of each volume, you will find a single letter or guide letters that tell you what subjects are covered in it. Look at the set of encyclopedias in your school library or public library.

Suppose that you were planning a composition on the effects of television. You might use the *World Book Encyclopedia, Collier's Encyclopedia,* or the *Britannica Junior Encyclopaedia.* Find the appropriate volume and look up the key word of your subject: television. You will find that the pages are marked with guide words. Like the guide words in a dictionary, these help you find your topic quickly.

An encyclopedia article on a major subject is usually organized into parts with subtitles. The article on television might include such parts as "Television in the Home," "The Television Industry," "How Television Works," and "Effects of Television." You may want to read only the parts about your specific topic. You may also want to look at the end of the article for a list of related articles in the encyclopedia or for a list of books for further reading.

Different encyclopedias have different reading levels. To find the one that is easiest for you to understand, choose a topic and look it up in several encyclopedias. You may want to ask the librarian to suggest an encyclopedia that would be best for you.

Check It Out   Look at an encyclopedia in your school library or public library. Answer the following questions.

- In what volume would you find information about Mexican food? space travel? folk music? Mark Twain? glaciers? Rhode Island? newspapers? Belgium? Mary Cassatt?

Try Your Skill Number your paper from 1 to 5. Write the key word in each question below that tells you where to find the answer in an encyclopedia.

1. What factors are important in choosing a career?
2. What unusual forms of transportation are used in other parts of the world?
3. In what state does the Mississippi River begin?
4. Did Edgar Allan Poe write a story called "The Black Cat"?
5. What treatment is recommended for burns?

Keep This in Mind

- An encyclopedia contains articles on many different subjects. Articles are arranged alphabetically in numbered volumes.
- Use key words to help find articles on your topic. Refer to the appropriate subtitle in an article to find specific information about your topic.
- Use an encyclopedia that you can read easily.

Now Write On your paper, write the title of this lesson, **It's All There.** Find an encyclopedia article on the job you chose in **Now Write** in the last lesson. List the following information: the name of the encyclopedia where you found the article, the number and guide letters of the volume, the guide words on the page, any related articles, and the title of any books on the subject. Put your work into your folder.

Study and Research Skills

Part 1

Before You Begin

Understanding the Assignment

Here's the Idea Do you ever wonder how you will be able to finish all your assignments correctly and on time? If you have good study and research skills, you will not have this problem. These skills will help you learn your lessons. They will also help you write your papers and complete projects.

Write down the important parts of an assignment when it is given. Use a special part of your notebook, or use a separate notebook. First, write the subject. Then write exactly what you are supposed to do. Also write the date the assignment was given. Finally, write the date it is due.

Subject	Assignment	Date Given	Date Due
English	Read Chapters 1 and 2 of Huckleberry Finn	5-3	5-5
Soc.Studies	Make map of Canada	5-3	5-6
Math	Read Chapter 10. Do exercises pp. 201-203	5-4	5-5

Before you begin an assignment, ask yourself these questions:

1. **What kind of assignment is it?** Will you have to study, read, memorize, write, answer questions, or make something?

2. **What should the final product be?** Will it be a composition, a report, a speech, answers to questions, or a skit?

3. **What do I need?** Will you need any special materials? Will you need certain books from the library?

4. **When is the assignment due?** How much time do you have to complete the assignment?

Check It Out   Read the following sample social studies assignment.

> Choose one American President. Write a two-page report on his life. Draw a picture of an interesting event that took place during his term of office. The assignment is due Thursday.

- What three things does the assignment ask you to do?
- What will the final products be?
- What special materials are necessary?
- When is the assignment due?

Try Your Skill   Read the sample science assignment below. What type of assignment is it? What will the final product be? What materials will you need? When is it due?

> By Friday, collect or draw pictures of the foods in the four basic food groups. Mount them in your notebook. Label them clearly. Write a short paragraph about each group, telling why those foods are important to good nutrition.

Keep This in Mind

- Be sure that you understand the assignments that you are given. Know what the final product should be. Know what materials you need. Also, know when the assignment is due.
- Write the details of your assignments and their due dates in your notebook.

Now Write   On your paper, draw a page from an assignment book like the one in this lesson. Label the columns as they are shown in the sample. Look at the sample assignments in **Check It Out** and **Try Your Skill**. Enter these assignments on your sample page. Save your work in your folder.

Part 2

What Do I Do Next?

Following Directions

Here's the Idea Have you ever gotten lost because you forgot or misunderstood the directions? Knowing how to follow directions is an important skill whether you are trying to find a building, play a game, or complete an assignment. Your assignments will be easier to complete if you follow directions carefully. Directions may be spoken or written.

These guidelines will help you follow spoken directions:

Listening to Spoken Directions

1. Listen carefully to what is said.
2. Notice how many steps are involved in the assignment. Also notice the order of the steps.
3. Listen for key words, such as *read, answer, collect, write, organize,* or *memorize.*
4. Ask your teacher questions if you do not understand a step.
5. Write down the directions when they are given.

These guidelines will help you follow written directions:

Reading Written Directions

1. Read all the directions carefully before you begin the assignment.
2. Ask questions if there is something that you don't understand.
3. Gather any necessary books and materials before you begin.
4. Break down the assignment into steps. Organize the steps in the order that you will complete them.

Check It Out   Read the directions for this assignment.

Make as many words as you can, using the letters in the word *airplane*. List the words neatly in alphabetical order on notebook paper. Use a dictionary to check the spelling of your words.

- Do you know exactly what to hand in? Do you know what form the assignment must be in?
- Are there any questions you might ask to make the directions clearer?
- How would you organize this assignment into steps?

Try Your Skill   Read and then follow this set of directions.

1. If you have green or brown eyes, write the place where you were born.

2. If your eyes are any other color, write the place where you live now.

3. If you are reading these directions correctly, you should have read all of them before beginning. Ignore directions 1 and 2. Write the name of a place where you would like to live someday.

Keep This in Mind

- Read or listen to all of the directions before you begin your assignment.
- Break down the assignment into steps.
- Ask questions if you do not understand some part of the assignment.

Now Write   Think about an activity that you do well. It might be preparing food, playing a game, or working on a hobby. Then, write directions for someone who does not know how to perform this activity. Be sure that you organize your directions into steps. Read your directions to a classmate. See whether he or she can follow your spoken directions. Save your work in your folder.

Where Can I Go?

A Time and a Place To Study

Here's the Idea   If you have a good place to study, you will find that it will be easier to get your assignments done. At home, you can set up a study area by clearing a table or a desk in your bedroom or some other room. At school, you can use the library or study hall. You can also find quiet places to study at your public library. Wherever you study, be sure that your space meets the following requirements:

Requirements for a Good Study Space
1. **It should be quiet.** You should not be disturbed by the TV, radio, telephone, or any other noise.
2. **It should be well lit.** Poor lighting can strain your eyes and give you headaches.
3. **It should be neat and organized.** You should not have to search for papers, books, and other materials.
4. **It should be equipped properly.** You should have paper, pens, and pencils handy. Your space should also have a dictionary.
5. **It should be available at a regular time.** Set aside a regular time to study each day. That way, others will know your study time and won't disturb you.

Check It Out   Here are examples of six study spaces.

1. A table in the library after school. There is space for your books and materials.

2. The kitchen table after dinner. Your books and materials are neatly arranged on the table.

3. The cafeteria during lunch hour.

4. Your bed. Your radio is playing loud music.
5. The living room floor near the TV.
6. A desk in your bedroom. There is a shelf for your books and a drawer for other materials.

- Which of these places would be good study spaces? Which would not be good? Explain your answers.

Try Your Skill   Decide how good your study space is. Rate your answers to these questions as follows:

A. Always (needs no improvement)
B. Sometimes (needs some improvement)
C. Rarely (needs much improvement)

1. Do you sit at a table or desk?
2. Is the light good for studying?
3. Is there too much noise nearby?
4. Are your books and materials organized?
5. Do you have all the supplies you need?

Compare your answers to the requirements listed for a good study space in this lesson. Use your answers to improve your study area.

Keep This in Mind

- A study space should be quiet, well-lit, and neat.
- Have paper, pens, pencils, and a dictionary available when you study.
- Establish a regular time each day to study.

Now Write   On your paper, list three good places in your home, at school, or in the public library where you could study. Also list when these places are available. Then tell how you could improve the study space you use now. Label your paper **Where Can I Go?** Save your paper in your folder.

Part 4

You Did It!

Achieving Goals with a Study Plan

Here's the Idea   Even if you have a perfect study space, your assignments won't get completed unless you plan your time carefully. How can you complete all of your assignments by their due dates? The best way to plan your time well is to set long-term and short-term goals.

At the end of each day, read over all of your assignments. Assignments that are due the next day are your **short-term goals.** Allow time each day to complete these assignments.

Assignments that will take longer than one day to complete are **long-term goals.** Divide all long-term goals into shorter tasks. Then arrange these tasks in the order in which they should be completed. Each day, you should do some of these shorter tasks. For example, suppose you have to write a science report about plants that grow in the ocean. You might break up this long-term goal into the following tasks:

1. Find three books in the library.
2. Read the sections on ocean plants in these books.
3. Write and organize some notes.
4. Find a picture of an ocean plant to include in the report.
5. Write the first draft.
6. Revise the first draft.
7. Prepare the final copy.

Once you have divided this long-term goal into shorter tasks, you need a **study plan** to help you complete them. A study plan is a calendar of all your daily activities. It includes school activities, social activities, and your homework. A study plan helps you to schedule your long- and short-term goals.

Check It Out   See how the science report about ocean plants is scheduled in a study plan.

Monday	Tuesday	Wednesday	Thursday	Friday	Saturday	Sunday
math problems	Library	research ocean plants	research ocean plants	organize notes	write 1ST draft	Review math
read poems	choir practice	piano lesson	basketball practice	basketball game	dinner, Aunt Sue's	Carol's party
revise draft	Dentist 3:30	Make final copy of report	ocean plants report due	English test	movie with Jan	write letter to Grandma
History assignment	choir practice	Math test	Review English	choir concert		

- Do you see how the work for the report has been organized so that it can be completed by the due date?
- Do you see that the student realized there were some days when no work could be done on the project?

Try Your Skill   Divide the following long-term goal into shorter tasks. Organize them in the order they need to be done.

Make a poster display that tells about five kinds of trees that grow in your state. Find at least one book about trees at the library. Read about the trees you have chosen. On each poster, draw a picture of one of the trees. Write a brief description of the tree below the picture.

Keep This in Mind

- Spend time each day completing short-term goals.
- Divide all long-term goals into shorter tasks. Arrange those tasks in a logical order.
- Make a study plan to help you schedule your time.

Now Write   On your paper, make a two-week calendar that shows your regular activities. Use the calendar in this lesson as a model. Then schedule your homework for this week and next week on the calendar. Use your completed study plan to help you finish your assignments during the week.

Part 5

Meet SQ3R

A Way To Study

Here's the Idea   For most activities that you do, you probably have a certain method or way of doing it that works best for you. The same goes for studying. If you use one study method regularly, it can help you to study more effectively.

One study method is called **SQ3R**. SQ3R stands for **S**urvey, **Q**uestion, **R**ead, **R**ecite, and **R**eview. These are the five steps that make up the study method.

SQ3R	
Survey	Look over the material quickly to get an idea of what you'll be reading. Read the titles, subtitles, introduction, and summary. Also look at any illustrations.
Question	Make a list of questions that you should be able to answer after reading the material. Include questions your teacher gives you, as well as those at the end of the chapter. You can also make questions out of titles, topic sentences, and illustrations.
Read	Pick out the main idea in each section as you read. Look for the answers to the questions you wrote.
Recite	Recite your answers to the questions. Take notes to help you remember the answers. Also take notes on any other important ideas.
Review	Quickly read over your notes and review the main ideas.

Check It Out   Reread the steps in the SQ3R Method.

- Which of these steps involves reading?

Try Your Skill   Apply the SQ3R method to the following passage. Turn the title and subheadings into questions. Take notes on any important information.

Ant Society

What insects live in organized communities, have wars, and work with their neighbors? The correct answer is *ants*.

The Classes of Ants.   Ants do not act alone. Instead, they do the same things as the other members of their class. The three major classes of ants are the queens, the workers, and the soldiers. The queen is the head of the ants. She spends most of her time laying eggs. The workers care for the nest and the young, and they also gather food. The soldiers attack other nests, and they defend their own colonies.

Activities of Ants.   Ants usually spend their lives within or near their nests. Ants can be friendly and live in other colonies. Ants can also feed each other. An ant can digest food for itself in one of its stomachs. It can also keep more food in a sac called the *social stomach*. This food is for the rest of the colony.

Ants can be warlike. Some species conduct slave hunts. Other ants quarrel constantly and rob other colonies.

Keep This in Mind

- The five steps in the SQ3R method are **S**urvey, **Q**uestion, **R**ead, **R**ecite, and **R**eview.
- Use the SQ3R method to study for all your classes.

Now Write   Apply the SQ3R method of studying to a homework reading assignment. You may choose math, science, social studies, or any other assignment. Write out your questions, answers, and notes. Label your paper **Meet SQ3R**. Save it in your folder.

Part 6

Write It Down

Taking Notes

Here's the Idea Do you sometimes have trouble remembering what you read or heard? If you take notes as you read or listen, you will be able to remember information more easily. Note-taking is an important study skill. Notes can help you to remember the main ideas of the material you are reading or hearing. Notes can also be used for study and review.

Keep your notes in a separate notebook. Divide this notebook into sections for each subject. Write the date and the subject at the top of each page of notes. List the main ideas covered in class. Also include notes and questions as you read your textbooks.

When you take notes while someone is speaking, be alert for clues that tell you what is important. These include phrases such as *most important, the main point, and to summarize.* Write this information in your notebook.

When you take notes as you read, include all the main ideas, key words, and definitions you find. Write the answers to any questions you think of as you read.

When you are taking notes, you will want to write quickly. Don't take the time to write complete sentences. Use phrases, abbreviations, and symbols to save time and space.

Common Abbreviations and Symbols					
w	with	*w/o*	without	*imp*	important
✳	important information	*b/c*	because	*d d*	due date
		=	is, are	&	and

You can make up your own abbreviations. Write your notes neatly and clearly so you can read them easily when you review.

Check It Out   Notice the use of symbols and abbreviations in the notes that follow this passage.

Some of the most intelligent creatures on earth are whales, dolphins, and porpoises. These mammals are born without a sense of smell and with poor eyesight. However, they have highly developed senses of hearing and touch. Because they communicate orally with each other, scientists believe that these animals have developed a form of language.

Whales, porpoises, & dolphins = among mst intell. creat. Communic w/ ea othr w/ lang.

- Has the writer taken notes on the main ideas?
- What symbols or abbreviations are in these notes? What do they mean?

Try Your Skill   Choose a passage from your science or social studies book. Read it and take notes. Use appropriate symbols or abbreviations. Then, exchange your notes with a classmate. See if you can understand each other's notes.

Keep This in Mind

- Take notes on important information to help you remember it.
- Use abbreviations and symbols when possible.
- Write notes in phrases, not sentences.
- Write your notes clearly.

Now Write   Take some notes on a major story in today's newspaper or on a story on the evening news on TV. Follow the guidelines suggested in this lesson. Tomorrow, see if you can write a paragraph about the news story, using your notes.

Part 7

Eye Openers

Using Graphic Aids

Here's the Idea Much of the information you learn is presented through language. However, you also receive much information through photographs, maps, tables and charts, graphs, and illustrations. These graphic aids present information quickly and clearly.

Photographs and illustrations can communicate moods or feelings quickly. Always read the captions that appear with these pictures.

Diagrams help you to identify parts of an object. They also show how the parts are related.

Maps are drawings of areas of land and water. A map can display facts about an area. For example, maps can show population, climate, or rainfall. A map can also show cities, roads, or the height of the land.

Tables and charts present groups of facts. These facts are usually arranged in columns.

Graphs are charts that show how one fact or set of facts is related to another. To understand a graph, first read the title of the graph. Then read the key to symbols used. Finally, read the information that appears above, beneath, or beside the graph.

Check It Out Study the graphic aids on the next page and then answer these questions.

- Which graphic aid is a map? a diagram? a chart? a graph? an illustration?
- How many calories does one cup of shredded raw carrot have?
- Is Rome on the east or west coast of Italy?

Food	Calories
apple, 1 large	117
carrots 1 cup	42
milk, whole 1 glass	124
CALORIES OF COMMON FOODS	

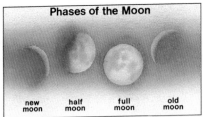

Phases of the Moon

new moon   half moon   full moon   old moon

Rome

ITALY

N
W — E
S

Cardinal

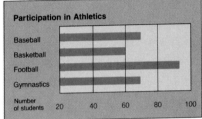

Participation in Athletics

Baseball
Basketball
Football
Gymnastics

Number of students   20   40   60   80   100

Try Your Skill   Which type of graphic aid would best present each type of information listed below?

1. Attendance at eight basketball games
2. The average temperature of an area
3. How two kinds of flowers differ in appearance

Keep This in Mind

- Graphic aids present information quickly and clearly.
- Graphic aids include photographs, diagrams, maps, tables and charts, and graphs.

Now Write   You have the following information about the countries that have won the most Olympic medals from 1896–1980.

United States   — 1,615 medals
USSR (Russia) — 1,028 medals
Great Britain   — 560 medals

Make a graph showing this information and label it.

Part 8

Get Set

Answering Objective Test Questions

Here's the Idea   Does the thought of taking a test make you a little nervous? Many people feel this way. However, remember that a test is an assignment. You can prepare for it as you would for any other assignment. This will help you to feel confident. Another way for you to feel confident is to understand the different kinds of test questions.

Objective test questions have only one answer. There are three different kinds of objective test questions. The following guidelines will help you to answer these kinds of questions.

Multiple Choice   In multiple choice questions, you must choose one answer out of the several given to you. Be sure to read all of the choices before you make your decision. Always choose the best answer.

True-False   In this kind of question, you must decide whether a statement is *true* or *false*. Watch for words like *always*, *never*, *all*, or *none*. These words often make a statement false.

Matching   In matching questions, you are given two lists. You must match items from one list with items in the other list. Always begin by matching the items you are surest of. Then it will be easier to match those that remain.

Check It Out   Read the following test questions.

1. True or False: The third planet from the Sun is Pluto. _F_

2. What is the first planet from the Sun?

   (A) Earth   (B) Venus   (C) Mercury   (D) Uranus

3. Match each planet with its position in relation to the sun.

Planet   **Position**

Uranus ——————— first

Mars ——————— fourth

Neptune ——————— seventh

Mercury ——————— eighth

- Do you see how different kinds of questions call for different kinds of answers?

Try Your Skill   Turn back to Part 5, **Meet SQ3R,** in this section. Write two true-false and two multiple choice test questions based on information in that part. Write the answers to the questions.

> **Keep This in Mind**
>
> - Objective test questions include multiple choice, true-false, and matching questions.
> - Read each question completely before you answer it.

Now Write   Write an objective test on a favorite sport, TV series, or book. Include three true-false questions and three multiple choice questions. Write a matching question with a list of four items to match with four other items. Exchange tests with a classmate. See how well you do on the test.

Part 9

Pencil or Pen?

Answering Written Test Questions

Here's the Idea   Some test questions require written answers. You might have to complete a sentence. You might have to write a short answer of a sentence or two. Finally, you might have to write an essay. Whenever you write, you must use good writing skills. Always check your spelling and punctuation.

There are three main types of written test questions.

Completion or **Fill-in-the-Blank**   For a completion question, you have to finish an incomplete statement with the correct word or phrase. If the answer comes at the end of the sentence, use correct punctuation. If the answer comes at the beginning, capitalize correctly.

Short Answer   This type of question asks you to write one or two sentences to answer the question. Be sure to use complete sentences. Also use correct capitalization and punctuation.

Essay   For an essay question, you must write your answer in one or more paragraphs. Always complete the pre-writing steps before you answer an essay question. First, decide what the question asks you to do. Look for clues in the directions, such as *explain* or *describe*. Then, list and organize your ideas on a separate sheet of paper. Finally, make sure each paragraph contains a good topic sentence.

Check It Out   See how the following questions are answered.

1. An angle that contains less than 90° is an ___*acute*___ angle.

2. What were the last two states allowed to join the USA?

The last two states admitted to the USA were Alaska and Hawaii.

3. Define the word *ballad*. Give the name of one ballad.

> *A ballad is a poem that tells a story. In the past, ballads were written to be sung. Ballads have four-line stanzas. Each stanza has the same rhythm and rhyme. Ballads usually tell about ordinary people who have had amazing adventures. An example of a ballad is "Brian O'Linn."*

- Do you see how these questions are answered differently?

Try Your Skill   Choose an article from the encyclopedia. Then, write three completion questions and two short-answer questions based on the article. Write the answers.

Keep This in Mind

- A completion question should be answered with a word or phrase.
- A short-answer question requires a one- or two-sentence answer.
- An essay requires an answer of one or more paragraphs.

Now Write   On your paper, answer this essay question:

Describe how you can use study and research skills in your science, social studies, or math class. Include at least three examples. Explain how these skills can help you.

Use good writing skills in your answer. Use correct capitalization and punctuation. Save your work in your folder.

Letters and Forms

Part 1

Write Soon

Writing a Friendly Letter

Here's the Idea Do you write many letters? A **friendly letter** is one that you write to someone you know. It should be interesting and easy to read. A friendly letter gives you the chance to write about what is important to you and interesting to a friend. Make your letter detailed and lively.

The form for a friendly letter has five main parts: the *heading,* the *salutation* or greeting, the *body* or main part, the *closing,* and the *signature.*

The **heading** tells where you are. The heading appears in the upper right corner of the page. It usually includes two lines for the address and one for the date.

The **salutation** is the way you greet your friend. It is written on the next line and begins at the left margin.

The **body,** the main part of the letter, starts on the next line. In this part of your letter you talk to your friend. Try to make your friend feel as though you were there in person. The first word of the body is indented. Each new paragraph of the body is indented, too.

The **closing** is the way you leave your friend. It is written on the line below the last sentence of the body. The closing should line up with the first line of the heading.

The **signature** is the last part of your letter. Skip a line after the closing and sign your name in line with the first word of the closing. Use your first name as your signature whenever you are writing a friendly letter to someone you know well. Otherwise, sign your full name.

Begin every main part of your letter with a capitalized word. Put a comma after the salutation and the closing.

1321 Hillcrest Avenue
Boulder, Colorado 80309
June 3, 1985

Dear Donna,

Your letter arrived this morning. It was good hearing from you. You certainly sound excited about astronomy, your new hobby. I've always wanted to know more about the stars. You can see quite a few tonight because the sky is so clear.

I'm reading up on amateur radio. There's certainly a lot to know in order to get a license! I think I'll start out with just a short-wave receiver. I hope to buy a kit and make it myself. It should be quite a challenge.

Please let me know when you've finished building your telescope. Can you bring it with you when your family comes to visit? Write again soon.

Yours truly,
Mark

- What details make this letter interesting?
- Identify the five parts of this letter.

Try Your Skill   Think of one event that has happened during the last week that you would enjoy telling a friend about. Try to recall as many details as you can, including how you felt about it. Imagine that you are writing a friendly letter. Write three or four sentences describing the event.

Keep This in Mind

- Friendly letters should be detailed, interesting, and easy to read.
- Friendly letters should follow the correct form. The heading, salutation, body, closing, and signature should each be written correctly.

Now Write   Write the title of this lesson, **Write Soon,** on your paper. Then write a friendly letter to a friend or relative. Try to include interesting details. Use the correct form.

When you have finished, put the letter into your folder. You may want to copy the letter so that you can mail it.

Handle with Care

Preparing Letters for the Mail

Here's the Idea When you have written your letter, fold it neatly. Use an envelope that matches the width of the stationery. Insert the letter into the envelope and seal the envelope.
  Follow these steps for preparing your envelope:

1. Address the envelope. Add your return address.
2. Check all numbers to make sure they are in the proper order.
3. Include the correct ZIP code and state abbreviation.
4. Put a stamp on your envelope.

Preparing the envelope correctly is an important step in letter writing. Always check letters and packages for accuracy. If you need more information, call your post office.

Check It Out Look at the envelope below.

Nora Barnes
18 Watson Place
Wichita, KS 67211

Joe Delgado
85 Elm Street
Philadelphia, PA 19116

- To whom is the letter being sent? Who sent the letter?
- How could you check to be sure that the state abbreviations and ZIP codes are correct?

Try Your Skill   On your paper, draw a rectangle the size of an envelope. Address it as though Louise Holmes were sending it to Peter Kaufman. Peter's address is 16 Wilson Street in San Francisco, California. Peter's ZIP code is 94105. Louise is writing from her home at 231 Sayers Place, Palo Alto, California. Her ZIP code is 94303.

Keep This in Mind

- Prepare your letters correctly. Fold your letter neatly, and use an envelope that matches the width of the stationery.
- Check addresses for neatness and accuracy. Check abbreviations of states and correct ZIP codes.
- Put your return address on the envelope.

Now Write   Write the title of this lesson, **Handle with Care,** on your paper. Draw a rectangle about the size of an envelope. Address it to the friend you wrote to in the last lesson. Make sure you include your return address.

Put your work into your folder when you have finished. You may want to copy the information onto a real envelope and mail it.

Special Occasions

Writing Social Notes

Here's the Idea   Social notes are written for specific reasons on special occasions. Invitations and thank-you notes are social notes. They are both short forms of friendly letters. They have the same five-part form. The heading may be shortened, however, to include only the date.

If you send an **invitation,** include details about *what, when,* and *where.* Make sure you include any special information a guest might need to know about the occasion. If you receive an invitation, you should reply as soon as possible. Tell whether or not you will attend.

You may also send thank-you notes. One kind of **thank-you** note is written after you have received a gift. If your gift was sent by mail, a thank-you note tells the sender that the gift arrived. If you liked the gift, tell the sender. In any case, always thank someone for his or her kindness.

A second kind of thank-you note is a **bread-and-butter** note. This social note is written to thank someone for his or her hospitality. If you stayed overnight at someone's house, you would write a thank-you note.

When you write either of these kinds of social notes, show your appreciation to the other person. Also be sure to write your notes as soon as you receive a gift or someone's hospitality.

Check It Out   Read the social note on page 260. Then answer these questions.

- What kind of social note is this? How is the form of this letter different from the friendly letter shown on page 255?
- What words and phrases are used to show appreciation?

259

April 12, 1985

Dear Aunt May,

Many thanks for the leather wallet you sent. I really appreciate your thinking of me each birthday. As you know, I often carry money around for lunch, busfare, and school supplies. Having a wallet will help to keep me from losing everything.

Thanks again for your present.

Love,
Jean

Try Your Skill   Your best friend Reuben gave you a gift certificate good for one record album at a local store. Write a note to Reuben thanking him for the gift certificate.

Keep This in Mind

- Social notes, such as invitations and thank-you notes, are short forms of friendly letters.
- An invitation should tell *what, when,* and *where.*
- Thank-you notes thank people for the thoughtfulness of their gifts and their hospitality.

Now Write   Write the title of this lesson, **Special Occasions**, on your paper. Now write an invitation, a thank-you note, or a bread-and-butter note to someone you know. Make up details. Use the correct form. Put your work into your folder.

Dear Sir or Madam:

Writing a Business Letter

Here's the Idea If you want to (1) request information, (2) order a product by mail, or (3) complain about a product to the manufacturer, you would write a **business letter.**

Business letters may be written in *modified block form* or *block form.* In the modified block form, the paragraphs are indented, and the closing and signature are in line with the heading, just as in a friendly letter. This form may be used for both handwritten and typed business letters.

The *block* form for a business letter is used only when the letter is typewritten. All the parts of the letter begin at the left margin. The paragraphs are not indented. Instead, there is a double space between paragraphs.

In both forms of a business letter, an inside address is included. An **inside address** is the name and address of the business to which you are writing. The inside address is placed above the salutation at the left margin. If you are writing to a specific person, use *Dear* and the person's name in the salutation. Otherwise, use a general greeting, such as *Dear Sir or Madam.* All salutations begin two lines after the inside address and end with a colon (:).

It is important to be brief and to the point in a business letter. It is also a good idea to make a copy of a business letter for your records. If you make a copy, mail the original.

Check It Out Read the letter on page 262. Then answer these questions.

- What is the purpose of this business letter?
- Identify the six parts of the letter.
- In what form is this letter written?

90 Robinson Avenue
New Orleans, Louisiana 70118
March 9, 1985

The Greylock Company
1570 Washington Street
Columbus, Ohio 43209

Dear Sir or Madam:

   In this month's issue of <u>Sky World</u> I
read your advertisement for model airplane
kits.   The ad also offered a free catalog.
I would like you to send me the free
catalog.   Please send it to me at the
address given above.

                    Sincerely yours,

                    Mario Rizzo

Try Your Skill   On your paper, write a short letter of complaint to the following imaginary company: Colorful Clothes Company, 35 Wildwood Drive, Atlanta, Georgia 30333. Tell them that the personalized T-shirt you ordered two months ago has not arrived. In your letter, be sure to mention the size, color, and style of T-shirt you requested. Also, be sure to mention the exact spelling of your name as you wanted it printed. Use today's date and your own name and address.

Keep This in Mind

- Business letters are written to request information, order products, or complain about products. They should be brief and to the point. Keep a copy for yourself.
- There are six parts to the form of a business letter. They are *heading, inside address, salutation, body, closing,* and *signature.*
- *Block* and *modified block* are two forms for a business letter.

Now Write   Find an advertisement in a magazine or newspaper for free information or a free booklet. On your paper, write the title of this lesson, **Dear Sir or Madam.** Write a business letter asking for the advertised item. Write the letter in one of the correct forms for a business letter.

Put your work into your folder. You may want to copy the letter and send it later.

Part 5

Information, Please

Writing Letters of Request

Here's the Idea You can receive valuable information by writing a business **letter of request.** This is one of the most common types of business letters. Companies are usually pleased to send information about their products. Schools and camps will send catalogs. Local officials in most towns will send maps, brochures, and sightseeing information, if you ask.

A well-written letter will usually receive a quick reply. Remember that you are asking someone to do something for you. Therefore, make sure your letter is polite and neat.

In your letter, include all the information that the company or person needs in order to send you what you request. If you are writing to a chamber of commerce for information, tell why you want to know about the town. Explain your request briefly and clearly. Be specific.

Also, be sure to send the letter to the right place. Many times you will find the name and address in an advertisement. Sometimes, though, you may have to do a little detective work. If you received a radio and want a parts list or wiring diagram, where should you write? Look carefully on the box and on the radio itself. Somewhere you will find the name and address of the company. If you write to *Customer Service* at that address, you should hear from someone. Other good places to find the right address are at the end of an instruction manual, on a tag, or in the yellow pages of a telephone book.

Check It Out Read the letter of request on the next page.

- Is this letter of request brief and polite?
- Is all the necessary information included?

21 Clark Street
Chicago, Illinois 60611
October 10, 19___

Guide Dog Foundation for the Blind
109-19 72 nd Avenue
Forest Hills, New York 11375

Dear Sir or Madam:

I am writing a report on Labrador retrievers and I understand that they are often used as guide dogs for the blind. Please send me information telling where you get the dogs, how they are trained, and how a blind person gets a guide dog. It is necessary that I receive the information by November 1 for my report.

Very truly yours,
Jessica Gould

Try Your Skill   Write a letter to the Lefthander's League, P.O. Box 89, New Milford, New Jersey 07646. Tell them that you would like information about joining their society. Find out what dues, if any, are charged, and what you must do in order to join. Use the modified block form for this letter.

Keep This in Mind

- Letters of request should be brief and polite.
- Ask only for the information you need. Be specific.

Now Write   Label your paper **Information, Please.** Plan a letter of request that you will actually mail. Write your letter. Make a copy. Keep one copy in your folder. Mail the other.

Part 6

Getting in Form

Filling Out Forms

Here's the Idea   Knowing how to fill out a form correctly is important. All your life you will have to fill out different kinds of forms. You must fill out a form to register your bicycle, to open a bank account, or to order something from a catalog. Study the following guidelines.

1. Skim the form. That is, look it over quickly, before you begin writing. This will tell you exactly what information you need to fill out the form. For example, you would need your social security number to open a bank account. Have any special information on hand before you begin.

2. Read the directions carefully. Are you supposed to write or print this information? Should you write your last name first? If you read the directions first, you will avoid making mistakes.

3. Have the correct writing tool. The form may require that you use blue or black ink. If a pencil is acceptable, be sure it is sharp. Have an eraser handy.

4. Fill out the form line by line. Do not skip about, for some information may depend on a previous answer. This will also prevent you from missing a question.

5. Proofread your work. Did you follow directions? Did you answer the questions correctly? Is your spelling correct?

Check It Out   Examine this completed savings account application and then answer these questions.

- Have all the instructions been followed correctly?
- Is the application form filled in neatly and carefully?
- Have all the items on the application been filled out?

REGULAR GOLD INDIVIDUAL ACCOUNT

Signature	*Marsha Wong*	
Address	1258 Foster	PHONE 555-0031

Place of Birth	San Francisco	DATE OF BIRTH	MONTH Jan.	DAY 23,	YEAR 1971

Employed by or School Attended	Sunnyside	MOTHER'S NAME BEFORE MARRIAGE	Sylvia Chin

Soc. Sec. No. 357-02-6324	DATE OPENED 2/15	INITIAL DEPOSIT $50.00	OPENED BY Marsha Wong
Lic. No. none			

BFC 21432   **SAVINGS ACCOUNT**

Try Your Skill   Suppose you want to open a savings account. You earned $250 this past summer babysitting and washing windows. On a separate sheet of paper, copy the application form as it is shown above. Then fill it out as you would actually complete it.

Keep This in Mind

- Skim any form before you begin filling it out. Have the needed information on hand.
- Read all of the instructions on the form.
- Have the correct writing tools.
- Complete all of the items neatly and accurately. Proofread your work.

Now Write   Get a pet license application from the local police or from your teacher. Complete the form neatly, using the guidelines from this lesson. Save this form in your folder.

Preparing a Talk

Part 1

Speaking Out

Informal and Formal Talks

Here's the Idea For some people, getting up to speak in class means an upset stomach and weak knees. You can overcome nervousness by learning good speaking skills. Such skills will help you to give speeches of all kinds with confidence.

One common kind of speech is the **informal talk.** It is used to give information quickly. An informal talk is usually short. It does not take a lot of preparation.

Informal Talks

Type of Talk	Purpose	Example
1. **Demonstrations**	to show how something is done	showing how to repair an air mattress or life raft
2. **Announcements**	to tell about some past or future event	telling about an upcoming concert or variety show
3. **Introductions**	to present people to an audience	presenting a visiting foreign exchange student to a class
4. **Directions**	to tell other people how to do something	telling how to get to a local museum

A **formal talk** takes more preparation than an informal one. It covers a specific subject in depth. Therefore, it is usually longer. Formal talks are also usually written out beforehand.

Check It Out Read the following talk.

Back in the days of the Greek myths, there were lots and lots of heroes. You couldn't go anywhere without bumping into one of them. They were all over the place, running up and down mountains, swimming oceans, saving people, and doing other mighty tasks. It was certainly a good time for heroes.

These days, though, there just aren't too many heroes left. That's what makes the next speaker so special. Kitty O'Neil Hambleton is a modern-day heroine. In 1976 she climbed into the seat of a rocket-powered, three-wheeled car. Then she raced across the Alvard Desert of Oregon at an incredible 512 miles per hour. Now, *that* was a mighty feat! Ladies and gentlemen, I am proud to present a genuine heroine, the holder of the world land speed record for women, Kitty O'Neil Hambleton.

- Is this an informal talk or a formal talk? Explain your answer.

Try Your Skill   Which of the following situations would require a formal talk? Which would require an informal talk? Write out your answers. Give a reason for each of your choices.

1. telling everyone the date for the school picnic
2. an art teacher showing how to use watercolor paints
3. giving a talk about Ray Bradbury to your reading class
4. introducing your out-of-town cousin to a class
5. a radio D.J. telling people how to send in for a free T-shirt

Keep This in Mind

- An informal talk is short. It provides information quickly. Announcements, introductions, directions, and demonstrations are all informal talks.
- A formal talk is longer than an informal talk. It takes more preparation and covers a specific subject in depth.

Now Write   Write a brief paragraph about any time when you gave a talk. Describe your subject and how you felt while you spoke. Tell whether yours was a formal or an informal talk. Discuss your paragraph with your classmates. Save your paper.

An Accurate Account

Preparing an Informal Talk

Here's the Idea Have you ever gotten lost because some-one gave you bad directions? If so, you know how important accurate information can be. To give an informal talk, you must gather information that is accurate and complete. The kind of information you need depends upon your talk.

Demonstrations must be well-organized and presented step-by-step. Any props should be kept close at hand. If, for exam-ple, you want to demonstrate how to change the strings on a guitar, you will need a guitar and a new set of strings. You should sit where your audience can see both you and the guitar clearly. Then, you should demonstrate the following steps:

1. Hold the guitar in your lap.
2. Remove the first string and throw it away.
3. Put on the new first string and tune it.
4. Repeat this procedure for each string.

Announcements answer the questions *who? what? where? when?* and *why?* Each question must be answered accurately and completely. Suppose, for example, that you were asked to announce the winners of a volleyball game. You might say, "Yes-terday, the girls' volleyball team played Central West on our home court. The spectacular serving of Emily Irving led our team to a fifteen-to-thirteen victory. Congratulations, Emily!" Notice that all five questions are answered in this brief talk.

Introductions should interest the audience in the person being introduced. They should be courteous, informative, and polite. If you do not already know a great deal about the person you are introducing, conduct an interview. Ask questions to find out interesting facts about the person. Use these facts in your talk. (See the sample introduction on pages 270–271.)

Directions should include all necessary details. No steps should be left out. If you do leave out a step, your listeners will get lost. Before giving directions, first think them through carefully. Then, you might say something like the following: "To get to the park from here, walk north two blocks on Walnut Street. Turn right on Tulip Avenue. Continue east on Tulip for three blocks. You will pass the bus station and then the Federal Building. The Federal Building faces the park."

Check It Out   Marc and Helene were asked to introduce the new gym coach to the student council. They decided to divide up the work. Marc was to get the background information about the coach. Helene was to give the informal talk. Marc gave Helene two pieces of information. Coach Richards played minor league baseball with the Chicago White Sox. He graduated from the University of Wisconsin.

- Was this enough material for an introduction?
- What additional information would be useful?

Try Your Skill   Write directions telling how to get from school to a local store. Follow a step-by-step order. (See Section 16, pages 186–187.) Read your directions to a classmate. Ask whether the directions are clear. Rewrite if necessary.

Keep This in Mind

- Informal talks require accurate and complete information.
- Gather all the information you need. Put it in the order that you will present it in your talk.

Now Speak   Prepare an announcement about some upcoming event in your community. Your subject can be a new movie or a sports event that will take place soon. Make sure your announcement tells *who? what? where? when?* and *why?* Make your announcement to your class.

Part 3

Formal Preparations

Planning a Formal Talk

Here's the Idea Planning a formal talk is much like planning a composition. Both require you to follow certain prewriting steps. The first three steps are as follows:

Choose and narrow your topic. The topic should interest both you and your audience. It should also fit the time available for your talk. For example, if you have only five minutes, you can't discuss every World Series game since 1933. However, you can discuss the three best plays in the history of the Series. (See Section 13, pp. 144–145, for more on how to narrow a topic.)

Determine your purpose. Decide on the effect that you want to have on your audience. Do you want to inform them? Do you want to persuade them to see things your way or to take some action? Do you want to entertain them? The purpose of your speech will determine what ideas you will present and how you will present them.

Identify your audience. Knowing your audience will help you to develop a speech that is suited to them. Ask yourself questions such as these: "What are the interests of my audience?" "How old are they?" "How much do they already know about the subject?" Remember, your final talk should not be too difficult for your audience to understand. It also should not be so simple that your audience gets bored.

Check It Out Ramon was asked to give a ten-minute talk to his music appreciation class. He and his classmates all enjoy popular music. They also like to watch videos. Ramon therefore picked *videos* as his topic. Then he had to narrow his topic.

He decided upon *How To Make Your Own Video*. This was still too broad. Finally, he narrowed the topic to *The Parts of a Video Script*.

- How did Ramon's audience influence his choice of topic?
- Is Ramon's purpose to inform, to persuade, or to entertain?

Try Your Skill   Read the following topics for five-minute formal talks.

1. sports   4. science fiction
2. automobiles   5. homework
3. movies   6. advertisements

Narrow each topic. Make sure that it is not too large or too small for the available time. On a piece of paper, write each narrowed topic. Next to each topic, tell whether it is for a talk that informs, persuades, or entertains.

Keep This in Mind

- Topics should be interesting and should fit the available time.
- A topic of the talk should suit the audience.
- The purpose of a formal talk may be to inform, to persuade, or entertain.

Now Write   Use brainstorming to choose a topic for a formal talk. On a piece of paper, write your topic and the purpose your talk will serve. Also tell who your audience will be. Label your paper **Formal Preparations.** Place it in your folder.

Part 4

What's the Big Idea?

Finding Information for a Formal Talk

Here's the Idea Once you know the topic, purpose, and audience for your talk, you must write out your main idea. State the main idea in a single sentence that tells the subject of the talk. Then gather and organize your information.

Gathering Information for a Formal Talk

1. Do some research to gather information. This information can come from books, magazines, newspapers, encyclopedias, other people, and your own experiences.

2. Take notes on note cards. Each note card should contain only one piece of information.

3. Make sure that the information you gather is related to your main idea.

4. Divide your notes into groups of related ideas. Leave out any information not related to your main idea.

5. Put the notes in the order that you want them to appear in the talk. Possible orders include the following:
   a. Least important to most important idea, or order of importance
   b. Step-by-step, or chronological order
   c. Most familiar to least familiar, or order of familiarity
   d. Spatial order (left to right, right to left, far to near, near to far, bottom to top, top to bottom)

6. Look for any gaps in your information. If necessary, do more research to fill in these gaps.

Check It Out Marianne decided to do a speech on the odd fish that live in the deepest parts of oceans. Her main idea was

"The fish that live at the bottom of the sea are the strangest creatures on earth."

- What written sources could she use?
- What people could she go to for information?

Try Your Skill The following are some notes for a speech on bottom-dwelling saltwater fish. Copy the notes onto note cards and arrange them in a logical order. Leave out any information that is not related to the main idea. Be prepared to defend your method of organization.

–Many ocean-bottom fish have huge mouths and fang-like teeth. These offer protection and a means of capturing food.

–The ocean bottom is dark.

–Most of the earth's surface is covered by oceans.

–The University of Florida offers courses in marine biology.

–The umbrella mouth gulper eel and the common blackdevil deep-sea angler are bottom-dwellers. They have large mouths and long, sharp teeth.

–Some ocean-bottom fish are blind. Others have enormous eyes that help them to see in the dark.

–The blue lantern fish has organs that produce light. It is one of many light-producing ocean-bottom fish.

Keep This in Mind

- State the main idea for your talk in a single sentence.
- Gather information related to your main idea.
- Organize your information logically.

Now Write Write a main idea statement for the topic that you chose in Part 3, **Formal Preparations.** Then, do research for your talk. Take notes on $3'' \times 5''$ note cards. Organize these notes for later use.

Part 5

Speaking Parts

Writing a Formal Talk

Here's the Idea   Once you have organized your information, you are ready to write your talk. A formal talk should contain each of the following parts:

The introduction.   This should be short. It should hold the attention of your listeners. It should end with the sentence that tells your main idea. Introductions may begin with surprising facts, interesting questions, comparisons, brief stories, or exhibits (objects shown to the audience).

The body.   This part contains the heart of the talk. Sentences in the body should support the main idea. They should also be organized in a logical way.

The conclusion.   This part should restate your main idea in different words. It should also summarize main points made in the body. If the purpose of your talk is to entertain, the conclusion may be a high point of entertainment. It may also be a lesson drawn from experiences told about in the talk.

Check It Out   Read the following introduction to a talk.

> People are a lot like plants. They need fresh air and room in which to grow. This is why our city should build a recreational park in this neighborhood.

- What is the purpose of this talk? Is it to inform, to persuade, or to entertain?
- What is the main idea of this talk?
- Does the introduction begin with a fact, a question, a comparison, a story, or an exhibit?

Try Your Skill The following sentences are main ideas from formal talks. Write introductions using each of these main ideas.

However, the best drama on television is in the commercials.
Entering high school also means making some adjustments.

Keep This in Mind

- The introduction should state the main idea of the talk. It should also hold the attention of the audience.
- The body should support the main idea of the talk.
- The conclusion often restates the main idea and summarizes the major points of the talk.

Now Write Write an introduction, body, and conclusion for a formal talk. Use the notes gathered in Part 4, **What's the Big Idea!** Then, revise your first draft. Check for good grammar, punctuation, and mechanics. Also check to make sure that the introduction, body, and conclusion contain the material described in **Here's the Idea** on page 278. Write a final draft of your talk. Label your first and final drafts **Speaking Parts.** Place these in your folder.

Part 6

Eye to Eye

Making a Good Impression

Here's the Idea   Do you sometimes become bored or restless when listening to a speaker? This may happen because the speech itself is weak. It may also happen when the speaker does not present the talk properly. The following guidelines will help you to make a good impression when giving a talk.

1. Look your best.   Dress neatly, and stand up straight. Try to appear confident. Do not move about nervously, but do not stand still like a statue, either.

2. Maintain eye contact.   This will help keep the attention of your audience. Look directly at audience members or slightly above their heads. Do not stare at one or two individuals. Do not look at your notes too often.

3. Control your voice.   Make sure everyone can hear you, but don't shout. Say your words clearly. Don't mumble, and don't speak in a monotone. Vary your volume and your rate of delivery. This will make your talk more interesting.

4. Use gestures and facial expressions.   These should be natural. They should also reflect what you are saying. If you say something funny, smile. If you make a series of points, count them off on your fingers. Natural, appropriate expressions and gestures will help your audience to understand your talk. They will also make you appear more confident.

Check It Out   Study the following situation.

Juanita was giving a talk on whaling. She felt that whales should be protected by international laws. First, she described a whale hunt. Then, she told how many whales are killed each year. As she spoke, her voice became louder. Her words came out faster and faster, but remained clear. Suddenly, she paused. She leaned forward and looked slowly around the room. She moved her head from left to right, looking everyone in the eye. As she did this, she said, slowly and quietly, "Only you can save the whales."

- What did Juanita do to emphasize her point at the end of her speech?
- What effect do you think Juanita's statement had on her audience?

Try Your Skill   Listen to the evening news on television. Notice how the newscasters speak and look. How many of the guidelines for presenting a talk do they follow? Write a paragraph telling about one newscaster's presentation.

Keep This in Mind

- How you look and sound is important to your audience.
- Look directly at your audience, and speak in a clear voice.
- Try to be natural and relaxed.

Now Write   Make a list of three emotions that a speaker might feel during a talk. Then, for each emotion, make a list of three ways that a speaker could communicate these emotions. Some of these ways include particular facial expressions, gestures, and tones of voice. Save your paper in your folder.

Part 7

Dress Rehearsal

Practicing a Talk

Here's the Idea   If you have ever learned a sport, a musical instrument, or a foreign language, you know the importance of practice. Through practice you can perfect the delivery of your talk and develop confidence. The more you practice, the better your final talk will be.

Guidelines for Practicing a Talk

1. Read your talk through several times. This will help you to become familiar with what you are going to say. It will also give you a chance to make any last-minute corrections.

2. Memorize your talk by reciting it over and over. You could also memorize most of your talk and refer to note cards for the rest. If you use note cards during the talk, simply glance at them occasionally. Maintain eye contact with your audience.

3. Practice your talk aloud. Use a tape recorder, if possible. Ask yourself the following questions: Do you speak too slowly or too quickly? Do you pronounce your words correctly? Do you pronounce them clearly? Does the tone of your voice show appropriate emotions? Do you vary your volume? Practice your talk again, correcting any errors.

4. Practice in front of family and friends. Study their reactions. Ask for suggestions about improving the content and delivery of your talk.

Check It Out   Read about the following situation.

Jon wrote a talk about safety rules for his shop class. He practiced in front of a mirror so he could see his gestures and facial expressions. He listened to a recording of his talk. He corrected and changed some parts that did not flow smoothly. After this, he felt ready to go before an audience.

- What methods did Jon use to practice his talk?
- What other methods could he have used?

Try Your Skill   The following is a selection from a talk. Practice this selection. Write down any problems that you notice in your delivery.

Americans produce some of the best food in the world. Our canned and packaged foods look good, smell good, taste good, and last a long time. However, some of these foods contain dangerous additives. Certain spices and food colorings make people sick. Certain preservatives have been linked to cancer and other diseases. Luckily, one federal agency keeps track of these additives and warns us about possible dangers. This agency is the Food and Drug Administration.

Keep This in Mind

- Always practice your talk before you give it.
- When you practice, study your voice, facial expressions, and gestures.
- Ask your family and friends to listen to your talk and to suggest improvements.

Now Speak   Practice the talk you wrote in Part 5, **Speaking Parts.** First practice by yourself. Then practice in front of someone else. List any improvements you can make on a piece of paper. Label this paper **Dress Rehearsal,** and place it in your folder. If your teacher directs, present your talk to your class.

Part 8

Lend Me Your Ears

Listening to a Talk

Here's the Idea It feels nice when someone takes the time to listen carefully to what you want to say. You can give other people the same feeling by practicing good listening skills.

1. Give the speaker your full attention.
2. Keep an open mind. Do not judge the speaker's ideas before you hear how they are supported.
3. Do not make distracting movements or noises.
4. Show your interest in what the speaker is saying. Look directly at the speaker.
5. Keep a positive expression on your face.
6. Listen for main ideas and supporting details in the talk.

Sometimes you may be asked to evaluate a talk given by someone else. If so, be polite and specific in your evaluation. Comment on the talk and how it was delivered, not on the personal qualities of the speaker.

CONTENT

Topic: Did the speaker make the main point clear?

Purpose: Was the purpose of the talk clear?

Audience: Was the talk suited to the audience?

Development: Was there enough information presented? Was there any unnecessary information?

Organization: Were the ideas presented in a logical order?

-**Introduction.** Did it arouse interest and state the main idea?

-**Body.** Did it support the main idea?

-**Conclusion.** Did the talk reach a satisfactory conclusion? Did it simply end abruptly?

PRESENTATION

Eye Contact: Did the speaker look at the audience?

Posture: Did the speaker stand up straight? Did he or she look relaxed?

Voice: Was the speaker easy to hear and understand? Did the speaker vary his or her volume and tone of voice?

Gestures: Were the speaker's gestures natural and appropriate?

Expressions: Were the speaker's facial expressions natural and appropriate?

Preparation: Did the speaker know the talk well? Did it seem as though the speaker had practiced?

Check It Out   Ricardo gave a talk on the dangers confronting American bald eagles. He then asked Paula what she thought of his talk. Paula said it was "good."

- What is wrong with Paula's reaction to the speech?
- How could Paula improve her response?

Try Your Skill   Copy the checklist for evaluating talks onto your own paper. Discuss this checklist with your classmates. What other items can you add to the list?

Keep This in Mind

- Be a polite, responsive listener.
- When you judge a talk, evaluate what was said and how it was said.
- Judge the talk, not the speaker.

Now Listen   Listen to a talk in your class. Use the checklist in this lesson to evaluate this talk. Compare your evaluation with those of your classmates.

Handbook

A detailed Table of Contents for the Handbook appears in the front of this book.

Learning About Sentences

When you learned to talk, you began slowly. You probably started out by saying the names of people around you. Then you added some action words to tell what the people were doing. Still later, you learned words to describe things you saw.

Now you know thousands of words. You know how to put many of them together to express your needs and ideas. Sometimes, however, you may still have trouble making others understand you. You must continue to grow in your ability to use your language.

This section will describe the rules for arranging words into good sentences. Learning these rules will help you understand more of the sentences you hear or read. It will also help you to express yourself more clearly to others when you speak and write.

Part 1 Complete Sentences

A sentence is a group of words that expresses a complete thought.

If people do not understand you when you talk, they can ask you questions. However, if they are reading a report, a letter, or a story you wrote, they cannot ask your paper any questions. Your report, letter, or story must make your thoughts clear.

When you are writing, make sure your sentences answer these two questions: *What happened?* and *Who or what did it?* If a group of words doesn't answer these questions, that group of words is not a complete sentence.

Read this group of words.

> The musicians in the park

Does this group of words tell *what happened?* No, it only tells *who.* It is only part of a sentence. It is a **fragment.**

You can make a fragment into a sentence. If the fragment only tells *who,* add a word or words to tell *what happened.* These two groups of words are complete sentences. They each tell *who* and *what happened.*

> The musicians in the park **sang.**
> The musicians in the park **played our favorite songs.**

Now read this group of words.

> Swam in the pool

Does this group of words tell *what happened?* Yes, it does. Does it tell *who* or *what?* No, it doesn't. It is a fragment. You can make this fragment into a sentence by adding a word or words to tell *who* or *what.*

> **Kristen** swam in the pool.
> **The seals at the zoo** swam in the pool.

Can you add words to the two fragments below to make them complete thoughts?

Threw out the first ball of the season
The TV special yesterday

Exercises   Recognize complete sentences.

A. Number your paper from 1 to 10. For each word group, write *Sentence* or *Fragment*.

1. A pocket of my jeans
2. Sold ten tickets
3. Two trucks blocked the intersection
4. The day before the school picnic
5. We visited Mount Rushmore
6. Between the laundromat and the corner
7. Carefully climbed up the ladder
8. Louis was asleep
9. A fountain in Lincoln Park
10. Three pounds of hamburger

B. Writing   All of the groups of words below are sentence fragments. Add words of your own to make complete sentences. Write the sentences.

1. On Friday
2. All the bus drivers
3. At six o'clock
4. Half the night
5. The automatic door at the supermarket
6. Across the bridge
7. Exploded in midair
8. Cautiously tried the ice on the pond
9. Too much water
10. A block from school

Part 2 Four Kinds of Sentences

You use sentences for many reasons. Sometimes you want to tell something. Sometimes you want to ask something. Sometimes you want to tell someone to do something. Other times you want to show how strongly you feel about something. There is a different kind of sentence for each of these four purposes.

1. A **declarative sentence** tells or states something. It ends with a period (.).

> Gwen bought a basketball.   These radishes are hot.

2. An **interrogative sentence** asks a question. It ends with a question mark (?).

> Are you positive?   Where are the forks?

3. An **imperative sentence** commands, instructs, or orders. It ends with a period (.).

> Count your change carefully.   Return your books on time.

4. An **exclamatory sentence** expresses joy, surprise, anger, excitement, or other strong feeling. It ends with an exclamation point (!).

> What a great cook you are!   How dark the sky is!

Begin every sentence with a capital letter.

Exercises   Identify the kinds of sentences.

A. These sentences do not have punctuation marks at the end. On your paper, write *Declarative, Interrogative, Imperative,* or *Exclamatory* to show what kind each sentence is.

1. Measure the length of the garter snake
2. May we go to the movies on Saturday
3. Birds' bones are hollow
4. Take a ten-minute break

5. How frightened I was
6. Do you have an eraser
7. Marie Curie received two Nobel prizes
8. Is there enough pressure in the tires
9. Does a chipmunk have a white stripe down its back
10. Tell me about your vacation to Alaska

B. Follow the directions for Exercise A.

1. John Singleton Copley painted portraits of Americans
2. Turn off the television, please
3. The watermelons lay ripening in the field
4. Can you walk on a balance beam
5. What a fast runner Barbara is
6. May I go to the movies, too
7. The magnolia is Mississippi's state flower
8. Wait for the next elevator, please
9. Did Samuel Morse develop the telegraph
10. Guava is a tropical fruit

Punctuating Sentences

The punctuation mark you put at the end of your sentence helps a reader understand your meaning. Remember these rules:

1. Use a period after a declarative sentence.
2. Use a question mark after an interrogative sentence.
3. Use a period after an imperative sentence.
4. Use an exclamation point after an exclamatory sentence.

Exercises **Use correct punctuation.**

A. Copy and punctuate these sentences.

1. Is Caracas the capital of Venezuela

2. Remember to bring a sweater tonight
3. Call Debbie to the phone, please
4. A meteor shower lit up the sky
5. Have you ever visited the Everglades
6. Write your name in the upper right-hand corner
7. How far can you swim underwater
8. The Swiss flag is red with a white cross
9. The planet Mars is named for the Roman war god
10. It's a home run

B. Follow the directions for Exercise A.

1. Proceed to gate G-7
2. What a great time we had at Disney World
3. Order your tickets today
4. Have you finished your homework
5. Elvis Presley Boulevard is a street in Memphis
6. Do twenty push-ups
7. Laura plays the tuba in our school orchestra
8. Does Michael wear contact lenses
9. Whales are huge yet gentle sea creatures
10. What is the Continental Divide

Part 3 Every Sentence Has Two Parts

Every sentence has a **subject** and a **predicate.**

1. The old car lost its tailpipe.

The old car	lost its tailpipe.
This part is the subject. It tells *what* the sentence is about.	This part is the predicate. It tells *what happened.*

2. The runner stumbled across the finish line.

The runner	stumbled across the finish line.
This is the subject. It tells *whom* the sentence is about.	This is the predicate. It tells *what the subject did.*

3. My friend Sue hit a home run.

My friend Sue	hit a home run.
Subject	Predicate

Finding the Subject and the Predicate

Every sentence states a complete thought. Every sentence has two parts: a subject and a predicate.

The subject of a sentence tells whom or what the sentence is about.

The predicate of a sentence tells what the subject did or what happened.

To find the subject of a sentence, ask whom or what the sentence is about. To find the predicate, ask what the subject did or what happened.

Read these examples. Notice the subject and predicate in each sentence.

Subject (whom or what the sentence is about)	Predicate (what the subject did, or what happened)
All my friends	came to the party.
The old elm tree	was destroyed by the storm.
Marcia's parents	met her at the airport.

Find subjects and predicates.

A. Copy these sentences. Draw a vertical line between the subject and the predicate.

Example: The astronaut   landed her spaceship safely.

1. Dad locked the keys in the house.
2. Thanksgiving falls on November 28 this year.
3. The first batter struck out.
4. My calculator needs a new battery.
5. A robin built a nest in the pear tree.
6. Jay's cat chases birds.
7. The second-string players watched from the bench.
8. Sunlight filled the room.
9. Lisa took her tennis racket with her.
10. Mandy leaped over the fence.

B. Follow the directions for Exercise A.

1. Maria found a gold pocket watch.
2. My brother collects stamps.
3. We bought three pounds of apples.
4. The President visited a junior-high classroom.
5. The sunlight sparkled on the water.
6. Terry baked whole wheat rolls.
7. The final whistle blew.
8. A butterfly danced from flower to flower.
9. The inventor experimented with the artificial heart.
10. The air conditioner in the cafeteria needs a new filter.

C. **Writing** Write an interesting predicate for each of these subjects. Begin each sentence with the words given.

1. the fire truck
2. a late snowstorm

3. my curious puppy
4. the evil witch
5. jackie's mom

D. **Writing**   Write a subject for each predicate.

1. stalled traffic for miles
2. arrived late
3. went to the zoo
4. bounced down the stairs
5. raced down the street

Part 4   The Verb

The subjects and predicates you have been studying so far are called **complete subjects** and **complete predicates.** The complete subject includes all of the words that tell *who* or *what.* The complete predicate includes all of the words that tell what was *done* or what *happened.*

One part of every complete predicate is more important than the rest. This part is the **verb.** It is sometimes called the **simple predicate.**

Finding the Verb

The verbs in these sentences are in *italics.*

We *ran* to the beach.   The tall girl *is* the winner.

Some verbs tell of an **action.**

The boys *ran* home.   Charlene *hit* the ball.

The action of the verb may be unseen.

Bo *forgot* the list.   Carmen *enjoys* music.

Verbs that tell of an action are called **action verbs.**

Other verbs state that **something is.**

That doctor *is* a surgeon.   You *are* so nervous.

Verbs that tell that *something is* are called **state-of-being verbs.**

A verb is a word that tells of an action or that something *is.*

Exercises   **Find the verb.**

A. Read these sentences. Write the verb in each sentence.

Example: The tornado carried Dorothy to Oz.
carried

1. Nobody believed Esther's story.
2. Reggie skates like a champion.
3. Diana Ross is a singer and a movie star.
4. In the spring, northern farmers boil maple sap into syrup.
5. The bike marathon lasts all day.
6. The guide told our tour group about the state capitol.
7. One of my cousins writes for *Newsweek*.
8. A hornets' nest is in that tree.
9. Sacagawea guided Lewis and Clark in their exploration of the Northwest Territory.
10. The Constitution guarantees freedom.

B. Follow the directions for Exercise A.

1. Queen Elizabeth I ruled England for forty-five years.
2. Water freezes at 0°C or 32°F.
3. All the students went home half an hour ago.
4. The mail arrived early this afternoon.
5. Barry rode his bike to school today.
6. The baby eats nothing but cereal.
7. Medicine Hat is the name of a town in Canada.

8. My mother teaches science at Carver Junior High School.
9. Alex found a dollar bill in the parking lot.
10. The lightning storm caused static on the radio.

Main Verbs and Helping Verbs

The verb is often only a single word. Read each sentence below and notice the verb.

> Eddie *made* some soup.   Georgia *whistled* a tune.

A verb may also be more than one word.

> Eddie *will make* some soup.
> Georgia *has been whistling* that tune all week.

In the first sentence the verb is *will make. Make* is the main verb and *will* is the helping verb. In the second sentence the verb is *has been whistling. Whistling* is the main verb, and *has* and *been* are helping verbs.

As you can see in these examples, the main verb sometimes changes form when helping verbs are used with it. The endings *-ing, -ed,* and *-en* are often added to main verbs. Using helping verbs and changing the ending of the main verb does not change the action that the main verb tells about. However, these changes do change the meaning slightly.

In the following examples, decide which words are main verbs and which words are helping verbs. Then look at the chart to see if you were right.

> Grace *was skating.*
> The old Ford *has been making* strange noises.
> The back door *should have been locked.*

Helping Verbs +	Main Verb =	Verb
was	skating	was skating
has been	making	has been making
should have been	locked	should have been locked

Some verbs can be used alone or as helping verbs.

is	am	were	has	do	did
are	was	have	had	does	

Examples: Tomorrow *is* a holiday. (verb)
The pump *is working*. (helping verb)

Some words can be used only as helping verbs.

can	will	should	may	might
shall	could	would	must	

When you are looking for verbs, keep these things in mind:

Some verbs are made up of a main verb and one or more helping verbs.

Some words can be used either as verbs by themselves or as helping verbs.

Some words can be used only as helping verbs.

Exercises   Find the main verb and helping verbs.

A. Make two columns on your paper. Label them *Helping Verbs* and *Main Verb*. Find all the parts of the verb in each sentence. Write each part in the proper column.

Example: Eighteen customers have demanded a refund.

Helping Verbs	Main Verb
have	demanded

1. I have seen the dinosaur bones in the museum.
2. The blizzard will have stopped all traffic in the city.
3. The Cubs might have beaten the Braves.
4. Pennsylvania is called the Keystone State.
5. Chris has completed four passes in this quarter.
6. Rick should be waiting for you.
7. Terri can do a somersault on the trampoline.
8. The chemical had polluted the river.
9. Lynn has been elected class president.
10. The fireworks in Candlestick Park will begin at eight.

B. Follow the directions for Exercise A.

1. You should have seen the game last Thursday.
2. Those hot peppers may burn your tongue.
3. The water was set at 26°C in the pool.
4. On Saturday the rides will cost a quarter.
5. Seattle was named for an Indian chief, Seathl.
6. The whole house would shake with each new earth-quake tremor.
7. The Grand Canyon is considered a wonder of the world.
8. My sister has moved to Cleveland.
9. I might go to the pet show tomorrow.
10. You must have taped that noise at the basketball game.

C. Writing Write a complete sentence for each of the following verbs. Underline the main verb and the helping verbs in each sentence.

1. were jumping
2. should have laughed
3. was done
4. is working
5. has been seen

Separated Parts of the Verb

The words that make up a verb are not always together in a sentence, like *could have been* and *might have seen*. Sometimes the helping verbs and the main verb are separated by other words that are not verbs.

can hardly **wait**	**could** not **have come**
has always **been**	**didn**'t **understand**
is usually **found**	**must have** already **gone**

Notice that *not* and the ending *n't* in contractions are not parts of the verb even though they do change the meaning of the verb.

Exercises   Find separated parts of the verb.

A.   Label two columns *Helping Verbs* and *Main Verb*. Find all the parts of the verb in each sentence. Write each part in the proper column.

Example: Did the kitten scratch you?

Helping Verbs	Main Verb
did	scratch

1. Jenny has always been my friend.
2. Bruce would often take the bus to hockey practice.
3. Jeans are usually found in the sportswear department.
4. Players are sometimes traded from one team to another.
5. We will probably see the movie this weekend.
6. Judy has just cut the lawn.
7. Nick is always playing that song.
8. The pool is usually cleaned once a week.
9. Sandy didn't understand the instructions in the booklet.
10. Maurice may have already finished his lunch.

B.   Follow the directions for Exercise A.
1. My mother is still looking for a new car.
2. The hot days of July and August are sometimes called the dog days.
3. That catbird is always mimicking all the other birds.
4. Ms. Washington doesn't assign homework often.
5. Valerie has never seen the ocean.
6. Mr. Lang must not have called very loudly.
7. A Venus' flytrap can really catch flies.
8. Greg doesn't want those travel posters.
9. In Australia, badgers are sometimes called bandicoots.
10. New York was originally named New Amsterdam.

Part 5 The Simple Subject

In a complete sentence, every verb has a subject.

Subject	Verb
I	laughed.
The chocolate	will melt.
The entire class	sang the song.

The subject of the verb is sometimes called the **simple subject** of the sentence. The simple subjects in the sentences above are *I, chocolate,* and *class.* From here on in this book, the simple subject will be called the *subject* of the verb.

To find the simple subject, first find the verb. Then ask *who* or *what* before the verb.

> **Examples:** The crowd at the concert cheered loudly.
> Verb: *cheered*
> *Who or what* cheered? crowd
> *Crowd* is the subject of *cheered.*
>
> The tall, red-haired boy is the best goalie.
> Verb: *is*
> *Who or what* is? boy
> *Boy* is the subject of *is.*

Exercises Find the verb and its subject.

A. Copy each sentence. Draw two lines under the verb. Then draw one line under the subject of the verb.

1. Ms. Carroll coached our team to the championship.
2. The spaceship has landed safely in the desert.
3. The clock struck twelve.
4. The hornets under the window buzzed angrily.
5. An architect designs buildings.
6. Joel is our next-door neighbor.

7. The treasures of King Tutankhamen were found in Egypt.
8. We circled the airport for an hour.
9. All three boys could play the guitar well.
10. A cat's eyes shine in the dark.

B. Follow the directions for Exercise A.

1. Aretha answered the test questions easily.
2. In July and August, the Dog Star rises with the sun.
3. Heavy traffic frequently jams the Holland Tunnel in New York City.
4. Everyone in the audience cheered the acrobats in the pyramid.
5. The steer in that pen was branded at the Lazy-T Ranch.
6. The smell of popcorn filled the theater.
7. Now Carl can dry the dishes.
8. The diner behind the factory was crowded at noon.
9. My older sister must have fixed my bicycle.
10. The lettuce in that salad was picked just this morning.

Part 6 The Subject in Unusual Positions

In nearly all the sentences you have studied so far, the subject has been at the beginning of the sentence. Sometimes however, the subject is in a different position.

The *shark* lingered offshore.
(The subject is at the beginning of the sentence.)
Offshore the *shark* lingered.
(The subject is in the middle of the sentence.)
Offshore lingered the *shark*.
(The subject is at the end of the sentence.)

It may be hard to find the subject when it is in an unusual position. Sometimes you can find the subject by turning the sentence around.

> Through the cloud shot the *rocket*.
> The *rocket* shot through the cloud.

Remember, always find the verb first. Then ask *who* or *what* before the verb.

Sometimes the subject must follow the verb, as in sentences that begin in these ways:

| Here is | There is | Where is |
| Here are | There are | Where are |

Here is your *guitar*. (*Guitar* is the subject of *is*.)
There is our *boat*. (*Boat* is the subject of *is*.)
Where are the *keys*? (*Keys* is the subject of *are*.)

Exercises Find the subject in unusual positions.

A. Copy each sentence. Draw two lines under the verb. Then draw one line under the subject of the verb.

1. There is a storm in the mountains.
2. Into the pool plunged the diver.
3. Before the storm, the girls closed the windows.
4. Where is the key to your locker?
5. From the haunted house came strange noises.
6. There were many interruptions during the program.
7. Across the street darted Mr. Walter's cat.
8. Finally Roger understood the question.
9. Up the tree scrambled the squirrels.
10. Three hours after dark, Kevin crept from his tent.

B. Follow the directions for Exercise A.

1. Here is my idea for our science project.
2. Overhead floated brightly colored helium balloons.

3. Down the Mississippi glided the coal barge.
4. Suddenly the rocket exploded.
5. In the tropical waters are many unusual and beautiful creatures.
6. There is room for five more people on the roller coaster.
7. In last year's competition, Al's team won easily.
8. Over the plains thundered the herd of zebras.
9. Here is my bracelet.
10. Where is a public telephone?

Part 7 Subjects and Verbs in Interrogative and Exclamatory Sentences

Some interrogative sentences are written in the usual order. That is, the subject comes first, followed by the verb.

Subject	Verb	
Who	brought	the fresh raspberries?

Sometimes, though, the order is changed. In the following interrogative sentence, the subject *Benji* comes between the two parts of the verb.

Has Benji heard the good news?

Some exclamatory sentences also have unusual word order. In the following exclamatory sentence, the subject *we* comes after the verb.

Were we scared!

Remember, some interrogative and exclamatory sentences have unusual word order. To find the subject and verb in sentences like these, try to reword the sentences as declarative sentences.

Benji has heard the good news.
We were scared.

Now these sentences have the usual word order. The subject and verb are easier to find.

Exercises **Find the subjects and verbs in interrogative and exclamatory sentences.**

A. Write the subject of each of the following sentences. To find the subject, first rewrite each sentence as a declarative sentence.

> Example: Did you clean your room?
> You did clean your room.

1. Were you a winner at the science fair?
2. Was Tom surprised!
3. Has the dog been fed?
4. Will you hurry!
5. Have they painted the library?
6. Did Carlos buy a new calculator?
7. Is Mr. Nelson mad!
8. May I help you?
9. Was I nervous!
10. Won't this snow ever melt!

B. Copy the sentences below. Draw two lines under the verb in each sentence. Draw one line under the subject of the verb. To help find the subjects and verbs, rewrite each sentence as a declarative sentence.

1. Did you find the right answer?
2. Does that hamburger have onions on it?
3. Were they shocked!
4. Did you write any poetry?
5. Have the Cubs played in a World Series?
6. Won't you ever learn!

7. Don't you ever forget it!
8. Did Angel Cordero ride in that race?
9. Has Marcia read today's newspaper already?
10. Am I hungry!

Part 8 When the Subject Is Not Given

Imperative sentences (commands) usually begin with a verb. For example, in the command *Close the door*, the verb is the first word, *close*. What is the subject? The subject in the sentence is *you*, even though it is not expressed. *You* is the person or group spoken to. The subject *you* is called the **understood subject.**

Examples: (*You*) Keep off the grass. (*You*) Stop!
(*You*) Hurry up! (*You*) Do not feed the animals.

Exercises **Find the subject.**

A. Copy the following sentences. Draw two lines under the verb in each sentence. Draw one line under the subject of the verb. If the subject is not given in the sentence, write it in parentheses in the place where it is understood.

Example: Memorize this poem.

(You) memorize this poem.

1. Play ball.
2. Marianne almost forgot her umbrella.
3. Take another turn before we have lunch.
4. Finish your game after class.
5. Did Joe bring the badminton net?
6. Give me your autograph, please.

7. Look out!
8. Is the story true?
9. Proceed with caution.
10. Do you know Steve Fowler?

B. Follow the directions for Exercise A.

1. Wait a minute!
2. Does Rosalie speak Spanish?
3. The violin players were not quite ready.
4. Did the explorers come from Portugal or Spain?
5. Listen to that rain.
6. Can everyone hear me?
7. How many points do triangles have?
8. Fix your bike tomorrow.
9. Turn left at the first stop light.
10. Some of my friends play handball every afternoon.

Part 9 Compound Subjects

Look at these two sentences:

Subject	Predicate
Tom	saw a traffic accident.
I	saw a traffic accident.

Since the predicates are the same, you can join the two sentences. The new sentence will be:

Subject	Predicate
Tom and I	saw a traffic accident.

Now the subject has two parts. When more than one subject is used with the same predicate, the subject is called a **compound subject.** *Compound* means "having more than one part."

Notice that the word *and* joins the two parts of the compound subject. The word *or* is also used to join parts of a subject. A word that is used to join words or groups of words is called a **conjunction.**

> Simple subject: *Darren* may win.
> Simple subject: *Alicia* may win.
> Compound subject: *Darren* **or** *Alicia* may win.

When more than two subjects are combined in a compound subject, use commas to separate them. Place the conjunction before the last subject.

> Example: The *trees,* the *bushes,* **and** the *flowers* were ruined by insects.

Exercises   Find compound subjects.

A.   Find the verb and its compound subject in each of the following sentences. Write the subjects and verb. Draw a vertical line between them.

> Example: The wind and the sudden rain ruined the picnic.
>
>   wind, rain   ruined

1. Emily, Charlotte, and Ann Brontë wrote novels.
2. The Knicks or the Celtics will win the playoffs.
3. Shirley, Della, and Pat are best friends.
4. In *Star Wars,* C3PO and R2D2 aided in the fight against Darth Vader.
5. Radishes, carrots, and potatoes grow underground.
6. That stuffed dog or the rubber duck would be a good gift for the baby.
7. John Lennon, Paul McCartney, George Harrison, and Ringo Starr became famous as the Beatles.
8. Marisa and Jorge tied for first place in the contest.

9. Cereal, milk, and juice make a nutritious breakfast.
10. The Mohawks and four other Indian tribes joined forces as the powerful Five Nations.

B. Writing Write a compound subject for each predicate listed below. Write the complete sentence. In some sentences, try to use a compound subject with three parts.

1. suddenly rounded the corner
2. are waiting outside
3. were my best subjects
4. have never been afraid of spiders
5. covered the ground
6. were not ready yet
7. ran for the last bus
8. are in the tool kit
9. were blocking the driveway
10. tied down the trunk of the car

Part 10 Compound Predicates

When two or more predicates are used with the same subject, the predicate is called a **compound predicate.**

When two or more sentences have the same subject but different predicates, you can often combine the sentences into one. Use a conjunction to join the parts of a compound predicate.

Subject	Predicate
The dog	growled at the letter carrier.
The dog	nipped at her heels.

Subject	Predicate
The dog	growled at the letter carrier and nipped at her heels.

When there are three or more predicates in a compound predicate, use commas to separate them. Place the conjunction before the last predicate.

> Example: Katherine *saw the bear, dropped the camera,* **and** *ran off.*

Exercises Write compound predicates.

A. Write each of the following sentences. Underline the subject once and each part of the compound predicate twice. Circle the conjunction.

1. I left the cake in the oven too long and burned it.
2. Ice covered the streets and caused many accidents.
3. My family went to the Grand Canyon, rode donkeys, and spent the night at the bottom of the Canyon.
4. The Angels lost one game but won the next three.
5. Frederick Douglass escaped from slavery and became a speaker for anti-slavery groups.
6. Our class rented a bus and visited the Museum.
7. King Kong escaped in New York City, climbed the Empire State Building, and fought for his life.
8. Bring your lunch or buy a hot dog at the cafeteria.
9. Mary Pickford starred in silent movies and was called "America's Sweetheart."
10. Ed came to the plate, ignored three wide pitches, and smashed the fourth pitch into the stands.

B. Writing Write a compound predicate for each subject listed below. Write the complete sentence. In some of your sentences, try to use a compound predicate with three parts.

1. The catcher
2. A clever detective
3. The Statue of Liberty
4. The school band
5. Stars and planets
6. The ice cream
7. An old house
8. Forest fires
9. A dolphin
10. The snowstorm

Sentences are made up of words. In order for a sentence to make sense, the words must be in a special order. Read the groups of words below. Which group makes sense?

> Ralph jumped up.
>
> Jumped Ralph up.

The first group makes sense. The words are in the right order for an English sentence. The second group does not make sense. Your ear tells you that the words are not in the right order.

Sometimes there is more than one right order for a group of words. Each order makes sense and expresses a message, but the messages may not be the same. Read this pair of sentences.

> Elaine saw Hugh.
>
> Hugh saw Elaine.

The words are the same in each sentence. Only the order of the words makes the sentences different. But the difference in order makes an important difference in meaning.

Exercise **Change the word order and meaning.**

Read each sentence. Then change the order of the words to change the meaning. Write each new sentence on your paper.

1. Tom spotted Phyllis.
2. Cake crumbs covered the dish.
3. The Tigers beat the Lions.
4. Carol knows my best friend.
5. Some insects eat plants.
6. Jack met the team.
7. Donna heard the cat.
8. Tim saw the dancer.

ADDITIONAL EXERCISES

Learning About Sentences

A. Sentences and Fragments   Number your paper from 1 to 10. For each word group, write *Sentence* or *Fragment*.

1. Cracked the egg
2. The top rung of the ladder
3. Emily studied for two hours
4. Across the Wells Street bridge
5. Received a special delivery letter
6. Lon practiced
7. The bank teller rang the burglar alarm
8. Invented the microwave oven
9. Mr. Sawyer chuckled
10. Shoveled the snow on the sidewalk and the driveway

B. Kinds of Sentences   For each of the following sentences, write *Declarative, Interrogative, Imperative,* or *Exclamatory* to show what kind it is. Add the punctuation mark that should be used at the end of each sentence.

1. Are all fables about animals
2. Try this new puzzle
3. The trout is a freshwater fish
4. What a heavy suitcase this is
5. Watch this last race
6. Where did Alice go
7. Tulips bloom in early spring
8. What fun that was
9. Turn on the projector, Sheila
10. Harry was absent today

C. Subjects and Predicates Copy these sentences. Draw a vertical line between the subject and the predicate in each sentence.

1. The coach videotaped the intermediate and senior wrestling matches.
2. My brother's bicycle has a flat tire.
3. Kristi lost her book bag.
4. Flowers filled the garden.
5. Icicles hung from the roof of the porch and over the windows.
6. We missed the last bus.
7. The pilot of the 747 radioed the control tower for landing instructions.
8. Our neighbors moved to Cleveland.
9. Cindy's design is colorful.
10. The park district sponsored the concert.

D. Main Verbs and Helping Verbs Label two columns *Helping Verbs* and *Main Verbs*. Write the parts of the verb in the proper column. Not every sentence will have both.

1. Sara typed the letter to her senator.
2. Ms. Black is the principal of our junior high.
3. Cora has a fever.
4. Mark is painting the fence.
5. The President may make an appearance at the rally on the Fourth of July.
6. Joe could barely see through the icy window.
7. David will probably walk to school today with Allen and Marcello.
8. Britta will be waiting at the bus stop.
9. Our team didn't make the play-offs.
10. Those bluejays are always chattering.

E. Subjects and Verbs Write the verb and its simple subject for each of the following sentences.

1. The newspaper reported the mayor's Inauguration Day speech.
2. The Phillipine Islands are located in the Pacific Ocean.
3. Jessica should have kept her promise.
4. The class will have a Halloween party.
5. The workers would have stayed longer.
6. A mirror is coated with silver paint.
7. A magnet will not attract plastic.
8. Mara will dive from the ten-meter platform.
9. You can buy two books for the price of one.
10. This camera doesn't work.

F. Subjects in Unusual Positions Write the verb and its simple subject for each of the following sentences.

1. Out of the closet tumbled the boxes.
2. There is the movie theater.
3. Where are my shoes?
4. Into the sky soared the jet.
5. Here is the box of oil paints.
6. Where is the nearest mailbox?
7. Onto the trampoline jumped the gymnast.
8. There are the snack trays.
9. Inside the locket was a picture.
10. Through the woods ran the fox.

G. Subjects and Verbs in Interrogative and Exclamatory Sentences Write the verb and its simple subject for each of the following sentences.

1. Did you see the eclipse of the moon?
2. Have Carla and Sue mowed the lawn yet?
3. Wasn't that great!

4. How old are these giant redwoods?
5. Should we bring our lunches along?
6. Am I angry!
7. Will you stop screaming!
8. Who was that masked man?
9. Was I relieved!
10. How many rings does Saturn have?

H. Understood Subjects Write the verb and its simple subject for each of the following sentences. If the subject is not given, write it in parentheses.

1. Choose your favorite story.
2. Will you sweep the porch?
3. Try this fresh apple juice.
4. Carl left his books on the counter.
5. Listen for the echo in this cave.
6. Ruth planted an herb garden.
7. Boil the eggs for three minutes.
8. Keep your dog on a leash.
9. The police arrived at the scene of the accident.
10. Remember your raincoat.

I. Compound Subjects Write the compound subjects in the following sentences.

1. Ramona and Susan transferred to a new school.
2. Magnolia trees and benches lined the walkway in the park.
3. Clark and Lois covered the story for the school paper.
4. The pencils and the markers rolled across the table and onto the floor.
5. Mom and Dad attended the meeting.
6. Peggy and I played paddle tennis at the health club.

7. The blue shirt or the red sweater would look nice with those jeans.
8. Lions, tigers, and leopards are kept in this part of the zoo.
9. The Royals and the Sox will play tonight.
10. Singers and musicians performed at the festival.

J. Compound Predicates   Write the compound predicates in the following sentences.

1. Cal lifted the boxes and loaded them onto the truck.
2. Scott swept the floor, washed the table, and emptied the trash.
3. I auditioned for the play but didn't get a part.
4. We pulled the taffy and cut it into pieces.
5. The officer blew the whistle and stopped traffic.
6. The ivy grew along the fence and started up the wall.
7. Carlos wrote the song and performed it.
8. The workers repaired the street and put in new curbs.
9. Sandy typed the information and made copies of it.
10. The movie started on time and lasted for three hours.

MIXED REVIEW

Learning About Sentences

A. Identifying fragments and kinds of sentences Read the following groups of words. Decide which are sentences and which are fragments. If the group of words is a fragment, write *Fragment*. If a group is a sentence, copy it and punctuate it correctly. Then write *Declarative, Interrogative, Imperative,* or *Exclamatory* to show what kind of sentence it is.

1. Kris enjoys mysteries and science fiction
2. Most of the voters
3. I got the job
4. Is the concert sold out
5. Alaska is our largest state
6. Energy from the sun
7. Call me tomorrow morning
8. The otter belongs to the weasel family
9. Carried the ball to the fifty-yard line
10. Have you read both chapters for the test on Friday

B. Recognizing subjects, predicates, and verbs Copy the following sentences. Draw a vertical line between the subject and predicate. Underline the verb. Remember that a verb can be more than one word.

1. The secretary has read the minutes to the council.
2. Tickets to the musical cost four dollars.
3. The green van ran out of gas.
4. This plant will need direct sunlight.
5. Tom bought a bookcase for his room.
6. We camped near Glacier National Park.
7. Ben can swim the length of the pool.
8. Sara forgot your phone number.
9. The ski jackets at this store are on sale.
10. Our local library will need volunteers this summer.

C. Finding the verb and the simple subject Copy the following sentences. Underline the simple subject once and the verb twice. Remember that the subject does not always come before the verb.

1. Scott usually leaves for school at eight o'clock.
2. Most of these houses have large yards.
3. You should have heard our school choir.
4. Virginia had never been on skis before.
5. Philadelphia was once the capital of the United States.
6. After the blizzard we shoveled the driveway.
7. New York City is sometimes called the "Big Apple."
8. Around the track roared the cars.
9. What time does the movie start?
10. Doreen always eats a good breakfast.
11. What an unusual car that is!
12. Do you want peanuts or sunflower seeds?

D. Recognizing compound subjects and compound predicates Number your paper from 1 to 10. Label two columns on your paper *Compound Subjects* and *Compound Predicates*. Write the compound subjects and compound predicates in the proper columns. Not every sentence will have both.

1. Jim sanded the chair and refinished the kitchen table.
2. Lois Lenski wrote that book and illustrated it.
3. London, Paris, and Rome are European capitals.
4. Korie and I babysit together.
5. Sylvia and Tony designed the mural and painted it.
6. The monkeys jumped and swung on the ropes.
7. Arizona and New Mexico have warm dry climates.
8. Rain or snow is predicted in today's weather forecast.
9. Ken and Julie auditioned for the play and got the lead roles.
10. Paul and Carla read and outlined each chapter.

USING GRAMMAR IN WRITING
Learning About Sentences

A. Think of someone you admire. It might be a favorite movie or TV star. It could be a well-known sports figure or an important leader of our country. What would you like to say to this person if you had the chance? What would you ask?

Write a fan letter to the person you admire. Include those things you especially like about him or her. Ask questions, too. The letter can be serious or funny. Write complete sentences. Include at least one of each kind of sentence: declarative, interrogative, imperative, and exclamatory. In each sentence, draw a line between the subject and the predicate.

B. One of the best things about summer is outdoor entertainment. Think about a summer event you have enjoyed. Was it a state or county fair? Was it a neighborhood party or a big festival? Maybe it was a rodeo or a beach picnic. Write a paragraph or two about this event. In each sentence underline the simple subject once and the verb twice. In at least one sentence, the subject should be in an unusual position.

C. Many people like to complain. They complain about the weather. They complain about their homework. They complain about the food they eat. In fact, some people always complain.

Imagine that you got stuck sitting next to one of these complainers on a long bus ride. He or she goes on and on about how bad everything is. See if you can convince this person that it's really *great* to be alive. What arguments can you use to convince your seat partner? Write a paragraph telling what's good about life.

Include one sentence in which the subject is not given. At least one sentence should contain a compound subject. One sentence should have a compound verb.

Using Sentences Correctly

There are many ways in which sentences are different from each other. They may have different purposes. They may express different ideas.

All sentences, however, have one thing in common. Every sentence expresses a complete thought.

> Ted's sister works in Boston.
> Are you going to the band concert?

Some groups of words do not express a complete thought. They express only part of a thought. These groups of words are called sentence **fragments.**

> Works in Boston
> Going to the band concert

Sometimes two or more sentences are written incorrectly as just one sentence. These sentences are called **run-on sentences.**

> Ted's sister works in Boston she is a reporter.
> Are you going to the band concert, do you need a ride?

You can see that sentence fragments and run-on sentences do not express ideas clearly. They are confusing when you read them.

When you write sentences, try to avoid confusion. Avoid fragments and run-on sentences. In this section, you will practice writing sentences correctly.

Part 1 Avoiding Sentence Fragments

A sentence fragment may express any part of a thought. A fragment might tell only *who* or *what*.

> Examples: My family
>   Otto the gorilla

Or a fragment might tell only what *happened* or what *is*.

> Examples: Lived on a farm
>   Is a star attraction

Or a fragment might tell any other part of a thought.

> Examples: In upstate New York
>   At the Lincoln Park Zoo

You can see that each of these sentence fragments expresses only part of an idea. Sentence fragments do not make sense.

A sentence that is clear and correct does make sense. A sentence expresses a complete thought.

> Examples: My family lived on a farm.
>   My family lived on a farm in upstate New York.

Otto the gorilla is the star attraction.

At the Lincoln Park Zoo, Otto the gorilla is the star attraction.

Exercises Recognize sentence fragments.

A. Read each of the following groups of words. Write *Sentence* or *Fragment* to tell what each group is.

1. Jumped into the water
2. Firefighters climbed onto the roof of the burning building
3. A stocking cap and waterproof mittens
4. I'll fix the salad
5. The outer layer of the tooth is enamel
6. Nomads often live in tents
7. Carrie laughed at the joke
8. Red, yellow, and blue are primary colors on the color wheel
9. Visited a museum in Detroit
10. Watched the Grammy Awards show on TV

B. Follow the directions for Exercise A.

1. Under the pile of firewood
2. The badly dented bicycle
3. Flash floods eroded the soil
4. Drove the tractor and plowed the fields
5. Vanessa read the message with a large magnifying glass
6. Stopped at a shady picnic spot
7. Mom had a toothache
8. The girls followed the map
9. Elizabeth Blackwell was the first woman doctor in the United States
10. The helicopter landed on the roof

C. Writing All of the following groups of words are fragments. Number your paper from 1 to 10. Make sentences from the fragments by adding whatever is needed. Write each sentence on your paper.

1. the door
2. the artist at her easel
3. a team of doctors
4. planted a garden
5. celebrated her birthday
6. have twenty cousins
7. a bolt of lightning
8. building a model car
9. traveled by jet
10. a Spiderman comic

Part 2 Avoiding Run-on Sentences

A run-on sentence is two or more sentences written as one. Sometimes a writer leaves out the capital letters and punctuation that show where each new idea begins. See how confusing these run-on sentences are.

It was a foggy night everything was still.
The group climbed up the hill, they camped for the night.

Now see how clear the ideas are when each sentence expresses a single thought.

It was a foggy night. Everything was still.
The group climbed up the hill. They camped for the night.

Whenever you write, be careful to put just one complete idea in each sentence. Mark the end of each sentence with a period, question mark, or exclamation point. Begin each new sentence with a capital letter.

Exercises   Recognize run-on sentences.

A.   Some of the following sentences are run-on sentences. Some are correct. Number your paper from 1 to 10. Read each sentence aloud. Then write either *Run-on* or *Correct*.

1. Lou and Bruce went to the game there was a huge crowd.
2. All of the books in that part of the library are nonfiction.
3. We had art class today I made a ceramic pin.
4. May I use your scissors I lost mine.
5. Scientists are developing ways to predict earthquakes.
6. Brazil is a very big country people speak Portuguese there.
7. Terry has a new calculator he got it for his birthday.
8. During Colonial times, children did not go to school very long.
9. Valerie and Susan took lessons in ballet and tap dancing.
10. Anita got an *A* on the science test, she studied for it all weekend.

B.   Follow the directions for Exercise A.

1. Betsy has a garden she grows flowers and vegetables.
2. Last week I went swimming it's too cold now.
3. Vasco de Balboa discovered the Pacific Ocean and claimed it for Spain.
4. John bought a sandwich it had beef, pickles, and tomatoes in it.
5. The strong wind made my eyes water.
6. Have you ever read this book by Madeleine L'Engle I enjoyed it.
7. Tammy kept careful records of all her experiments.
8. Two companies of firefighters fought the fire on my street.

9. Edith and her family visited Idaho, they went in a camper.
10. Bill "Bojangles" Robinson was a popular dancer he also appeared in movies.

C. Writing Number your paper from 1 to 10. Correct each of the following run-on sentences. Read each run-on aloud. Then rewrite each one, adding the correct capitalization and punctuation.

1. Have you ever seen this program is it good?
2. In that bakery, a machine kneads the bread dough the baker makes the cookie dough by hand.
3. The bricklayer applied mortar, she stacked another brick.
4. Chuck read *Freaky Friday* it's a funny book.
5. Pam jumped into the pool she swam six laps.
6. Annie likes to play Royal Rummy Evan likes Monopoly.
7. The jury gave its verdict the man was guilty.
8. Gordon replaced the antenna on the TV set now it works fine.
9. The waterfall splashed down the rocks it sprayed us.
10. This soil has too much clay plants don't grow well here.

ADDITIONAL EXERCISES

Using Sentences Correctly

A. Sentences and Fragments Write *Fragment* or *Sentence* for each of the following groups of words to show what each group is.

1. Glowed red at sunset
2. Adam studied hard for the math test
3. The menu with cartoon drawings on it
4. A hydroplane skims over the surface of the water
5. A tornado thirty miles away
6. Has a two-party system of government
7. The Feldmans won a trip to Atlanta
8. Peter threw his curveball across the plate
9. Wore brightly striped socks
10. Figure skaters glided and twirled on the smooth ice

B. Sentences and Run-ons Write *Sentence* or *Run-on* for each of the following groups of words to show what each group is.

1. There are volcanoes in the Hawaiian Islands one is active
2. Sarah's bicycle tire went flat on the bumpy road
3. Kate took her first piano lesson she learned to play a short song
4. Jupiter was a Roman god Athena was a Greek goddess
5. Mom runs every morning at dawn
6. Sheila played ringtoss at the carnival, she won a prize
7. Do you play checkers
8. The advisors met with the President, they discussed energy
9. The yellow roses are blooming
10. Play this record first

C. Sentences, Fragments, and Run-on Sentences Write *Fragment, Sentence,* or *Run-on* for each of the following groups of words to show what each group is.

1. What programs do you enjoy
2. A package from Nome, Alaska
3. People call the radio program they talk to the disk jockey
4. My uncle is a nurse at our community hospital
5. Karen added the list of figures quickly
6. Scared by a sudden blast
7. Read this poem, it's one of my favorites
8. Doesn't like blueberry yogurt
9. Keith spent all his money on a new bike
10. We missed the train, the bus has gone, too

MIXED REVIEW

Using Sentences Correctly

A. Identifying sentences, fragments, and run-ons Write *Fragment, Sentence,* or *Run-on* for each of the following groups of words. Then correct any fragments by adding words to make a complete sentence. Correct run-ons by adding capitalization and punctuation.

1. A funnel cloud touched down it destroyed a barn
2. Itzhak Pearlman studied the violin for many years now he is a world-famous musician
3. Amy, Raoul, and Derek served on the committee
4. Ran the mile in record time
5. Oranges are grown in both Florida and California
6. Along the coast of northern Africa
7. The factory closed many workers were laid off
8. Texas grows the most cotton in the United States, Iowa grows the most corn
9. Loretta Lynn and Willie Nelson sang at the concert
10. A valuable member of our soccer team

B. Correcting fragments and run-on sentences Copy this paragraph. Correct any fragments and run-ons.

Igloo is the Eskimo word for shelter. An igloo is a dome-shaped house, it is built from blocks of packed snow. Eskimos cut blocks of snow. About three feet long and about two feet wide. They fit these blocks together into a dome shape about ten feet wide, there is a hole at the top for air. Eskimos build a platform inside the igloo. This is where the family eats and sleeps, an igloo may have a window made from a thin slab of ice. The doorway to the igloo is a tunnel. The tunnel prevents the cold air from getting inside. Also, a fire. Burns inside the igloo to keep the family warm.

USING GRAMMAR IN WRITING
Using Sentences Correctly

A. You were at a party last weekend. The sandwiches that were served were delicious. You asked if you could get the recipe. The friend who gave the party calls and gives you instructions for the sandwiches over the phone. You scribble the instructions down quickly as he reads. Here is what you write:

> Grind up one pound of bologna add three-fourths of a pound of sharp American cheese mix the ingredients together add half an onion and three tablespoons pickle relish stir in one-fourth cup of mustard and one-third cup of mayonnaise. Or salad dressing. Mix well butter the hot dog buns. Spread the buns with the bologna mixture. Wrap each bun. In aluminum foil. Bake the sandwiches at 300 degrees for twenty-five minutes the recipe makes about eighteen sandwiches.

Now try to make sense of the instructions that you copied. Rewrite the instructions. Correct all run-on sentences and fragments.

B. An old corked bottle has washed ashore. Inside, you find a note. Water has seeped into the bottle, so some of the words have disappeared. Write what you think the note once said. Turn each of the fragments from the note into a sentence.

> The name of my ship
> on Friday, the thirteenth
> the only survivors
> an island in the Pacific
> Please send
> too late

Using Nouns

Part 1 What Are Nouns?

Who are you?

You are a person, a human being, a student. You are a girl or a boy, a daughter or a son, perhaps a sister or a brother. You may be a cyclist, a chess-player, a cook. You are a friend.

All of these answers are different names for you. They are all **nouns.**

Nouns are words that are used to name persons, places, or things. Here are a few examples of nouns:

Names of Persons

child   painter   Max   Lois Lane

Names of Places

city   home   Australia   North Dakota

Names of Things

fence   spinach   dinosaur   Eiffel Tower

A noun is a word that names a person, place, or thing.

Nouns name things that you can see, such as *desk* and *bicycle*. They also name things that you cannot see or touch—such as *kindness, honesty, skill,* and *courage.*

Exercises   Find the nouns.

A.   Write the nouns in each sentence below.

1. Three porpoises jumped high above the water.
2. Does Betty know the title of that song?
3. The heel of my boot is caught on a nail.
4. Mrs. Holmes kept her promise to the class.
5. Which contest did the twins win?
6. An alert lifeguard sat on the platform at the beach and watched the swimmers.
7. Many large cities have problems with pollution.
8. My older sister moved to Georgia because of her job.
9. Texas is the second largest state in the United States.
10. The rules for this game are simple.

B.   Follow the directions for Exercise A.

1. The prices of the coats are marked on the tags.
2. Sally went to Memphis and saw many old streets and houses.
3. Pepper is a little dog with black spots.
4. A foil is a sword with a button on the point.
5. The cheese on this cracker tastes delicious.
6. Alaska and Hawaii are the newest states.
7. People from Cuba speak Spanish.
8. Buttercups and daisies were growing in the field behind the house.
9. The strength of the runners impressed the fans.
10. Mr. Martin won't take any nonsense or excuses.

In this exercise, you will write only nouns.

   a. Write the names of four persons you know.
   b. Write the names of four places you have visited.
   c. Write the names of four things you can see at this mo-
      ment.
   d. Write the names of four things you cannot see or
      touch, such as *truth* or *love*.

Part 2   Common Nouns and Proper Nouns

When you call yourself a student, you are giving yourself a name that you share with all of your classmates. When you call yourself a boy or a girl, you are giving yourself a name that you share with about half your classmates. *Student, boy,* and *girl* are general names for people. They are called **common nouns.**

Playground, town, and *lake* are general names for places. They, too, are common nouns. Many words are general names for things, like *book, tool,* or *animal.* These words are also common nouns.

A common noun is a general name for a person, place, or thing. A common noun begins with a small letter.

You are not just any person. You have a name that is specifi-cally yours. Margaret Thatcher, Judy Blume, and Captain James T. Kirk are specific people. These specific names for people are called **proper nouns.**

Proper nouns can also name specific places, like Houston and Lake Erie. Proper nouns may name specific things, like the *Mayflower* and a *Schwinn.*

A proper noun names a particular person, place, or thing. A proper noun always begins with a capital letter.

	Common Nouns	Proper Nouns
Persons	doctor children judge	Dr. Jonas Salk Jane Banks, Michael Banks Sandra Day O'Connor
Places	street park city	Jefferson Street Yosemite National Park Richmond
Things	bridge country religion	George Washington Bridge Canada Christianity

Notice that a proper noun may include more than one word. Capitalize all of the words in a proper noun. Do not capitalize the words *a, an,* or *the* before a proper noun.

Exercises **Find common and proper nouns.**

A. Make two columns on your paper. Title them *Common Noun* and *Proper Noun.* Write each of the following nouns in the correct column. Be sure to capitalize the proper nouns.

1. school
2. woolworth's
3. colorado
4. mountain
5. the rocky mountains
6. jennifer parsons
7. chair
8. geraldo
9. the hudson river
10. actor
11. country
12. lake erie
13. elmwood elementary school
14. harbor
15. cowboy
16. atlantic ocean
17. ohio river
18. martin luther king
19. elizabeth
20. daughter

B. Follow the directions for Exercise A.

1. philadelphia
2. the white house
3. cleveland
4. man
5. the chicago black hawks
6. europe
7. bridge
8. france
9. the new york stock exchange
10. high school
11. theresa
12. the jefferson memorial
13. south america
14. crossword puzzle
15. coca-cola
16. world war II
17. detective
18. horse
19. madison
20. fort

C. Writing Copy these sentences. Capitalize each proper noun.

1. Mr. mackey rode his bike through florida last winter.
2. Ms. moore told us about islands in the pacific ocean.
3. Potatoes are grown in the state of idaho.
4. My uncle andrew works in the sears tower.
5. Brenda's birthday is in january.

Part 3 Singular and Plural Nouns

Look at these two nouns.

player   players

They are exactly the same except for the last letter. The noun *player* refers to one person. It is called a **singular** noun.

A singular noun names just one person, place, or thing.

The noun *players* ends in *s*. It refers to several persons. It is called a **plural** noun. The word *plural* means "more than one."

A plural noun names more than one person, place, or thing.

336

Here are seven rules for forming the plurals of nouns:

1. To form the plural of most nouns, just add -s.

hats	streets	hamburgers	animals
tables	miles	shakes	movies

2. When the singular ends in s, sh, ch, x, or z, add -es.

gases	brushes	boxes
dresses	matches	waltzes

3. When the singular ends in o, add -s.

radios	solos	banjos	Eskimos

Exceptions: For the following nouns ending in **o**, add **-es:**

echoes	heroes	potatoes	tomatoes

4. When the singular noun ends in y with a consonant before it, change the y to i and add -es.

pony→ponies	baby→babies
lady→ladies	daisy→daisies

5. For most nouns ending in f or ff, add -s. For some nouns ending in f or fe, however, change the f to v and add -es or -s.

beliefs	thief→thieves	leaf→leaves
roofs	knife→knives	half→halves
staffs	wife→wives	shelf→shelves

6. Some nouns are the same for both singular and plural.

deer	sheep	trout	salmon	bass

7. Some nouns form their plurals in special ways.

child→children	man→men	tooth→teeth
mouse→mice	woman→women	foot→feet

Using a Dictionary To Find Plurals

On the next page is a dictionary entry for the word *echo*. Notice that the entry shows the plural ending -oes. The plural form is *echoes*. Most dictionaries show the plural or plural ending of a noun, if the plural is formed in an irregular way.

When you are not sure about the correct plural form of a noun, look up the noun in a dictionary.

Dictionary Entry for *Echo*

ech·o (ek′ō) *n., pl.,* **-oes** [< L. < Gr. *ēchō*] **1.** *a*) the repetition of a sound that occurs when sound waves are reflected from a surface *b*) a sound so made **2.** *a*) any repetition or imitation of the words, ideas, etc. of another *b*) a person who repeats or imitates in this way **3.** sympathetic response **4.** a radar wave reflected from an object, appearing as a spot of light on a radarscope —[**E-**] *Gr. Myth.* a nymph who pined away for Narcissus until only her voice remained —**vi. o-ed -o.ing 1.** to be filled with echoes [the long hall *echoed* with their laughter] **2.** to be repeated as an echo [his words *echoed* in the valley] —**vt. 1.** to repeat (the words, ideas, etc.) of (another) **2.** to repeat or reflect (sound) from a surface

---

Exercises   Form plurals of nouns.

A. Write all of the plural nouns in each of the following sentences. After each noun, write the number of the rule that tells how the plural was formed.

Examples: Representatives from three countries signed the treaty.

Representatives—1, countries—4

1. The halves of the melon were filled with blueberries.
2. Three deer and some foxes live in the forest.
3. On the trip, I caught two bass and several trout.
4. In some countries, adults believe in witches and elves.
5. The gardener trimmed the bushes.
6. Set the potatoes and tomatoes on the tables.
7. The girls heard echoes in the cave.
8. The germs were examined by the scientists.
9. Do geese have teeth?
10. The dairies in the cities suffered losses.

B. Write the plural form for each of these nouns.

1. wish   5. candy   9. life
2. guppy   6. porch   10. company
3. watch   7. leaf   11. wife
4. foot   8. hero   12. woman

Part 4   How Nouns Show Possession

When you speak of something that belongs to someone, you need a way to show that relationship. You do not want to say "the dog that belongs to Tom" every time you refer to it. Instead, you can use the *possessive form* of a noun. The possessive form of *Tom* is *Tom's*. The simplest way to refer to the dog that belongs to Tom is to call it *Tom's dog*.

Possessive nouns show possession, or ownership, of the noun that follows.

Forming Possessives of Singular Nouns

The difference between *Tom* and the possessive form *Tom's* is the ending. *Tom's* has an apostrophe (') and an **s.**

To form the possessive of a singular noun, add an apostrophe and s.

Singular Noun	Possessive Form
baby	baby's
Charles	Charles's

Forming Possessives of Plural Nouns

There are two rules to remember for forming the possessive of a plural noun.

1. If the plural noun ends in s, simply add an apostrophe after the s.

Plural Noun	Possessive Form
flowers	flowers'
pirates	pirates'
cats	cats'
doctors	doctors'
students	students'

2. If the plural noun does not end in s, add an apostrophe and an s after the apostrophe.

Plural Noun	Possessive Form
men	men's
women	women's
children	children's

Be careful when you are adding possessive endings. The position of the apostrophe affects the meaning of the possessive noun.

> The *student*'s idea means the idea belongs to *one* student.
> The *students*' idea means the idea belongs to *two or more* students.

If you are not sure how to write the possessive form of a noun, do this:

1. Write the noun.
2. Decide if the noun is singular or plural.
3. Follow the rules you have learned.

Exercises   Write the possessive form.

A.   Write the possessive form of the word in italics in each of the following sentences.

1. The doctor took the *runner* pulse.
2. Is that the *manager* phone number?

3. The *model* hair was long and curly.
4. Follow your *mother* advice.
5. A parade honored the *astronauts* homecoming.
6. *Jim* books are in the library.
7. The *sailors* raincoats protected them from the spray.
8. The *statue* hands looks real.
9. My *dog* ears perked up.
10. *Tess* butterfly collection has two dozen specimens.

B. Follow the directions for Exercise A.

1. The *children* presents are in the hall closet.
2. *Ann* store sells maps and travel books.
3. The golf bags are in my *father* car.
4. That *architect* designs have won awards.
5. Many *camper* tents were destroyed in the forest fire.
6. We used *Megan* scarf as a bandage.
7. *Andrea* painting was sold.
8. The *mice* whiskers twitched nervously.
9. The *governor* mansion was lit by floodlights.
10. On *Ms. Conway* desk is a no-smoking sign.

C. Write the possessive forms of the following nouns.

1. king
2. Jill
3. referees
4. Barney
5. owls
6. Anita
7. Mr. Barrett
8. Louis
9. women
10. sister

In an English sentence, the words are put together in a certain order to make sense. The word order of most sentences follows a pattern. In this book, you will study four **sentence patterns**.

Every sentence has a subject and a verb. The subject is usually a noun. In this chart, *N* stands for the noun in the complete subject. *V* stands for the verb in the complete predicate.

N	V
Margie	cheered.
Carl	ate quickly.
The baby	smiled.
The red balloon	popped.
Our puppy	snores.

The word order in these sentences follows a pattern. That pattern is noun-verb, or N V. This pattern is called the **N V pattern**.

Exercises **The N V Pattern**

A. Make a chart like the one above. Label one column *N* and the other *V*. Write these sentences on the chart.

1. Clouds formed.
2. Jenny skates every day.
3. The teams struggled.
4. Strong winds howled.
5. The dogs barked loudly.
6. Alex whistled.

B. Make a chart of your own for the N V pattern. Write five sentences using the N V pattern.

ADDITIONAL EXERCISES

Using Nouns

A. Common and Proper Nouns There are common nouns and proper nouns in each of the following sentences. Write the nouns in each sentence. Capitalize every proper noun.

1. Praise and encouragement helped the child gain confidence.
2. Rhode island is the smallest state in the nation.
3. In the fog, we could barely see the lighthouse at portland.
4. During class, andrew told a very funny joke.
5. Dr. alexander treated her patients at the hospital.
6. Tracey found beautiful seashells on the beaches of sanibel island.
7. Robert fulton designed the earliest steamboats.
8. People wonder about life on other planets, especially mars.
9. Charlie chaplin was an actor and director in the early days of the movies.
10. Bowls, spoons, plates, and pots covered the counters.

B. Proper Nouns Write the proper nouns in each of the following sentences. Capitalize them.

1. We saw the statue of liberty on our way to staten island.
2. My mother made a business trip to australia and new zealand.
3. The christmas party was given by emma and jean.
4. Our class will visit abraham lincoln's home at new salem state park.

5. They sailed from island to island in the pacific ocean.
6. Pélé played soccer as a boy in brazil.
7. Our troop visited stone mountain, which is near atlanta, georgia.
8. There are many redwoods in california.
9. Carol met june at sears.
10. Alison and todd climbed the sandy dunes on cape cod.

C. Plurals Write the plural form of each noun in italics.

1. *Paper* lined the floor of the hallway.
2. Rita ate the *sandwich*.
3. We picked the *tomato* and *strawberry* from our garden.
4. The *knife* lay on the shelf.
5. The child petted the *deer* and the *goose*.
6. Aunt Mary visited the *church* in Italy.
7. Look at the new *calf*!
8. Jason played the *hero* of the *story*.
9. The *county* reported its *vote* to the election *judge*.
10. The speaker defended her *belief*.

D. Possessives Write the possessive form of each *italicized* noun.

1. The *sightseers* tour included the museum.
2. My *family* camper sleeps six people.
3. *Russ* pony trotted around the track.
4. The *robot* chores were cooking and cleaning.
5. The politician wanted the *people* trust.
6. The *members* dues were collected annually.
7. My *brother* motorcycle is parked in the drive.
8. Our *boss* office is nicely furnished.
9. The *women* names were announced on the radio.
10. The *runner* pace quickened as she neared the finish.

MIXED REVIEW

Using Nouns

A.   Identifying common and proper nouns   Make two columns on your paper. Label them *Common Nouns* and *Proper Nouns*. Write the nouns in the correct columns. Capitalize all of the proper nouns.

> Most *countries* in *africa* have national *parks*. These *parks* protect the *wilderness* and *wildlife*. The *serengeti national park* in *tanzania* is one such *park*. It is estimated that over a million *wildebeest* live there. There are also large *preserves* in *kenya*. *People* and *animals* benefit from these *parks*. *Tourists* from *america* and *europe* can view the African *wildlife*. Also, the *animals* are protected from the growing *farms* and *cities*.

B.   Using plural and possessive nouns   The following paragraph contains errors in the use of plural and possessive nouns. Copy the paragraph, correcting those errors.

> Our schools Balloon Race is all of the student's favorite event. The race is organized by the science and social studies teachers'. It is designed to teach us about the winds current's and also about our areas cities' and towns'. Each students' balloon is tagged with a stamped, self-addressed postcard. The message on the card requests the finders cooperation. The finder writes the balloons exact location and mails the postcard. Romero Vazquezs' card was returned from Savannah, Georgia. That is nearly 400 mile's from here! Several student's balloons' were not found, including mine. Perhaps it hasn't yet reached its journeys' end.

USING GRAMMAR IN WRITING
Using Nouns

A. You've decided you want to be alone for a while. You are going to live by yourself on a deserted island. Space is limited on the little boat that will get you to your island. You can only take a few things with you. You can take three books, three records for your record player, three movies, and six of your favorite foods. Write a paragraph about what you will take with you. Underline the common nouns once. Underline the proper nouns twice. Circle any plural nouns.

B. Imagine that one of your friends had an unusual Halloween party. Everyone was told to dress-up as someone famous. Write a little story about the party. Who came dressed as whom? What did they wear? What music did you dance to?

Underline all the common nouns once. Underline the proper nouns twice. Include several sentences in which nouns show possession.

C. Many people enjoy collecting things. Stamp collecting, for example, is popular. Some people collect unusual things like license plates or bottle caps. Some collect autographs or baseball cards. Do you collect anything? If not, is someone in your family a collector? Does one of your friends collect something interesting or unusual? Write about a collector you know. Tell about his or her collection.

Use nouns in different ways in your sentences. Include at least one noun that is a direct object, one that is an indirect object, and one that is a predicate noun. Label each noun according to the way it is used.

Using Verbs

Read these words.

Becky _____ the dog.

These words almost express a complete thought. By putting words in the blank, you can complete the thought in several ways.

Becky *fed* the dog.
Becky *washed* the dog.
Becky *owned* the dog.

Now the groups of words express complete thoughts. The words *fed, washed,* and *owned* say what Becky did.

The words *fed, washed,* and *owned* all belong to a group of words called **verbs**. No sentence is complete without a verb. This section will tell you about verbs. It will also show you know to use them.

Part 1 Kinds of Verbs

Some verbs tell about action. They are **action verbs**.

Sue *hit* the ball.   Bill *ran* to the window.

Some verbs tell about an action that you cannot see. That is, there is no actual movement taking place.

Barbara *thought* about school.   Jack *wanted* a puppy.

Some verbs are not action verbs. They simply state that something *is*. They express a state of being. These verbs are **state-of-being verbs**.

Your book *is* on the table.   The slacks *were* too big.

The most common state-of-being verbs are these:

is	are	were	being
am	was	be	been

Verbs are words that tell of action or a state of being.

Exercises **Find action verbs and state-of-being verbs.**

A. Copy these sentences. Underline the verb in each sentence.

1. The mood at the party was joyful.
2. I took my dog to obedience school.
3. Colorful ceramic pots lined the tables.
4. A band played music in the plaza.
5. Our school held an art fair.
6. Students displayed their artwork.
7. We reward Scamp with dog biscuits.
8. Sharon remembered her umbrella.
9. Last summer the weather was hot and humid.
10. Rosario missed the bus this morning.

B. Make two columns on your paper. Title one column *Action Verbs* and the other *State-of-Being Verbs*. Find the verb in each sentence and place it in the correct column.

Example: That is Kevin's music stand.
Beth drank the lemonade.

Action Verbs	State-of-Being Verbs
	is
drank	

1. The leaves were red and yellow.
2. This old dress is perfect for the costume party.
3. Judy likes dill pickles.
4. We rode our bikes down to the canal and across the bridge.
5. The fourth question on the test was tricky.
6. Suddenly Syd's dark eyes lit up.
7. I know the names of all the Presidents.
8. Valentina Tereshkova was the first woman in space.
9. The kingfisher swallowed a frog and two fish.
10. Richard repaired his bike by himself.

C. Follow the directions for Exercise B.

1. In 1927, Charles A. Lindbergh flew from New York to Paris.
2. He was alone.
3. He faced many hardships.
4. After many hours in flight, he landed in France.
5. The French people welcomed him.
6. He came home on a United States cruiser.
7. The American people gave him many honors.
8. His solo flight was a great event.
9. It aided the development of aviation.
10. Lindbergh is an important aviation hero.

Part 2 Main Verbs and Helping Verbs

Many verbs are made of more than one word. They are made up of a main verb and one or more helping verbs.

Read these examples:

I *am going* to the concert tonight.
Molly *is going* deep sea fishing.
Bea and Jessie *will go* to North Carolina.
Mrs. Casey *has gone* to New York on business.
The snow *has been gone* for a week.
Sam *could have gone* to Mexico.

Helping Verbs	+	Main Verb	=	Verb
am		going		am going
is		going		is going
will		go		will go
has		gone		has gone
has been		gone		has been gone
could have		gone		could have gone

The most common of the helping verbs are these forms of *be, have,* and *do:*

be	am, are, is, was, were
have	has, have, had
do	does, do, did

These words can also be used by themselves as main verbs.

Used as Helping Verb	Used as Main Verb
Bob *is going* to New York.	Bob *is* the pitcher.
Sally *has gone* home.	Sally *has* a moped.
They *did go* to the zoo.	They *did* a duet.

There are several other helping verbs that you will often use with main verbs:

be	been	can	would	shall	might
being	may	could	should	will	must

A verb may be a single word. It may also be a group of words, made up of a main verb and one or more helping verbs.

Separated Parts of the Verb

The main verb and helping verbs are not always together. They may be separated by other parts of the sentence.

> The batter **was** not **watching** for signals.
> Frankenstein **couldn**'t **control** his monster.
> Max **had** completely **recovered** from the flu.
> **Did** the boys **make** spaghetti?

Notice that *not* and the ending *n't* in the contraction are not verbs, although they do change the meaning of the verbs.

Exercises **Find main verbs and helping verbs.**

A. Number your paper from 1 to 10. Make two columns. Label the first column *Helping Verbs*. Label the second *Main Verb*. Write the verbs for each of these sentences in the correct column. (Watch out for separated parts of the verb.)

Example: The books could not be found anywhere.

Helping Verbs	Main Verb
could be	found

1. Where can we find a book about marine life?
2. You should have seen the flames from the bonfire.
3. I am expecting a phone call.
4. The old chestnut tree was hit by lightning.
5. This contest entry might be the winner.
6. The tent had completely collapsed.
7. Skip has never had the measles.
8. That bottle could have floated here from Greenland.
9. We have already eaten our sandwiches.
10. The team had been hoping for a sunny day.

B. Follow the directions for Exercise A.

1. Curt might be joining the hockey team.
2. Computers will soon be performing many tasks.
3. The Bears are beating the Vikings, 7–0.
4. People should always eat a nutritious breakfast.
5. Cartoons can sometimes be violent.
6. Did Momoko bring her skateboard?
7. Have you ever written a poem?
8. The red wolf is becoming extinct.
9. Coach Perez had called a timeout.
10. A President can't be elected more than twice.

Part 3 Verbs and Direct Objects

In many sentences the thought is complete with just a verb and its subject:

Subject	Verb
The audience	applauded.
Mary Ann	coughed.
Donald	worked.

In other sentences the thought is not complete until other words have been added. Read these words. Are they complete thoughts?

Paul dropped
Lucy liked

Words must be added to complete these thoughts.

Paul dropped the *plates*.   Lucy liked the new *coach*.

In the first sentence, the word *plates* receives the action of the verb *dropped*. It completes the meaning of the verb. It is the **direct object** of the verb.

In the second sentence, *coach* receives the action of the verb *liked*. It completes the meaning of the verb. It also is a **direct object**.

The direct object tells whom or what receives the action of the verb.

Recognizing Direct Objects

To find the direct object in a sentence, first find the verb. Then ask *what* or *whom* after the verb.

Examples: Christy likes math.

Christy likes *what*?   math
The direct object is *math*.

Mrs. McKenna hired Kim.

Mrs. McKenna hired *whom*?   Kim
The direct object is *Kim*.

Direct objects only answer *what* or *whom* after the verb. They do not tell *when* or *where* or *how*. You can see that there are no direct objects in the following sentences.

Liz studies in the morning.
They drove to the beach.
Julio reads quickly.

Exercises   Find direct objects.

A.   Copy the following sentences. Underline the verb. Draw a circle around the direct object.

Example: The accident <u>stopped</u> all (traffic.)

1. The scuba divers found the shipwreck.
2. Bruce won the race.
3. The pilot steered his craft onto the airfield.
4. I am studying science now.

353

5. The boys have carved a big pumpkin.
6. The Bureau of the Mint manufactures all coins.
7. Katy will repair the brakes on her bike.
8. Dolores made posters for the walkathon.
9. On Thanksgiving Day we eat turkey with gravy.
10. The United States exports grain to the Far East.

B. Find and write the direct objects in these sentences.

1. Sonia made pizzas for the party.
2. The sailors unfurled the mainsail.
3. Our basketball team won its first game.
4. In 1785, Jean Pierre Blanchard invented the parachute.
5. Janet Guthrie drove the Corvette.
6. Jody will answer these letters.
7. We saw a movie about Australia.
8. The zookeeper fed the lions.
9. Did you drop the carton of eggs?
10. Beth placed the saddle on the horse's back.

Exercises   Write direct objects.

A. Write direct objects that will complete these sentences.

1. The reporter wrote a good _____ .
2. The Cardinals scored a _____ .
3. Newspapers littered the _____ .
4. Jolita rode the _____ with ease.
5. Leroy planted _____ in his front yard.
6. Nicky read a _____ yesterday.
7. Harvey wore a bright yellow _____ .
8. Kristin put the _____ in her wallet.
9. My favorite radio station plays good _____ .
10. Did you close the _____ ?

B. Writing Write sentences using these verbs. Put a direct object in each sentence. Circle the direct object.

1. have caught
2. filled
3. would have stopped
4. was twisting
5. painted
6. will open
7. has invented
8. ruined
9. should buy
10. might use

Part 4 Linking Verbs

State-of-being verbs are often called **linking verbs**. Here are some examples.

> The sky *was* blue.
> The omelet *smells* delicious.
> The table *looked* unsteady.

Linking verbs connect the subject with a word in the predicate. In the examples, *was* connects *sky* with *blue*, *smells* connects *omelet* with *delicious*, and *looked* connects *table* with *unsteady*.

The words *is, am, are, was, were, be, being, been,* and *become* are often used as linking verbs. The words *seem, look, appear, smell, taste, feel, grow,* and *sound* are sometimes linking verbs.

The words that follow linking verbs tell something about the subject. They may be nouns or adjectives. These words complete the meaning of sentences that contain linking verbs.

Here are some examples of nouns that follow linking verbs. These nouns are called **predicate nouns**. See how each predicate noun is connected to the subject.

> My mother *is* a **coach**.

> The Beatles *were* a very popular **group**.

> He *will be* the **pitcher**.

Here are some examples of adjectives that follow linking verbs. These adjectives are called **predicate adjectives**. See how each predicate adjective describes the subject.

Leslie *looked* **unhappy**.

The roads *were* very **slippery**.

Greg *is being* **stubborn**.

Exercises   Find the linking verbs.

A.   Make three columns on your paper. Title them *Subject, Linking Verb*, and *Word Linked to Subject*. Find the three parts in each sentence. Write them in the proper columns.

Example: The contestants in the marathon appeared weary.

Subject	Linking Verb	Word Linked to Subject
contestants	appeared	weary

1. Jane Fonda is an actress.
2. That clown's hat looks ridiculous.
3. The fresh bread smells delicious.
4. A young kangaroo is a joey.
5. Don't bullfights seem dangerous?
6. Samuel's story sounds unbelievable.
7. That mask looks scary.
8. The old man felt weary.
9. Scrooge is a character in *A Christmas Carol*.
10. We should be quiet during the rehearsal.

B.   Follow the directions for Exercise A.

1. The edge of this knife is dull.
2. My skates are becoming rusty.
3. This chili tastes spicy.

4. The fastest animal is the cheetah.
5. I don't feel sleepy.
6. Those huge trees are sequoias.
7. Our country's oldest national park is Yellowstone.
8. The Vikings may have been Scandinavian pirates.
9. Mother must be very upset about the flat tire on the car.
10. A popular breed of dog is the poodle.

Direct Objects or Predicate Words?

What are the differences between these two sentences?

> Kate called the doctor.
> Kate is a doctor.

You have learned about two kinds of verbs. There are action verbs and linking verbs. You have also learned about two kinds of words that follow verbs and complete their meaning. There are direct objects. There are also predicate words.

How can you tell which words are direct objects and which words are predicate words?

First, find the verb in a sentence. Is the verb an action verb or a linking verb?

1. If an **action verb** is followed by a noun that tells *what* or *whom*, that noun is a **direct object**.

   Examples: Bob *plays* **tennis**.
   Sally *won* the **contest**.

2. If a **linking verb** is followed by a word that tells about the subject, that word is a **predicate noun** or a **predicate adjective**.

   Examples: Bob *is* an **athlete**. (predicate noun)
   Sally *is* **clever**. (predicate adjective)

Now compare these two examples:

Kate called the doctor.

> *Called* is an action verb.
> *Doctor* is the direct object.

Kate is a doctor.

> *Is* is a linking verb.
> *Doctor* is the predicate noun.

Exercises Find direct objects and predicate words.

A. In some of the following sentences linking verbs are followed by predicate words. In other sentences action verbs are followed by direct objects. Copy the sentences. Circle the linking verbs and predicate words. Underline the action verbs and direct objects.

> Examples: Emmett Kelly (was) a famous (clown.)
> Congress approved the treaty.

1. The campers carried firewood to the campsite.
2. Marina is a good pianist.
3. Vacations always seem too short.
4. The police detective found a clue.
5. A down quilt feels cozy in winter.
6. The golfer hit the ball into the water.
7. According to legend, Betsy Ross made the first American flag.
8. The bill may soon become a law.
9. Mopeds use gas efficiently.
10. Mopeds are efficient vehicles.

B. Follow the directions for Exercise A.

1. The cashier added the figures.
2. The Soviet Union is the largest country in the world.

3. Rain delayed the baseball game.
4. The floor of the gym seems sticky.
5. Jason smelled smoke down the hall.
6. The peaches tasted sweet.
7. Cheryl's story was good.
8. The auditorium quickly became noisy during basketball practice.
9. The goalie stopped the puck just in time.
10. Some Eskimos use snowmobiles instead of dog sleds.

Part 5 Verb Tenses

A verb is a time-telling word. It not only tells of an action or a state of being. It also tells *when* something takes place. By changing its form, it tells whether the action or state of being it expresses is past, present, or future. This change in form to show time is called **tense**.

The **present tense** shows an action or state of being happening now.

> I *play* basketball.   I *am* a basketball player.

The **past tense** shows an action or state of being completed in the past.

> I *played* all last winter.   I *was* a guard.

The **future tense** shows an action or state of being that will happen in the future.

> I *will play* again next year.   I *will be* a forward.

Tense is shown by a change in the form of a verb. These changes are made in three ways:

1. by a change in spelling: *know, knew*
2. by a change in ending: *look, looked*
3. by a change in helping verbs: *did work, will work*

Forming Tenses

Present Tense

In general, the present tense of a verb is the same as the name of the verb: *call, do, race*. An *-s* or *-es* is added to the verb when it is used with *he, she, it,* or a singular noun.

I	call	we	call
you	call	you	call
he, she, it, Tom	calls	they, boys	call
I	do	we	do
you	do	you	do
he, she, it, Lisa	does	they, girls	do

Past Tense

The past tense of most verbs is formed by adding *-d* or *-ed* to the present tense. These verbs are called **regular verbs**.

> save—save*d*   pull—pull*ed*

The past tense of other verbs is shown by a change of spelling. These verbs are called **irregular verbs**.

> write—*wrote*   bring—*brought*

Future Tense

The future tense is formed by using the helping words *will* or *shall* with the present tense:

> *will* save   *shall* pull   *will* write   *shall* bring

Exercises   **Recognize and use verb tenses.**

A.   Number your paper from 1 to 10. Write the verb in each of the following sentences. Name the tense of each verb.

1. Alison does crossword puzzles.
2. Students will take a bus home from the game.

3. Tracy Austin plays fine tennis.
4. We saw a porpoise show at Brookfield Zoo.
5. The fans cheered the rock star.
6. Wellington is the capital of New Zealand.
7. Sir Edmund Hillary climbed Mount Everest.
8. Our class will plan a winter carnival.
9. I will return this book to the library.
10. Indians first explored this wilderness.

B. Number your paper from 1 to 10. Write the form of the verb asked for in each of the following sentences.

Example: The runner (past of *cross*) the finish line.
crossed

1. Scott O'Dell (past of *write*) *Island of the Blue Dolphins.*
2. Eric and Teresa (past of *pick*) raspberries.
3. We (present of *roast*) chestnuts in the fireplace.
4. Tyrone (past of *make*) a lamp for his room.
5. The airplane (future of *land*) in a few minutes.
6. I (future of *read*) all of the Hardy Boys mysteries.
7. The lawyer (past of *argue*) her case.
8. A cricket game (present of *confuse*) most American spectators.
9. Sponges (present of *live*) in the deep seas.
10. The track team (future of *run*) in a meet tomorrow.

C. Writing Write a sentence for each of the verbs below. Use the verb in the tense indicated.

1. hurry (future)
2. think (past)
3. enjoy (present)
4. call (past)
5. remove (past)
6. finish (future)

The **N V N pattern** describes a sentence with three parts. The first *N* stands for the subject noun. The *V* stands for the verb. The second *N* stands for the direct object noun.

N	V	N
Rosa	ordered	waffles.
Henry	plays	chess.
The carpenter	pounded	the nails.
The class	presented	a play.

Exercises   The N V N Pattern

A.   Make a chart like the one above. Label the three columns *N*, *V*, and *N*. Write these sentences on the chart.

1. Diana collects seashells.
2. Plants need sunlight.
3. My brother likes toffee.
4. Yuri climbed that peak.
5. The judges awarded prizes.
6. Eric bakes tasty bread.
7. NASA launched a rocket.
8. Our team won the game.

B.   Copy this chart. Add a word to each blank to complete the sentence in the N V N pattern.

N	V	N
1. _____	shook	the house.
2. King Kong	grabbed	_____.
3. _____	saw	_____.
4. Tony	_____	two hamburgers.
5. _____	called	Lou Ann.
6. The goat	rammed	_____.

C.   Make a chart of your own. Label the columns *N*, *V*, and *N*. Write five sentences in the N V N pattern.

The **N LV N pattern** describes a sentence with three parts. The first *N* stands for the subject noun. *LV* stands for the linking verb. The second *N* stands for the predicate noun.

N	LV	N
Chimpanzees	are	mammals.
Allen	is	my friend.
My favorite dessert	is	pudding.
The blizzard	was	a disaster.

Exercises   The N LV N Pattern

A. Make a chart like the one above. Label the three columns *N, LV,* and *N.* Write these sentences on the chart.

1. Dee is my sister.
2. Pumpkins are vegetables.
3. This chair is an antique.
4. The Tortugas are islands.
5. Pete is an artist.
6. My dad was coach.
7. The sun is a star.
8. My aunt is a jogger.

B. Copy the chart below. Add a word to each blank to complete the sentence in the N LV N pattern.

N	LV	N
1. _____	is	a useful tool.
2. My best friend	is	_____ .
3. _____	are	reptiles.
4. The Riveras	_____	my neighbors.
5. _____	are	_____ .

C. Make a chart of your own. Label the columns *N, LV,* and *N.* Write five sentences in the N LV N pattern.

There are three parts to sentences that have the **N LV Adj pattern.** The *N* stands for the subject noun. *LV* stands for the linking verb. *Adj* stands for the predicate adjective. Each of the sentences in the following chart is in the N LV Adj pattern.

N	LV	Adj
Peter	is	friendly.
The water	looks	murky.
Your voice	sounds	hoarse.
This melon	tastes	sweet.

Exercises   The N LV Adj Pattern

A. Make a chart like the one above. Label the three columns *N*, *LV*, and *Adj*. Write these sentences on the chart.

1. Lottie seems cautious.
2. This ice is slippery.
3. Cherry pie is delicious.
4. Skydivers are brave.
5. Jeff seemed lucky.
6. The trees were bare.
7. The sky looked gloomy.
8. My father will be late.

B. Copy the chart below. Add a word to each blank to complete the sentence in the N LV Adj pattern.

N	LV	Adj
1. _____	is	cheerful.
2. The snow	became	_____ .
3. Clowns	look	_____ .
4. The detectives	_____	busy.
5. _____	was	_____ .

C. Make a chart of your own. Label the columns *N*, *LV*, and *Adj*. Write five sentences in the N LV Adj pattern.

ADDITIONAL EXERCISES

Using Verbs

A. Action Verbs and State-of-Being Verbs Write each verb. Beside the verb, write *Action* or *State-of-Being.*

1. A band led the parade.
2. Our youth club elected officers last night.
3. The team seems ready for the big game.
4. Deena borrowed my basketball.
5. The patient's condition has become critical.
6. Before a rain, the air feels heavy.
7. Mangoes are tropical fruits.
8. Steve carefully crossed the footbridge.
9. The gymnast practiced on the ropes.
10. Jeopardy is a game for three or more players.

B. Parts of the Verb Write the complete verb in each sentence.

1. Dry ice is sometimes used in ice-cream machines.
2. Bears at Yellowstone will often come up to cars.
3. The rescue party must have searched the woods.
4. Ms. Andretti has not given any homework.
5. Have you ever been on a motorcycle?
6. Mark isn't going on the field trip.
7. The mail should have arrived by now.
8. Will you be swimming in the meet?
9. Snow has been falling all day.
10. Sue had completely forgotten about the test.

C. Verbs and Direct Objects Copy the following sentences. Underline the verbs. Circle the direct objects.

1. Beth won a blue ribbon in the competition.
2. Ms. Berzinski directed the play.

3. Bonny prepared tacos for dinner.
4. Zeke remembered the address.
5. Joe played golf with Harry today.
6. That corporation donated money to the university.
7. The batter hit the ball into the stands.
8. Susan can fix the leaky faucet.
9. I am writing a letter to the mayor.
10. Chris paid the bill for the repairs.

D. Linking Verbs and Predicate Words Write *Subject*, *Linking Verb*, and *Word Linked to Subject*. Find the three parts in each sentence. Write them in the proper columns.

1. Paul Zindel is a writer.
2. Was the meeting important?
3. The stew tastes bland.
4. Robert is being helpful.
5. Aren't sunsets on the ocean beautiful?
6. The cookies in the tin are crisp.
7. I am the editor of the school newspaper.
8. The witness seems nervous.
9. That plant is a cactus.
10. This record sounds scratchy.

E. Verb Tenses Write each verb and its tense.

1. Carlotta saw the eclipse.
2. Mr. and Mrs. Lewis train watchdogs.
3. Sportswriters will name the all-star team.
4. Admiral Peary explored the North Pole.
5. Brian expects an apology.
6. The Titans will win the game!
7. I shall say the magic words.
8. The singer had a cold.
9. Grandmother collects stamps.
10. Hal missed the deadline for the contest.

MIXED REVIEW

Using Verbs

A. Identifying verbs Number your paper from 1 to 10. Label three columns on your paper *Helping Verbs*, *Main Verbs*, and *Kinds of Verbs*. Write the parts of the verbs from these sentences in the first two columns. In the third column, write whether the main verb is an *Action* or *State-of-Being* verb.

Example: The climbers will signal at dawn.

Helping Verbs	Main Verbs	Kinds of Verbs
will	signal	action

1. It might be our bus.
2. Have you ever slept in a pup tent?
3. I should have finished this work yesterday.
4. Gina will be our next class treasurer.
5. Mr. Phillips is staying for dinner.
6. Denver is called the "Mile High City."
7. Their plane will be arriving at three o'clock.
8. Winter can be a difficult time for animals.
9. Todd should have been more careful.
10. The girls are practicing their jump shots.

B. Identifying verbs, direct objects, and predicate words Number your paper from 1 to 10. Label three columns *Verbs*, *Direct Objects*, and *Predicate Words*. Write the verbs, direct objects, and predicate words from these sentences in the proper columns. No sentence will have both a direct object and a predicate word.

1. This test seems easy.
2. Jane held the leash tightly.
3. Edgar Allen Poe was a skillful writer.

4. Jeff put the groceries into the bag.
5. Jimmy Carter is a former President of the United States.
6. Rhode Island is our smallest state.
7. Kate became ill after the party.
8. I need film for my camera.
9. Carol believes your story.
10. We didn't forget her birthday.

C. Using verb tenses correctly Copy the following sentences, using the verb and tense given in parentheses.

1. Marnie (past of *see*) *The Nutcracker* three times.
2. We (future of *look*) for your contact lens.
3. The police artist (past of *draw*) a picture of the lost child.
4. Our family (present of *watch*) "60 Minutes" every Sunday night.
5. Charles Schultz (past of *create*) the *Peanuts* cartoon characters.
6. Who (future of *clean*) up this mess?
7. Sam always (present of *lock*) his bike.
8. The ranger (past of *drive*) us to our campsite.
9. Ben (present of *drink*) a quart of water every day.
10. JoAnn (future of *bring*) the dessert.

D. Using sentence patterns Write two sentences for each of the following sentence patterns.

1. N V
2. N V N
3. N LV N
4. N LV Adj.

USING GRAMMAR IN WRITING
Using Verbs

A. If you could be any animal, which one would you choose? Think about the reasons you would like to be that animal. Would you like to be fast like the cheetah? Would you like to soar in the mountain wilderness like an eagle? Does living underwater like a dolphin appeal to you? Maybe you would prefer to be a pampered poodle! In a paragraph write about why you would choose the life of a certain animal.

Include action verbs and state-of-being verbs in your paragraph. Underline every action verb once and every state-of-being verb twice. At least one sentence should contain a direct object. Circle the direct objects you use.

B. Write five sentences about ways to earn money during summer vacation. Include a main verb and a helping verb in each sentence. In at least one of your sentences, separate the main verb and helping verb. Underline the main verb once and the helping verb twice in each sentence.

C. It is New Year's Eve, and you have decided to make some resolutions. Resolutions are the things you promise to do in the coming years. Write two paragraphs. The first will contain five things you did last year that you don't want to repeat. The second paragraph will be about five good things you hope to do this year.

Include at least three sentences that contain linking verbs. Underline the linking verbs. Circle all predicate words.

Using Irregular Verbs

Part 1 Principal Parts of Verbs

A verb can take many forms. The verb *walk*, for example, can have these forms:

> I *walked* through the park.
> Sharon *has walked* to the library.
> Dennis *will walk* the dog.
> We *could have walked* home.

While *walk* can be used in many ways, the verb has just three main forms. These three forms are known as the **principal parts**. Every verb has three principal parts: the **present**, the **past**, and the **past participle**.

Present	Past	Past Participle
walk	walked	(have) walked

Here are the principal parts of some familiar verbs:

Present	Past	Past Participle
call	called	(have) called
look	looked	(have) looked
hurry	hurried	(have) hurried
race	raced	(have) raced
stop	stopped	(have) stopped

The *present* part of the verb is its present tense. (Add *-s* or *-es* when it is used with a singular noun or *he, she*, or *it*.) The present part used with *will* or *shall* forms the future tense.

The *past* part of the verb is its past tense.

The *past participle* is used with helping verbs to make other forms of the verb. Here are some examples of these other forms:

has stopped	was being stopped
have stopped	shall be stopped
had stopped	has been stopped
was stopped	will have stopped
were stopped	should have been stopped

Part 2 Regular Verbs

The verbs in the list of principal parts given above are **regular verbs**. A regular verb forms its past tense by adding *-ed* (*called*) or *-d* (*raced*) to the present form. The past participle is the same as the past form and is always used with a helping verb. Most verbs in English are regular.

Exercise Form principal parts.

Number your paper from 1 to 10. Write the verb form indicated for each of the following regular verbs. Use one or more helping verbs with each past participle.

1. print (past)
2. ask (present)
3. dream (past participle)
4. want (past)
5. use (past participle)
6. help (past participle)
7. confuse (present)
8. list (past)
9. cover (past participle)
10. like (future)

Part 3   Irregular Verbs

Some verbs do not form their pasts and past participles in the regular way. These verbs are called **irregular verbs**. Here are five examples:

Present	Past	Past Participle
go	went	gone
feel	felt	felt
know	knew	known
see	saw	seen
think	thought	thought

There are about sixty of these irregular verbs in English. The best way to learn them is to memorize their three principal parts. A list of the most commonly used irregular verbs is given on page 374.

When you use irregular verbs, remember these two rules:

1. The past form is always used by itself, **without** a helping verb.

   We *went* to the movies last Saturday.

2. The past participle is always used **with** a helping verb.

   We *have gone* to the movies every Saturday this month.

Helping Verbs

Forms of *be* and *have* are the helping verbs most often used with past participles. Here are the forms of *be* and *have*.

Be					
Singular	**Present**	**Past**	**Plural**	**Present**	**Past**
I	am	was	we	are	were
you	are	were	you	are	were
he, she, it	is	was	they	are	were

Be, been, and *being* are forms of *be* that must be used with helping verbs.

> Janice *will be* running in this race.
> My father *has been* working overtime.
> Your name *is being* called.

Have					
Singular	**Present**	**Past**	**Plural**	**Present**	**Past**
I	have	had	we	have	had
you	have	had	you	have	had
he, she, it	has	had	they	have	had

Using a Dictionary To Find Principal Parts

If you are not sure about the principal part of a verb, look it up in a dictionary. If the verb is regular, usually only the present form will be listed.

If the verb is irregular, the dictionary will give the irregular forms. It will give two forms if the past and past participle are the same: *say, said.* It will give all three principal parts if they are all different: *see, saw, seen.*

Dictionary Entry for *Begin*

present
|

be·gin (bi gin′), **v.** to start being, doing, acting, etc.; get under way [Work *begins* at 8:00 A.M. His cold *began* with a sore throat.] —**be·gan′**, *p.;* **be·gun′**, *p.p.*

past ——————┘   └——————— **past participle**

Principal Parts of Common Irregular Verbs

Present	Past	Past Participle
begin	began	(have) begun
break	broke	(have) broken
bring	brought	(have) brought
choose	chose	(have) chosen
come	came	(have) come
do	did	(have) done
drink	drank	(have) drunk
eat	ate	(have) eaten
fall	fell	(have) fallen
freeze	froze	(have) frozen
give	gave	(have) given
go	went	(have) gone
grow	grew	(have) grown
know	knew	(have) known
ride	rode	(have) ridden
ring	rang	(have) rung
rise	rose	(have) risen
run	ran	(have) run
say	said	(have) said
see	saw	(have) seen
sing	sang	(have) sung
sit	sat	(have) sat
speak	spoke	(have) spoken
steal	stole	(have) stolen
swim	swam	(have) swum
take	took	(have) taken
teach	taught	(have) taught
throw	threw	(have) thrown
wear	wore	(have) worn
write	wrote	(have) written

Part 4 Practice Pages on Irregular Verbs

The past and past participle forms of regular verbs are made by adding *-ed* or *-d* to the present form.

Irregular verbs, however, often have different forms for the past and past participle. The only way to learn the past and past participle form of irregular verbs is to study them.

The exercise below will help you find out which irregular verbs you need to study. Following this exercise, there is a page of exercises for each verb tested. When you know which verbs you want to practice, you can then turn to the exercise pages on those verbs.

Exercise Use irregular verbs.

Number your paper from 1 to 15. For each sentence, write the correct word from the two given in the parentheses.

1. We (drank, drunk) the juice after football practice.
2. Jesse's notebook has (fell, fallen) off the desk.
3. Last month, six thousand visitors (came, come) to the museum.
4. Kate (did, done) her best.
5. Andrew has (did, done) all his assignments.
6. The puppy has (ran, run) into the flower garden.
7. Mr. Lee (spoke, spoken) to us about the teen center.
8. All this loud music has (gave, given) me a headache.
9. My father has (went, gone) to the grocery store.
10. Our team has (swam, swum) in the state meets.
11. Have you ever (ran, run) in a relay race?
12. My father (saw, seen) me in the class play.
13. Somebody has (took, taken) my lunch.
14. We have (drank, drunk) the lemonade.
15. Morgan has already (wrote, written) to his friend.

Use the Right Word

Say It Right Hear It Right

Say these sentences until they sound correct to you.

1. It *came* early this morning.
2. We *had come* to the end of the road.
3. The traffic *had come* to a standstill.
4. Why *have* so many people *come* to the park?
5. They *came* to see the fireworks.
6. *Has* the mail *come* yet?
7. *Haven't* the Lombardis *come* home from their trip?
8. Yes, they *came* home last night.
9. The gift *came* in a huge cardboard box.
10. New members *should have come* to the first meeting.

Write It Right

Write the correct verb from the two forms given. Check your answer by saying the complete sentence to yourself.

1. Wendy (came, come) to the variety show last week.
2. Our kitten (came, come) home from the vet yesterday.
3. Who (came, come) to the door?
4. A messenger had (came, come) with a note.
5. John (came, come) to school late again.
6. Lisa has (came, come) to visit you.
7. The notice from school (came, come) yesterday afternoon.
8. Have you (came, come) from Denver?
9. Philip (came, come) early to help with the refreshments.
10. Has Jeannette (came, come) in yet?
11. The delivery men (came, come) with the packages.
12. The fire chief (came, come) to the Boy Scout meeting.
13. He had (came, come) to discuss fire safety.
14. You should have (came, come) to the basketball game.
15. The President had (came, come) to give a speech.

Use the Right Word

Do
Did
Done

Say It Right   Hear It Right

Say these sentences until they sound correct to you.

1. What *was done* about the broken window?
2. Wendy *did* more than her share.
3. Tell me what you *did* on your vacation.
4. Sally *had done* two extra–credit projects.
5. Jeff *did* the wrong math problems.
6. What *have* you *done* with my books?
7. Robert *did* everything he could to help, too.
8. Didn't you think they *had done* a good job?
9. The acrobats *did* tricks on the high wire.
10. These card tricks *are done* with ordinary cards.

Write It Right

Write the correct verb from the two forms given. Check your answer by saying the complete sentence to yourself.

1. Has Roberto (did, done) all of his homework?
2. I could have (did, done) another lap around the track.
3. Haven't you (did, done) your homework?
4. Nothing has been (did, done) about the gutted building.
5. Who (did, done) that drawing of Rod Carew?
6. Midge had never (did, done) a cartwheel before.
7. Our dog (did, done) every trick we taught him.
8. Who (did, done) the dishes last night?
9. Peggy certainly (did, done) a good job on her speech.
10. What was (did, done) with the extra newspapers?
11. The diver (did, done) a back flip off the high dive.
12. Have you (did, done) oral book reports this year?
13. Myra (did, done) a tap dance for the talent show.
14. Who (did, done) the paint job on that car?
15. Those paintings were (did, done) by Andrew Wyeth.

377

Use the Right Word

Say It Right   Hear It Right

Say these sentences until they sound correct to you.

1. Tony *must have drunk* the rest of my soda.
2. On the farm we *drank* water from the well.
3. I *drank* two glasses.
4. My cat *has* always *drunk* apple juice.
5. The knights *drank* a toast to their king.
6. Dad left before he *had drunk* his coffee.
7. Who *drank* my milkshake?
8. The dog *has drunk* all of its water.
9. No one *drank* the warm milk.
10. *Have* you *drunk* your lemonade?

Write It Right

Write the correct verb from the two forms given. Check your answer by saying the complete sentence to yourself.

1. Why haven't you (drank, drunk) your orange juice?
2. My dog Peppy (drank, drunk) from the garden hose.
3. In England tea is (drank, drunk) more often than coffee.
4. The hot chocolate we had (drank, drunk) warmed us up.
5. The sparrows (drank, drunk) from the bird bath.
6. The parched hikers (drank, drunk) the cool water.
7. Matt couldn't have (drank, drunk) all of the punch.
8. Pam has never (drank, drunk) buttermilk.
9. I could have (drank, drunk) a gallon of milk.
10. After exercising, Jean (drank, drunk) a glass of juice.
11. The elephants (drank, drunk) from the stream.
12. Our kittens (drank, drunk) all the cream from the saucer.
13. Could Milly have (drank, drunk) all the cola?
14. The camels (drank, drunk) from the pond in the oasis.
15. Formula is (drank, drunk) by small babies.

Say It Right   Hear It Right

Say these sentences until they sound correct to you.

1. *Has* that picture *fallen* off the wall again?
2. My grades *fell* when I stopped doing my homework.
3. Sherry tripped and *fell* on the stairs.
4. Rain *had* not *fallen* for several weeks.
5. The vase *fell* from the shelf.
6. I *have fallen* over your shoes three times now.
7. The temperature *fell* sharply last night.
8. All the leaves *had fallen* by late October.
9. The show's ratings *have fallen* sharply.
10. A potted plant *fell* from the windowsill.

Write It Right

Write the correct verb from the two forms given. Check your answer by saying the complete sentence to yourself.

1. Six inches of snow have (fell, fallen) since this morning.
2. The dictionary has (fell, fallen) to the floor.
3. Some ashes had (fell, fallen) from the chimney.
4. Amy has (fell, fallen) in love again.
5. Chuck (fell, fallen) into the pool by accident.
6. The satellite must have (fell, fallen) to the earth.
7. The shirts have (fell, fallen) from the hangers.
8. The horse stumbled over a rock and (fell, fallen).
9. Stock market prices have (fell, fallen) again today.
10. Those keys must have (fell, fallen) out of his pocket.
11. Dad slipped on the ice and (fell, fallen).
12. When the chef opened the oven door, the cake (fell, fallen).
13. All the leaves have (fell, fallen) from the trees.
14. Lois Lane (fell, fallen) in love with Superman.
15. The price of soybeans should have (fell, fallen) this season.

Use the Right Word

Say It Right   Hear It Right

Say these sentences until they sound correct to you.

1. My older sister *had given* me a ride to the track meet.
2. Ms. Reynolds' piano students *have given* concerts.
3. Judy *hasn't given* her speech.
4. Raymond *gave* me a puzzle for my birthday.
5. I *have given* Mary all of her assignments.
6. Who *gave* you the new record?
7. The princess *was given* a gold ring.
8. The doctor *gave* me a flu shot.
9. *Have* you ever *given* a dog a bath?
10. The sudden crash *gave* me a scare.

Write It Right

Write the correct verb from the two forms given. Check your answer by saying the complete sentence to yourself.

1. Mr. Fabri has (gave, given) us our band uniforms.
2. The President (gave, given) a speech to Congress.
3. All the actors have (gave, given) excellent performances.
4. Hasn't Michael (gave, given) your pen back?
5. Uncle Dave (gave, given) me two passes to the game.
6. This award is (gave, given) to the best students.
7. Rick has (gave, given) away all his old comic books.
8. I (gave, given) my sister the keys to the clubhouse.
9. I have (gave, given) her directions to the theater.
10. The Drama Club (gave, given) the play last night.
11. Our club (gave, given) a going-away party for Louise.
12. The millionaire has (gave, given) much money to charity.
13. Has Jill (gave, given) you the directions?
14. She (gave, given) them to me today.
15. Dad must have (gave, given) Mom those flowers.

Say It Right   Hear It Right

Say these sentences until they sound correct to you.

1. The cheesecake *was gone* in no time.
2. *Has* Roxanna *gone* camping?
3. An hour *had gone* by.
4. My grades *went* up this term.
5. *Have* you ever *gone* trout fishing?
6. I *went* once with my family.
7. She *went* with her family this mornng.
8. We *should have gone* to the air show.
9. Marla *went* through the fun house.
10. The art classes *have gone* on a field trip.

Write It Right

Write the correct verb from the two forms given. Check your answer by saying the complete sentence to yourself.

1. Have you (went, gone) to a professional hockey game?
2. Karen (went, gone) on the hiking trip.
3. Allen (went, gone) to Missouri last summer.
4. Have you ever (went, gone) camping in the mountains?
5. After everyone had (went, gone), Victor did the dishes.
6. Jo and Beth (went, gone) to the meeting.
7. We (went, gone) to the park for a picnic.
8. Have you (went, gone) jogging lately?
9. I (went, gone) just this morning.
10. We (went, gone) to do the laundry after dinner.
11. Joel has (went, gone) to the library.
12. Rita (went, gone) to a soccer clinic today.
13. The children have (went, gone) to sleep already.
14. We (went, gone) to Six Flags, an amusement park.
15. The rain clouds have finally (went, gone) away.

Use the Right Word

Say It Right   Hear It Right

Say these sentences until they sound correct to you.

1. Jane's dog *ran* after my cat.
2. The grandfather clock *had* finally *run* down.
3. We *ran* all the way home.
4. The Kentucky Derby *is* always *run* in May.
5. *Has* Sandy ever *run* the movie projector?
6. She *ran* it the last time we saw a movie in class.
7. Which way *have* the boys *run?*
8. The trains *ran* on time.
9. The police *must have run* out of clues.
10. The parents' association *ran* the school fair.

Write It Right

Write the correct verb from the two forms given. Check your answer by saying the complete sentence to yourself.

1. The twins (ran, run) in the sack race.
2. Bonny had (ran, run) the hurdles and the relay.
3. He also (ran, run) marathons in two Olympics.
4. Our bus had (ran, run) out of gas.
5. Have you ever (ran, run) that fast before?
6. My digital watch has always (ran, run) well.
7. I (ran, run) two miles before school this morning.
8. Who (ran, run) against Lyndon Johnson in 1964?
9. The Indianapolis 500 wasn't (ran, run) because of rain.
10. Raise your hand if you haven't (ran, run) a mile.
11. Which trains (ran, run) late today?
12. The batteries in your calculator may have (ran, run) down.
13. Bill Rodgers has (ran, run) in the Boston Marathon.
14. Lewis (ran, run) a fever of 102° all night.
15. The secretary has (ran, run) off seven copies of the report.

Say It Right   Hear It Right

Say these sentences until they sound correct to you.

1. Randy *saw* the finish line just ahead of her.
2. The divers *had seen* a sunken ship.
3. A tall, bearded man *was seen* leaving the bank.
4. No one ever *saw* him again.
5. *Have* you ever *seen* a triple play?
6. No, but I once *saw* a grand-slam home run.
7. Mona *saw* the All-Star game.
8. Giant Pandas *are* seldom *seen* outside China.
9. *Has* Mrs. Levy's class *seen* the crafts show?
10. We *saw* a great dolphin show at Marineland.

Write It Right

Write the correct verb from the two forms given. Check your answer by saying the complete sentence to yourself.

1. Has anybody (saw, seen) my sweatshirt?
2. We (saw, seen) a filmstrip about the Civil War.
3. Our class (saw, seen) the Cousteau special about Atlantis.
4. I haven't (saw, seen) Maria all day.
5. Have you ever (saw, seen) the Olympics on television?
6. You look as if you had (saw, seen) a ghost.
7. Lee (saw, seen) the variety show last night.
8. He could have (saw, seen) it with us tonight.
9. Betty (saw, seen) an accident on her way downtown.
10. Have you ever (saw, seen) any ducks in this pond?
11. Has your class (saw, seen) the movie *The Red Pony?*
12. Bill (saw, seen) a spider catch a fly in its web.
13. I may have (saw, seen) that episode before.
14. Jerry (saw, seen) the Statue of Liberty on his vacation.
15. Have you ever (saw, seen) a twenty-dollar gold piece?

Use the Right Word

Say It Right   Hear It Right

Say these sentences until they sound correct to you.

1. Wendy *should have spoken* sooner.
2. The lecturer *spoke* about schools in France.
3. Raymond *spoke* with a Southern accent.
4. Ms. Weber *has spoken* to me about my project.
5. The greeting *was spoken* in several languages.
6. The actor *spoke* in a deep voice.
7. Carlotta *has* always *spoken* Italian at home.
8. The pledge *was spoken* solemnly.
9. Kelly *spoke* to Ms. Evans on the phone.
10. The foreign student *spoke* Portuguese.

Write It Right

Write the correct verb from the two forms given. Check your answer by saying the complete sentence to yourself.

1. Kris has (spoke, spoken) to the neighbors about babysitting.
2. The first word the baby (spoke, spoken) was "Mama."
3. When the boss (spoke, spoken), we listened.
4. The coach (spoke, spoken) in an even, calm voice.
5. The lawyer has (spoke, spoken) to the judge.
6. Darren's lines were (spoke, spoken) with great force.
7. Dr. Taylor (spoke, spoken) at my sister's graduation.
8. The girls (spoke, spoken) in Chinese.
9. We should have (spoke, spoken) to the mayor.
10. Carol (spoke, spoken) into the microphone.
11. Spanish is (spoke, spoken) at this store.
12. Angry words were (spoke, spoken) by the two men.
13. French is (spoke, spoken) by the people in Quebec.
14. Dirk has (spoke, spoken) to his boss about a raise.
15. Dad (spoke, spoken) to Lisa about her report card.

384

Say It Right   Hear It Right

Say these sentences until they sound correct to you.

1. *Have* you ever *swum* in salt water?
2. The trained porpoises *swam* in formation.
3. The counselors *swam* with the campers.
4. The relay race *was swum* first.
5. That child *should have swum* closer to shore.
6. Snorkelers *swam* in the clear waters.
7. The girls *swam* to the deep end of the pool.
8. Barry *has swum* across the lake.
9. Several whales almost *swam* ashore.
10. Deena *had swum* faster than Laura.

Write It Right

Write the correct verb from the two forms given. Check your answer by saying the complete sentence to yourself.

1. Some of the crew members (swam, swum) ashore.
2. The water ballet group (swam, swum) to music.
3. Curt has (swam, swum) on the team for two years.
4. A scuba diver (swam, swum) to the ship's wreckage.
5. The trout (swam, swum) right to my hook.
6. We (swam, swum) from our canoe to the dock.
7. The shark (swam, swum) in circles.
8. Diana Nyad has (swam, swum) long distances.
9. We (swam, swum) in the ocean.
10. The marathon swimmer (swam, swum) alongside a boat.
11. The minnows (swam, swum) into my net.
12. Mark Spitz has (swam, swum) in the Olympics.
13. Paul and Sean have (swam, swum) out to the sand bar.
14. Our dog Molly (swam, swum) in the lake.
15. That race was (swam, swum) in record time.

Use the Right Word

Say It Right   Hear It Right

Say these sentences until they sound correct to you.

1. *Have* you ever *taken* a boat ride?
2. We *took* one when we went to New York.
3. My brother *has taken* my bike to Hill Park.
4. He *took* it early this morning.
5. The second graders *were taken* to the circus.
6. What *took* you so long?
7. You must *have taken* a wrong turn at the stoplight.
8. Who *took* my pencil?
9. Jenny *took* her sister's advice.
10. The photographer *has taken* pictures of each student.

Write It Right

Write the correct verb from the two forms given. Check your answer by saying the complete sentence to yourself.

1. It has (took, taken) Brad an hour to get ready.
2. Leona (took, taken) the science test this morning.
3. Who (took, taken) the Ping-Pong paddles?
4. Ted's family (took, taken) a plane to San Diego.
5. Have you (took, taken) your medicine?
6. I had already (took, taken) mine.
7. It (took, taken) us two hours to get through the traffic.
8. Bonita (took, taken) her brother to the movies.
9. We should have (took, taken) the shortcut home.
10. Julie was (took, taken) to the nurse's office.
11. We should have (took, taken) the train.
12. Have you (took, taken) your vitamins?
13. The secretary (took, taken) notes during the meeting.
14. Leroy has (took, taken) his skateboard to the park.
15. Anita (took, taken) two aspirin and went to bed.

Say It Right   Hear It Right

Say these sentences until they sound correct to you.

1. This book *was written* by Robert Louis Stevenson.
2. Louise *wrote* a very funny story.
3. Who *wrote* that song?
4. Kevin *wrote* Mother another letter.
5. He *has written* to her every week.
6. Raoul *had written* the letter in both Spanish and English.
7. Carole King *has written* many popular songs.
8. Ms. Novak *wrote* our assignments on the chalkboard.
9. Rick *has written* a script for a TV show.
10. Jan *wrote* the message beside the phone.

Write It Right

Write the correct verb from the two forms given. Check your answer by saying the complete sentence to yourself.

1. Has anyone (wrote, written) to Darren?
2. Was the note (wrote, written) or typed?
3. Mark Twain (wrote, written) *Tom Sawyer.*
4. Stacy has (wrote, written) a letter to the newspaper.
5. Lennon and McCartney (wrote, written) many songs.
6. Kevin (wrote, written) some poems.
7. Was *The Pigman* (wrote, written) by Paul Zindel?
8. Yes, it was Paul Zindel who (wrote, written) that novel.
9. Have you (wrote, written) your report yet?
10. I (wrote, written) half of it.
11. Mom (wrote, written) a letter to Aunt Marion.
12. It was (wrote, written) on the stationery I gave her.
13. Who (wrote, written) the book *Crazy Eights?*
14. Marti has (wrote, written) a report about telephones.
15. Bob and Jed both have (wrote, written) their paragraphs.

387

ADDITIONAL EXERCISES

Using Irregular Verbs

Irregular Verbs Write the correct verb from the two forms given in parentheses. Check your answer by reading the sentence to yourself.

1. We (saw, seen) the model plane in an open field.
2. The birds (drank, drunk) from the fountain.
3. We haven't (swam, swum) much this year.
4. The bull (came, come) close to the matador.
5. Trish (did, done) a handspring on the exercise mat.
6. Have you ever (saw, seen) a polar bear?
7. Each student had (did, done) a good job.
8. The fortune teller (gave, given) his predictions.
9. A rock (went, gone) through the window.
10. George has (gave, given) me a message for them.
11. Judy has (fell, fallen) behind in her work this week.
12. Jason has (went, gone) to the track championships.
13. Blaine has never (saw, seen) a marathon.
14. Davis dodged the tackle and (ran, run) toward the goal line.
15. Roberto (saw, seen) his relatives during the holidays.
16. Lindsay has (took, taken) weekly guitar lessons.
17. The troops (took, taken) orders from the captain.
18. I have (spoke, spoken) to my parents about my plans.
19. Mr. Kaminski (wrote, written) a riddle on the board.
20. You should have (saw, seen) that movie!
21. Our cat has (came, come) home.
22. The soda shop has (ran, run) out of whipping cream.
23. The governor (spoke, spoken) to the Junior Achievers.
24. Candy has (wrote, written) a song.
25. The horses have (drank, drunk) all of the water.

MIXED REVIEW

Using Irregular Verbs

A. Using irregular verbs correctly   Number your paper from 1 to 20. Write the correct verb from those in parentheses.

1. What have you (did, done) with my ice skates?
2. The sun (rose, risen) at 5:52 this morning.
3. The mayor (spoke, spoken) to our graduating class.
4. Cindy has (threw, thrown) a perfect pitch.
5. I (saw, seen) a red-winged blackbird in the woods.
6. Ed has (broke, broken) his wrist.
7. Judy Blume has (wrote, written) many books.
8. Our track coach has (ran, run) every day for years.
9. I (gave, given) my vote to Mitch.
10. Craig easily (stole, stolen) second base.
11. The temperature has (fell, fallen) rapidly.
12. Bob has (took, taken) Spanish lessons.
13. Sylvia (knew, known) the answer to that question.
14. The bear (stole, stolen) the food at our campsite.
15. Wade (took, taken) the shortcut through the woods.
16. Has she (went, gone) home already?
17. Ms. Tomas (spoke, spoken) about computers.
18. Olivia Newton-John (sang, sung) her greatest hits.
19. I haven't (wore, worn) that sweater all week.
20. The pioneers (rode, ridden) west in covered wagons.

B. Identifying the principal parts   Label three columns *Present*, *Past*, and *Past Participle*. List the three principal parts of the following irregular verbs.

1. go	5. see	9. rise
2. drink	6. eat	10. begin
3. choose	7. ring	
4. fall	8. take	

USING GRAMMAR IN WRITING
Using Irregular Verbs

A. Mrs. Greengarden is your neighbor. She can grow anything. Her tomatoes are as big as melons, and her pumpkins are as big as bushel baskets. You want to find out her secret. You watch her in her garden as she works. What do you discover? Write about Mrs. Greengarden's secret of success and how you discovered it.

Use some of these irregular verbs in your paragraph. Write in the past tense.

give	have
begin	grow
see	freeze
throw	rise

B. Do you believe in ghosts? Some people believe there are spirits called *poltergeists*. Poltergeists are full of mischief. They cause trouble, even though they are invisible. Imagine that it's Saturday. You have just finished cleaning up your room. Even your closet is in order. You feel great because everything looks neat.

You go to a friend's house for the rest of the day. When you return, you hardly recognize your room. A poltergeist has attacked while you were away. Describe the scene. Tell about the funny note the poltergeist wrote on the ceiling.

Use some of these irregular verbs in your paragraph.

see	take
spill	throw
tear	do
break	fall

Using Troublesome Verbs Correctly

Using irregular verbs can be a problem until you learn their principal parts. Other kinds of verbs can also be troublesome. Some are pairs of verbs that are often confused. Others are verbs that are often misused.

This section will help you to sort out the confusion so that you can use verbs correctly.

Part 1 Pairs of Verbs That Are Often Confused

See how the following pairs of verbs are used. Study the difference in their meanings. Avoid making mistakes when you use them.

Can and May

Use **can** when you are talking about being able to do something. *Can* has no principal parts. Another form of *can* is *could*.

Use **may** when you are asking or giving permission. *May* is used only as a helping verb. It has no principal parts. Another form of *may* is *might*.

Can you see me?   *Might* we leave early?
Tara *could* not see the screen.   You *may go* to the party.

Exercise   Use can and may correctly.

Number your paper from 1 to 10. Write the correct verb from the two given in parentheses.

1. (May, Can) you write backwards?
2. (May, Can) I help you with anything for the Halloween party?
3. Yes, you (can, may) go to Robert's party.
4. (Can, May) that little stove heat this whole room?
5. (May, Can) Melinda and I go out in the canoe?
6. (May, Can) you read the bottom line without your glasses?
7. A catbird (can, may) imitate other birds.
8. (May, Can) I please be excused?
9. (Can, May) Eduardo go to the park with us?
10. My little brother (may, can) count up to forty-nine.

Leave and Let

Leave means to go away from a person, place, or thing. The principal parts are **leave, left, left.**

Let means to permit or allow. The principal parts are **let, let, let.**

Leave the room.	*Let* me see your ring.
Jim *left* his hat here.	I *let* go of the reins.
Sue *has left* for Mexico.	*Has* Dad *let* you steer the boat?

Exercise   Use *leave* and *let* correctly.

Number your paper from 1 to 10. Write the correct verb from the two given in parentheses.

1. Betty (let, left) me see her stamp collection.
2. (Let, Leave) Jim have the last piece of the cake.
3. (Leave, Let) Tanya help you.
4. I must have (let, left) my wallet at home.
5. Don't (let, leave) the baby fall backwards.
6. Who (let, left) the lid off the paint can?
7. (Leave, Let) me handle the refreshments.
8. That licorice has (let, left) a bad taste in my mouth.
9. (Leave, Let) me take your coat.
10. Somebody must have (let, left) the door open.

Lie and Lay

Lie means "to rest in a reclining position." The principal parts are **lie, lay, lain.**

Lay means "to put or place." The principal parts are **lay, laid, laid.**

Lie still and rest.	*Lay* your books here.
The cat *lay* on the porch.	Max *laid* the brush down.
How long *has* he *lain* there?	Pam *has laid* aside her work.

393

Exercise   Use *lie* and *lay* correctly.

Number your paper from 1 to 10. Write the correct verb from the two given in parentheses.

1. The dog likes to (lay, lie) on the rug.
2. My dad (lay, laid) his ties over the hanger.
3. (Lay, Lie) your cards face up.
4. The trainer can make the lions (lie, lay) still.
5. Where did you (lie, lay) the newspaper?
6. (Lay, Lie) on the deck and take a nap.
7. The child wouldn't (lie, lay) down.
8. Don't ever (lie, lay) plastic dishes on the hot stove.
9. The sunbathers had (lain, laid) on the beach.
10. Papers (laid, lay) all over the ball diamond.

Review Exercises   Use the right verb.

A.   Write the correct verb from the two given.

1. Don't (lay, lie) in the sun too long.
2. (May, Can) Marcia and Fred really read that fast?
3. Certainly Jean (may, can) leave her bike in our garage.
4. (Leave, Let) the needle of the compass settle.
5. A sea turtle will (lie, lay) her eggs in the sand.
6. (May, Can) I borrow your tape recorder?
7. Cindy always (lets, leaves) the icing till last.
8. Bricklayers never (lie, lay) bricks without a trowel.
9. Will Ms. Cordero (let, leave) you plan the award ceremony?
10. (May, Can) you hold all the groceries?

B.   Follow the directions for Exercise A.

1. The explorers had (left, let) an oil lamp burn all night.
2. (May, Can) we use the auditorium for our rehearsal?

3. Have you (lain, laid) the spoons on the right side of the plates?
4. (Can, May) you figure out what's inside the box?
5. The brake will not (leave, let) the wheels spin freely.
6. You and she (may, can) take a copy of the play.
7. My cat (lay, laid) near the heater.
8. You (can, may) often see for forty miles from this lookout.
9. (Leave, Let) Grandpa help you.
10. Have you (lain, laid) in the new hammock?

Rise and Raise

Rise means "to get up or go upward." The principal parts are **rise, rose, risen.**

Raise means "to lift or make something go up." It also means "to grow something." The principal parts are **raise, raised, raised.**

The dough *rises* slowly.	Do you *raise* strawberries?
The sun *rose* later today.	Brad *raised* the flag.
Has the curtain *risen* yet?	*Have* they *raised* the price?

Exercise Use *rise* and *raise* correctly.

Number your paper from 1 to 10. Write the correct verb.

1. All the ducks (raised, rose) into the air at once.
2. (Raise, Rise) your foot while I straighten the rug.
3. In this vampire movie, Count Dracula (raises, rises) from the dead.
4. Has the temperature in the room (raised, risen)?
5. The Kellogg boys (raise, rise) rabbits.
6. Turn off the burner when steam (rises, raises) from the kettle.
7. Marcy and Clare will (raise, rise) the curtain at eight.

8. Did the moon (rise, raise) yet?
9. It's not so hard to (raise, rise) tomatoes.
10. Did the drum major (raise, rise) his baton?

Sit and Set

Sit means "to rest in one place." The principal parts are **sit, sat, sat.**

Set means "to place or put." The principal parts are **set, set, set.**

Sit and rest awhile.	*Set* the groceries here.
Our guests *sat* down.	Jill *set* the film on the ledge.
Have you *sat* on stage?	*Did* you *set* your keys down?

Exercise   Use *sit* and *set* correctly.

Write the correct verb from the two given.

1. Muffer barked suddenly and (sat, set) up.
2. Elizabeth (sat, set) out the milk for the cats.
3. Jud had (sat, set) in the waiting room all afternoon.
4. (Set, Sit) the books on the table.
5. The baby (set, sat) there chewing his spoon.
6. Mary climbed up the rock and (sat, set) down.
7. They had (set, sat) out lanterns for the festival.
8. Come in and (set, sit) down for a while.
9. (Set, Sit) down the groceries and help me.
10. (Set, Sit) the fudge in the refrigerator to cool.

Teach and Learn

You **teach** somebody to do something. The principal parts are **teach, taught, taught.**

You **learn** to do something with practice. The principal parts are **learn, learned, learned.**

Mr. Adams *teaches* history. *Learn* this part.
He once *taught* science. Nina *learned* to ski.
Have you *taught* dancing? *Have* you *learned* to swim?

Exercise   Use *teach* and *learn* correctly.

Write the correct verb from the two given in parentheses.

1. Can you (learn, teach) me to swim?
2. Fay has (taught, learned) her parakeet to talk.
3. My little sister has (learned, taught) the alphabet.
4. Marilyn will (learn, teach) her nephew about bicycle safety.
5. I just (learned, taught) to play chess.
6. Will you (learn, teach) me to braid my hair?
7. Juanita (learned, taught) us Spanish.
8. Patty would like to (teach, learn) to fly.
9. The pioneers (taught, learned) their children to be independent.
10. I can't (learn, teach) my puppy any tricks.

Review Exercises   Use the right verb.

A.   Number your paper from 1 to 10. Write the correct verb.

1. (Teach, Learn) me how to make bread.
2. Jeff (sat, set) the alarm for 5 A.M.
3. Kathy will (rise, raise) and take a place on stage.
4. (Set, Sit) still while I cut your hair.
5. I (learned, taught) five year olds to swim during summer camp.
6. Do farmers (raise, rise) corn in Kansas?
7. (Learn, Teach) Jessica and me how to throw a lasso.
8. The box (set, sat) right where I had left it.
9. Mr. Wu had (taught, learned) us to use chopsticks.
10. Did Jill (raise, rise) the flag this morning?

B. Follow the directions for Exercise A.

1. During a standing ovation, the audience (raises, rises) and applauds.
2. You have to (sit, set) still to fish.
3. (Set, Sit) the balance beam along this side of the gym.
4. The cardinal had (taught, learned) its young to fly.
5. Louise didn't even (rise, raise) her voice.
6. (Learn, Teach) the class how to hold their rackets.
7. The barometer is (raising, rising).
8. My Uncle Frank (set, sat) up waiting for me.
9. (Raise, Rise) the hood and look at the engine.
10. Please (teach, learn) me how to play the guitar.

Part 2 Using Negatives Correctly

Negatives are words that say "no." *Not, none, nobody, nowhere, nothing,* and *never* are negatives. Contractions such as *can't, don't, doesn't, wouldn't, won't, isn't,* and *aren't* are also negatives. Each contains a shortened form of the word *not.*

A **double negative** is using two "no" words in the same sentence. Avoid double negatives in speaking and writing. Using double negatives is always incorrect.

Read the following sentences. Notice that there are two ways to correct a double negative. Both correct ways use only one negative in a sentence.

Incorrect: Dan doesn't have no paper.
Correct: Dan doesn't have any paper.
      or
      Dan has no paper.

Incorrect: He doesn't have none.
Correct: He doesn't have any.
      or
      He has none.

Incorrect:	Can't nobody solve this puzzle?
Correct:	Can't anybody solve this puzzle?
	or
	Can nobody solve this puzzle?

Exercises Use one negative.

A. Write the following conversation, or take turns reading it aloud. Choose the correct word from the parentheses.

RUTH: Thank you, but I can't eat (no, any) more chicken.

JACK: Didn't you have (none, any)?

RUTH: Yes, I did. I just can't eat (any, no) more. It's delicious, but I don't (ever, never) eat more than one piece.

PAUL: I don't know of (nothing, anything) I like better than chicken.

JANE: Won't (somebody, nobody) finish the chicken?

PAUL: I wouldn't (never, ever) want to see chicken wasted. I'll finish it.

B. Number your paper from 1 to 10. Write the correct word from the two given in parentheses.

1. We aren't going (nowhere, anywhere) this summer.
2. I don't (never, ever) want to see another Kung Fu movie.
3. Sandra wouldn't have taken the album (nowhere, anywhere).
4. Albert won't climb (any, no) ladder more than three feet tall.
5. Gary can think of (nobody, anybody) else.
6. Don't you want (any, no) orange juice?
7. Sara doesn't go (anywhere, nowhere) without her bike.
8. I haven't heard (nothing, anything).
9. We have (no more, any more) string.
10. Wouldn't you like (no, some) cake?

Part 3 Good Speech Habits

Don't say *ain't*. Use *am not, isn't, aren't, haven't,* or *hasn't*.

> Say: I *am not* going fishing.
> Kevin *isn't* here.
> Those *aren't* my fishing poles.
> We *haven't* seen her.
> Lynn *hasn't* come home yet.

Never use *don't* with the pronouns *he, she,* and *it,* or with a singular noun. Use *doesn't*.

> Say: She *doesn't* fish often.
> He *doesn't* like fishing.
> It *doesn't* appeal to him.

Don't use *was* or *wasn't* with the pronouns *we, you,* and *they,* or with a plural noun. Use *were* or *weren't*.

> Say: We *weren't* swimming.
> *Were* you fishing?
> They *were* catching big fish.

Exercises Form good speech habits.

A. Number your paper from 1 to 10. Read each sentence. Choose the correct word from the two given. Then read the completed sentence to yourself.

1. These books (ain't, aren't) Ginger's.
2. Why (was, were) the ducks in the cage?
3. The weather (don't, doesn't) look that bad.
4. (Was, Were) you at the circus last week?
5. There (ain't, isn't) anything I'd rather do than swim.
6. What (was, were) you thinking about?
7. She (doesn't, don't) ever say anything.
8. (Ain't, Aren't) you ready yet?

9. You (ain't, aren't) going to fall.
10. This card trick (don't, doesn't) ever fail.

B. Here are ten questions and answers. Write the correct word from the two given in parentheses. Then read the completed pair of sentences to yourself.

1. It (doesn't, don't) matter to me, but (wasn't, weren't) you using my soccer ball?
   No, I (ain't, haven't) used it, but the twins (was, were) using it.
2. (Don't, Doesn't) Sandra's friends hike any more?
   Yes, they (was, were) on a hike last Saturday.
3. (Were, Was) your cousins at the class picnic?
   Yes, they (was, were) at the picnic.
4. We (was, were) invited, (weren't, wasn't) we?
   Yes, we (were, was) invited.
5. (Doesn't, Don't) he know the address?
   No, he (don't, doesn't) remember it.
6. (Was, Were) you fishing last week?
   No, I (ain't, am not) a fisherman.
7. (Isn't, Ain't) Eric a friend of yours?
   No, he (don't, doesn't) even know me.
8. You (ain't, haven't) seen my jacket, have you?
   No, I (haven't, ain't) seen it (nowhere, anywhere).
9. (Wasn't, Weren't) you and your brothers on a trip?
   Yes, we (was, were) gone for six weeks.
10. Why (was, were) you three girls the ones chosen?
    We (were, was) the first volunteers.

ADDITIONAL EXERCISES

Using Troublesome Verbs Correctly

A. Troublesome Verbs Write the correct word from the two given in parentheses. Check your answer by reading the completed sentence to yourself.

1. (Can, May) you read this messy writing?
2. (Can, May) we please use the earphones?
3. Amanda has (left, let) the windows open.
4. Who (left, let) the fire burn out?
5. Baby seals (lay, laid) on the ice.
6. Hunters (lay, laid) moss and grass over the trap.
7. The hot-air balloons (rose, raised) smoothly.
8. (Sit, Set) the plants on the windowsill.
9. The three friends (sat, set) on the steps and talked.
10. My brother has (taught, learned) me how to play rugby.
11. I am going to (lie, lay) down.
12. Some people (can, may) write with either hand.
13. (Let, Leave) the baby play with the pots and pans.
14. Dad (lay, laid) in the lounge chair all afternoon.
15. Tom has already (laid, lain) the tile floor.
16. Mel (rose, raised) the hood of the car.
17. Kathy has (taught, learned) to speak French.
18. She (sat, set) down and visited for a while.
19. Smoke (rises, raises) from the chimney.
20. (Can, May) we decorate our lockers?

B. Negatives Write the correct word from the two given in parentheses.

1. The shorter players couldn't get (no, any) rebounds.
2. Don't whales (never, ever) swim close to shore?

3. Hasn't (anybody, nobody) heard this album?
4. The ambulance didn't stop for (anything, nothing).
5. I can't see the Big Dipper (anywhere, nowhere).
6. The store has (no, any) more milk.
7. We couldn't find the puppy (nowhere, anywhere).
8. Isn't (anybody, nobody) going to the concert?
9. Wasn't (nothing, anything) taken in the burglary?
10. Didn't you (ever, never) visit a farm?

C. Good Speech Habits Write the correct word from the two given in parentheses.

1. Carlos (ain't, isn't) on that committee.
2. She (don't, doesn't) swim the backstroke.
3. Seth (doesn't, don't) want to go along.
4. We (was, were) playing badminton.
5. You (wasn't, weren't) looking at the camera.
6. They (was, were) practicing free throws.
7. (Don't, Doesn't) Marsha play tennis?
8. The hamburgers (ain't, aren't) cooked yet.
9. (Was, Were) you in the band last year?
10. Lisa (don't, doesn't) agree with you.

MIXED REVIEW

Using Troublesome Verbs Correctly

A. Using the correct verb Number your paper 1 to 10. Write the correct verb from those given in parentheses.

1. My brother has (lain, laid) aside money for a camera.
2. My sister and I (rise, raise) hamsters.
3. (May, Can) I borrow your calculator?
4. Mrs. Kahn (lets, leaves) us play ball in her yard.
5. The President (rose, raised) to his feet.
6. (May, Can) you reach the top shelf?
7. I (let, left) the cat play with the yarn.
8. Chuck (lay, laid) still while the nurse bandaged his foot.
9. We have (sat, set) here too long.
10. Miss Arnold (learned, taught) us to dance the waltz.

B. Using contractions and negatives correctly Five of the following sentences contain errors in the use of contractions and negatives. If a sentence contains an error, rewrite it correctly. If a sentence is already correct, write *Correct*.

1. Rob doesn't go nowhere without his brother.
2. I've never seen any UFOs.
3. Isn't Wisconsin called the "Badger State?"
4. She don't live very far from the library.
5. Kelly doesn't ever practice her violin.
6. They was unable to read the map.
7. The dog won't obey anyone but his owner.
8. Mr. Roland doesn't want anything from the market.
9. Terri can't play football no more.
10. Why don't she wear this costume for the play?

USING GRAMMAR IN WRITING
Using Troublesome Verbs Correctly

A. Here is a brief scene from a Western movie. The script contains several errors. See if you can spot the troublesome verbs that are used incorrectly. Also look for double negatives. Rewrite the script correctly.

"Come and set by the fire awhile," said the old prospector to his partner.

"Sure. Just leave me sit this down first." Jake sat the kettle of stew in the coals to simmer. He lay his hat next to his saddle.

The two prospectors watched the smoke as it rised from the fire. Clyde raised up and tossed another log on the blaze. In the west the sun was just sitting. Before it would raise again, the men would head out for Sacramento. Their sights were set on gold.

"Sacramento's just another twelve hour's ride, ain't it?" asked Jake.

"I don't have no idea," replied Clyde. "I ain't never been there. Besides, no one ever learned me to judge distances."

Jake fell silent. He had been raised in Sacramento, but he didn't want Clyde to know about none of his past.

Over supper they laid their final plans. They set and talked about how rich they would be. When the stars came out they laid back and dreamed about gold.

B. Write a story about what happens to Jake and Clyde when they finally get to gold country. Do they find gold? Do their dreams come true? Use these verbs correctly in your story. Underline them.

learn	let	left	raise	sat
teach	leave	rise	sit	set

Using Pronouns

Part 1   What Pronouns Do

Which of these paragraphs sounds better?

Jane loaded Jane's boat and rowed the boat to a quiet spot. Jane fished with Jane's special bait. Jane caught five big salmon and grilled the salmon for Jane's family.

Jane loaded her boat and rowed it to a quiet spot. She fished with her special bait. She caught five big salmon and grilled them for her family.

You probably decided that the second paragraph sounded better. Why did you think so? Perhaps you felt that using the name *Jane* over and over again became boring or irritating.

How did the second paragraph avoid repetition? Did you notice how it used the pronouns *she* and *her* in place of the name *Jane* and *it* in place of *boat*? Pronouns didn't change the meaning. They did improve the sound of the paragraph.

A pronoun is a word used in place of a noun.

You learned to use pronouns as soon as you learned to talk. You learned to use certain pronouns to do three things.

1. To refer to yourself:
   I pulled the heavy cart behind *me*.
2. To refer to the person you are talking to:
   Did *you* forget *your* books?
3. To refer to other persons, places, or things:
   The cat blinked *its* eyes.
   The girls won *their* game, 5–3.

Like nouns, pronouns can be singular or plural. Usually, the pronoun changes to make different forms. Study this chart of all the forms of pronouns.

Singular Pronouns			
Person Speaking:	I	me	my, mine
Person Spoken To:	you	you	your, yours
Other Persons, Places and Things:	he she it	him her it	his her, hers its

Plural Pronouns			
Persons Speaking:	we	us	our, ours
Persons Spoken To:	you	you	your, yours
Other Persons, Places and Things:	they	them	their, theirs

Exercises Recognize pronouns.

A. Number your paper from 1 to 10. List the pronouns used in each sentence.

1. The ship dropped its anchor.
2. Donna promised she would give me her old bike.
3. Take us to the boat show, please.
4. Your notebook is much neater than mine.
5. We told them about the walkathon.
6. You should find Ramon's books and return them to him.
7. He coaxed the chickens out of their coop.
8. I saw the geese as they flew over my yard.
9. A swan cleaned its snowy feathers.
10. We ran past her house.

B. Write the pronouns in italics in the following story. After each pronoun, write the word it stands for.

Since Ted is old enough this year, *he* can enter the Soap Box Derby. Mr. Williams gave *him* a copy of the rules for the race. Ted is building the racer in the garage. Ted's parents are proud that Ted wants to build *it* himself. *They* often give *him* advice. Ted paid $29.95 for the wheel and axle set, but the steering gear cost *him* only $5.75. Ted hopes to win the race. *He* thinks *he* can win *it* easily.

C. Writing Write the pronoun or pronouns you would use to refer to each of the following nouns.

1. lake
2. father
3. cats
4. teachers
5. Ms. Howard
6. friends
7. sister
8. brother
9. pencils
10. doctors

Part 2   Pronouns as Subjects

Which of these sentences sounds right to you?

> Her went to the game.
> She went to the game.

You probably had no trouble in picking the second sentence. Now suppose you add the name of someone else who went to the game. Which of these sentences is correct?

> Her and David went to the game.
> She and David went to the game.

The second sentence is right. *She and David* is a compound subject. To figure out what pronoun to use in a compound subject, try each part separately.

> David went to the game.
> She went to the game.

Then put the two subjects together, using the same pronoun.

Follow the same steps when there are two pronouns in the subject. Read these sentences to yourself:

> (He, Him) and (I, me) built a radio.
> He built a radio. I built a radio.
> He and I built a radio.

Here is another simple problem with pronouns. Which would you say: *We had a picnic* or *Us had a picnic?* As you probably know, the first sentence is right.

Now, which of these sentences is correct?

> We girls organized a field trip.   (Right. *We* is correct.)
> Us girls organized a field trip.   (*Us* is not a subject pronoun. It should never be used in the subject.)

Only these pronouns may be used as **subject pronouns.**

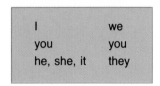

I	we
you	you
he, she, it	they

Exercises   Use pronouns in the subject.

A. Write the correct pronoun for each sentence.

1. (We, Us) boys planted a four-foot pine tree.
2. Ms. Tandy and (he, him) bicycled to the store.
3. The other players and (me, I) got drenched.
4. Did you find the mittens? (Them, They) are mine.
5. (They, Them) and the other gloves were on the chair.
6. (Us, We) girls hiked to Daw's Bridge.
7. My dog and (me, I) ran through the park.
8. (He, Him) and Carol clocked the runners.
9. Brian and (she, her) spotted the Little Dipper.
10. (We, Us) players are in a hurry.

B. Follow the directions for Exercise A.

1. Randy and (me, I) finished the cornflakes.
2. Kitty and (she, her) went up in the ski lift.
3. (Us, We) girls won the raffle.
4. (Him, He) and (her, she) both come from Louisville.
5. Those boots can't be the ones I lost. (They, Them)
    don't look like mine.
6. (We, Us) three got all the blame.
7. In the snapshot, (he, him) and Carla had no heads.
8. (He, Him) and (me, I) were talking to the crossing
    guard.
9. Susie and (I, me) ran the cold drink stand.
10. (He, Him) and John feed the ducks at Hillcrest Pond.

Part 3 Pronouns After Linking Verbs

Read these two sentences.

The captain is *he*.   *He* is the captain.

These sentences mean the same thing. As you can see, the pronoun following the linking verb *is* can be made the subject without changing the meaning of the sentence.

Pronouns used after linking verbs are called **predicate pronouns.** Predicate pronouns are the same as subject pronouns. Read the following pairs of sentences.

Our new doctor is *she*.
She is our new doctor.
The winners were Ralph and *I*.
Ralph and *I* were the winners.
The new officers are *she* and Ken.
She and Ken are the new officers.

Remember to use these pronouns after linking verbs:

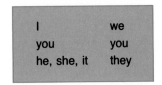

I	we
you	you
he, she, it	they

Exercises   Use pronouns after linking verbs.

A. Write the correct pronoun for each sentence.

1. The leaders are (he, him) and Valerie.
2. The first customer was (he, him).
3. The guests of honor will be (we, us) girls.
4. Our club sponsors are Ms. Martin and (he, him).
5. The runners-up were (we, us) boys.

6. The directors for the talent show were (her, she) and Maria.
7. The only people in the pool were Wayne and (me, I).
8. The earliest arrivals were (him, he) and Ron.
9. Our doctor is (her, she).
10. The stage managers for our play are Paul and (them, they).

B. Follow the directions for Exercise A.

1. The soloists are Wendy and (I, me).
2. My teammates were Isabella and (they, them).
3. The winners of the relay race were Rich and (me, I).
4. The fastest outfielders are (her, she) and George.
5. The referees were Carla and (he, him).
6. Our dinner guests were John and (she, her).
7. The speakers at the assembly will be you and (he, him).
8. The brightest student in our class is (her, she).
9. Faith's back-up singers were Jenny and (he, him).
10. The only person with new skates was (she, her).

Part 4 Pronouns as Objects

A noun does not change its form when it is an object in a sentence. Pronouns, however, have special forms when they are objects. These forms are called the **object pronouns.**

These pronouns are used as object pronouns.

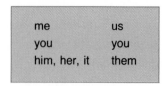

me	us
you	you
him, her, it	them

Notice the object pronoun in each of these sentences.

Mom took *us* to the rodeo.
Jeff wrote to *them* at Thanksgiving.
Connie saw *him* at the store.
Mr. Gonzalez gave *me* the award.

Be on guard when one or more pronouns are parts of a compound object.

Mom took Jane and *us* to the rodeo.
Connie saw *him* and *her* at the store.

If you are not sure which pronoun to use, say each part separately.

Kay stopped (he, him) and (I, me).
Kay stopped *him.*
Kay stopped *me.*
Kay stopped *him* and *me.*

Exercises Use pronouns as objects.

A. Number your paper from 1 to 10. Write the correct pronoun from the two given in parentheses.

1. Please call Jim and (I, me) in the morning.
2. The principal asked (them, they) and their parents for suggestions.
3. Mom dropped Matt and (me, I) off at City Hall.
4. The Kiwanis Club sponsored (he, him) in the race.
5. Judy's dog chased Pat and (she, her).
6. Ms. Talbot complimented the class and (he, him).
7. That owl scared Doug and (I, me) out of our wits.
8. The coach trusted (them, they) and (we, us).
9. Help Brenda and (I, me), please.
10. Will you give Roger and (they, them) a hand?

B. Follow the directions for Exercise A.

1. Hold (them, they) at the ten-yard line.
2. Didn't the waitress bill Todd and (I, me) correctly?

3. Will you pull (she, her) on this sled?
4. Snowballs hit David and (we, us).
5. The radio announcer interviewed Doug and (he, him).
6. We left Shelley and (she, her) at the park.
7. A raft carried Tammy and (I, me) downstream.
8. Meet Michelle and (me, I) at the ticket booth.
9. That joke embarrassed Wes and (him, he).
10. The clerk showed Tony and (I, me) the newest model.

Part 5   Possessive Pronouns

To make the possessive form of a noun, you add an apostrophe or an apostrophe and an *s* to the noun. Pronouns, however, have special possessive forms. These forms do not use apostrophes at all.

These are the possessive pronouns.

my, mine	our, ours
your, yours	your, yours
his, her, hers, its	their, theirs

Read these sentences that use possessive pronouns:

This is *my* locker.   We have *our* friends.
This locker is *mine.*   These friends are *ours.*

Is that *your* ticket?   Are those *your* skis?
Is that *yours?*   Are those *yours?*

Here is *his* coat.   Do you know *their* plans?
The coat is *his.*   The plans are *theirs.*

Where is *her* lunch?
This lunch is *hers.*

Some people confuse the possessive pronoun *its* with the contraction *it's. Its* (without an apostrophe) is the possessive form of *it. It's* (with an apostrophe) means *it is* or *it has.*

The museum opened *its* new wing.
(The wing belongs to the museum.)
It's almost noon and I'm hungry.
(*It is* almost noon and I'm hungry.)

Exercises   Use possessive pronouns.

A.   Copy the following sentences. Where there is a blank, write the appropriate possessive pronoun.

1. This lunchbag is _____ . (The lunchbag belongs to me.)
2. The dog lost _____ bone. (The bone belongs to it.)
3. That glove must be _____ . (The glove belongs to you.)
4. Kate took _____ advice. (The advice belongs to him.)
5. That house is _____ . (The house belongs to us.)
6. The sweater is _____ . (The sweater belongs to her.)
7. The helmets are _____ . (The helmets belong to them.)
8. Jim made _____ bed. (The bed belongs to him.)
9. We watered _____ plants. (The plants belong to us.)
10. The cat ate _____ food. (The food belongs to it.)

B.   Write each of these sentences. Whenever you write *its*, insert an apostrophe only if it is needed.

1. I hate gum when its flavor is gone.
2. The school started its basketball season last week.
3. Change the thermostat if its set too low.
4. That stuffed dog lost a lot of its stuffing.
5. Butter that toast while its still hot.
6. Leary's store ends its sale on school supplies today.
7. Leave the puzzle in its box.
8. The rat lost its way in the maze.
9. Its snowing throughout the Northeast.
10. Its too late to go swimming now.

ADDITIONAL EXERCISES

Using Pronouns

A. Pronouns Number your paper from 1 to 10. Write the pronouns you find in each of the following sentences. After each pronoun, write the noun or nouns it stands for. Some sentences have more than one pronoun.

1. Mary gave her sister a hug.
2. Mr. and Mrs. Morgan sold their house last week.
3. The rabbit wiggled its nose.
4. Tim was late. He had missed his train.
5. Mark said, "Jason and I gave our report on Egypt today."
6. Did you find your sweater?
7. Sally said, "Hand me my book, please."
8. Chrissy tripped over the hurdle. She sprained her ankle.
9. Here's a rubberband. Put it around the deck of cards.
10. The twins rode their bikes to the meet.

B. Subject Pronouns Write the correct pronoun from the two given in parentheses.

1. (He, Him) and Sue Ellen worked with stained glass.
2. Colleen and (me, I) timed the swimmers.
3. (We, Us) older kids were asked to help.
4. Watch those plates. (They, Them) break easily.
5. (She, Her) and her sister often trade clothes.
6. (They, Them) and their friends sold tickets.
7. (He, Him) and David built the treehouse.
8. Nora and (I, me) took the bus.
9. (We, Us) weeded the vegetable garden this morning.
10. Mike and (them, they) returned the bottles.

C. Pronouns After Linking Verbs Write the correct pronoun from the two given in parentheses.

1. The top scorers were Joshua and (me, I).
2. The silliest people at the party were (we, us) three.
3. The sports reporters for the school paper are Kevin and (she, her).
4. Our guests were the Prestons and (he, him).
5. The two guitarists are Wendy and (him, he).
6. The winner of the race was (she, her).
7. The ushers will be (us, we) students.
8. The lifeguards at the community pool were Miranda and (I, me).
9. Our coaches are Ms. Andrews and (he, him).
10. My assistants during the pageant were Jesse and (she, her).

D. Object Pronouns Write the correct pronoun from the two given in parentheses.

1. The pitcher threw (she, her) a fast ball.
2. The lifeguard rescued Curt and (he, him) from the overturned raft.
3. Mom quizzed Jeff and (me, I) on the math problems before the exam.
4. Do you remember Kirsten and (we, us)?
5. Do the experts favor (her, she) or Chris Evert Lloyd to win the match?
6. The bus took Heather and (I, me) to the door of the ice rink.
7. Ms. Lopez questioned Lupe and (she, her) about the class play.
8. The movie starred Jack Nicholson and (he, him).
9. Do you believe (they, them) or (we, us)?
10. Give Matt and (I, me) some help, too.

E. Possessive Pronouns Copy the following sentences. Where there is a blank, write the correct possessive pronoun.

1. These skis are _____. (The skis belong to us.)
2. Two actors gave us _____ autographs. (The autographs belong to the actors.)
3. Tim cleaned _____ desk. (The desk belongs to Tim.)
4. The snake shed _____ skin. (The skin belongs to the snake.)
5. The drawings are _____. (The drawings belong to you.)
6. This coat is _____. (The coat belongs to her.)
7. That locker is _____. (The locker belongs to me.)
8. The sailboats are _____. (The sailboats belong to them.)
9. Give us _____ tickets, please. (The tickets belong to us.)
10. The bird flew to _____ nest. (The nest belongs to the bird.)

MIXED REVIEW

Using Pronouns

A. Choosing the correct pronouns Number your paper from 1 to 14. Read the following paragraph. Write the correct pronoun from the two given in parentheses. After each pronoun, write the noun it stands for.

Ellen is (my, mine) name. (My, Mine) sister Sal and (I, me) wanted to do something really different for the Cycle Show. So (we, us) did. The unicycles were (her, she) idea. Holding hands while riding was (me, mine). (Our, Ours) parents were quite nervous. (They, Them) couldn't even watch (we, us) practice. (We, Us) made (they, them) proud, however, at the Cycle Show. (I, Me) could hear (their, them) applause as (we, us) accepted (our, ours) prize—a bicycle built for two!

B. Using subject, object, and possessive pronouns Number your paper from 1 to 10. Write the pronouns used in the following sentences. After each, write S (Subject), O (Object), or P (Possessive) to show what kind it is.

1. He memorized the Gettysburg Address for Lincoln's birthday.
2. The teacher chose Michael and her.
3. Mr. Guthrie found him in the chemistry lab.
4. The cat licked its paw.
5. My report is about the first settlers in our town.
6. The wasp chased me around the yard and out the gate.
7. The mailman knew Mrs. Herman and them.
8. Is she the girl from Japan?
9. My parents and their friends are playing Monopoly.
10. The cashier didn't give you or me the correct change.

C. Using possessive pronouns correctly Copy the following sentences. Write the correct possessive pronoun.

1. Don't run in _____ garden. (The garden belongs to them.)
2. Nine must be _____ lucky number. (The number belongs to her.)
3. The boat lost _____ sail during the storm. (The sail belongs to it.)
4. _____ team has lost four games in a row. (The team belongs to us.)
5. Queenie is _____ dog. (The dog belongs to me.)
6. The judge made _____ decision. (The decision belongs to her.)
7. Here is _____ receipt. (The receipt belongs to you.)
8. The old wooden racket is _____. (The racket belongs to him.)
9. The rusty yellow bike is _____. (The bike belongs to me.)
10. _____ ideas are the most original. (The ideas belong to them.)

D. Using pronouns correctly Five of the following sentences use pronouns incorrectly. Rewrite those sentences correctly. If a sentence is already correct, write *Correct*.

1. Did Roger collect dues from her?
2. I talked to she about the skit.
3. He and I photographed the funnel cloud.
4. We helped them fix the flat tire.
5. The first guests at the dinner were them.
6. Scott and me are cutting lawns this summer.
7. We soccer players need rest and exercise.
8. The dog lost it's rubber ball.
9. His tacos and my pizza tied for first place.
10. Last night I cooked mine own dinner.

USING GRAMMAR IN WRITING
Using Pronouns

A. Imagine that you are out wandering one day in the park or along the edge of a forest. Suddenly something quite strange steps from behind a tree. The creature has enormous, pointed ears. Its face is very wrinkled, but not quite human. When it speaks to you, your fears quiet down. You realize that you are facing an intelligent creature from another planet. The creature has made an amazing journey from its own galaxy. Now it has some questions to ask you. Before the creature leaves, it gives you a message for the rest of the world. Write the five questions that the creature asks you. Answer each question with a complete sentence. Then write the message the creature tells you.

Include interrogative, demonstrative, and personal pronouns in your questions, answers, and message.

B. Your class at school has decided to raise money for an end-of-year party. The boys will compete against the girls to see who can earn the most money. You could have a car wash, for instance. You might have a bike-a-thon or a volleyball tournament. You decide. Then write a paragraph to the principal explaining your plan. Use the phrases *we girls* and *us girls* or *we boys* and *us boys* correctly at least once. Use compound personal pronouns and indefinite pronouns in your paragraph.

Using Adjectives

Part 1 What Are Adjectives?

Does the sentence below tell you very much about what Mr. Rafael drives?

Mr. Rafael drives a van.

Can you tell more about what Mr. Rafael drives when you read the following sentence?

Mr. Rafael drives a small, black van.

Which words in the second sentence tell you what kind of van Mr. Rafael drives? *Small* and *black* describe the van. They are **adjectives**.

Adjectives are words that describe nouns and pronouns. They are called **modifiers** because they limit, or modify, the meaning of the word they describe. Read these examples:

> Kathy drove along the *scenic* highway.
> Kathy drove along the *wide* highway.
> Kathy drove along the *narrow* highway.
> Kathy drove along the *dusty* highway.

An adjective is a word that modifies a noun or pronoun.

One or more adjectives may be used before the noun or pronoun being modified. Usually, when you use two or more adjectives together, separate them with commas.

> We had our picnic under a *tall, shady* tree.

Adjectives telling numbers do not have to follow this rule.

> We had *two big* baskets of food.

Adjectives may also follow the noun or pronoun they modify.

> I met Jeff, *hungry* and *weary*, at the end of the trail.

Some Adjectives Tell *What Kind*

Adjectives describe persons, places, and things. Some adjectives tell *what kind* of person, place, or thing.

> Henry wore *woolen* gloves and a *colorful* scarf.

> The alligator's *sharp* teeth are *dangerous* weapons.

> Lately we have had *warm, rainy* weather.

> These are *comfortable* seats.

Many adjectives that tell *what kind* are formed by adding an adjective ending to a noun. Here are some examples:

Noun		Adjective Ending		Adjective
rain	+	y	=	rainy
color	+	ful	=	colorful
danger	+	ous	=	dangerous
wool	+	en	=	woolen
comfort	+	able	=	comfortable

Some Adjectives Tell *How Many*

Adjectives can tell *how many* persons, places, or things you are talking about. The adjectives in the following sentences tell *how many*.

Mr. and Mrs. Ellsworth own *twenty* trucks.

Their trucks travel across *several* states.

Some trucks have *many* license plates.

They have *frequent* breakdowns but *few* accidents.

Some Adjectives Tell *Which Ones*

Some adjectives tell *which* person, place, or thing you are talking about.

These trucks hold nine rooms of furniture.

Those trucks transport new automobiles.

This truck is used for hauling coal or dirt.

That truck is used to tow away wrecks.

Exercises   Use adjectives.

A.   Copy these sentences. Draw an arrow from each adjective that tells *what kind* to the noun it modifies.

1. Did you find a brown wallet?
2. Ronnie scraped sticky gum from her shoe.
3. Do you know how to give artificial respiration?
4. An unearthly howl made Rich tremble.
5. Small pink flowers covered the ground.
6. Peculiar noises came from the closet.
7. The sky was filled with puffy white clouds.
8. Tina complained of a stiff neck.
9. Mary's new camera has a red filter.
10. The boys looked for small starfish.

B.   Number your paper from 1 to 10. Make two columns. Title one column *Which Ones*. Title the other *How Many*. Find the adjectives in these sentences and place them in the appropriate column. Not every sentence has both kinds of adjectives.

Example: Those trees have grown two feet this year.

Which Ones	How Many
those	two

1. Janet has used this saw many times.
2. Many people prefer this brand of cereal.
3. Look at these beautiful seashells.
4. Mr. Harvey received six boxes of books.
5. Is this saddle for Sara?
6. These cards belong to that game.
7. That light flashed a signal to some men on the shore.
8. We have ordered several cakes from that bakery.
9. The voice on that tape doesn't sound like yours.
10. It took four hours to sand those desks.

Part 2 The Articles

The words *a, an,* and *the* are called **articles**. Since they always modify nouns, they are also adjectives.

1. Use *a* before words beginning with consonant sounds:

   a box   *a* hat   *a* moth

2. Use *an* before words beginning with vowel sounds:

   an apple   *an* engineer   *an* island   *an* uncle

3. Use *the* before words beginning with any sound:

   the actor   *the* center   *the* race   *the* audience

Some words begin with a silent *h*. In these words, you do not say the *h* sound. Instead, you begin the word with the sound of the vowel after the *h*. Therefore, you follow the rule for the vowel sound, and use *an*:

   an honor   *an* hour   *an* honest person

Exercises   Use articles.

A. Read the following sentences carefully. Copy the sentences. Fill in the blanks with the articles *a* or *an*.

1. I just peeled _____ onion.
2. _____ acrobat could do that.
3. Carlos was riding _____ bicycle.
4. Is that _____ iceberg near the horizon?
5. Can you ride _____ horse?
6. Dennis is known as _____ honest person.
7. Mom's gone to _____ important meeting.
8. Does the car have _____ undercoating to prevent rust?
9. The bird on the cliff was _____ eagle.
10. The boat drifted in _____ aimless pattern.

B. Writing Write a sentence using each of the following nouns. Place an article and an adjective before each noun.

1. person
2. mountains
3. friend
4. meal
5. clothes
6. vacation
7. animal
8. books
9. family
10. house

Part 3 Predicate Adjectives

When an adjective follows a linking verb like *is* or *seemed*, it is part of the predicate. However, it modifies a noun or pronoun in the subject. This kind of adjective is called a **predicate adjective**. Read these examples.

The trees are *tall*.

Donna will be *happy*.

He is *right*.

The patient seemed *sleepy*.

An **adjective** that follows a linking verb and modifies the subject is called a **predicate adjective**.

Exercises Use predicate adjectives.

A. Writing Copy these sentences, putting a predicate adjective in each blank. Draw an arrow from the predicate adjective to the word it modifies.

1. Lemons are _____ .
2. Before the test, I was _____ .
3. The boys were _____ after the game.
4. Every day at noon, I am _____ .

5. The sun was _____ this morning.
6. With the new addition, the house will be _____ .
7. You are _____ than any other student here.
8. This rose is _____ .
9. Rhonda will be _____ when she sees your present.
10. From far away, the bell sounded _____ .

B. Follow the directions for Exercise A.

1. The loaves of fresh bread smell _____ .
2. Without water, the plants will become _____ .
3. Your new suit looks _____ .
4. That book was _____ .
5. The plane to Omaha will be _____ .
6. The early settlers were very _____ .
7. Vincent's violin sounds _____ .
8. This apple tastes _____ .
9. After several days, the leftovers became _____ .
10. This movie is too _____ .

Part 4 Proper Adjectives

You have already used many adjectives formed from common nouns, such as *rainy, comfortable,* and *woolen.* Some adjectives are formed from proper nouns. These adjectives are called **proper adjectives.**

You know that a proper noun names a particular person, place, or thing. By adding adjective endings to some proper nouns, you change them into proper adjectives. Here are some examples:

Proper Noun	Proper Adjective + Noun Modified
Britain	British royalty
Japan	Japanese yen
Mexico	Mexican jewelry
Bible	Biblical quotation

Some proper nouns are used as adjectives without the addition of adjective endings. Here are some examples.

the California sunshine   a Chevrolet engine
a Streisand movie   a Brahms symphony

A proper adjective is an adjective that has been made from a proper noun. A proper adjective begins with a capital letter.

Exercises   Use proper adjectives.

A. Write each proper adjective. Capitalize correctly.

1. Is that an irish sheep dog?
2. The austrian ski team won the downhill competition.
3. My sister bought a japanese car.
4. This delicatessen sells polish sausage.
5. When was the alaskan pipeline started?
6. The jewish community is celebrating Rosh Hashana.
7. The olympic committee met with the President.
8. The canadian Rockies are higher than the american Rockies.
9. Napoleon's army was defeated partly by the russian winter.
10. The museum just purchased a spanish painting.

B. Follow the directions for Exercise A.

1. We studied roman numerals in math today.
2. The nigerian capital is Lagos.
3. Cleopatra ruled the egyptian people.
4. I like italian, blue cheese, and french dressings.

5. Lawrence is taking german lessons.
6. My aunt bought some indian turquoise jewelry.
7. Mrs. Haas was a dutch immigrant.
8. When was the gregorian calendar developed?
9. Valerie had a siamese kitten and a persian cat.
10. Eduardo's father drove his italian car across the swiss border.

Part 5   Demonstrative Adjectives

The adjectives *this*, *that*, *these*, and *those* tell which one or which ones. *This*, *that*, *these*, and *those* are called **demonstrative adjectives.**

> *This* melon tastes sweeter than *that* one.
> *These* notebooks cost a quarter each. *Those* notebooks cost a dollar each.

Use *this* and *that* with singular nouns. Use *these* and *those* with plural nouns.

this Frisbee	these Frisbees
that field	those fields

The nouns *kind* and *sort* are singular. Therefore, you say *this kind* and *this sort*. Use *these* and *those* only with the plurals: *these kinds* or *those sorts*.

this kind of pizza	these kinds of sweaters
that sort of movie	those sorts of ribbons

Using *Those* and *Them*

Those is a word with many uses. It may be used as an adjective:

> Where did you find *those* skates?

Those may also be used as a pronoun. As a pronoun it can be the subject of a verb or it can be a direct object.

> *Those* are my sisters. (subject)
> Paint *those* tomorrow. (direct object)

Them is always an object pronoun. It is never used as an adjective. You shouldn't say *them books* or *them tickets*. Always use *those* when you want the adjective form of *them*.

> My uncle gave me *those* stamps.

As a pronoun, *them* is never used as the subject. You would use *them* only as an object, as in these examples:

> He gave *them* to me.
> I added *them* to my collection.

Exercises   Use demonstrative adjectives and *them*.

A.   Number your paper from 1 to 10. Write the correct word from the two given in parentheses. Then read the completed sentence to yourself.

1. Robert needs (that, those) kind of car to finish his model train set.
2. (Them, Those) flowers across the street are snapdragons.
3. Do you like (this, these) kind of notebook?
4. (These, Them) girls with me are my cousins.
5. (Those, These) swimming lessons last summer taught me a lot.
6. Lois often buys (them, these) sorts of rings.
7. Can you see (those, them) geese flying south?
8. I think (those, them) kinds of programs are the best.
9. These muffins have chopped walnuts in (those, them).
10. (Them, These) albums are by a new group.

B. Copy these sentences. Use *them* or *those* in the blanks. Then read the completed sentence to yourself.

1. _____ songs were sung in Spanish.
2. I want those calendars. How much do you charge for _____ ?
3. Tell _____ to come back tomorrow for their typewriter.
4. These slacks fit me better than _____ .
5. Joan made the boxes and painted _____ .
6. Where did you get all _____ old magazines?
7. You can't ask _____ for all _____ labels.
8. Are _____ posters dry yet?
9. All of _____ boys play on Marvin's team.
10. _____ were the most expensive shoes.

Part 6 Making Comparisons with Adjectives

Lions are big. Zebras are big. Elephants are big. All three of these animals are big. But they are not all the same size. If you want to say that the animals are of different sizes, you will have to change the word *big*.

You use the word *bigger* to compare two persons or things.

> A zebra is *bigger* than a lion.
> An elephant is *bigger* than a zebra.

Bigger is called the **comparative form** of *big*.

You use the word *biggest* to compare more than two persons or things.

> An elephant is the *biggest* of the three animals.

Biggest is called the **superlative form** of *big*.

Use the comparative form of an adjective to compare two persons, places, or things.

Lake Michigan is *deeper* than Lake Huron.

Use the superlative form of an adjective to compare more than two persons, places, or things.

Lake Superior is the *deepest* of all the Great Lakes.

Usually, you make the comparative form of a short adjective by adding -*er*. You make the superlative form by adding -*est*. If the adjective ends in *e*, drop the *e* before adding -*er* or -*est*. If the adjective ends in *y*, change the *y* to *i* before adding -*er* or -*est*.

Adjective	Comparative Form	Superlative Form
long	longer	longest
old	older	oldest
tall	taller	tallest
big	bigger	biggest
funny	funnier	funniest

For longer adjectives, you form the comparative by using the word *more*. You form the superlative by using the word *most*.

Adjective	Comparative Form	Superlative Form
ridiculous	more ridiculous	most ridiculous
noticeable	more noticeable	most noticeable
careful	more careful	most careful
terrible	more terrible	most terrible

Use only one form of comparison at a time. Do not use *more* and *-er*, or *most* and *-est* together.

Incorrect:	This pillow is *more softer* than that one.
Correct:	This pillow is *softer* than that one.
Incorrect:	That dress is the *most prettiest* of all.
Correct:	That dress is the *prettiest* of all.

The Forms of *Good* and *Bad*

A few adjectives change their forms in other ways. Some adjectives have completely different words for the comparative and superlative forms. Here are two important ones to remember:

good	better	best
bad	worse	worst

Donna is my *good* friend.
She is a *better* cook than I am.
Her spaghetti sauce is the *best* I've tasted.

David suffered a *bad* sprain.
He was in *worse* pain today than yesterday.
"I have the *worst* luck of anyone," he moaned.

Exercises **Use adjectives to make comparisons.**

A. Number your paper from 1 to 10. Write the correct form of the adjective from the two given in parentheses. Then read the completed sentence to yourself.

1. Todd is (stronger, strongest) than I.
2. This sausage pizza tastes (better, more better) than the cheese pizza.
3. Who is the (youngest, most young) in your family?
4. I was wearing my (bestest, best) jeans.
5. The weather in Sky Harbor is (badder, worse) than ours.

6. Have you heard the (latest, most late) news?
7. Claire is the (carefulest, most careful) person I know.
8. Cindy has the (most, mostest) beautiful guitar.
9. The snow was (worse, worser) in the mountains.
10. That is the (best, better) picture in the whole book.

B. Follow the directions for Exercise A.

1. That is the (funnier, funniest) show of the season.
2. Marguerita's briefcase was (heavy, heavier) than her mother's suitcase.
3. A new raincoat will be (expensiver, more expensive) than I expected.
4. Superman is (stronger, strongest) than ordinary humans.
5. Doc was the (smarter, smartest) of the Seven Dwarfs.
6. Between Andrea and Luis, Luis is (taller, tallest).
7. A balanced meal is (gooder, better) for your health than junk food.
8. Tomorrow will be (colder, more colder) than today.
9. Who is the (most old, oldest) in your family?
10. Jody thinks radishes have the (worst, worstest) taste of any vegetable.

ADDITIONAL EXERCISES

Using Adjectives

A. Recognizing Adjectives Write the adjectives in each sentence. Beside each adjective, write the noun it modifies. Put the noun in parentheses. Do not include articles.

1. These candles make an eerie glow on the bedroom wall.
2. Two batters used the lightweight metal bats.
3. We went to the top floor of the tall building.
4. Those twelve cheerleaders led the crowd in the school cheer.
5. That wild horse tossed the first rider.
6. We picked these crisp red apples.
7. Poor Charlie Brown didn't get any Valentines.
8. Ted covered the ten puppies with a fuzzy blue blanket.
9. We ate many pancakes with butter and syrup.
10. Lynn heard the dry rattle of the poisonous snake.

B. Use Articles Copy these sentences. Fill in the blanks with *a* or *an*.

1. Would you like _____ apple or some grapes?
2. _____ huge rainbow appeared in the sky.
3. Does Janet have _____ older sister?
4. I drank _____ cup of chicken noodle soup.
5. We saw _____ owl in the old oak tree.
6. Dad made _____ salad of lettuce and tomatoes.
7. Tim waited _____ hour for the mail delivery.
8. What _____ beautiful sunset we saw!
9. Chris ordered _____ hot dog with mustard.
10. All the guests had _____ enjoyable visit.

C. Predicate Adjectives   Write the predicate adjective in each sentence.

1. The koala bear is Australian.
2. That clock must be wrong.
3. The sky was cloudy today.
4. These baseball uniforms are filthy.
5. Are those boots comfortable?
6. The new receptionist seems pleasant.
7. The attic was dusty.
8. Peanut brittle is crunchy.
9. Those students seem friendly.
10. Is that jacket warm?

D. Proper Adjectives   Write each proper adjective. Capitalize correctly.

1. Are american cars as fuel-efficient as japanese cars?
2. That dog is part german shepherd.
3. We will read and discuss some greek myths this week.
4. Mr. Aden bought a navajo rug on an indian reservation.
5. Which do you prefer, new england clam chowder or manhattan clam chowder?
6. Ted gave us some mexican jumping beans.
7. The dune buggy had a volkswagen engine.
8. Is that hot or mild italian sausage?
9. The Amazon River flows through the brazilian jungle.
10. Is this a florida avocado or a california avocado?

E. Demonstrative Adjectives   Write the correct word from the two given in parentheses.

1. Clara won't wear (them, those) boots.
2. Dad likes (this, these) kind of tie.
3. (Them, Those) bills should be paid promptly.

4. (That, Those) sorts of pastries are rich.
5. Swallows prefer (this, these) kind of birdhouse.
6. (That, Those) sort of mistake can be avoided.
7. (Those, Them) jeans are expensive.
8. Give (them, those) notes to Harry.
9. (This, These) kinds of sweaters are on sale.
10. Who brought (them, those) packages?

F.   Adjectives in Comparisons   Write the correct form of the adjective from the two given in parentheses.

1. This puzzle is (harder, more hard) than that one.
2. Cindy's voice is (higher, highest) than Diane's.
3. This puzzle is the (more complex, most complex) of all.
4. Which of these two lines is (straighter, straightest)?
5. Julio had a (better, more better) time than Connie did.
6. Which horse is the (bigger, biggest) of the two pulling the wagon?
7. Your problem seems (worse, worst) than mine.
8. That snapshot is the (clearer, more clearer) of the two.
9. Which of these three paintings is the (older, oldest)?
10. My cold is (badder, worse) today.

MIXED REVIEW

Using Adjectives

A. Identifying adjectives List all of the adjectives in the following sentences. Include articles, proper adjectives, predicate adjectives, and demonstrative adjectives. After each adjective, write the word it modifies.

1. Toronto is the largest Canadian city.
2. Dark clouds threatened the annual Greek picnic.
3. Creamy chocolate mousse is a delicious French dessert.
4. We ate a spicy meal at the new Mexican restaurant.
5. Does Samantha own a small black poodle?
6. This article about bats is excellent.
7. Stewart bought five tickets for the Chinese exhibition.
8. These old boots are comfortable.
9. The solitary spacecraft explored Venus.
10. The last train is leaving in thirty minutes.

B. Using adjectives correctly Six of the following sentences contain errors in the use of adjectives. If a sentence contains an error, rewrite it correctly. If a sentence is already correct, write *Correct*.

1. The pizza will be ready in a hour.
2. These kind of dog is very intelligent.
3. The Sudan is the largest country in Africa.
4. Be carefuller when you cross the street next time.
5. Earthball is an unusual game.
6. The Swedish bakery sells delicious potato bread.
7. Which is more hard, diamond or glass?
8. Them coupons are worth three dollars.
9. That was the worse movie I have ever seen.
10. This restaurant serves authentic Indonesian food.

USING GRAMMAR IN WRITING
Using Adjectives

A.   Think about a large shopping center that you are familiar with. Imagine that the manager of the center has told you he would like more teenagers to shop there. Decide which of the stores or other places in the center you like best. Then write a story about the center for the school newspaper. Your story should appeal to teens. Tell about four or five places in the shopping center that you know people your age would like.

Your story should include vivid adjectives that will make the shopping center sound appealing. Include proper adjectives, articles, and demonstrative adjectives.

B.   When you are riding a bus or the subway, do you ever watch the other passengers? Most of us are curious about where other people might be going and what their lives are like. Sometimes it's fun to guess about people from the way they look or from what they are wearing or reading. Imagine that you are on a crowded bus. Describe someone who looks unusual and interesting. Write a paragraph that tells what the person looks like. Write a second paragraph that tells what you think the person's life might be like. Use his or her appearance and clothing as clues. Use good, strong adjectives to describe this stranger.

Using Adverbs

Part 1 What Are Adverbs?

Adjectives modify nouns and pronouns. **Adverbs** modify verbs, adjectives, and other adverbs. Read these examples.

Jerry worked *quickly*.
We *always* go there.
The cat ran *away*.
It was *very* windy.

Adverbs usually tell *how, when, where,* or *to what extent* about the words they modify. If you are not sure whether a word is an adverb, ask yourself if it answers one of these questions.

Adverbs Modify Verbs

Joe whistled.

How?　Joe whistled *loudly.*

Where?　Joe whistled *outside.*

When?　Joe whistled *constantly.*

Adverbs Modify Adjectives

That is a *bright* light.

How bright?　That is a *very* bright light.

This stunt is *dangerous.*

How dangerous?　This stunt is *too* dangerous.

Adverbs Modify Other Adverbs

John dances *well.*

How well?　John dances *extremely* well.

The horse ran *away.*

To what extent?　The horse ran *far* away.

Generally, an adverb that modifies an adjective or another adverb comes before the word it modifies.

very bright
extremely well

An adverb that modifies a verb can sometimes be placed in more than one position in the sentence.

He reads books *often.*
Often he reads books.
He *often* reads books.

Many adverbs are formed by adding *-ly* to an adjective:

bad—badly	slow—slowly
quick—quickly	happy—happily
careful—carefully	suspicious—suspiciously

Adverbs modify verbs, adjectives, and other adverbs.

Exercises **Find and use adverbs.**

A. Number your paper from 1 to 10. Write every adverb used in each sentence. After each adverb, write the word it modifies.

1. Roberto took the exam yesterday during study period.
2. Suddenly Jill looked up.
3. Soon the sun came out.
4. Because of his cold, Dennis can hardly talk.
5. The eighth grade class entered the auditorium quickly but quietly.
6. Did you ever hear Louisa play?
7. Those two boys are never late.
8. The explosion happened suddenly.
9. David sanded the table very carefully with two kinds of sandpaper.
10. Soon the mist over the lake cleared.

B. Writing Write a sentence for each of the following adverbs. Underline the adverb in each sentence. Circle the word the adverb modifies.

1. here	3. outside	5. too	7. almost	9. soon
2. slowly	4. now	6. never	8. very	10. early

Part 2　Making Comparisons with Adverbs

Adverbs, like adjectives, have comparative and superlative forms. You use the **comparative form** when you consider two persons or things:

Jack ran *faster* than the giant.

You use the **superlative form** when you consider more than two persons or things:

The cheetah is the *fastest* of all animals.

The comparative and superlative forms of adverbs are formed in three ways.

1. Some short adverbs add -*er* for the comparative and -*est* for the superlative.

Adverb	Comparative Form	Superlative Form
fast	faster	fastest
hard	harder	hardest

2. Most adverbs that end in -*ly* form the comparative with the word *more*. They form the superlative with the word *most*.

Adverb	Comparative Form	Superlative Form
easily	more easily	most easily
carefully	more carefully	most carefully

3. Some adverbs make their comparative and superlative forms by complete word changes.

Adverb	Comparative Form	Superlative Form
well	better	best
much	more	most
little	less	least
badly	worse	worst

Exercises   Make comparisons with adverbs.

A. Number your paper from 1 to 10. Label three columns: *Adverb, Comparative,* and *Superlative.* List all of the adverbs below in the first column. Then write their comparative and superlative forms.

1. often   3. soon   5. quickly   7. easily   9. little
2. heavily   4. carefully   6. well   8. slowly   10. hard

B. Number your paper from 1 to 10. Write the correct word from the two given in parentheses.

1. Push the car (more hard, harder) if you want to get it out of the snowbank.
2. I did (worse, more bad) than you on the quiz in science class.
3. That stunt driver is driving (more recklessly, most recklessly) than ever before.
4. This lid came off (more easily, most easily) of all.
5. Sheila pitches (most fast, fastest) when the pressure is the greatest.
6. Gayle skates (more gracefully, most gracefully) than Kenneth.
7. Power brakes will stop a car (more quickly, quicklier) than regular brakes.
8. Ned is the (less, least) noisy person in the room.
9. That dog performs (worse, worst) than any other dog in the act.

10. Among the racers in his age group, Ricky swam (more quickly, most quickly).

Part 3   Adjective or Adverb?

You learned that some adverbs are made by adding *-ly* to an adjective. Read these examples:

My sister is a *careful* driver.   My sister drives *carefully.*

Patty is *happy.*   Patty smiled *happily.*

Because many adjectives and adverbs look and sound similar, it is sometimes hard to know whether to use the adjective or adverb. Which would you say?

Anita worked very *careful.*   *or*   Anita worked very *carefully.*

To find the answer, ask what you are trying to say. Are you trying to say:

which one Anita worked?
what kind Anita worked?
how many Anita worked?

Or are you trying to say:

how Anita worked?

You are trying to say *how.* The kind of word that tells how something happened or how something was done is an adverb. This adverb modifies the verb *worked.* You would use the adverb *carefully* in this sentence.

Anita worked very *carefully.*

When you are choosing the correct modifier, ask yourself:

1. Which word does the modifier tell about?
2. What does the modifier tell?

The chart below will help you to answer these questions.

An adverb tells	An adjective tells
how	what kind
when	how many
where	which one
to what extent	
about a verb, an adjective, or another adverb.	**about a noun or pronoun.**

Exercises **Choose the right modifier.**

A. Copy each sentence, putting in the correct modifier. Underline the modifier. Draw an arrow from the modifier to the word it modifies. Then write *Adjective* or *Adverb* to show how the modifier is used.

Examples: Mike looked (happy, happily) after the race.

Mike looked happy after the race. adjective

The choir sang (good, well).

The choir sang well. adverb

1. That barn looks (empty, emptily).
2. This cliff is (sure, surely) too steep for me to climb.
3. Karen didn't feel (really, real) sure of her answer.
4. Those mountains look (beautiful, beautifully).
5. Our test wasn't (real, really) hard.
6. After the fight, the cat looked pretty (bad, badly).
7. You print so (neat, neatly).
8. The actor sang too (poor, poorly) to get the role.
9. The team felt (bad, badly) about losing the game.
10. Dan pitched (wild, wildly).

Follow the directions for Exercise A.

1. The price of the car sounded (incredible, incredibly).
2. The teams were matched pretty (even, evenly).
3. I go to the library (regularly, regular) on Friday.
4. This vegetable soup tastes (bad, badly).
5. You sang (remarkable, remarkably) well.
6. The sun set (slow, slowly).
7. The edge of the paper was (real, really) crooked.
8. That map was drawn (bad, badly).
9. The line was drawn (uneven, unevenly).
10. Our guests arrived (promptly, prompt) at ten.

Using *Good* and *Well*

The words *good* and *well* are often confused. They form their comparative and superlative forms in the same way:

good	better	best
well	better	best

Good is always an adjective that describes a noun or pronoun. It is never used as an adverb.

> You are a good student.
>   (*Good* modifies *student*.)

> That cake looks good.
>   (*Looks* is a linking verb; *good* modifies the noun *cake*.)

Well is an adjective when it describes a noun or pronoun and means "healthy."

> If you take your medicine, you will be well.
>   (*Well* modifies the pronoun *you*.)

> I feel well.
>   (*Feel* is a linking verb; *well* modifies the pronoun *I*.)

Well is an adverb when it modifies a verb, adverb, or adjective, and tells *how* something is done.

You cook *well*.
   (*Well* modifies the verb *cook*.)

Margo explained the game *well*.
   (*Well* modifies the verb *explained*.)

Exercises   Use *good* and *well* correctly.

A. Write *Adjective* or *Adverb* to tell how each word in italics is used. Then write the word or words that it modifies.

1. Kelly is *good* at tennis.
2. Can you see *better* without sunglasses?
3. Ted takes *good* care of his bicycle.
4. In training camp, the football players eat *well*.
5. Dana gave the *best* answer.
6. These shoes fit me *best*.
7. The woman had a *good* look at the robber.
8. You are *better* at baseball.
9. Andy writes *good* reports.
10. These ski boots don't fit *well*.

B. Follow the directions for Exercise A.

1. Dave is the *best* catcher on our block.
2. Ramona has a *good* recipe for brownies.
3. The team did *well* in the exhibition games.
4. Your homemade pies are *better* than bakery pies.
5. Fernando has a *better* idea.
6. Andrea speaks *well* before large groups.
7. The map showed a *better* route than Fran's.
8. Did you have a *good* time?
9. Anyone plays *better* after some practice.
10. My dad wore his *best* tie.

ADDITIONAL EXERCISES

Using Adverbs

A. Adverbs Copy each sentence. Circle each adverb. Draw an arrow from each adverb to the word it modifies.

1. The campers slept outside.
2. Carol quickly ate her breakfast.
3. The stage crew looked everywhere for the props.
4. The conductor never collected our tickets.
5. Today a guide showed us the space capsule.
6. Ants completely covered our picnic blanket.
7. Tom works quite slowly.
8. We hiked too far from the camp.
9. Instantly, the coach jumped up.
10. Sherry almost always sinks free throws.

B. Adverbs in Comparison Choose the correct form of the adverb from the two given in parentheses.

1. Penny's toss came (closer, closest) than Pam's.
2. Sam scored (higher, more high) on the last test.
3. Andrea practices (less, least) than her sister.
4. Of all the planets, Venus can be seen (more clearly, most clearly).
5. Dave and Jerry have been friends (longer, more longer) than you and I.
6. This engine works (more efficiently, efficientlier) than that one.
7. This new detergent cleans (best, better) of all.
8. Of all the team members, Loren shoots (most accurately, more accurately).
9. Sean sings (worse, worst) than I do.
10. Hang the picture (more low, lower).

C. Adjective or Adverb? Write the correct modifier from the two given in parentheses.

1. The snow fell (steady, steadily).
2. The pianist played (beautiful, beautifully).
3. The gymnast seemed (graceful, gracefully).
4. That movie is (real, really) funny.
5. Jeff felt (bad, badly) after the quarrel.
6. The carpenter hung the cabinets (skillful, skillfully).
7. The food tasted (delicious, deliciously).
8. Our coach spoke (serious, seriously) to us about training.
9. Detective Howard looked around the room (curious, curiously).
10. We cleaned the room very (thorough, thoroughly).

D. *Good and Well* Write the correct modifier.

1. Marcy performed (good, well) in the meet.
2. Those uniforms look (good, well).
3. Dad and Mom dance (good, well) together.
4. Do you know Sandy very (good, well)?
5. Chuck plays the drums (good, well).
6. Sally is a (good, well) guitarist.
7. Ralph skates (well, good) enough for the Olympics.
8. That car handles curves (well, good).
9. Marta has a (good, well) chance for a scholarship.
10. The secret documents were protected (good, well).

MIXED REVIEW

Using Adverbs

A. Identifying adverbs   List all of the adverbs in the following sentences. Then write the word each modifies. Finally, write *how*, *when*, *where*, or *to what extent* to show what each adverb tells.

1. Yesterday I rode my bike to school.
2. This bike rides more smoothly than that one.
3. The fans cheered enthusiastically.
4. That is a very unusual painting.
5. Now we can start the motor.
6. The cadets slowly raised the flag.
7. The waves lapped gently against the shore.
8. Pat never eats between meals.
9. Monica skis well.
10. Roy walked cautiously across the rope bridge.

B. Using adverbs correctly   Five of the following sentences contain errors in the use of adverbs. Rewrite correctly any sentence that contains an error. If a sentence is already correct, write *Correct*.

1. It's quite cold in this room.
2. I feel worst than I did yesterday.
3. You swim so good.
4. Sasha planted the flowers evenly along the path.
5. Print your name neat in the boxes.
6. You can type more fast on an electric typewriter.
7. This soup tastes too salty.
8. I have looked everywhere for my ring.
9. Did you answer the question correct?
10. Josh left the meeting very early.

USING GRAMMAR IN WRITING
Using Adverbs

A. Below is a description of a scene. The writer could have made the description much more exciting. See if you can improve the paragraph. Add adverbs to make the scene come alive.

> I was walking along the ocean. My dog trotted beside me. The waves were rolling in. The sun was shining through the morning mist. I was barefoot, and the sand slid through my toes. I heard a noise behind me. Turning, I saw a horse galloping toward me. I stood and watched as it approached. A girl about my age was riding him. She waved as they passed. The horse tossed his mane. His rider spoke to him, and he broke into a canter. I watched until they disappeared in the mist. I wished the rider were me.

Underline each adverb that you add. Place at least three of the adverbs before the words they modify.

B. Imagine that you went to the last Olympic Games. Choose the sport that you most enjoyed watching. Write a letter to a friend describing the action. Make the action come alive for your friend by using lively and exciting adverbs. For instance:

> The gymnast flipped *gracefully* from the beam.
> The runners sprinted *quickly* from the starting blocks.

Using Prepositions and Conjunctions

Little words can do big jobs. In this section, you will learn about some little words that join other words in a sentence. These useful words are called **prepositions** and **conjunctions**. Without them, the meaning of many sentences would not be clear.

Part 1 What Are Prepositions?

Prepositions are words that show how one word is related to another word. Read these sentences. Notice how each shows a different relationship.

Jill's gloves are *on the table.*
Jill's gloves are *beside the table.*
Jill's gloves are *under the table.*

Ralph studied *before dinner.*
Ralph studied *during dinner.*
Ralph studied *after dinner.*

The book was written *for my father.*
The book was written *about my father.*
The book was written *by my father.*

In the first group of sentences, you can see that the words *on, beside,* and *under* show how *table* is related to *gloves. On, beside,* and *under* show location.

In the second group of sentences, *before, during,* and *after* show how *dinner* is related to *studied. Before, during,* and *after* show time.

In the third group of sentences *for, about,* and *by* show how *father* is related to *was written. For, about,* and *by* show other relationships.

All these words that show relationships are **prepositions.**

You can see that prepositions do not show relationships by themselves. They begin a **prepositional phrase,** a group of words that belong together but have no subject and verb. *On the table, before dinner,* and *for my father* are some examples of prepositional phrases in the sentences you've just read. What are the other prepositional phrases in these sentences?

A preposition is a word used with a noun or pronoun, called its object. A preposition shows how the noun or pronoun is related to some other word in the sentence.

A prepositional phrase consists of a preposition, its object, and any modifiers of the object.

Here is a list of words often used as prepositions. Most of these prepositions show relationships of place or time. Some show other relationships among people and things. Study these prepositions and see the relationship that each of them shows.

Words Often Used as Prepositions

about	before	down	of	throughout
above	behind	during	off	to
across	below	except	on	toward
after	beneath	for	onto	under
against	beside	from	out	until
along	between	in	outside	up
among	beyond	inside	over	upon
around	but (*except*)	into	past	with
at	by	like	since	within
		near	through	without

Exercise **Recognize prepositional phrases.**

Number your paper from 1 to 10. Write the prepositional phrase in each sentence.

1. The runners sprinted across town.
2. Marshall caught the long pass from Stevenson.
3. During practice Kendra sprained her ankle.
4. Westerns on TV often use stunt people.
5. Without sunlight the plants will die.
6. Where is the line of scrimmage?
7. We make ice cream at home.
8. At midnight the power failed.
9. Students gathered in the hallway.
10. Why did David get into trouble?

Using Prepositional Phrases

The group of words that includes a preposition and its object is a **prepositional phrase.** All the words that modify the object are also part of the phrase.

> Examples: We ate lunch *by a stream*.
> We ate lunch *by a clear blue stream*.

If a preposition has more than one object, all the parts of the object are included in the prepositional phrase.

> Example: He placed the flowers *in the dining room, the living room, and the front hall*.

Exercises   Find the prepositional phrases.

A.   Number your paper from 1 to 10. Write the prepositional phrases in each of the following sentences.

1. Have you ever played tennis on a grass court?
2. Up the spiral staircase is a secret room.
3. Leaves floated on the pond.
4. A tornado swept across the flat land.
5. The murderer confesses in the third act.
6. The stunt planes performed over the lake.
7. We followed a path through the dark forest.
8. Mike had a magician at his party.
9. Two swimmers leaped into the dark, icy waters.
10. I enjoy spaghetti with meatballs.

B.   Writing   On your paper, write a preposition to complete each sentence. Refer to the list on page 456.

1. The plane landed _____ 7:30 P.M.
2. We hiked _____ the lake.
3. A pencil fell _____ the desk.
4. The captain looked _____ us.

5. The ball landed _____ the stands.
6. Jill sang _____ me.
7. Our canary flew _____ the house.
8. Carolyn sat _____ Bob and me.
9. A posse rode _____ town.
10. Wait for me _____ the gate.

Part 2   Objects of Prepositions

Using Nouns as Objects of Prepositions

You have seen that nouns may be used as subjects or objects of verbs. You will now see how nouns are used as objects of prepositions. Read the following examples. The object of each preposition is in heavy type.

> The tomatoes are *from our* **garden.**
> A message arrived *for* **Gloria.**
> The team practiced *in the* **park.**

Exercise   Find nouns used as objects of prepositions.

Number your paper from 1 to 10. For each sentence, write the prepositional phrase. Then underline the noun used as the object of the preposition.

1. We drove through the scenic park.
2. Sandy repaired her bike with a wrench.
3. We added wood to the huge bonfire.
4. The fans crowded onto the bleachers.
5. In the lab is a real skeleton.
6. Stacey tried for the lead role.
7. After dinner, we took a drive.
8. We ran laps around the gym.
9. The train stopped past the station.
10. Before the final bell, the champ scored a knockout.

Using Pronouns as Objects of Prepositions

When a pronoun is used as the object of a preposition, its object form must be used. The object forms are these:

Object Pronouns

me	us
you	you
him, her, it	them

Examples: The package was sent *to* **us**.
Is there a ticket *for* **me**?

Using Pronouns in Compound Objects of Prepositions

Usually you make few mistakes in using the object form of a pronoun as the object of a preposition. But you may become confused when the object of a preposition is compound.

Simple Object	**Compound Object**
Study *with* **her**.	Study *with* **David** *and* **her**.
Wait *for* **me**.	Wait *for* **him** *and* **me**.

If you are not sure which form to use, first say the sentence with the pronoun alone following the preposition.

Example: We're working for Tom and (she, her).
We're working for *her*.
We're working for Tom and *her*.

Using *Between* and *Among*

The prepositions *between* and *among* are often confused. Use *between* to speak of two persons or things. Use *among* to speak of more than two. Read these examples:

Did you see the match **between** *Jeff and him*?
Wendy could not choose **between** *the two gifts*.

The money was divided **among** *Tess, Julia, and her.*
The bees flew **among** *the roses, the daisies, and the marigolds.*

Exercises   Use pronouns as objects of prepositions.

A.   Choose the correct pronoun from the two given in paren-theses. Write the complete prepositional phrase. Check your answer by reading the sentence to yourself.

Example: The villain shot at the sheriff and (he, him).

at the sheriff and him

1. There was a tie between Andy and (him, he).
2. Will you take a picture of Britt and (I, me)?
3. Mr. Hernandez ate lunch with Bonnie and (I, me).
4. Mom wrote notes for my sister and (me, I).
5. Prizes were awarded to Keith and (she, her).
6. Jan did magic tricks for (us, we).
7. A firecracker exploded near (they, them).
8. The chores were divided among Tina, Becky, and (she, her).
9. Beneath (we, us) the ground shook.
10. I wrapped presents for (him, he) and his brother.

B.   Follow the directions for Exercise A.

1. Sing along with (I, me).
2. A jeep bumped toward (they, them).
3. The librarian glared at Shawn and (us, we).
4. The curtain fell behind Danielle and (her, she).
5. Two snakes slithered past Bob and (me, I).
6. The bike beside Lowell and (her, she) is for sale.
7. Coach Wheatley motioned to Carlotta and (she, her).
8. The play-offs will be between Jefferson Junior High and (we, us).

9. There was a rivalry between Pete and (him, he).

10. Have you practiced the skit with Denise and (her, she)?

Part 3 Preposition or Adverb?

Several words that are used as prepositions are also used as adverbs.

Examples: The doctor is *in*.   (adverb)
The doctor is *in her office*.   (preposition)
The chickens ran *around*.   (adverb)
The chickens ran *around the yard*.   (preposition)

If you aren't sure whether a word is an adverb or a preposition, see how it is used. If it begins a phrase, it is probably a preposition. If it is used alone, it is probably an adverb.

Exercises   Find prepositions and adverbs.

A.   In each pair of sentences that follows, one word is used as an adverb and as a preposition. Number your paper from 1 to 10. After each number, write *a.* and *b.* After each letter, write *Preposition* or *Adverb* depending on which you find in that sentence.

Example: a. Look out!   b. Look out the window.
a. Adverb   b. Preposition

1. a. The collie rolled over.   b. That ball went over the fence.

2. a. Two children hid behind the bushes.   b. One hiker lagged behind.

3. a. Sharks waited below.   b. Below deck is the Captain's cabin.

4. a. We are going inside.   b. Have you been inside a cockpit?

5. a. Ramona's brother tagged along.   b. Ants crawled along the windowsill.
6. a. Our plane flew through the storm.   b. Our plans fell through.
7. a. Above, cranes hoisted steel beams.   b. Is the temperature above zero?
8. a. The cat jumped out the window.   b. The fire has gone out.
9. a. Let's ski down this slope.   b. That battery has run down.
10. a. A police car drove past.   b. Our guests stayed past midnight.

B. Follow the directions for Exercise A.

1. a. My pencil rolled under the desk.   b. The diver went under.
2. a. We built a fence around our ranch.   b. Larry went downtown and looked around.
3. a. What lies beyond our solar system?   b. Beyond, a rainbow appeared.
4. a. Terry finally gave in.   b. Jessica sings in the chorus.
5. a. The red paint is used up.   b. Can you climb up this rope?
6. a. An ambulance raced by.   b. The weaving is by Leslie.
7. a. The press gathered outside city hall.   b. We have gym class outside.
8. a. Beneath is a parking garage.   b. Beneath the rug is a trapdoor.
9. a. My report is about apes.   b. Tourists wandered about.
10. a. Carol waded along the shore.   b. A trail guide rode along.

Part 4 Prepositional Phrases as Modifiers

Prepositional phrases do the same work in a sentence as adjectives and adverbs.

A phrase that modifies a noun or pronoun is an adjective phrase. An adjective phrase tells *which one, what kind,* or *how many* about the noun or pronoun it modifies.

> Examples: The window *in the garage* is broken.   (which one)
>
> A few yards *of silk* are expensive.   (what kind)
>
> We saw statues *of several Presidents.*   (how many)

A phrase that modifies a verb is an adverb phrase. An adverb phrase tells *where, when,* or *how* about the verb.

> Examples: Jason lived *in Utah.*   (where)
>
> I had a cake *on my birthday.*   (when)
>
> The crowd ate *in shifts.*   (how)

Exercises   Find adjective and adverb phrases.

A.   Make three columns marked *Word Modified, Phrase,* and *Kind of Phrase.* For each prepositional phrase in the following sentences, fill in the information under the three columns. (You may want to review the kinds of questions that adjectives and adverbs answer.)

1. Kay and Lee rode on the tandem bike.
2. The actor rehearsed in costume.
3. The locker by the stairs is mine.
4. Tracey walked across the bridge.
5. Vanessa gave a speech at the meeting.
6. Men at Work is a group from Australia.
7. Is the first row of the theater full?

8. The book of ghost stories is scary.
9. The runner stopped at third base.
10. Cal crawled under the fence.

B. Follow the directions for Exercise A.

1. Ted opened a bag of peanuts.
2. The skaters jumped over barrels.
3. Ms. Connors drove to Minneapolis.
4. The movie portrays life on Mars.
5. We basked in the hot sun.
6. Enter through the side door, please.
7. Two fire trucks sped up the street.
8. The reward for our lost dog is ten dollars.
9. The girl on the bench is my sister.
10. Thousands of people attended the outdoor concert.

Part 5 Using Prepositional Phrases in the Right Places

Some prepositional phrases can be moved from one position in a sentence to another without changing the meaning of the sentence. Here is an example:

We visited Florida *during our vacation.*
During our vacation, we visited Florida.

To give your writing variety, begin a sentence with a prepositional phrase now and then. However, too many sentences that begin with prepositional phrases can become boring. Don't use phrases too often at the beginnings of sentences.

Some prepositional phrases do not move easily from one position in the sentence to another. The position of the phrase can make a great deal of difference in the meaning of the sentence.

Example: The plant *with the red flowers* is for sale.
The plant is for sale *with the red flowers*.

The second sentence is confusing. The prepositional phrase *with the red flowers* should not be moved away from *plant*.

Example: The letter is from Jane *on the table*.
The letter *on the table* is from Jane.

The second sentence puts the prepositional phrase where it belongs, next to *letter*. This makes the meaning much clearer.

A prepositional phrase should be placed either directly before or directly after the word it modifies.

Exercises   Use prepositional phrases correctly.

A.   The following sentences are confusing. By changing the position of one phrase in each sentence, you can make the meaning clear. Rewrite each sentence to make it clear.

1. The patient needs a blanket with a fever.
2. The book is yours in my locker.
3. Blue jeans are popular with straight legs.
4. Buy your tickets as soon as possible for the concert.
5. The handlebars rusted on my bike.
6. The album is by Steve Martin on that shelf.
7. Annie was praised for her work by the teacher.
8. The thief was caught after the robbery by the police.
9. The class played on Mr. Pauley a joke.
10. The train neared the station from Miami.

B.   Follow the directions for Exercise A.

1. Kate bought some slippers for her mom with tassels.
2. The pictures fell on the wall.
3. This album is good by Billy Joel.
4. Keith read about outer space during the summer.
5. The bird left the cage with yellow feathers.

6. My room is small but comfortable at home.
7. Tom slipped and sprained his ankle on the ice.
8. The poodle won a prize with the diamond collar.
9. The water won't drain in the sink.
10. The car had to pull over with a flat tire.

Part 6 What Are Conjunctions?

You have learned that prepositions show relationships between words in a sentence. Relationships are also shown by another kind of word: **conjunctions.**

How is the word *and* used in each of these sentences?

> *Tom* **and** *David* went to a movie.
> The plane *circled* **and** *landed.*
> Sarah *sketched the scene* **and** *painted it.*
> Monica hit a *double* **and** two *singles* in the game.

Do you see that in each sentence, *and* connects words or groups of words of the same type? In the first example, *and* joins two subjects. In the second example, *and* joins two verbs. In the third example, *and* joins two predicates. In the last example, *and* connects two direct objects. The word *and* is a conjunction.

A conjunction is a word that connects words or groups of words.

Two other conjunctions you use often are *but* and *or.* Like *and,* they may be used to connect sentence parts.

> **Andy** *or* **Gail** will bring the records.   (compound subject)
> The performers **danced** *and* **sang.**   (compound verb)
> The forward **shot for the basket** *but* **missed it.**   (compound predicate)
> Buy some **bread** *or* some **rolls.**   (compound direct object)
> The soup was **spicy** *but* **delicious.**   (compound predicate adjective)

The pianist performed **in London** *and* **New York.** (compound object of a preposition)

Exercises   Use conjunctions correctly.

A. Copy each sentence. Underline the words that are connected by a conjunction. Circle the conjunction.

Example: The Celtics survived that season and gradually improved.

The Celtics survived that season (and) gradually improved.

1. The pitcher and the catcher exchanged signals.
2. French and English are spoken in Canada.
3. This gadget dries and styles my hair.
4. Nancy or Gail will finish first.
5. Do you play soccer or football?
6. We ate bacon and eggs.
7. The students made clay pots and wooden boxes.
8. Running shorts and a T-shirt are our uniform.
9. The toboggan hit the wall and rolled over.
10. The cafeteria serves breakfast and lunch.

B. Writing Write sentences with compound subjects, predicates, or objects as the directions state. Use *and, but,* or *or.*

Example: Compound subject. Use a noun and a pronoun.
Kate and I made the salad.

1. Compound subject. Use two nouns.
2. Compound predicate.
3. Compound direct object. Use two nouns.
4. Compound subject. Use a noun and a pronoun.
5. Compound direct object. Use two pronouns.

ADDITIONAL EXERCISES

Using Prepositions and Conjunctions

A. Prepositional Phrases Write the prepositional phrases in these sentences. Circle each object of the preposition. Some sentences have more than one prepositional phrase.

1. Bonita is the last person in line.
2. Mary Pickford starred in silent films.
3. The library has rooms for meetings.
4. We donated a box of old toys to a charity.
5. Grace handed the tickets to Ken and me.
6. Put the bucket under the sink.
7. Jets flew over the desert.
8. Water spilled from the pitcher and onto the kitchen floor.
9. Morris stood between us.
10. The cat sat at the top of the stairs.

B. Pronouns as Objects of Prepositions Choose the correct pronoun from the two given in parentheses. Write the complete prepositional phrase.

1. Nancy baked bran muffins for (us, we).
2. Ted's dog ran beside (he, him).
3. Mr. Dale shouted to Craig and (I, me).
4. We divided the grapes among Barb, Jill and (I, me).
5. The audience applauded for Tom and (she, her).
6. The argument was between (we, us) and (they, them).
7. The chimpanzee threw bananas at Jan and (I, me).
8. The cost of the flowers was shared by (they, them) and (I, me).
9. Get the information from Pat or (he, him).
10. Curt waved to Scott and (they, them).

C. Using Prepositional Phrases Correctly

The following sentences are confusing. By changing the position of one phrase in each sentence, you can make the meaning clear. Rewrite each sentence to make it clear.

1. The clown fell down with the purple hair.
2. Your jacket is ripped with the hood.
3. From the drain Mark rescued the diamond necklace.
4. Tony made oatmeal cookies for dessert with raisins.
5. The photo is old and cracked in my wallet.
6. The man got on the train with sunglasses.
7. Ann put the invitations into the mailbox for the party.
8. Linda ordered spaghetti for lunch with clam sauce.
9. The car needs a tow truck with a flat tire.
10. With butter Henry ordered popcorn.

D. Conjunctions and Compound Sentence Parts

For each of the following sentences, write the compound sentence parts and their conjunction. Circle each conjunction.

1. The interviewer and her guest discussed movies.
2. We don't have any chalk or erasers.
3. The skater slipped and fell.
4. Football players should wear helmets and pads.
5. Dinosaurs roamed the land and swam in the sea.
6. Some people are intelligent but lazy.
7. Dr. Michaels spoke to the students and their parents.
8. The lion and its trainer delighted the crowd.
9. Sheila checked out the book and read it immediately.
10. Did you lose your gloves or your hat?

E. Preposition or Adverb?

Write *Adverb* or *Preposition* to tell what each word in italics is.

1. Don't turn *around*.
2. Fish swam *beneath* the ice.

3. Children *under* twelve are admitted free.
4. It is warm *inside* a sleeping bag.
5. The fog rolled *in*.
6. We turned the heat *up*.
7. The mirror fell *off* the wall.
8. Please turn the stereo *down*.
9. The Alaskan sled dog slept *outside*.
10. Mom spread ham salad *on* the bread.

F. Prepositional Phrases as Modifiers Write *Adjective* or *Adverb* to tell what each prepositional phrase is.

1. Randy dashed *toward home plate*.
2. Ginny drew a cartoon *about our baseball team*.
3. The first signs *of spring* are here.
4. A branch fell *into the pool*.
5. The wind whistled *through the trees*.
6. The waiter bumped *into the swinging door*.
7. The wicker chair *on the porch* is broken.
8. Our train sped *through a tunnel*.
9. Claudia took a picture *of the parade*.
10. This bowl *of ice cream* is melting.

MIXED REVIEW

Using Prepositions and Conjunctions

A. Identifying prepositions and adverbs Some of the following sentences contain prepositional phrases. Others contain adverbs. Number your paper from 1 to 10. Write the adverb or the prepositional phrase from each sentence. Circle the object of each preposition.

1. The bright stars shone above.
2. The squirrel scampered up the tree.
3. Paul looked up and saw the spacecraft.
4. The kites soared over the field.
5. Below is a garden apartment.
6. Please come in.
7. The crowd listened to the candidate's speech.
8. What resources lie beneath the sea?
9. Decorated floats passed by.
10. The campers slept in pup tents.

B. Using prepositional phrases as modifiers Rewrite the following sentences, adding the prepositional phrases shown in parentheses. Be careful to put the phrase in the correct place. After each sentence, write whether the prepositional phrase is used as an *Adverb* or *Adjective* phrase.

1. Atlanta is the largest city. (in Georgia)
2. The study is called astronomy. (of the stars)
3. Henry took notes. (during the lecture)
4. We can't decide. (without a vote)
5. The flowers are peonies. (in that garden)
6. The clothes are mostly hand-me-downs. (in this closet)
7. The archeologists searched for bits of pottery. (through the ruins)
8. The bread is usually fresh. (from that bakery)

9. The president wrote the editorial. (of the school board)
10. Temperatures are cooler. (in the morning)

C.   Using conjunctions and compound sentence parts
Write sentences using compound sentence parts according to the directions.

1. Compound direct object. Use a noun and a pronoun.
2. Compound subject. Use two pronouns.
3. Compound predicate.
4. Compound subject. Use two nouns.
5. Compound predicate adjective.
6. Compound adverb.
7. Compound direct object. Use two nouns.
8. Compound subject. Use a noun and a pronoun.
9. Compound verb.
10. Compound object of a preposition. Use two nouns.

USING GRAMMAR IN WRITING
Using Prepositions and Conjunctions

A. Have you ever thought it would be fun to be a detective? Imagine that you are a famous private eye. Your abilities to find missing people and stolen property are well known. You have just completed another successful case. Write a report about what you were looking for. Tell how and where you searched, and where you finally found the missing object. Use several of these prepositions in your reports.

above	below	down	in	near
against	beneath	over	down	of
among	beside	through	inside	off
around	between	under	into	onto
behind	by	upon	to	outside

B. Circuses are exciting, especially the big cats' show. It's thrilling to watch the lions, tigers, leopards, and panthers respond to their trainer's commands. Write a paragraph describing this exciting show. Include prepositional phrases used as modifiers.

C. Most of us resemble someone in our family. Maybe we have an uncle's nose. Perhaps we have our father's great sense of humor. Maybe our mother's interest in science has rubbed off on us. Whom do you think you are most similar to in your family? How are you alike? Write a paragraph telling how you resemble a member of your family. Use the conjunctions *and, but,* or *or* to connect subjects, objects, verbs, and predicates.

Using the Parts of Speech

Part 1 The Parts of Speech

In previous sections, you have become familiar with these groups of words:

nouns	verbs	adverbs	conjunctions
pronouns	adjectives	prepositions	

You have been learning to recognize words in each group and to use them correctly. These seven groups of words are called the **parts of speech.**

The eighth part of speech is the **interjection.** In this section, you will learn about interjections. You will also review all eight parts of speech.

What Are Interjections?

In addition to the seven important groups of words you have studied, there is also a group of words called interjections.

An interjection is a word or short group of words used to express strong feeling. It may express surprise, joy, anger, or sadness. An interjection is often followed by an exclamation mark (!).

Look at these examples of interjections:

> *Oh no!* The fire has gone out.
> *Hooray!*
> *Wonderful!*
> *Quick!* Get a bandage.

Now you have learned about all eight parts of speech.

The Parts of Speech			
nouns	verbs	adverbs	conjunctions
pronouns	adjectives	prepositions	interjections

A word fits into one of these groups because of the way it is used in a sentence.

Exercises Recognize the parts of speech.

A. Number your paper from 1 to 10. Read each sentence. Then write the underlined word. Beside each word, write what part of speech it is.

1. Jack speaks very slowly.
2. The rocket zoomed upward.
3. The parade came down Maple Avenue.
4. An usher walked down the aisle.
5. The batter has two strikes.
6. Fireworks lit the sky.
7. Look! It's Superman!

8. Wow! That water is cold.
9. Will you write to me?
10. My dogs begs and shakes hands.

B. Follow the directions for Exercise A.

1. The Scouts learned first aid and water safety.
2. Madame Solga looked into her very large crystal ball.
3. Kirsten has a bank account.
4. Careful! Those rocks are loose.
5. These pictures are fuzzy.
6. We always go to Grandma's house on holidays.
7. The group ate lunch near the fountain.
8. They tracked the plane on radar.
9. Bill worries too much.
10. The hikers sang folksongs as they walked.

Part 2 Using Words as Different Parts of Speech

In order to tell what part of speech a word is you must see how the word is used in a sentence. Often, one word can be used as different parts of speech.

In **Section 10,** you learned that certain words can be used as an adverb or a preposition. For example, read this pair of sentences:

Hang *on*.
(In this sentence, *on* is an adverb.)

My watch is *on* the table.
(Here, *on* is a preposition.)

Other words may be used as different parts of speech. Here are several more examples for you to study.

We left the dishes in the *sink*.

(In this sentence, *sink* is used as a noun.)

I can't float; I *sink*.

(Here, *sink* is used as a verb.)

Plant these seeds in the garden.

(In this sentence, *plant* is used as a verb.)

This *plant* is from the desert.

(In this sentence, *plant* is used as a noun.)

We gave the flowers some *plant* food.

(Here, *plant* is used as an adjective.)

Jack doesn't feel *well*.

(Here, *well* is used as an adjective.)

Sandy dances *well*.

(In this sentence, *well* is an adverb.)

There is only one sure way to decide what part of speech a word is. That way is to see how the word is used in a sentence.

Exercises   Recognize the parts of speech.

A. In each pair of sentences that follows, one word is used as two different parts of speech. Number your paper from 1 to 10. After each number, write *a*. and *b*. After each letter, write the word that appears in italics. Tell how it is used. It may be a *noun*, *verb*, *adjective*, *adverb*, or *preposition*.

Example: a. Open a *can* of beans.   b. My cousins *can* tomatoes.

a. can, **noun**   b. can, **verb**

1. a. Turn off the *light*, please.   b. Jeff, *light* the candles.
2. a. I brought the dog *in*.   b. The horse is *in* the stable.
3. a. There are two new *houses* in our neighborhood.
   b. The university *houses* football players in this dormitory.

4. a. Vince went *outside* for a walk.   b. We saw several deer *outside* the cabin.

5. a. Ms. Rosen made a *pencil* drawing of the park.
   b. I sharpened my *pencil*.

6. a. Carla put the umbrella *over* the table.   b. Those thunderclouds will soon blow *over*.

7. a. My brother usually *drives* to work.   b. Nellie enjoys *drives* in the country.

8. a. The class president *ended* the meeting.   b. This *end* of the couch is dirty.

9. a. A soprano sings *high* notes.   b. The team's fortunes have reached a new *high*.

10. a. Look *up*!   b. Alice rode her horse *up* the hill.

B. Follow the directions for Exercise A.

1. a. The Little League game drew a big *crowd*.
   b. Some people *crowd* into elevators.

2. a. There are diamonds in that *crown*.   b. England's *crown* jewels are extremely valuable.

3. a. Please *hand* me my coat.   b. Do these gloves fit your *hands*?

4. a. Have you gone *down* the giant slide?   b. Isabella fell *down*.

5. a. When it started to rain, we went *below*.   b. The captain is *below* deck.

6. a. The king had a *fool* to entertain him.   b. Magicians often *fool* the audience.

7. a. Gather *around*!   b. Ricky tied tape *around* the handle of the bat.

8. a. This book lists many sports' *records*.   b. She *records* her songs on tape.

9. a. Some workers *strike* for more pay.   b. The union will call a *strike* tomorrow.

10. a. *Lower* the picture an inch or two.   b. The *lower* shelves of this bookcase need paint.

ADDITIONAL EXERCISES

The Parts of Speech

A. Parts of Speech   Read each sentence. Write the word in italics. Then write what part of speech that word is.

1. *She* has a pet snake.
2. *Oops*! I spilled the paint all over the garage floor.
3. A luscious *smell* filled the kitchen.
4. Don *read* three books last week.
5. Are you going to the *rock* concert?
6. Ed and Steve arm-wrestled *on* the table.
7. *Ingrid* speaks three languages.
8. What is a *platypus*?
9. Ginger wore a mask *and* disguised her voice during the play.
10. Barry looked *hungrily* at the barbequed chicken.
11. Chlorine *kills* germs in a swimming pool.
12. *Everyone* enjoyed the movie.
13. Did you *or* Jeff pay that library fine?
14. *Stop*! You're too close to the edge.
15. *Soon* Mom will have a realtor's license.
16. Museums display great works of *art*.
17. Jonathan tripped *over* the hose.
18. The new *center* shows old films.
19. Suddenly the fish flipped *over*.
20. We walked *through* the high school building.
21. That salad dressing is *tangy*.
22. Dad made a huge pot of *vegetable* soup.
23. Mr. Murphy *walks* his dog every morning.
24. The hostess gave *them* menus.
25. The temperature is *extremely* cold in the Arctic.

MIXED REVIEW

Using The Parts Of Speech

Identifying the parts of speech Number your paper from 1 to 20. Write the underlined words in the following paragraph. Then write the part of speech that each word is used as.

You may think that gorillas are fierce, but you are wrong. Gorillas are quiet, peaceful animals. They live in groups of two to thirty in the rain forests of east and west central Africa. Gorillas eat bark, leaves, and fruit. Only gorillas that live in zoos eat meat. Most of the first gorillas kept in zoos died quickly. Many people think that these gorillas died of loneliness. Gorillas are friendly, and they like to be with other gorillas. That is why in many zoos today you will not see a gorilla alone in a cage. Instead, you will see gorillas sharing a large area with other members of their "family."

USING GRAMMAR IN WRITING
Using the Parts of Speech

A. Do you know what Tom Sawyer was most famous for? He was supposed to paint his Aunt Polly's fence. He started the job, but he hated doing it. As his friends stopped by, he pretended he was having great fun. In this way he got his friends to paint the fence.

Is there some chore you hate doing? Try Tom Sawyer's approach. Make the chore seem like fun to someone else. If you are clever enough, maybe you can convince someone else to do the chore for you. Write an ad for the Help Wanted section of your local newspaper.

Include at least one example of each part of speech. Then make a list with eight columns. Label each column with the name of a different part of speech. Write one or two words from your ad in each column.

B. Think about the first time you were on ice skates, roller skates, a skateboard, or a two-wheel bicycle. Can you remember what it was like? In a paragraph, describe your first experience. Use at least six of the words below in your paragraph. Try to use some of the words twice, as different parts of speech. Here's an example.

Even though I slammed on my **brakes** [noun], I couldn't **brake** [verb] fast enough.

skate	pedal	try	struggle	fall	hit
run	jump	break	slip	hurt	bruise

CUMULATIVE REVIEW
The Parts of Speech

A. Identifying parts of speech   There are twenty underlined words in the following paragraph. Decide what part of speech each word is used as. Number your paper from 1 to 20. Write *Noun, Verb, Pronoun, Adjective, Adverb, Preposition,* or *Conjunction* for each word. Be sure to notice *how* the word is used in the sentence.

There is a new sports event for <u>athletes</u> who have [1] mastered <u>the</u> challenge <u>of</u> marathon running. It [2] [3] is <u>called</u> the triathlon. A <u>triathlon</u> consists of <u>three</u> [4] [5] [6] events: swimming, bicycling, and running. <u>You</u> need [7] <u>endurance</u> to compete in a triathlon. For example, <u>in</u> [8] [9] the Ironman Triathlon, you swim for 2.4 <u>miles</u>, <u>bicycle</u> [10] [11] for 112 miles, and <u>then</u> run 26.2 miles. Triathletes [12] have <u>extraordinary</u> training sessions. Dave Scott, a [13] winner of the Ironman, starts his daily training by running ten to fifteen miles. Then <u>he</u> bikes seventy-five [14] miles and swims three miles. Triathletes <u>feel</u> that this [15] <u>extremely</u> demanding sport pays off for <u>them</u>. Their [16] [17] bodies are strong and <u>healthy</u>, <u>and</u> their spirits soar [18] [19] when they <u>successfully</u> complete a race. [20]

Each of the following sentences contains an underlined word. Decide how that word is used. Number your paper from 1 to 15. Write *Subject, Verb, Direct Object, Indirect Object, Object of the Preposition, Predicate Noun,* or *Predicate Adjective* to show what each word is.

1. Platinum is a precious <u>metal</u>.
2. A strong wind blew across the <u>valley</u>.
3. Has the <u>alarm</u> rung yet?
4. The earthquake <u>was centered</u> in Idaho.
5. Honolulu was once a whaling <u>port</u>.
6. The audience gave the <u>cast</u> of the play a standing ovation.
7. The farmer <u>plowed</u> the field.
8. Coach White gave <u>him</u> the game football.
9. Carol's chili tastes <u>spicy</u>.
10. In the kitchen, the <u>chef</u> prepared the dinner.
11. Give the <u>conductor</u> your train ticket.
12. Dirk found the <u>receipt</u> at the bottom of the bag.
13. The flowers in those pots are <u>geraniums</u>.
14. Mr. Bucci <u>plastered</u> the ceiling.
15. Laurie seems <u>upset</u> about something.

Making Subjects and Verbs Agree

Read these sentences.

A clerk sorts the mail.
Two clerks sort the mail.
Many clerks sorts the mail.

In two of the above sentences, the subject and verb agree. In other words, they match. In one sentence the subject and verb do not agree. Which sentence sounds wrong to you?

If you said the third sentence, you are correct. Its subject (*clerks*) and verb (*sorts*) do not agree. The result is like trying to jam together two puzzle pieces that don't belong together.

In this section, you will learn how to make subjects and verbs agree.

Part 1 Rules for Making the Subject and Verb Agree

If a noun names one person, place, or thing, it is **singular.** If a noun names more than one person, place, or thing, it is **plural.**

boy	field	coin
boys	fields	coins

Verbs, too, have singular and plural forms. In a sentence, the verb must always agree in number with its subject. *Number* means that a word is singular or plural.

Read these examples:

Singular	**Plural**
Ruth **sings** in the next act.	The girls **sing** this part.
My mother **runs** daily.	We **run** two miles together.
That boy **speaks** German.	Those boys **speak** Spanish.

When you talk about one girl, you say she *sings.* When you talk about more than one girl, you say the girls *sing.* One person *runs,* but many people *run.* One boy *speaks,* but many boys *speak.*

The *s* at the end of a verb, as in *sings, runs,* and *speaks,* shows that the verb is singular. It is used with a singular noun. In the examples, the singular nouns *Ruth, mother,* and *boy* are the subjects. When the subject is plural, the verb is plural. *Girls, we,* and *boys* are plural. The *s* on the verb is dropped.

Remember these rules:

1. If the subject is **singular,** use the singular form of the verb.
2. If the subject is **plural,** use the plural form of the verb.

Prepositional Phrases After the Subject

Be careful with prepositional phrases that come between the subject and the verb. Do not confuse the subject of the verb with the object of the preposition.

Examples: The members of the band (practices, practice) on Friday.

> Who practices? *members* (subject)
> *Of the band* is a prepositional phrase describing *members*.

The verb must agree with the subject.

The *members* of the band *practice* on Friday.

A pair of tickets (were, was) lost.

> What was lost? *pair* (subject)
> *Of tickets* is a prepositional phrase describing *pair*.

The verb must agree with the subject.

A *pair* of tickets *was* lost.

Exercises   Recognize singular and plural forms.

A.   On your paper, write the subjects listed below. After each subject, write *Singular* or *Plural* to tell whether it will take the singular or the plural form of the verb.

1. the apples
2. a carnival
3. Shelia
4. the wristwatch
5. autumn leaves
6. the mice
7. the passengers
8. a box
9. the men
10. wild geese

B.   Number your paper from 1 to 10. Find the subject and the verb in each sentence below. Write the subject and verb and tell whether they are singular or plural.

> Example: The dogs in the yard were barking at us.
> dogs, were barking (plural)

1. A set of books is missing.
2. Angela likes the seat near the window.
3. The cheese in these sandwiches is delicious.

4. We are using clay in this art project.
5. Woody plays shortstop or second base.
6. Students in the hall are auditioning for the show.
7. I walk two miles to school.
8. The brakes on this bike need adjustment.
9. The high winds have blown that trailer over.
10. A long-distance phone call costs less on weekends.

Special Forms of Certain Verbs

A few verbs have special forms that you should keep in mind.

Is, Was, Are, Were. The verb form *is* and *was* are singular. The forms *are* and *were* are plural.

> Singular: Carlos *is* here.   Carlos *was* here.
> Plural: The Smiths *are* here.   The Smiths *were* here.

Has, Have. The verb form *has* is singular. The form *have* is plural.

> Singular: Martha *has* the answer.
> Plural: They *have* the answer.

Does, Do. The verb form *does* is singular. The form *do* is plural.

> Singular: Dennis *does* the laundry.
> Plural: They *do* the laundry.

Exercises   **Make the verb agree with the subject.**

A.   Number your paper from 1 to 10. Write the correct verb from the two given in parentheses. Check your answer by reading the sentence to yourself.

1. My cousin (has, have) been singing in the choir.
2. Bob's teeth (has, have) never had a cavity.
3. The locker rooms (is, are) newly painted.
4. Two ski poles (was, were) standing in the drift.

5. At high tide, those boats (is, are) floating on the water.
6. The girls (was, were) diving for oysters.
7. How many people (is, are) in your family?
8. Tony's swollen knee (is, are) getting better.
9. Rico (doesn't, don't) waste time.
10. The two stores on Central Street (is, are) closed.

B. Follow the directions for Exercise A.

1. Our bus (has, have) a flat tire.
2. My feet (is, are) too big for these shoes.
3. (Is, Are) the Boy Scouts in the parade?
4. The noises in this cave (has, have) weird echoes.
5. Some friends of my sister (is, are) coming for dinner.
6. (Is, Are) the towels dry?
7. All along the street (was, were) Japanese lanterns.
8. (Does, Do) the canary ever sing?
9. The gears on this bike (is, are) not working properly.
10. In *Peter Pan,* all the children (is, are) lost.

Part 2 Special Problems with Subjects

Sometimes making subjects and verbs agree is difficult. Some subjects are tricky to use. In this part, you will be learning to use these tricky subjects with the correct verbs.

Certain Pronouns

The following words are singular. Use each with a singular verb form.

each	either	everyone	anyone
one	neither	everybody	nobody

Read these examples several times until they sound correct and natural to you.

Each of the boats *has* a motor.
One of the stories *was* scary.
Is either of the answers right?
Neither of the dogs *was* friendly.
Everyone helps with the dishes.
Everybody is thirsty.
Is anyone there?
Nobody was home.

Watch out for these pronouns, especially when they are used as subjects and are followed by a prepositional phrase. If the object of the preposition is plural, don't make the mistake of using a plural verb form.

Example: Neither of the chairs (was, were) comfortable.

What is the complete subject? *Neither of the chairs*
What is the prepositional phrase? *of the chairs*
What is the subject? *Neither*
Neither is singular, so the verb must be singular.

Neither of the chairs *was* comfortable.

Exercises   Make the verb agree with the subject.

A.   Copy these sentences, leaving a space for the verb. Circle the prepositional phrase that follows the subject. Then choose the right form of the verb and write it. Check your answer by reading the sentence to yourself.

Example: Neither of the bolts (fit, fits).
Neither (of the bolts) fits.

1. Nobody in our class (swim, swims) in this race.
2. One of the propellers (was, were) broken.
3. Each of you girls (is, are) allowed five minutes for your speech.
4. Neither of the cats (has, have) been fed.

5. One of the faucets (are, is) leaking.
6. Each of the uniforms (has, have) the school's name on it.
7. Neither of the teams (has, have) a coach.
8. Either of those games (is, are) easy.
9. Each of the displays (is, are) of a different country.
10. (Has, Have) either of you brought the hammock?

B. Follow the directions for Exercise A.

1. Either of the digital clocks (tell, tells) perfect time.
2. Everybody from both classes (was, were) invited.
3. One of my keys (are, is) missing.
4. Everybody in the stands (yell, yells) loudly.
5. Each of the vendors (sell, sells) hot dogs.
6. One of my shoes (is, are) untied.
7. (Do, Does) anyone on the bus have change?
8. Nobody with braces (eats, eat) taffy apples.
9. Neither of the pitchers (throw, throws) curve balls.
10. Each of those elephants (weighs, weigh) six tons.

There Is, Here Is, Where Is

Many sentences begin with *There, Here,* or *Where.* These words are never subjects. In sentences beginning with these words, the subject usually comes after the verb.

Before you can choose the right verb form, you have to know what the subject is. You have to know whether it is singular or plural.

There are your books.   (*Books* is the subject; the plural form *are* is correct.)

Here is the path.   (*Path* is the subject; the singular form *is* is correct.)

Where do the pencils belong?   (*Pencils* is the subject; the plural form *do belong* is correct.)

A.   Write the correct form of the verb.

1. Here (is, are) four more pieces for the puzzle.
2. Where (are, is) that cushion with the stripes?
3. There (was, were) no salt in the salt shaker.
4. Where (was, were) you waiting?
5. Where (is, are) everybody?
6. Where (does, do) this road go?
7. Here (is, are) your pencils.
8. There (was, were) many reasons for the President's action.
9. Here (is, are) one of the oars.
10. Where (does, do) the books on the table belong?

B.   Follow the directions for Exercise A.

1. Where (is, are) the entrances to the mall?
2. Here (is, are) the prettiest wildflowers.
3. There (is, are) five good shows on TV.
4. Here (is, are) the dog food.
5. Where (has, have) the time gone?
6. There (was, were) a penalty on that play.
7. Here (is, are) two of my scrapbooks.
8. (Has, Have) there been any problems?
9. Where (does, do) the sightseeing helicopters land?
10. There (is, are) a light on each video camera.

Compound Subjects

When the parts of a compound subject are joined by the conjunction *and,* use the plural form of the verb.

> The mayor and the police chief **were** in the parade.
> **Are** your hat and gloves in your locker?

When the parts are joined by *or*, *either—or*, or *neither—nor*, use the form of the verb that agrees with the nearer subject.

> Carol or *Janet* **is singing**.
> Neither Mathew nor his *brothers* **are** here.
> Either six pencils or one *pen* **costs** a dollar.

Exercises   Use the right verb form.

A.   Number your paper from 1 to 10. Write the correct form of the verb from the two given in parentheses. If a conjunction with *or* or *nor* is used in the subject, also write the part of the compound subject nearer the verb.

> Example: Neither my dog nor my cats (has, have) been fed.
>
> cats, have

1. Gerry and her teammates (was, were) there for the championship game.
2. Maria and her mother (grows, grow) fresh herbs in their garden.
3. Ted and Victoria (has, have) new cameras.
4. Either Mr. Lind or his children (walks, walk) the dog every afternoon.
5. Neither the girls nor the boys (has, have) the right answer.
6. Duchess and her pups (sleeps, sleep) on the back porch.
7. Neither Mary nor I (like, likes) fried foods.
8. The swimmers and their coach (practices, practice) every day.
9. Neither the lights nor the phone (works, work) since the wind storm.
10. Either Vincent or the other orchestra members (is, are) setting up the chairs.

B. Follow the directions for Exercise A.

1. Superman or Spiderman (is, are) on the case.
2. Red and orange (is, are) warm colors.
3. Switzerland and Italy (shares, share) a border.
4. Neither snow nor cold (keeps, keep) our team from practicing.
5. Pancakes or waffles (is, are) tasty for breakfast.
6. Either skates or a skateboard (goes, go) fast.
7. Gary and Wayne (has, have) the flu.
8. Either Lynn or her sisters (has, have) the comic book.
9. Neither the clocks nor my watch (is, are) right.
10. Either chimes or a buzzer (signals, signal) the guard.

Using *I*

Although *I* stands for a single person, it does not usually take a singular verb form. The only singular verb forms used with it are *am* and *was*.

> I *am* the goalie.   I *was* here yesterday.

Otherwise, the verb form used with *I* is the same as the plural form.

> I *do* my work.   I *live* on the next block.
> I *have* a cold.   I *throw* a good fastball.

Using *You*

The word *you* can stand for one person or for several persons. It may be either singular or plural. Whether it is singular or plural, always use the plural verb form with the pronoun *you*.

> You **were** the only *person* with a bike.
> You **were** the only *students* in the room.

Exercises   Make the verb agree with the subject.

A. Write the correct verb from the two given in parentheses. Check your answer by reading the sentence to yourself.

1. You (was, were) ready, weren't you?
2. I (am, are) going for a walk.
3. In that closet (is, are) the tools.
4. With your new bike, you (rides, ride) faster than before.
5. Among the library aides, I (is, am) the youngest.
6. You (is, are) welcome at the party.
7. (Has, Have) you brought in the flag?
8. I (am, is) the best speller in the class.
9. (Was, Were) you afraid?
10. My mother and I (am, are) going to the supermarket.

B. Follow the directions for Exercise A.

1. (Was, Were) you going to the library?
2. I (were, was) the only swimmer in the pool.
3. (Does, Do) you know sign language?
4. I (am, is, are) afraid of heights.
5. I (knows, know) three chords on the guitar.
6. You (has, have) a great record collection.
7. I (is, am) learning a new song on the guitar.
8. You (was, were) in the play.
9. I (was, were) a caddy last summer.
10. At camp you (was, were) our best counselor.

ADDITIONAL EXERCISES

Making Subjects and Verbs Agree

A. Subject and Verb Agreement Write the correct form of the verb for each sentence.

1. Rockets (blasts, blast) off at Cape Canaveral.
2. A police officer (directs, direct) traffic here.
3. One sport of the Canadians (is, are) curling.
4. The dogs at the dog pound (looks, look) cute.
5. The members of the team (practice, practices) here.
6. Those horses (is, are) thoroughbreds.
7. Jane (has, have) a cast on her leg.
8. My brothers (does, do) their chores after school.
9. The branches on that tree (needs, need) trimming.
10. Those geese (honk, honks) at the cows.

B. Special Problems with Subjects Write the correct form of the verb for each sentence.

1. Neither of these buses (stops, stop) near home.
2. Everyone in the fields (is, are) harvesting crops.
3. Where (does, do) the subway line start?
4. There (is, are) raccoons in the attic.
5. Samantha and Cara (is, are) sunburned.
6. Either pants or a skirt (is, are) appropriate.
7. Neither the luggage nor the passengers (has, have) arrived.
8. I (sees, see) the North Star.
9. You (was, were) the only runner on the track.
10. I (am, is, are) expecting a phone call.

MIXED REVIEW

Making Subjects And Verbs Agree

A. Using the correct verb Write the correct verb from those given in parentheses.

1. Gail (walk, walks) to the library every Saturday morning.
2. A pint of blueberries (cost, costs) one dollar.
3. The Browers (is, are) our new neighbors.
4. One of the Twin Cities (is, are) Minneapolis.
5. Mitch's grades in math (have, has) improved this year.
6. Florida's warm climate (attract, attracts) many winter vacationers.
7. The list of winners (was, were) printed in the paper.
8. Parts of the puzzle (was, were) hard to do.
9. Jenny (practice, practices) the flute every afternoon.
10. Anita's parents (was, were) born in Puerto Rico.

B. Making subjects and verbs agree Five of the following sentences contain errors in subject-verb agreement. Find and rewrite correctly the sentences that do. If a sentence is already correct, write *Correct*.

1. Where is the best seats in the stadium?
2. Are these your books?
3. Neither of the actors were prepared for the rehearsal.
4. I swim on the varsity team.
5. Everyone in our class have completed the assignment.
6. You was the best candidate for the job.
7. Young foxes and young bears are called cubs.
8. Nobody wants an argument.
9. Bees and wasps builds nests quickly.
10. Here is the money for the tickets.

USING GRAMMAR IN WRITING
Making Subjects and Verbs Agree

A. Clowns usually have enormous smiles painted on their faces. They look and act like the happiest people on earth. It is often said that clowns "laugh on the outside and cry on the inside."

Write two paragraphs. In the first one, describe a clown's appearances and actions. In the second paragraph, pretend you are the clown. Begin your paragraph with, "No one really knows what is behind my painted smile."

Be sure all verbs agree with their subjects. Be especially careful to use the correct forms of these verbs:

> is, was, were, are
> has, have
> does, do

B. Think of two popular performers. Both people should perform in the same general field. In other words, don't pick one rock star and one comedian. Now think of the ways that the two performers are similar. Also think about how they are different. Write about their similarities and differences. Use some of the following words as subjects. Be sure that each verb agrees with its subject.

each	she/he	everyone
both	one	the other
neither	nobody	they
either	no one	anybody

At least one sentence should have a compound subject.

CUMULATIVE REVIEW
Usage

A. Choosing the correct word Write the correct word from the two given in parentheses.

1. Aaron can't have (no, any) more pizza.
2. Where did you get (them, those) socks?
3. (Its, It's) hot and humid in Florida during the summer.
4. (Them, Those) girls shouldn't (lay, lie) in the sun so long.
5. Mr. Schmitt looks (good, well) with a beard.
6. (May, Can) I (rise, raise) the curtain now?
7. Mr. Revere plays the flute quite (good, well).
8. Don't (let, leave) the dog (lay, lie) on the new couch.
9. (Sit, Set) the globe on the round table.
10. The dog scratched behind (its, it's) ear.
11. Marty doesn't feel (good, well) after eating all those tacos.
12. (Their, They're) new uniforms looked (good, well).
13. Ivan will (learn, teach) us the Russian alphabet.
14. (Its, It's) difficult to (lie, lay) carpeting.
15. Ellen feels (bad, badly) about breaking (them, those) plates.
16. (This, These) kind of apple makes a good pie.
17. We (set, sat) on the grass and ate our lunch.
18. Neither of the television sets (was, were) working.
19. Will you (leave, let) me use the electric drill?
20. (Those, Them) boys swam (good, well) at the meet.
21. Choose (among, between) the four books on the shelf.
22. David and Regina went to the farmers' market with Katie and (me, I).

23. She drove the car (slowly, slow), and then she came to a stop.
24. Marc felt (really, real) tired after the aerobic class.
25. Are you the (older, oldest) in your family?

B. Using words correctly   Twenty words are underlined in the following paragraph. Ten of the underlined words contain errors in the use of verbs, nouns, pronouns, adverbs, and adjectives. Ten of the words are correct. Proofread the paragraph. Rewrite it, correcting the errors.

Painting our room was a bigger job than I had planned on. My sister Gayle hadn't never painted before, which was a problem. When I brought out all the equipment, she said, "What are all them things for?" I explained to she the purposes of all the tool. I then asked Gayle to start painting the trim. She dripped paint bad all over the floor. "She don't know what she's doing!" I thought, and I quick showed her how to wipe the edge of the brush off. It was quite a job to be patient with her. When I started using the roller, she said, "Them things are funner to use than paint brushes. Each of us should have their turn using the roller." Two days and many spills and arguments later, we finished the room. Next time I'll do it myself!

Using Compound Sentences

Part 1 A Review of the Sentence

In this book you have studied different kinds of sentences. Most of them have been simple sentences. In this section you will learn about another kind of sentence called the **compound sentence**.

Before studying the compound sentence, you should review what you know about sentences. You know that a sentence has two basic parts, a subject and a predicate.

Subject	Predicate
The players	rested.
The players	are weary.
Six weary players	rested quietly.
Six weary players	rested in the locker room.

You know that the **subject** of a sentence names the person or thing the sentence is about. The **predicate** tells what *is* or what *happens*.

Compound Parts of the Sentence

You also know that all parts of the sentence may be **compound.** That is, all the parts of the sentence may have more than one part. Look at these examples.

Compound Subject:
The *President* and the *Prime Minister* met.

Compound Verb:
Dave Cowens *played* and *coached.*

Compound Predicate:
The firefighters *heard the alarm* and *dashed to the trucks.*

A Definition of the Sentence

You can see that each of these sentences expresses one main idea. The sentences you have just read, like all of those you have been studying, are called **simple sentences.**

Now you are ready for a definition of the simple sentence.

A simple sentence contains only one subject and predicate.

Both the subject and the predicate may be compound.

A. Write the simple subject and verb in each simple sentence. Draw a vertical line between them. (Remember to look for compound sentence parts.)

Example: Chris and Bill cooked dinner.

Chris, Bill | cooked

1. Mom and Julie painted the porch.
2. Meg's fingers and toes are frostbitten.
3. Our class uses the metric system.
4. Did the Raiders score a field goal?
5. The troops arrived by ship.
6. West High School has three thousand students.
7. We learned and practiced first aid.
8. Nancy and Rebecca took a shortcut.
9. Greg is practicing the clarinet.
10. The cat clawed and chewed our furniture.

B. Follow the directions for Exercise A.

1. I like this album and play it often.
2. The store and the theater are closed for the summer.
3. A new Italian restaurant opened downtown.
4. Some people need very little sleep.
5. Fans filled the ballpark and cheered wildly.
6. Ms. Lee poured the acid and did the experiment.
7. Mr. Homer writes in an elegant script.
8. The magician and his assistant rehearsed backstage.
9. In Iowa, high winds and heavy rain destroyed the crop.
10. Jill bought an old bike and fixed it herself.

C. Writing Write five simple sentences. Underline the simple subject and verb in each sentence. Use capital letters and correct punctuation.

Part 2 What Are Compound Sentences?

Sometimes two sentences are so closely related in thought that you join them together. Then you have a different kind of sentence. You have a sentence that has more than one subject and more than one predicate. You have a sentence with more than one main idea. This is called a **compound sentence.** Read these examples:

Snow fell all night, **and** it buried everything.
Beth likes all sports, **but** she enjoys tennis the most.
Study this map of the city, **or** you will get lost.

Now look at the parts of these compound sentences:

Subject	Verb	Conjunction	Subject	Verb
Snow	fell	and	it	buried
Beth	likes	but	she	enjoys
(*you*)	Study	or	you	will get

A compound sentence consists of two or more simple sentences joined together. Usually a conjunction joins the parts.

When To Use Compound Sentences

When would you want to use a compound sentence? Why not just write simple sentences? You will know why as soon as you read this paragraph.

It was a hot, humid day. The sky was gray. We were looking out the window. We saw something blurry. It was funnel-shaped. It looked cloudy. It seemed to be moving toward us. Finally, we realized what it was. We moved away from the window. It was a tornado coming our way.

You can see that a long series of short sentences is dull and choppy. Combined into compound sentences, they sound much better.

It was a hot, humid day, and the sky was gray. We were looking out the window, and we saw something blurry. It was funnel-shaped, and it looked cloudy. It seemed to be moving toward us. Finally, we realized what it was, and we moved back from the window. It was a tornado coming our way.

Exercises   Use compound sentences.

A.   Number your paper from 1 to 10. Label three columns *Subject/Verb, Conjunction,* and *Subject/Verb.* For each sentence, fill in the columns.

Example: Diane left for school, but I stayed home.

Subject / Verb	Conjunction	Subject / Verb
Diane / left	but	I / stayed

1. We have a jar of paste, but it is too dry.
2. Patchwork is an old craft, but it is popular once again.
3. Fur traders go to Alaska, and they look for skins.
4. We take the bus, or we walk home.
5. The heart is a muscle, and it pumps blood.
6. Seaweed is a food, and it is nutritious.
7. The teacher called on Michelle, but she had forgotten the answer.
8. Vic owes me two dollars, but he is broke.
9. A bottle washed ashore, and a note was inside.
10. The Winter Olympics have started, and they are spectacular.

B.   Follow the directions for Exercise A.

1. Wear your winter jacket, or you will be cold.
2. Mary saddled her horse first, and then she helped me with mine.
3. Peters is the star center, but he did not play well today.

4. Sarah wanted a new record album, but she couldn't decide on one.
5. Take ski lessons, and you will feel more confident.
6. Handle the eggs carefully, or they will break.
7. The library has many science fiction books, and I have read most of them.
8. Jennifer felt lonely, and she called a friend.
9. Brad organized a team, and Mr. Chan coached.
10. Clay and Steve must leave now, or they will miss dinner.

Punctuating Compound Sentences

Because compound sentences combine two or more simple sentences, they may be long. To help the reader keep the thoughts clear, put a **comma** before the conjunction in a compound sentence. The comma alerts the reader to the end of the first idea, and it prepares the reader for the second idea.

Emily mowed the lawn, *and* Carl washed the windows.
Brian enjoys most music, *but* jazz is his favorite.
Terri must speak more clearly, *or* the audience won't hear her.
Grapefruits and oranges are citrus fruits, *and* they contain vitamin C.

You may leave out the comma only when the two sentences are very short and are joined by *and*.

Beth danced and Carol watched.
It was late and we were tired.

Exercises **Punctuate compound sentences.**

A. Copy the following compound sentences. Add a comma wherever one is needed. Circle the conjunction that joins the parts of the sentence.

1. Ted dusted and Ernestine swept.

2. Steve jumped from the plane and his parachute opened.
3. I read the front page and Don read the comics.
4. Marietta heard the news but she couldn't believe it.
5. My sister wants a job but she hasn't found one yet.
6. We turned on the light and the mouse ran away.
7. A tire burst and the car swerved.
8. The TV dial is broken but Mom will fix it.
9. Have you finished your homework or will you study in the library?
10. I run one mile every day but my brother runs three miles.

B. Follow the directions for Exercise A.

1. The two boys collided but neither was hurt.
2. Jocelyn felt happy and she smiled at everyone.
3. Bells rang and people cheered.
4. Rattlesnakes bite but pythons don't.
5. The bullfighter twirled his cape and the bull charged.
6. Judy rowed to the middle of the lake and then the boat started leaking.
7. Americans use dollar bills but the English use pound notes.
8. Are you left-handed or are you right-handed?
9. New York is the home of the Statue of Liberty and Philadelphia has the Liberty Bell.
10. Would you like a sandwich or would you rather have soup?

C. Writing Write five compound sentences. Punctuate them correctly. Circle the conjunction that joins the parts of each sentence. Underline the subject once and the verb twice in each part of the sentences.

ADDITIONAL EXERCISES

Using Compound Sentences

A. Simple Sentences Write the subjects and verbs in these simple sentences.

1. Lifejackets are used for water safety.
2. Boats docked in the harbor.
3. The Governor and the Senator spoke at the rally.
4. Chris waited and worried.
5. Jane Goodall went to Africa and studied chimpanzees.

B. Compound Sentences Copy each sentence. Add the punctuation needed to make the sentence correct. Underline the subject once and the verb twice in each part.

1. Bird blocked another shot and the Celtics won.
2. We washed the car and it looked like new.
3. A van pulled up and my friends jumped out.
4. The airport closed and many people were stranded.
5. Use a lock on your bike or it could be stolen.
6. Are you going to camp or will you stay home this summer?
7. The pool will open soon and we will swim often.
8. Sue smiled and Tom smiled back.
9. There was a fire but firefighters quickly put it out.
10. Six inches of snow fell and we shoveled the walk.
11. Vacation will begin soon and everyone is ready for it.
12. A light flashed and the police car began a chase.
13. An astronaut talked to us and we learned about the space program.
14. We need a ladder or we will never reach the roof.
15. A thermometer measures temperature and a barometer measures air pressure.

MIXED REVIEW

Using Compound Sentences

A. Identifying simple and compound sentences Copy each of the following sentences. If a sentence is a simple sentence, write *S*. If a sentence is compound, write *C*. Underline all subjects once and all verbs twice. If a sentence is compound, add any necessary commas.

1. Frank and Judy sang a duet.
2. I called Foster but he wasn't home.
3. We can grill hamburgers or we can make a pizza.
4. Carol washed and waxed the old station wagon.
5. We planted lettuce but the rabbits ate it.
6. Most buildings use gas or electric heat.
7. Mom and I visited New York and Boston.
8. Popcorn is nutritious and it is inexpensive.
9. Scott read and outlined the entire chapter of his science textbook.
10. Write yourself a note or you might forget the meeting.

B. Combining sentences Combine the following parts of simple sentences into compound sentences. Punctuate them correctly.

1. You can wait for Dr. Alther.
   You can come back later.
2. These crossword puzzles are difficult.
   They are fun.
3. We went to the bike shop.
   It was closed.
4. Val tried the combination.
   It worked.
5. I can save up for two months.
   I can borrow the money now.

USING GRAMMAR IN WRITING
Using Compound Sentences

A. This paragraph was written with only simple sentences. Improve it by combining the simple sentences into compound sentences.

> Mom pitched the tent. Ray helped her. Tanya chopped wood. She built the campfire. Dad was fishing at the lake's edge. Michelle was fishing from the boat. Suddenly the sky began to darken. The wind bent the trees low. Michelle came running. Dad followed close behind. The fire went out. The tent blew over. We ran to the van. We waited inside during the storm. Finally the wind and rain stopped. It was too wet to camp. We collected our soggy tent. We gathered up our camping equipment. Our dinner at Paul Bunyan's was delicious. Our beds in the Lone Pines motel were nice. They were dry.

B. You have won a camera in a contest. Part of the prize is an all-expenses-paid weekend anywhere in the U.S. to take photographs. First decide where you would like to spend your photo holiday. Then write about the pictures you would take there. You may want to look up the place in an encyclopedia or travel book before you write. Use compound sentences in your paragraph.

C. Imagine that you are watching a race. It may be between runners on a track team or between race car drivers. It might be a dirt bike or a speed skating race. Describe the action in a paragraph. Make at least three of the sentences compound sentences.

Using Complex Sentences

Simple and compound sentences are not the only kinds of sentences that you use. Another kind of sentence is the **complex sentence**. In this section, you will see how ideas are expressed in complex sentences.

Part 1   What Are Complex Sentences?

Before you can know what a complex sentence is, you must know what a clause is.

A clause is a group of words that contains a verb and its subject.

According to this definition, a simple sentence is a clause. It has both a verb and subject.

> s.   v.
> This poster glows in the dark.

> s.   v.
> Naomi James is a skilled sailor.

How about compound sentences? Do they contain clauses? Do they contain groups of words that have a subject and a verb? Read these examples:

> s.   v.   s.   v.
> Bradley chopped a hole in the ice, and then he fished.

> s.   v.   s.   v.
> Six of our swimmers made the finals, but only two won.

The answer is clear. Compound sentences do contain groups of words that have their own subjects and verbs. That is, compound sentences do contain clauses.

Main Clauses

A clause that can stand as a sentence by itself is a **main clause**. The clauses in compound sentences are main clauses. They can stand as simple sentences by themselves. That is why main clauses are sometimes called **independent clauses**.

From these definitions, you can see that you have already been working with clauses. A simple sentence is actually a main (independent) clause. A compound sentence is really two or more main (independent) clauses joined together.

Subordinate Clauses

Now look at clauses of a different kind:

s.   v.
after he chopped a hole in the ice

s.   v.
when I become an electrician

s. v.
who sail around the world

Each of these clauses has a subject and verb. However, none of the clauses can stand alone as a sentence. Each clause must have something added to make a complete thought. Such clauses are called **subordinate clauses** or **dependent clauses**. The word *subordinate* means that these clauses depend on another group of words to make a complete thought. Read these subordinate clauses. Think of ways to complete the thoughts.

because I helped my brother
after Dawn missed the bus
whenever we visit my aunt

A Definition of the Complex Sentence

Now that you know about main clauses and subordinate clauses, you are ready to learn what a complex sentence is.

A complex sentence is a sentence that contains one main clause and one or more subordinate clauses.

Main Clause	Subordinate Clause
Thomas Adams is the person	who invented chewing gum.
The fireworks began	after the parade was over.
Ed says	that he is a contestant.

Subordinate Clause	Main Clause
Before she cut it,	Meg had waist-length hair.
Since the library is closed,	we must study at home.
While you were away,	this package arrived.

Exercise **Recognize main clauses and subordinate clauses.**

Number your paper from 1 to 10. Each of the clauses below has been written without punctuation. Read each clause. Then write *Main* or *Subordinate* to tell what kind each clause is.

1. after we washed the car
2. water sparkled in the sunlight
3. Vinnie likes cereal and toast
4. whenever Lionel giggles
5. although it is the right size
6. someone left the window open
7. where Madison Avenue is
8. who makes stained glass
9. the ship sank during the storm
10. while the new house is being built

Part 2 More About Subordinate Clauses

Look at the following groups of words. Are they subordinate clauses?

until tomorrow   after the storm   since vacation

These examples are not subordinate clauses because they do not have subjects and verbs. These groups of words are prepositional phrases.

Phrases and Clauses

Can you tell the difference between a phrase and a subordinate clause? Look at these examples.

Phrases	Clauses
until tomorrow	until Mary arrives
after the storm	after the painters have finished the house.

A clause has a subject and a verb. A phrase does not. When you work with subordinate clauses, remember to look for a subject and verb.

Exercise **Recognize phrases and clauses.**

Read each of the following groups of words. Then write *Phrase* or *Clause* to tell what each group is.

1. in the alley
2. because he was late
3. since last September
4. before the bell rings
5. inside the cave
6. when the tide rises
7. before class
8. since we all agree
9. when we got our report cards
10. where the judge sits

Words Often Used To Begin Subordinate Clauses

Read these subordinate clauses:

when the door opened   *after* the concert is over

Now, cover the first word in each clause, and read the clause again. What happens? Each group of words becomes a complete sentence. You can see, then, that words such as *when* and *after* are important in a subordinate clause. When a word such as *when* or *after* introduces a clause, it *subordinates* the clause. That is, it makes the clause depend on a main clause to complete its meaning. Here is a list of words that often introduce subordinate clauses:

after	because	than	when
although	before	though	whenever
as	if	unless	where
as if	since	until	wherever
as long as	so that	whatever	while

Subordinate clauses may also begin with these words:

that	who, whom, whose	which
what	whoever, whomever	how

Caution: All of these words are subordinating words only when they introduce a clause. Some of them can be used in other ways.

Exercises   Recognize subordinate clauses.

A. Find the subordinate clause in each complex sentence. Write the clause. Then underline its subject once and its verb twice.

1. The horse fell before the race began.
2. Lincoln Park is the place where we will ride.
3. Find out when the game starts.
4. This is the family that has triplets.
5. Since she was six, Donna has played tennis.
6. Robert trembled because he was scared.
7. As we talked, the politician smiled.
8. *Summer of Fear* is the book that I liked best.

B. Follow the directions for Exercise A.

1. After choir practice ended, we went to Laurel's house for a snack.
2. A new toy that I saw tosses a football.
3. Beth wondered how actors are trained.
4. Alana shopped while Mom and I waited.
5. Jeff rested before the play began.
6. Tracy Austin, who plays pro tennis, was the youngest player ever at Wimbledon.
7. Their dog barks whenever the doorbell rings.
8. Although it looks easy, a back flip is difficult.
9. Few people know what makes them happy.
10. Can you babysit after school is out?

C. Writing Write five complex sentences. Underline each main clause once and each subordinate clause twice in each sentence.

Part 3 More About Sentence Fragments

The sentence fragments that you studied in **Section 2** were easy to spot. They were fragments because they lacked a verb or the subject of a verb.

Now you'll learn about another kind of sentence fragment, the subordinate clause. A subordinate clause has both a verb and a subject. It is still a fragment, however, because its meaning is not complete. Look at the groups of words below.

> when he was young
> where young people go
> that Dallas would win the game

A subordinate clause must not be written as a complete sentence. It must always be joined to a main clause.

Fragment:	When he was young.
Sentence:	When he was young, Einstein did poorly in math.
Fragment:	Where young people go.
Sentence:	The drop-in center is a place where young people go.
Fragment:	That the Falcons would win the game.
Sentence:	We were hoping that the Falcons would win the game.

Exercises   Recognize sentence fragments.

A. Decide whether the groups of words below are sentences or fragments. Write *S* for *Sentence* or *F* for *Fragment*. Add words to make each fragment a complete sentence. Punctuate and capitalize each sentence correctly.

1. we played basketball until the sun set
2. I saw a man who was juggling oranges
3. although the bike is old
4. where I live
5. Tina told Jack that he was a good worker
6. as she shoveled snow
7. when he paints
8. if I need help, I'll call you
9. since you weren't home
10. as the deadline approached

B. Follow the directions for Exercise A.

1. Carla thought that she must be dreaming
2. when the storm uprooted a tree
3. the hamster escaped when I opened the cage
4. although he ran for President
5. because the gates were locked
6. if you work hard

7. we ate popcorn while we watched the old time movie
8. this station plays the top ten songs
9. eat breakfast before you leave
10. while the bread cools

Part 4 A Review of Sentences

In this book you have learned about three kinds of sentences that you use.

• You know that a **simple sentence** contains one subject and one predicate. A simple sentence expresses one main idea. You will remember, however, that parts of the simple sentence may be compound.

s.   s.   v.

Examples: The baseball team and the lacrosse team won yesterday.

s.   s.   v.   v.

Dan and Mary read and discussed the history assignment.

• You have learned that a **compound sentence** consists of two simple sentences. These simple sentences are joined by a conjunction. A compound sentence expresses two main ideas that are related in thought.

s.   v.

Examples: The baseball team won yesterday, *but* the wrestling

s.   v.

team lost.

s.   v.   s.   v.

Dan studied history, *and* Mary did her math.

• You have also learned that a **complex sentence** contains one main clause and one or more subordinate clauses. A complex sentence expresses one main idea and one or more other ideas that depend on the main idea.

Examples: *Although the baseball team won yesterday,*

s. v.

s. v.

the lacrosse team lost.

s. v. s. v.

Dan studied history *while Mary watched television.*

Exercises   **Recognize the kinds of sentences.**

A. Number your paper from 1 to 10. For each sentence, write *Simple, Compound, or Complex* to tell what kind it is.

1. The movie is a space thriller, and a robot is the star.
2. What Megan said makes sense.
3. Because Vanessa sensed danger, she left.
4. I helped Mandy with the crossword puzzle.
5. Models paraded in the new spring fashions.
6. Justin hit a single, and then he stole second base.
7. When Tracy serves, she often wins the game.
8. The dog with the pointed ears is a Doberman.
9. Vacation begins on Friday, and my family is going to the lake.
10. Clark made a skateboard, and it has a motor.

B. Follow the directions for Exercise A.

1. Arnold screamed when he opened the box.
2. If the weather is warm, we'll go to the beach.
3. Where is the nearest fire extinguisher?
4. Franklin bumped into Diane, and she dropped her books.
5. Our neighbors play volleyball in an empty lot.
6. The next solar eclipse will be in 2017.
7. The comedian told jokes, but no one laughed.
8. The Amazing Wanda rides a unicycle as she juggles.
9. Many people say that they are shy.
10. The commercials that I like best are the funny ones.

ADDITIONAL EXERCISES

Using Complex Sentences

A. Complex Sentences Write the subordinate clause in each complex sentence.

1. Although we were tired, we couldn't sleep.
2. Marco, who comes from Italy, doesn't speak English.
3. I didn't know that your ears were pierced.
4. Before I was six, we had moved four times.
5. When Dad is angry, he is silent.
6. A teller rang the alarm after the robbers had fled.
7. I jog along the lake whenever the weather is good.
8. Tom, who is my oldest brother, works in a bank.
9. Call me if you need a ride.
10. We saw a movie that was terrifying.
11. Pam asked where the best beaches are.
12. We climbed a mountain that was twelve hundred feet high.
13. Julie listened while the chef explained.
14. I disagree with the referee who called that penalty.
15. We met a girl who reminded us of Jeff's sister.

B. Clauses, Phrases, and Sentences Decide whether the following groups of words are clauses, phrases, or sentences. Write C for *Clause*, P for *Phrase*, or S for *Sentence*. Capitalize and punctuate any sentences correctly.

1. before you change your mind
2. for the last three months
3. we cheered when we heard the score
4. ask Seth if you need some help
5. at the very last minute
6. that they would need more food for a one-week-trip

7. whenever you turn on the radio
8. Laura whistled as she repaired her bicycle
9. in the trunk of Dad's car
10. Jack didn't know who had left the message

C.   Review of Sentences   For each sentence, write *Simple*, *Compound*, or *Complex* to tell what kind it is.

1. Ms. Adams teaches math at the high school.
2. The President threw out the first ball, and the game began.
3. Although the bike chain works, it needs oil.
4. I've heard of a zoo where there are no cages.
5. Some cars were buried in snow for weeks after the blizzard.
6. Mary practiced the violin, and John read a book.
7. Lois Lane and Clark Kent worked for the *Daily Planet*.
8. We found what we needed.
9. Thunder boomed and shook the house, and lightning lit up the sky.
10. Jim and Louise washed and groomed the dog.

MIXED REVIEW

Using Complex Sentences

A. Identifying kinds of sentences Copy the following sentences. Add punctuation wherever it is necessary. After each sentence, write *Simple, Compound,* or *Complex* to show what kind it is.

1. Before we leave we must turn off the lights.
2. I can't wait until Friday.
3. Pam felt something under her feet.
4. Give Beth this message if you see her.
5. Kent caught a strange butterfly but he let it go.
6. We found a lantern and we lit it.
7. The North and South reunited after the Civil War.
8. The Senator spoke to us as if we were voters.
9. Read this book and then return it to me.
10. If you see Casey tell her about your vacation.

B. Identifying fragments and sentences Decide whether the following groups of words are sentences or fragments. Write *S* for *Sentence* and *F* for *Fragment.* Then, add a main clause to any fragments to make complex sentences.

1. Steve is hoping that he will win the trophy.
2. Whatever you do.
3. As soon as the meeting began.
4. Although Chicago is a large city, it has many small neighborhoods.
5. Bob has been more careful since he lost his watch.
6. As long as I can.
7. Bev watered the plants while we were away.
8. Whenever Marty sees a scary movie.
9. You may have this shell since you saw it first.
10. Although Kara enjoys sports.

USING GRAMMAR IN WRITING
Using Complex Sentences

A. A new clothing store, *Teen Jeans*, has opened near you. To advertise, the store has passed out hundreds of balloons at their grand opening. Inside the balloons are messages. Each balloon contains half of a message. When you get your balloon, you must find the person who has the other half of the message. If you find each other, you each claim a new pair of jeans.

Here are eight halves of messages. Notice that each is a subordinate clause. Write matching halves for each one. Add main clauses to complete the messages.

When you buy _____
Whatever you do _____
_____ whenever you want to look great
_____ until the sale ends
Before you shop anywhere else _____
Since everyone loves jeans _____
_____ so that we can meet you
_____ that you'll tell your friends

B. You probably have some friends who are in high school. What kinds of things do they say about school? Does it seem different from your school? Write a paragraph about the ways you think high school will be different from junior high. Include some complex sentences. These words can be used to begin the subordinate clauses:

because	until	where	whoever
if	whatever	wherever	which
than	when	that	what
unless	whenever	who	how

CUMULATIVE REVIEW
The Sentence

A. Identifying kinds of sentences Copy the following sentences. Insert the correct punctuation. After each sentence, write *D* for declarative, *INT* for interrogative, *IMP* for imperative, or *E* for exclamatory. Underline each subject once and each verb twice.

1. Did the water boil yet
2. Melody develops her own photographs
3. Turn off the hall light
4. A shark is circling our boat
5. Ryan wore a ski sweater
6. The clown dashed into the audience
7. Put some air in those tires
8. What a lovely voice she has
9. When does the concert begin
10. Crows perched on the telephone lines

B. Understanding agreement in sentences Number your paper from 1 to 15. Write the correct word from the two given in parentheses.

1. Everyone wore (his or her, their) costume to the dress rehearsal.
2. There (is, are) a swarm of bees near the clover patch.
3. She (don't, doesn't) agree with me.
4. The shelves in this bookcase (is, are) six inches deep.
5. The soup in those jars (is, are) homemade minestrone.
6. Each of the girls brought (her, their) camera on the field trip.
7. Here (is, are) the hammer and the nails.
8. Rumors about the stock market (interest, interests) Mr. Houseman.

9. One of the puppies (has, have) a sore paw.
10. You (is, are) on my bowling team this year.
11. Either Molly or her friends (want, wants) this poster.
12. The spruce tree and the hedges (need, needs) pruning.
13. Where (is, are) the keys to the shed?
14. Each of the actors (want, wants) that part in the play.
15. The color of these sweatshirts (is, are) brilliant.

C. Correcting fragments and run-on sentences The following paragraph contains fragments and run-on sentences. Rewrite the paragraph. Use capitalization and punctuation to correct the fragments and run-ons. Do not add or change any words.

Many people are surprised. To learn that the Pony Express lasted only eighteen months. However, it filled a need it moved the mail from St. Joseph, Missouri, to Sacramento, California, in ten days. Mail delivery by stagecoach or ship took from three to six weeks. The Pony Express used a system of horsemen riding in relays, the horses were mostly mustangs. Usually each man. Rode seventy-five miles a day. The mail was carried in a waterproof leather pouch. Progress ended the need for the Pony Express, the first telegraph line from coast to coast was completed in 1861. Messages and news could now be sent. In minutes instead of days.

D. Writing good sentences Rewrite each of the following sentences. Follow the directions in the parentheses.

1. Drew read that article for science class.   (Add the prepositional phrase *about sea otters*.)
2. Miriam will ride her bike to my house. Her mother will drive her.   (Combine these two simple sentences into a compound sentence using **, or**.)

3. Clem went to the sporting goods store. (Add the prepositional phrase *near the courthouse.*)

4. Jean planted the saplings. She watered them. (Combine these two simple sentences into one with a compound verb.)

5. Luther was voted the most valuable player in the game. Luther is the quarterback. (Combine these simple sentences into one complex sentence using *who.*)

6. Josh searched his locker. He couldn't find his pen. (Combine these two simple sentences into a compound sentence using **, but**.)

7. Natalie ran for student council president. Mark ran, too. (Combine these two simple sentences into one with a compound subject.)

8. Matthew studied in study hall. (Change this N V sentence to one with a N V N pattern.)

9. Professor Bradley is an intelligent man. (Change this N LV N sentence into one with a N LV ADJ pattern.)

10. All the guests have arrived. The dinner is ready. (Combine these two simple sentences into a compound sentence using **, and**.)

Diagraming the Sentence

Part 1 What Is Diagraming?

A street map is a clear picture of the roads in a town. An X-ray is a clear picture of the parts of the body. Like a map or an X-ray, a **diagram** of a sentence is a picture of the sentence and its parts. A diagram of a sentence shows clearly how each word in a sentence is related to every other word. A diagram shows how each word functions in a sentence.

When you make diagrams, you follow patterns. It is important to follow the patterns exactly. Be careful to put words in the right places. Make vertical lines, horizontal lines, or slanted lines carefully. Copy words exactly as they appear in a sentence, with capital letters or without them. Do not copy any punctuation marks except the apostrophes within a word.

In this section, you will learn how to diagram parts of a sentence. You'll see how diagraming can help you to understand how sentences work.

Part 2 Diagraming Verbs and Their Subjects

A sentence diagram always begins on a horizontal line. A vertical line cuts the horizontal line in two. It separates the subject from the verb. The subject is placed to the left of the vertical line. The verb is placed to the right of it.

The clerk helped.

clerk	helped

Michael Jackson sang.

Michael Jackson	sang

Exercise **Diagram the verbs and their subjects.**

Diagram the verb and its simple subject in each of the following sentences. (Ignore all other words.)

1. Mr. Rosen skis.
2. Marcy sneezed.
3. Bulls charge.
4. Darren laughed at my joke.
5. Horns honked loudly.
6. Tammy Dillon left.
7. The ice melted in the sun.
8. The floors creaked.
9. Mayor Best campaigned.
10. The Bulldogs will play on Friday.

Part 3 Diagraming Subjects in Unusual Order

The positions of subjects and verbs on diagrams do not change when a sentence is in unusual order.

Above the clouds soared the jet.

jet	soared

Out of the darkness walked a stranger.

stranger	walked

Exercise Diagram subjects in unusual order.

Diagram the subjects and verbs in the following sentences. (Ignore all other words.)

1. Down the ice skated Miller.
2. Behind the door lay a newspaper.
3. On Casey's pants were patches.
4. Across the sky shot a star.
5. Under a blanket rested the cat.
6. Through the harbor roared the boat.
7. Around the branch wound the snake.
8. Across the Olympic-sized pool raced the swimmers.
9. In the back of the mahogany desk was a secret drawer.
10. In the distance blared a foghorn.

Part 4 Diagraming Questions

When you diagram a question, put the subject and verb in normal order. Notice the capital letters in these diagrams.

Did Sara ride her bike?

Have you sent for tickets?

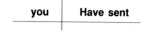

Exercise Diagram questions.

Diagram the subject and verb in each of the following questions. Include capital letters wherever necessary. (Ignore all other words.)

1. Will Natalie Cole sing?
2. Have you noticed a change?
3. Did the paint dry?
4. Shall we sit in a booth?
5. Has the sherbet melted?
6. Would you like a snack?
7. When will school begin?
8. Did you get a booster shot?
9. Has Jennifer learned her lines for the Thanksgiving program?
10. Did you enjoy the movie?

Part 5 Diagraming Imperative Sentences

When the subject of an imperative sentence is understood, show it on your diagram by writing *(you)* in the subject position.

Put air in this tire.

Show your pass to the guard.

Exercise Diagram imperative sentences.

Diagram the subjects and verbs in the following imperative sentences. (Ignore all other words.)

1. Remember your locker combination.
2. Consider this problem.
3. Throw the ball with your left hand.
4. Find more recent information.
5. Hold your breath underwater.
6. Close all of the windows.
7. Change the radio station.
8. Watch that documentary on TV.
9. Observe this stunt carefully.
10. Store those old toys in the large trunk in the garage.

Part 6 Diagraming Sentences with *There*

There is often just an "extra" word. Write it on a separate line above the subject in a sentence diagram.

There were three lifeguards on duty.

Is there a map of this museum?

Exercise **Diagram sentences with *there*.**

Diagram the subjects and verbs and the word *there* in the following sentences.

1. There are eight notes in the scale.
2. There were hundreds of people in line.
3. There are two pounds of Golden Delicious apples in the sack.
4. Is there a punch line to that joke?
5. Was there a package on our porch?
6. There is no room at this motel.
7. Were there sand-crabs on the beach?
8. Is there time for another match?
9. There are seventy horses on this ranch.
10. Are there fifty-two weeks in a year?

Part 7 Diagraming Compound Subjects and Verbs

To diagram the two or more parts of a compound subject, split the subject line. Put the conjunction on a connecting dotted line.

Tanya and her brother missed the bus.

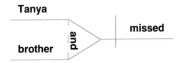

To diagram the two or more parts of a compound verb, split the verb line. Put the conjunction on a connecting dotted line.

Carol cleaned, sanded and painted the desk.

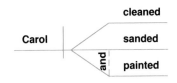

Exercise **Diagram compound subjects and verbs.**

Diagram the compound subjects and verbs in the following sentences. (Ignore all other words.)

1. The captain and crew swam to shore.
2. Margie stayed and helped with decorations.
3. Ron and I rode in a seaplane.
4. Kara and her mother raked the leaves.
5. Staple or clip your papers together.
6. Annie waited and hoped for a chance.
7. The leaders met and discussed a truce.
8. Kevin and Marvin wrestled in the meet.
9. Have Maggie and Lisa planned a party?
10. Inside my pocket were two nails and a thumbtack.

Part 8 Diagraming Sentences Containing Direct Objects

When you diagram a sentence, place a direct object on the horizontal line following the verb. Separate it from the action verb by a vertical line that does not cut through the subject-verb line.

My friends buy discount records.

For compound direct objects, continue the horizontal line a little way beyond the verb and then split it. Make as many parallel direct object lines as you need. Put the vertical line before the split, to show that all the words that follow are direct objects.

I trust Michelle, Steve, and Toby.

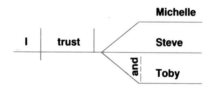

Exercise Diagram sentences containing direct objects.

Diagram the subjects, verbs, and direct objects in the following sentences. Some direct objects may be compound. (Ignore all other words.)

1. Dawn plays the saxophone.
2. The stars guide sailors at sea.
3. Noel makes jewelry from driftwood.
4. Did you weave this cloth?
5. People built castles and statues in the sand.

6. Is Jamie using the telephone?
7. My family uses a van for camping.
8. Dogs can hear high-pitched sounds.
9. Put your name and address on the application.
10. Mark has played defense and offense.

Part 9 Diagraming Sentences Containing Predicate Nouns

The diagram for a sentence containing a predicate noun is different from the diagram for a sentence containing a direct object.

A Cyclops was a one-eyed monster.

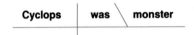

Notice that the predicate noun is on the horizontal line in the same position as the direct object. But the line that separates the predicate noun from the linking verb slants back toward the subject. This is to show its close relationship to the subject.

For sentences containing compound predicate nouns, use parallel lines. Put the slanting line after the verb.

Seth is a good student and a fine athlete.

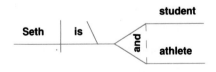

Diagram sentences containing predicate nouns.

Diagram the subjects, linking verbs, and predicate nouns in the following sentences. (Ignore all other words.)

1. Those girls are skaters.
2. That boy is a model.
3. Canoes are light, slender boats.
4. Was Hoyt the pitcher?
5. Diana and Minerva were Roman goddesses.
6. The Milky Way is a galaxy of stars.
7. Langston Hughes was a poet.
8. The Navajos are a tribe of the Southwest.
9. Kate became a better player and a good sport during the last game.
10. Jesse James and Billy the Kid were outlaws in the Old West.

Part 10 Diagraming Sentences Containing Predicate Adjectives

Show a predicate adjective on a diagram just as you show a predicate noun. Place it on the horizontal line following the linking verb, and separate it from the verb by a line slanting back toward the subject.

Good workers are reliable.

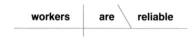

For sentences with compound predicate adjectives, use parallel lines. Put the slanting line after the verb.

The earth feels damp and spongy.

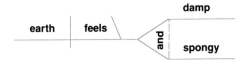

Exercise **Diagram sentences containing predicate adjectives.**

Diagram the subjects, verbs, and predicate adjectives in these sentences. (Ignore all other words.)

1. Inez seems ambitious.
2. That taco smells delicious.
3. Our teacher is patient and enthusiastic.
4. Contact lenses should feel comfortable.
5. Jamaica is lush and lovely.
6. Is Vitamin C good for colds?
7. Be still.
8. Will the photos be ready today?
9. A coral reef feels sharp and brittle.
10. The coach and players are exhausted.

Part 11 Diagraming Sentences Containing Adjectives

Show an adjective in a diagram on a line that slants down from the noun or pronoun it modifies. Articles, which are also adjectives, are shown in the same way.

The new school has a large, bright gym.

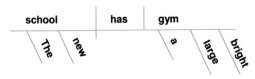

Carol Brown is a strong, steady swimmer.

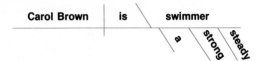

Diagram sentences containing adjectives.

Diagram the subjects, verbs, and adjectives in the following sentences. Also diagram any direct objects, predicate nouns, and predicate adjectives.

1. Mike wears plaid suspenders.
2. A new student entered the classroom.
3. A special squad defused the black bomb.
4. Forest fires do tremendous damage.
5. A sari is a long Indian dress.
6. Two green snakes protected five eggs.
7. The lost child was frightened.
8. Does the track team have a new coach?
9. The reddish plant has poisonous leaves.
10. Mr. Wayne has a pleasant face and a friendly smile.

Part 12 Diagraming Sentences Containing Possessive Nouns and Pronouns

In a diagram, possessive nouns and pronouns are diagramed in the same way that adjectives are.

Those are Penny's skis.

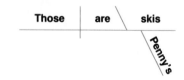

His little brother was hungry.

Exercise **Diagram sentences containing possessive nouns.**

Diagram the subjects, verbs, and possessive nouns and pronouns in these sentences. Also diagram any direct objects, predicate nouns, predicate adjectives, and adjectives.

1. I washed your new car.
2. Samantha's serve is accurate.
3. Have you heard Eric's joke?
4. Ingrid is their babysitter.
5. Alex beat Steve's time.
6. Steve Cauthen's horse took the lead.
7. Georgia's weather is mild.
8. My uncle has a pilot's license.
9. Watch the champion's difficult new dive.
10. Her mother is a dentist.

Part 13 Diagraming Sentences Containing Adverbs

Adverbs, like adjectives, are shown in diagrams on slanting lines attached to the words they modify. The following diagram shows the adverb *suddenly* modifying a verb.

Suddenly, a small plane radioed the tower.

```
   plane   | radioed  |  tower
 a   small    Suddenly    the
```

The next diagram shows adverbs modifying a verb, an adjective, and an adverb. The adverb *truly* modifies the adjective *great*. *Truly* is attached to *great*. The adverb *quite* modifies another adverb *late*. Notice how *quite* is attached to *late*.

Some truly great athletes began competition quite late.

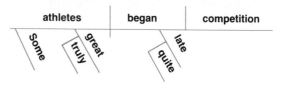

Exercise **Diagram sentences containing adverbs.**

Diagram the subjects, verbs, and adverbs in the following sentences. Also diagram any adjectives, predicate adjectives, predicate nouns, and direct objects.

1. JoAnn carefully avoided an argument.
2. This store usually has good bargains.
3. Now Sandy's racer rides smoothly.
4. Lena and Rachel dive well.
5. This stereo's sound is very clear.
6. Dad and Mom jog here daily.
7. Does Ellery Queen always solve the crime?
8. Handle these plates carefully.
9. You must visit me very soon.
10. Doctors sometimes treat really serious injuries.

Part 14 Diagraming Prepositional Phrases

In diagrams, a prepositional phrase is placed below the word it modifies. The preposition is shown on a line slanting down from the modified word. Attached to the slanting line is a horizontal line on which the object of the preposition is written. Modifiers are shown below the object on a slanted line.

Remember that a prepositional phrase can be an adjective phrase or an adverb phrase. A prepositional phrase that modifies a noun or pronoun is an adjective phrase. A prepositional phrase that modifies a verb is an adverb phrase. In the following example, *with red hair* is an adjective phrase. It modifies the noun *girl*. *In our band* is an adverb phrase. It modifies the verb *plays*.

The girl with red hair plays in our band.

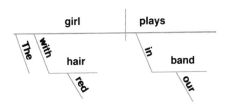

Exercise **Diagram sentences containing prepositional phrases.**

Diagram the following sentences. Be sure to diagram the prepositional phrases correctly.

1. Marlene sits in the second row.
2. Everyone in the room laughed.
3. Toby wandered down the alley.
4. Several cars had stopped near the corner.
5. Mary Ann waited at the station.
6. Have you walked past the new theater?
7. The legal owner of that abandoned car has been found.
8. Will you sit beside me?
9. The nineteen workers inside the coal mine were rescued.
10. A large evergreen tree fell during the thunderstorm.

Part 15 Diagraming Compound Sentences

It is not difficult to diagram compound sentences if you can already diagram simple sentences. A compound sentence is really two or more simple sentences joined together. Therefore, you draw the diagram for the first half of the sentence, draw a dotted-line "step" for the conjunction, and then draw the diagram for the second half.

Irma is a skillful artist, and she has won many prizes.

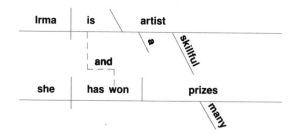

Exercise Diagram compound sentences.

Diagram the following compound sentences. Diagram each part of the sentence. Then join the parts.

1. Terry sealed the envelope, and Claudia stamped it.
2. Natalie was very busy, but she took a break.
3. Sally is blonde, but her sister is brunette.
4. Amy's plan was unusual, but it was practical.
5. There are four trophies, but we have five winners.
6. Bring a lunch, or buy one here.
7. Is the movie good, or shall we skip it?
8. Have you started your project, or will you begin soon?
9. Some Indian jewelry is silver, and it is very beautiful.
10. The Nobel Prize is awarded annually, and it is a great honor.

ADDITIONAL EXERCISES

Diagraming the Sentence

Diagraming Sentences Diagram the following sentences.

1. Jody shivered.
2. From the palms hang coconuts.
3. Do truckers drive through the night?
4. Try this key.
5. There are no stores on the island.
6. Is there a leash for your puppy?
7. Neal and Scott traded lunches.
8. Maria makes wooden toys.
9. We recycle cans, bottles, and papers.
10. John Glenn is a politician and former astronaut.
11. That cartoon is funny but true.
12. Can you answer that difficult riddle?
13. Some apes have learned sign language.
14. The court's decision is final.
15. Mr. Van talks gruffly but acts gently.
16. Very few people understand highly technical language.
17. Use this penknife carefully.
18. The Bears' fans are loyal, but the team is still losing.
19. The principal introduced the graduates, but a student gave the speech.
20. The glacier moved slowly, and finally it covered the mountainside.

MIXED REVIEW

Diagraming the Sentence

Diagraming sentences   Diagram the following sentences.

1. Japan is a small country, but it has many people.
2. Rudy washed the beach towels.
3. Frogs croaked softly during the night.
4. That plaid blanket is too warm.
5. Nicole reads poetry in her spare time.
6. What is the weather forecast?
7. We found a map and it was helpful.
8. Has the band played your favorite song?
9. There are five players on a basketball team.
10. Many exotic birds live on that tropical island.
11. I found Carla's wallet under the cushions.
12. My family went to the museum, and we enjoyed the exhibit about China.
13. The sailboat glided quickly out of the harbor.
14. The circus animals and performers delighted everyone.
15. Linda chose a huge, round pumpkin for Halloween.
16. Tim's uncle lives in Tennessee, and he raises horses.
17. David's favorite books are mysteries and biographies.
18. Washington has a mild, rainy climate.
19. The woman in the blue coat is my grandmother.
20. Karen's mom is a lawyer, and she works in the city.

USING GRAMMAR IN WRITING
Diagraming the Sentence

A. Some strange things have been occurring at home. You suspect your house or apartment may be haunted. Then one day you find a note tucked in your shoe. The next day a note is taped to the bathroom mirror. The notes are very odd. You realize that the sender has a sense of humor. He knows you have been diagraming sentences at school, so he has written all his notes to you in diagram form. If you can decipher the notes, you will learn about your visitor from the spirit world. Write out each sentence.

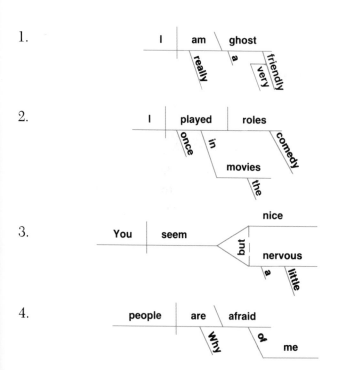

1.

2.

3.

4.

5.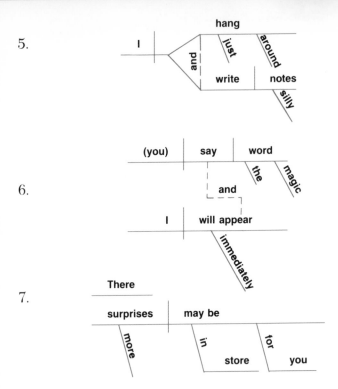

6.

7.

B. What would you like to reply to the ghost? Answer him in three sentences. Put each one in diagram form.

Capitalization

Capitalization is the use of capital letters. When you capitalize the first letter of a word, such as a proper noun, you call attention to that word.

Capital letters are also used to call attention to other special words. For instance, words that begin sentences are capitalized. In that way, capital letters make reading easier.

In this section, you will learn when to capitalize words. Study the rules and their examples. Refer to these rules whenever you have a question about capitalization.

Proper Nouns and Adjectives

Capitalize proper nouns and proper adjectives.

A **common noun** is a general name for a person, place, or thing.

> man   country   book

A **proper noun** is the name of a particular person, place, or thing.

> **T**homas **J**efferson   **S**weden   **B**ible

A **proper adjective** is an adjective formed from a proper noun.

Jeffersonian ideas   Swedish meatballs   Biblical story

There are many kinds of proper nouns. Some of them are made up of more than one word. Capitalize the first word and all other words in a proper noun except articles (*a, an, the*), conjunctions (*and, but, or*), and prepositions of four or fewer letters.

London Bridge   Museum of Science and Industry
Santa Fe   Gulf of Mexico

Names and Titles

Capitalize the names of people and pets.

Capitalize each word in a person's name. An **initial** is the first letter of a person's name. An initial stands for a name. Capitalize initials and follow them with a period.

Susan B. Anthony   A. J. Foyt   S. F. B. Morse   Lassie

Capitalize a title used with a person's name.

Dr. Chavez and Coach Bell discussed exercise.
Have you seen Ms. Gray or Mr. Townsend?

Capitalize the word *I*.

Mary and I planted sunflower seeds.

Capitalize the name of a family relationship when it is used with a person's name or in place of a person's name.

Ask Mother or Aunt Leslie for directions.
My sister visited Grandma in Atlanta.

Do not capitalize names of family relationships if possessive nouns or pronouns come before them, as in *Brad's dad* or *my brother.*

A. Write the words that should be capitalized, using the necessary capital letters.

1. This series was based on books by laura ingalls wilder.
2. The name spencer p. marks was on the plaque.
3. Some people think that thomas a. edison was a genius.
4. Chris and mom prepared a greek dinner.
5. Dr. george washington carver was born a slave.
6. Bob and i read a mystery by theodore taylor.
7. Susan and i played tennis against kenny and my sister.
8. We live next door to mr. and mrs. robert f. torres.
9. Was the speech given by professor eileen black?
10. Annette made an appointment with dr. adams.

B. Follow the directions for Exercise A.

1. David, grandpa, and i ate at a mexican restaurant.
2. Tomorrow i will cut mr. quinlan's lawn.
3. President lincoln met harriet beecher stowe.
4. Sandy and dennis visted their uncle, mr. ralph t. cage.
5. The teacher of althea's italian class is ms. hartley.
6. Did dr. rosenberg and his family go to italy?
7. When did marian anderson begin her opera career?
8. Either lottie or i can take you to ms. franklin's office.
9. One of the speakers was senator edward kennedy.
10. The boxer cassius clay changed his name to muhammad ali.

Months, Days, and Holidays

Capitalize the names of months, days, and holidays.

On **F**riday, **D**ecember 16, our **C**hristmas vacation begins.

Do not capitalize the names of the four seasons.

My favorite season is winter.

Particular Places and Things

Capitalize the names of cities, states, and countries.

> Which is larger, Portland, Oregon, or Detroit, Michigan?
> Brazil is the largest country in South America, and Canada is the largest country in North America.

Capitalize the names of streets, buildings, and bridges.

> The Chambers Building is at the corner of Greenlawn Avenue and High Street.

Capitalize all geographical names.

Also capitalize the words *north, south, east,* and *west* when they refer to a particular section of a country.

> Most of the area between the Rocky Mountains in the West and the Appalachian Mountains in the East is drained by three rivers, the Mississippi, the Ohio, and the Missouri.

Exercises   Use capital letters correctly.

A.   Number your paper from 1 to 10. For each sentence, write the words that should be capitalized. Capitalize them correctly.

1. The first king of hawaii was king kamehameha.
2. Does interstate highway 80 go to des moines, iowa?
3. Is the amazon river in brazil or in argentina?
4. Dean's dairy bar isn't open on holidays.
5. Doreen was in the west, visiting relatives in arizona.
6. We passed by the ewing ranch just before sunset.
7. If you can't come at thanksgiving, come this summer.
8. We could see long island and new jersey from the top of the world trade center.
9. The famous irwin hospital is in the east.
10. Five states border the gulf of mexico.

B. Follow the directions for Exercise A.

1. The golden gate bridge is in san francisco.
2. What is the oldest city in the west?
3. The snowy peaks of the grand tetons are gorgeous.
4. The astronauts will speak in houston on tuesday.
5. The altitude of denver, colorado, is one mile above sea level.
6. I have never visited any states in the south except kentucky.
7. We are spending easter in macon, georgia.
8. Do we celebrate thanksgiving on the fourth thursday of november?
9. People gathered on cathedral square in the kremlin in moscow.
10. The ship will land in puerto rico on thursday, july 12.

Races, Religions, Nationalities, and Languages

Capitalize the names of races, religions, nationalities, and languages.

Modern American Indian artists often use traditional designs in their work.

Judaism, Christianity, and Islam share a belief in one God.

The Russians and the Chinese have frequent arguments about their border.

Does this junior high offer French?

Clubs, Organizations, and Businesses

Capitalize the names of clubs, organizations, and business firms.

My uncle belongs to the Centerville Garden Club.

Where is the headquarters of the Boy Scouts of America?

Don's mother works for General Motors.

Exercises   Use capital letters correctly.

A.   Number your paper from 1 to 10. Copy each of the following groups of words. Wherever necessary, change small letters to capitals.

1. polish sausage
2. a methodist minister
3. german potato salad
4. the cub scouts
5. a dutch windmill
6. african art
7. chinese food
8. the campfire girls
9. bell telephone company
10. the arab oil fields

B.   Number your paper from 1 to 10. Copy each of the following sentences. Capitalize correctly.

1. Dolores's mother is a systems analyst for digital equipment company.
2. The elmwood photography club meets every monday in the carnegie library.
3. Gabriel joined the united states marine corps after he graduated from high school.
4. Were those tourists speaking japanese?
5. Many people in india practice hinduism.
6. Our school has language classes in french, italian, and spanish.
7. The olmecs were an ancient indian tribe in mexico.
8. Roberto is active in the peoria chamber of commerce.
9. The museum exhibits include an egyptian mummy, some roman statues, and several greek vases.
10. The irish writer jonathan swift wrote a great english novel about a man named gulliver.

First Words

Sentences

Capitalize the first word of every sentence.

> Workers digging the foundation found an ancient burial-ground.
> When will the eclipse begin?
> Look out!

Poetry

Capitalize the first word in most lines of poetry.

> The wind was a torrent of darkness among the gusty trees,
> The moon was a ghostly galleon tossed upon cloudy seas,
> The road was a ribbon of moonlight over the purple moor,
> And the highwayman came riding—
>   Riding—riding—
> The highwayman came riding, up to the old inn-door.
>   —from "The Highwayman" ALFRED NOYES

Sometimes, especially in modern poetry, the lines of a poem do not begin with capital letters.

> Will I remember
> how I looked
> and what I did
> when I was young
> (when I am old)?
> Will I remember what I wondered?
> When I am old,
> who will I be?
> Still me?
>   —RICHARD J. MARGOLIS

Exercises   Use capital letters correctly.

A.   Number your paper from 1 to 10. Find the words in the following sentences that should be capitalized. Copy each sentence or poem, using the necessary capital letters.

1. do you like italian food? we can have pizza at tina's restaurant.
2. there is a program about japan on television tonight.
3. listen, my children, and you shall hear
   of the midnight ride of paul revere,
   on the eighteenth of april, in seventy-five;
   hardly a man is now alive
   who remembers that famous day and year.

   —from "Paul Revere's Ride" HENRY WADSWORTH LONGFELLOW

4. last year we had a dry summer and a rainy fall.
5. the third sunday in june is father's day.
6. is cotton still an important crop in the south?
7. dr. frances gilbert teaches english at carroll university.
8. on tuesday i will celebrate my birthday.
9. this month has five saturdays.
10. have you seen any movies by woody allen?

B.   Follow the directions for Exercise A.

1. we celebrate flag day on june 14.
2. are you visiting montreal, in quebec? there, canadians speak french.
3. on wednesday i'll be late for dinner. the girl scouts are having a meeting at four o'clock.
4. what is the spanish word for *hello*?
5. our new address is 141 miller avenue.
6. the orchestra will play two works by wolfgang amadeus mozart.
7. mom is going to dearborn, michigan, on friday.

8. yesterday rabbi silver spoke at the synagogue in newton.

9. the setting of the book is new orleans, louisiana.

10. **The Rhinoceros**

the Rhino is a homely beast,
for human eyes he's not a feast,
but you and i will never know
why Nature chose to make him so,
farewell, farewell, you old rhinoceros,
i'll stare at something less prepoceros.

—OGDEN NASH

Direct Quotations

When you write the exact words somebody else said, you are **quoting** that person. The words are a **direct quotation**.

Capitalize the first word of a direct quotation.

"Tomorrow we can expect heavy rain," said the forecaster.

Usually, when you are writing what a person said, you use explaining words, like *he asked* or *she said*, before or after the direct quotation. If these explaining words come before the direct quotation, capitalize the first explaining word. Then capitalize the first word of the direct quotation.

"The game is starting now," my brother said.
My mother asked, "Do you have any homework?"

Letters

Capitalize the greeting and the first word of the closing of a letter.

Examples: Dear Sir: Very truly yours,
         Dear Madam: Sincerely,
         Dear Linda,   Your friend,

Outlines

Capitalize the first word of each item in an outline.

Capitalization and Punctuation

I. Use of capital letters
    A. Proper nouns and adjectives
    B. First words
       1. Sentences
       2. Poetry
       3. Direct quotations
       4. Letters
       5. Outlines
       6. Titles
II. Use of periods

Exercises   **Use capital letters correctly.**

A.   Copy the following. Use correct capitalization.

1. Ms. Berg asked, "where is my train ticket?"
2. Rona commented, "you're a good basketball player."
3. "the pineapple is delicious," Stu said.
4. he asked, "is Gordon a nurse?"
5. "where is my mistake?" Amy asked.
6. the fortune teller said, "pick a card."
7. "try these crutches," the doctor said.
8. she asked, "is a violin a fiddle?"
9. "the park is closed," the guard told us.
10. "where is a salesperson?" the customer asked.

B.   Follow the directions for Exercise A.

1.   indians of the Northeast
    I. groups
       A. lake indians
       B. woodland indians

II. important foods
   A. lake indians
      1. wild rice
      2. fish
   B. woodland indians
      1. corn
      2. deer and other game

2.   September 12, 1985
   dear kathleen,
      thank you for showing me the sights of washington,
   d.c. nothing here in cleveland seems as exciting as the
   white house, the capitol, or the smithsonian institution.
      in one of my classes, i showed my photos of george
   washington's home. we talked about mount vernon.
      i hope that next august you will come to visit me. i'll
   make sure that you have a good time here in the midwest.

                                    very truly yours,
                                    alison

Titles

Capitalize the first word and all important words in chapter titles, titles of magazine articles, titles of short stories or single poems, and titles of songs.

Use quotation marks for these titles.

Chapter:	"The Troubled City"
Magazine article:	"Winning and Losing"
Short story:	"The Monkey's Paw"
Poem:	"Annabel Lee"
Song:	"Home on the Range"

Capitalize the first word and all important words in titles of books, newspapers, magazines, titles of television programs, and movies.

Underline these titles. (When printed, they are *italicized*.)

Book:	*Roots*
Newspaper:	*The New York Times*
Magazine:	*People*
Television program:	*60 Minutes*
Movie:	*The Right Stuff*

Do not capitalize articles, conjunctions, or prepositions of four or fewer letters unless they are the first words in a title.

Exercises   Use capital letters correctly.

A. Copy these titles. Capitalize correctly.

1. "making friends"   (magazine article)
2. *teen*   (magazine)
3. "the ransom of red chief"   (short story)
4. *the sound of music*   (movie)
5. "the underwater world"   (chapter title)
6. *los angeles times*   (newspaper)
7. "dust of snow"   (poem)
8. "dixie"   (song)
9. *masterpiece theatre*   (television program)
10. *all creatures great and small*   (book)

B. Follow the directions for Exercise A.

1. *the evening news*   (television program)
2. *the pigman*   (book)
3. *superman*   (movie)
4. "the spirit of democracy"   (chapter title)
5. *miami herald*   (newspaper)
6. "the bat"   (poem)
7. "to build a fire"   (short story)
8. "born free"   (song)
9. *time*   (magazine)
10. "what do your dreams mean?"   (magazine article)

ADDITIONAL EXERCISES

Capitalization

A. Proper Nouns and Adjectives Copy each of the following sentences. Change small letters to capital letters wherever necessary.

1. When is barry manilow's next concert?
2. After lunch, judge chase addressed the jury.
3. Jack's birthday is during the summer, but mine is november 8.
4. This tuesday will be groundhog day.
5. Did chicago, illinois, have a record cold spell last winter?
6. People attend bullfights in madrid, spain.
7. The two largest states are alaska and texas.
8. We met mayor minsky at city hall.
9. Is thornton junior high on ridge avenue and main street?
10. The snake river runs through a deep gorge.
11. We camped at glacier national park and yellowstone national park during our vacation in the west.
12. We traveled south to the grand canyon.
13. The japanese welcomed ambassador graf.
14. The catholic priest recited the prayer in latin.
15. Did you play in the lakeville little league?
16. The ralston-purina company makes food for animals.
17. My dentist is dr. m. j. cullinan.
18. For lunch i had a spanish omelette, french bread, and salad with italian dressing.
19. The sunshine state parkway runs through central florida.
20. The marquette building is on dearborn street.

B. First Words and Titles

Copy each of the following sentences. Change small letters to capital letters wherever necessary.

1. "here is the royal gorge bridge," the guide said.
2. bill asked, "have you ever had a greek salad?"
3. i read *the outsiders* and *that was then, this is now*.
4. "the land of happy" is a poem by shel silverstein.
5. wow! there's a falling star!
6. my sister said, "there are only ten days until vacation."
7.
      Winter Morning

   winter is the king of showmen,
   turning tree stumps into snow men
   and houses into birthday cakes
   and spreading sugar over lakes.
   smooth and clean and frosty white
   the world looks good enough to bite.
   that's the season to be young,
   catching snowflakes on your tongue.

   —OGDEN NASH

8.
                                    january 2, 1985
   dear brian,

       thank you for the great christmas gift. how did you
   know i wanted a backgammon game? when you come
   to kansas city, i'll teach you how to play.

                              your friend,
                              curt

9.   popular sports in the midwest

   I. winter sports
       A. cross-country skiing
       B. ice skating
   II. summer sports

       A. bicycling
       B. fishing
       C. boating

10. is *hill street blues* your favorite television program?

MIXED REVIEW

Capitalization

A. Using capitalization correctly   Copy the following sentences, changing small letters to capitals where necessary.

1. Is lake ontario connected to lake erie?
2. Is mount rushmore in south dakota or north dakota?
3. Mr. stevens applied for a job with general motors.
4. Does lisa attend the oak ridge school of folk music?
5. The indianapolis 500 is run on memorial day.
6. My aunt is going to south america this spring.
7. The league of women voters sponsored a debate last tuesday night.
8. The cotton bowl is played in dallas, texas.
9. Was t. s. eliot an american poet or an english poet?
10. The air conditioner in dad's office is made by general electric.

B. Using capitalization correctly in proofreading   Proofread the following. Rewrite it, correcting capitalization.

the first Ferris wheel was built for the 1893 world's fair in chicago. the planners of the fair wanted a spectacular attraction, like the eiffel tower had been for the fair in paris four years earlier. a man named george ferris drew plans of a gigantic wheel that people could ride. this original Ferris wheel makes today's version seem small. each full ride gave over 2,000 people a view of chicago and lake michigan. the wheel was then moved to st. louis for another fair. finally, a chicagoan named w. e. sullivan designed a smaller version that could be taken apart and put together. the Ferris wheel then became a popular feature in amusement parks, fairs, and carnivals all over america.

USING MECHANICS IN WRITING
Capitalization

A. You have a new pen pal. She has written to you about her country. Now she has some questions for you. Write a letter to her, answering the questions. Capitalize where necessary.

> Dear Pen Pal,
>
> Would you tell me some things about your home state? What is the capital of the state? I know that your country has a national anthem. Does your state have an official song, too? If so, what is it? What other towns are important in your state? I am interested in history. Can you tell me the date when your state gained its statehood? I would also like to know the names of two or three important people in the history of your state. Geography is my other favorite subject. Please tell me the names of any mountains, deserts, lakes, or rivers that you think are important. Thank you very much. I look forward to your answer.

You will probably have to look up the answers to some of these questions in the library.

B. Imagine that your uncle owns a movie theater. For your birthday, he surprises you with this offer: you may choose any five of your favorite movies and select the dates they will run. He will show each one for three days. Write out a schedule for your uncle so he can order the movies. Capitalize correctly.

C. You have decided to write to a local disc jockey to request that she play some of your favorite songs. Name three singles and one album that you would like to hear more often. Include the names of groups and singers as well as the song and album titles. Be sure to capitalize correctly.

Punctuation

Punctuation is the use of commas, periods, apostrophes, and other marks in writing. The marks, called **punctuation marks,** make the meanings of sentences clear.

Good punctuation is an aid to the reader. It helps the reader to understand whether a sentence is a statement, a question, or an exclamation. Periods and commas keep words and sentences from running together and confusing the reader. Punctuation marks also show that a word has been abbreviated, or short-ened. Without punctuation marks, a piece of writing would be as difficult to read as a coded message.

In this section, you will learn how to use punctuation marks. Whenever you write, these rules will help you write correctly. Look at them whenever you need help with punctuation.

End Marks

The signal that shows where a sentence begins is a capital letter. The punctuation marks that show where a sentence ends are called **end marks.**

There are three important end marks: (1) the **period,** (2) the **question mark,** and (3) the **exclamation point.**

The Period

Use a period at the end of a declarative sentence. A declarative sentence makes a statement.

> The Great Salt Lake is in Utah.

> Sarah and Josh are going to the dance.

Use a period at the end of an imperative sentence. An imperative sentence requests, instructs, or orders.

> Put your poster on the bulletin board.

> Read the directions carefully.

Use a period after an abbreviation.

Words are often written in a shortened form to save time and space. These shortened forms of words are called **abbreviations.** On calendars, for example, the names of the days are often abbreviated, as in *Mon.* for *Monday.*

You use the abbreviation *A.M.* to stand for the two Latin words, *ante meridiem,* which mean "before noon." The abbreviation *P.M.* stands for *post meridiem,* meaning "after noon."

Here are examples of other common abbreviations. Notice that some abbreviations have two or three parts, with each part standing for one or more words. A period is then used after each part of the abbreviation.

St. =	Street or Saint		in. =	inch
Mt. =	Mount or Mountain		doz. =	dozen
R.R. =	Railroad		Dr. =	Doctor
P.O. =	Post Office		Mr. =	Mister
U.S.A. =	United States of America			
D.C. =	District of Columbia			

Periods are not used after some abbreviations. Here are some examples:

        m = meter
        g = gram
        l = liter
        CB = Citizens' Band
        ZIP = Zone Improvement Plan

Note: Check with your local post office for the correct state abbreviations used with ZIP codes. All of the two-letter abbreviations are approved by the United States Postal Service. These special abbreviations are to be used only for the mail. Here are three examples of these special abbreviations:

        CA = California   OH = Ohio   VT = Vermont

If you are not sure whether an abbreviation should be written with or without periods, look up the abbreviation in a dictionary.

It is important to know the most common abbreviations. It is also important to use abbreviations correctly.

Most abbreviations may be used only in lists, addresses, arithmetic problems, or other special forms of writing. Abbreviations should not be used in sentences, paragraphs, or compositions. For example, on an application for a library card, or on an envelope, you may write your address in this way:

        152 W. Madison Rd.

In a sentence, you should write this:

        I live at 152 West Madison Road.

As a general rule, the only abbreviations you should use in sentences are *A.M.* and *P.M.*, *B.C.* and *A.D.*, and titles with names, such as *Dr.* Brothers.

Use a period after an initial.

A name is often shortened to its first letter, which is called an **initial.** Always use a period after an initial.

U.S. Grant   (Ulysses Simpson Grant)

Robert E. Lee   (Robert Edward Lee)

Use a period after each numeral or letter that shows a division of an outline or that precedes an item in a list.

An Outline

Punctuation
I. End marks
  A. The period
    1. Sentences
    2. Abbreviations and initials
    3. Outlines and lists
  B. The question mark
  C. The exclamation point
II. The comma

A List

Shopping list
1. apples
2. eggs
3. bread
4. lettuce

Exercises   Use periods correctly.

A. Number your paper from 1 to 10. Copy the following phrases, putting periods where necessary.

1. 4 ft 10 in
2. Washington, D C
3. 1 c sugar
4. Bedford Ave
5. Aug 30

6. Butterford Chocolate Co, Inc
7. Dr H M Ritchie
8. Los Angeles, CA 90053
9. (list) First five Presidents

     1 George Washington
     2 John Adams
     3 Thomas Jefferson
     4 James Madison
     5 James Monroe

10. (outline) Super-8 movie-making

    I   Major equipment needed
       A   Camera
          1   For silent movies
          2   For sound movies
       B   Projector
    II   Other materials needed
       A   Film
       B   Splicer

B. Write abbreviations for the following groups of words.

1. Eastern Standard Time
2. Buffalo, New York
3. Reverend John Marsh
4. 4 gallons
5. Mount Snow
6. Raleigh, North Carolina
7. December 9
8. Benander Game Company
9. 10 square feet
10. Durapools, Incorporated

C. Writing List five abbreviations used in your math book. Beside each abbreviation, write the word it stands for.

The Question Mark

Use a question mark at the end of an interrogative sentence.
An interrogative sentence is a sentence that asks a question.

Where are we?   Are you going to the game?

The Exclamation Point

Use an exclamation point at the end of an exclamatory sentence. An exclamatory sentence is a sentence that expresses strong feeling or excitement.

Jackie struck out!   Be careful!

Use an exclamation point after an interjection. An interjection is a word or group of words used to express strong feeling. Words often used as other parts of speech may become interjections when they express strong feeling.

Oh! How beautiful!   Wow! What an ending!

Exercises   Use periods, question marks, and exclamation points correctly.

A.   Copy the following sentences. Supply the missing punctuation.

1. My new address is 600 W 24 St
2. Don't touch that broken glass
3. Dr Evans will be in his office until 4:30
4. What circus did P T Barnum manage
5. Ms Carol F Kiley will speak at the N H S graduation
6. Mr and Mrs Gregory go to Miami every winter
7. Ouch This pan is hot
8. We stopped at an L C Carran gas station
9. How many empty bottles are you returning
10. Help These packages are too heavy for me

B. Follow the directions for Exercise A.

1. Is Dr Howard your dentist
2. The poet Hilda Dolittle signed her poems H D
3. W E B DuBois was a writer and a professor of sociology
4. Jump out of the way of that car
5. Mail the letter to Miss Deborah K Sobol
6. Terrific We got the last four tickets
7. How much does that album cost
8. Oh, no You didn't forget the picnic lunch, did you
9. Did Vanessa try out for the team last night
10. We met Dr Rusnak at her cousin's home

The Comma

Commas in Sentences

Commas tell the reader to pause slightly. The pause keeps the reader from running together words that should be kept apart. Commas are a great help in reading.

Use commas to separate a series of words. Two words are not a series. There are always more than two words in a series.

The boys entered dogs, cats, and hamsters in the show.
The day was sunny, hot, and humid.

In a series, commas are placed *after* each word but the last.
You can see how important it is to separate the parts of a series by reading these sentences.

At the party Bob ate cheese, pizza, ice cream, sandwiches, and milk.

At the party Bob ate cheese pizza, ice cream sandwiches, and milk.

Both sentences could be right. It depends upon what Bob did eat. The writer has to use commas correctly to tell the reader what Bob ate.

Use a comma after introductory words, such as *yes* or *no*.

Yes, I'm going.

No, I can't go out tonight.

Use a comma in a compound sentence. Place the comma at the end of the first complete thought.

Clark Kent disappeared, and Superman arrived.

We ran fast, but we nearly missed the bus.

When a subordinate clause begins a complex sentence, use a comma to separate it from the main clause.

When Clark Kent disappeared, Superman arrived.

Although we ran fast, we nearly missed the bus.

Exercises **Use commas correctly.**

A. Copy these sentences. Place commas where they are needed.

1. Yes we went to the zoo last summer.
2. You can take a bus to the zoo but we bicycled there.
3. We took our lunches and we spent the whole day.
4. We saw a hippopotamus a gorilla and an anteater.
5. Since the zoo was built a building was added.
6. After the seals performed their trainer fed them.
7. There were monkeys of every size color and shape.
8. Two monkeys started a fight and another watched.
9. We took pictures had a boat ride and saw a movie.
10. The movie was good but it wasn't as much fun as the animals at the zoo.

B. Follow the directions for Exercise A.

1. Will you drive us or should we take the subway?
2. The spaghetti tomato sauce and spices are in that cabinet.
3. Motels are all right but I like campgrounds better.
4. Robert and Anna weeded the garden and Doug and Nancy repaired the fence.
5. Although it was raining we still went for a walk.
6. Denmark Norway and Sweden are called Scandinavian countries.
7. No it's not raining.
8. We measured cut and sewed the curtains.
9. Because Joe was sick he missed the test.
10. My three sisters' names are Linda Donna and Jean.

Use commas to set off the name of a person spoken to. If the name begins or ends the sentence, one comma is enough. If the name comes in the middle of the sentence, place one comma before the name and another comma after it.

Please answer the phone, Jim.

Ginny, may I use your pen?

I believe, Mark, that you are right.

Set off an appositive with commas. An **appositive** is a word or group of words that means the same as the noun just before it. The appositive gives more information about the noun.

The words in italics in the following sentences are appositives. Notice that they tell more about *Mr. Lopez* and *the two teams*. Notice also that they are set off by commas.

Mr. Lopez, *the scoutmaster,* moved away.

The two teams tied for first place, *the Angels and the Royals,* will play tonight.

Use a comma after each part of a date. Place a comma between the date and the year. Use a comma after the year, too, unless it ends the sentence.

On November 7, 1962, Eleanor Roosevelt died.

The license expires on Thursday, June 1, 1987.

Note: Do not place a comma between the month and the number of the day: April 4.

Use a comma between the name of a city and the name of a state or country. If the two names come in the middle of a sentence, place a comma after the second name.

My grandmother was born in Dublin, Ireland.

We left Concord, New Hampshire, at noon.

Exercises **Use commas correctly.**

A. Copy these sentences. Place commas where they are needed.

1. Hold the line Gerry and I'll ask her.
2. On Saturday January 25 the excavation was begun.
3. We all met the new principal Ms. Gomez.
4. At Kitty Hawk North Carolina the Wright brothers successfully flew three gliders.
5. Dad this is Al Cresco a friend of mine.
6. The weather was hot in Corpus Christi Texas.
7. Last summer we went to Richmond Virginia.
8. Friday May 5 was our opening night.
9. Joey and Sandra lunch is ready.
10. The famous comedian Charlie Chaplin won the award.

B. Follow the directions for Exercise A.

1. Rhonda were you born in September 1972?

2. Albany New York is on the Hudson River.
3. Mary Shelley's famous novel *Frankenstein* was published in 1818.
4. Mr. Gray let's have the exhibit on Friday February 19.
5. The candidate Ms. Wingreen made a speech.
6. On October 4 1957 the Soviet Union launched the first satellite.
7. Did you know Adele that I'll be away tomorrow?
8. In Duluth Minnesota there is a statue of Jay Cooke the financier.
9. No Mrs. Lucas I have never lived in Dayton Ohio.
10. On September 25 1981 Sandra Day O'Connor was sworn in as an associate justice of the Supreme Court.

C. Writing Write your own sentences, using commas as indicated by these directions.

1. Write two sentences using commas to set off the names of persons.
2. Write two sentences using commas to set off appositives.
3. Write two sentences using commas to separate the parts of a date.
4. Write two sentences using commas to separate the name of a city from name of a state.

Commas with Quotations

Use a comma to set off the explaining words for a direct quotation.

When you use a quotation, you are giving the words of a speaker or writer. You are *quoting* the words of the speaker or writer. If you give *exact* words, you give a direct quotation.

Usually you include explaining words of your own, like *Mary Kay said, JoAnne answered,* or *Phil asked.*

> Courtney announced, "The movie will begin in ten minutes."

In the above sentence, the explaining words come *before* the quotation. A comma is placed after the last explaining word. Now read this quotation:

> "I want to go home," moaned Lisa.

In the above sentence, the explaining words come *after* the quotation. A comma is placed within the quotation marks after the last word of the quotation.

Sometimes the quotation is separated into two parts.

> "One of the people in this room," the detective said, "is the murderer."

The sentence above is an example of a **divided quotation.** It is called "divided" because it is made up of two parts that are separated by the explaining words. A comma is used after the last word of the first part of the quotation. Another comma is used after the last explaining word.

A quotation can be either *direct* or *indirect.* The quotations you have just looked at are all direct quotations. In an **indirect quotation** you change the words of a speaker or writer to your own words. No commas are used.

> Courtney announced that the movie would begin in ten minutes.
>
> Lisa said that she wanted to go home.

Commas in Letter Parts

Use a comma after the greeting of a friendly letter and after the closing of any letter.

> Dear Alice,   Sincerely yours,

Commas To Avoid Confusion

Some sentences can be confusing if commas are not used in them. Here are two examples of such sentences. Read them aloud.

> Going up the elevator lost power.
> In the grocery bags were in demand.

Now notice how much clearer these sentences are when commas are used.

> Going up, the elevator lost power.

> In the grocery, bags were in demand.

Use a comma whenever the reader might otherwise be confused.

Exercises   **Use commas correctly.**

A.   Copy the following sentences. Add commas where they are needed.

1. In the story books were forbidden.
2. After we ate the neighbors came to visit.
3. When Sheila typed the table shook.
4. "It seems to me" Carol said "that this puzzle is missing some pieces."
5. Benjamin said "I'd like to visit Boston some day."
6. "This soup is delicious" said my father.
7. "Who" the caterpillar asked Alice in Wonderland "are you?"
8. According to the paper cups of coffee will cost a dollar each.
9. In the garden flowers were blooming from May through September.
10. "Come here Midnight" Ned called.

Follow the directions for Exercise A.

1. When our team lost the players felt depressed.
2. In the kitchen chairs were rearranged.
3. For dinner Tony had a salad spaghetti and fruit.
4. Ms. Miller announced "The concert begins at seven."
5. "The radio is too loud" my mother complained.
6. While Vickie painted Eric sanded the table.
7. "Tomorrow's weather" the forecaster said "will be sunny and warm."
8. Yvette asked "What's on TV tonight?"
9. After Mr. Knowles left his puppy whined.
10. "Three weeks ago today" Meg said "I got a bike."

The Apostrophe

The Apostrophe To Show Possession

A **possessive** is a word that shows that someone or something owns something else.

To form the possessive of a singular noun, add an apostrophe and s after the apostrophe.

$$\text{dog} + \text{'s} = \text{dog's}$$
$$\text{man} + \text{'s} = \text{man's}$$
$$\text{lady} + \text{'s} = \text{lady's}$$
$$\text{James} + \text{'s} = \text{James's}$$

To form the possessive of a plural noun that does not end in s, add an apostrophe and an s after the apostrophe.

$$\text{men} + \text{'s} = \text{men's}$$
$$\text{geese} + \text{'s} = \text{geese's}$$

Form the possessive of a plural noun that ends in s, by adding only an apostrophe.

$$\text{dogs} + \text{'} = \text{dogs'}$$
$$\text{ladies} + \text{'} = \text{ladies'}$$

Exercises Use apostrophes in possessives.

A. Copy the groups of words below. Make the italicized word in each group show possession.

1. *children* games
2. *family* vacation
3. *bird* nest
4. *babies* toys
5. *announcer* voice
6. *goalies* saves
7. *Chris* lunch
8. *golfer* shots
9. the *girl* sweater
10. *mechanics* tools

B. Make these words show possession. Write the possessive form.

1. bikers
2. Ms. Smith
3. policemen
4. women
5. Louisa
6. poets
7. painter
8. cats
9. horse
10. cyclist
11. Dr. Bliss
12. partner

The Apostrophe in Contractions

A **contraction** is a word made by combining two words and omitting one or more letters. The apostrophe shows where a letter or letters have been omitted. Here are some contractions you use often:

cannot = can't
will not = won't
you will = you'll
must not = mustn't
they are = they're

we are = we're
does not = doesn't
he had, he would = he'd
she had, she would = she'd
are not = aren't

Be careful with *it's* and *its*. Remember:

It's always means *it is* or *it has*.

> *It's* going to rain today.

Its is the possessive of *it*.

> The racehorse broke *its* leg in a fall.

Remember that no apostrophe is used with the possessive pronouns *yours*, *hers*, *ours*, and *theirs*.

> The black checkers are *yours*. These drawings are *ours*.
> The red ones are *hers*. I like *theirs* better.

Here are some contractions and other words that are often confused.

Who's means *who is* or *who has*.

> *Who's* at the door?

Whose is the possessive of *who*.

> *Whose* bike is that?

You're means *you are*.

> *You're* coming to the library now, aren't you?

Your is the possessive of *you*.

> Hang *your* coat there.

They're means *they are*.

> *They're* waiting for us at the mall.

Their is the possessive form of *they*.

> The girls left *their* towels at the pool.

There means a place, or is used to begin sentences.

> *There* is an elephant over *there*.

Exercises   Use apostrophes in contractions.

A.   Write the contractions of these words.

1. I am   3. has not   5. we will
2. are not   4. I will   6. is not

7. it is	9. she is	11. that is
8. will not	10. we would	12. had not

B. Rewrite the following sentences. In each sentence make a contraction of the words in italics.

1. *I am* ready to go.
2. *We are* going to play miniature golf.
3. Darren *will not* come out this afternoon.
4. I *have not* delivered the papers yet.
5. Wanda and Mike said that *they are* working tomorrow.
6. *Who is* going to the library this afternoon?
7. *It is* your turn, Joy.
8. *It is* a great day for a picnic.
9. *What is* your name?
10. *I had* never seen so many tourists before.

The Hyphen

Use a hyphen to divide a word at the end of a line.

Before you choose a career, inves-
   tigate many fields.

Only words of two or more syllables can be divided at the end of a line. Never divide words of one syllable, such as *slight* or *bounce*. If you are in doubt about dividing a word, look it up in a dictionary.

Do not leave a single letter at the end of a line. For example, this division would be wrong: *a- mong*. A single letter must not appear at the beginning of a line, either. It would be wrong to divide *inventory* like this: *inventor- y*.

Use a hyphen in compound numbers from twenty-one through ninety-nine.

seventy-six trombones   Twenty-third Psalm

Exercises Use hyphens correctly.

A. Copy the following phrases. Decide whether you can divide the word in italics into two parts, each part having more than one letter. If you can, divide the word as you would at the end of a line. Also, add other necessary hyphens. If the word can be correctly divided more than one way, show all the ways.

> Examples: the thirty eight *runners*
>
> the thirty-eight run-
> ners

1. twenty nine *cents*
2. the sixty fourth *experiment*
3. the Twenty Second *Amendment*
4. thirty four *years*
5. eighty one *trailers*
6. seventy nine years *ago*
7. ninety three *skateboards*
8. forty five *minutes*
9. the fifty ninth *correction*
10. forty *clarinets*

B. Follow the directions for Exercise A.

1. seventy nine *students*
2. the thirty sixth *card*
3. seventy five *invitations*
4. the twenty two *classrooms*
5. ninety seven *cups*
6. the fifty fourth *contestant*
7. the eighty fifth *problem*
8. the forty eighth *state*
9. your ninety third *birthday*
10. the twenty ninth *story*

Quotation Marks

Direct Quotations

When you write what someone has said or written, you are using a **quotation.** If you write the person's exact words, you write a **direct quotation.** If you do not write his or her exact words, you have an **indirect quotation.** Study these sentences.

> Direct quotation: Steven said, "I don't want to go."
>
> Indirect quotation: Steven said that he didn't want to go.

Use quotation marks before and after the words of a direct quotation.

Quotation marks [" "] consist of two pairs of small marks that resemble apostrophes. They tell a reader that the exact words of another speaker or writer are being given.

Quotation marks are *not* used with indirect quotations.

> Direct quotation: Molly said, "I'm leaving."
>
> Indirect quotation: Molly said that she was leaving.

Separate the words of a direct quotation from the rest of the sentence with a comma or end mark, in addition to quotation marks.

> Jane said, "This glass is chipped."
>
> "This glass is chipped," Jane said.

Notice that in the first sentence above, the comma comes *before* the quotation marks. The second sentence starts with the quoted words, and the comma falls *inside* the quotation marks.

Now look carefully at these sentences:

> Mom asked, "Are you hungry?"
>
> "We're starving!" Bill replied.

You can see that in these sentences the question mark and exclamation point fall *inside* the quotation marks.

Place question marks and exclamation points inside quotation marks if they belong to the quotation itself.

The baby said, "I see Mama!"

Place question marks and exclamation points outside quotation marks if they do not belong to the quotation.

Did Dad say, "Come home at 7:00"?

Remember to capitalize the first word of a direct quotation.

Exercises **Punctuate direct quotations.**

A. Read these sentences to yourself. Copy them. Then add all the punctuation marks that are needed.

1. Do you really believe in ESP asked Tammy.
2. Did Lillian say I'll be at the pool soon?
3. The cashier asked Will there be anything else?
4. Call me when you finish said Ms. Walters.
5. Kevin replied I am finished now.
6. My parents said I can't go Pablo complained.
7. Drop anchor bellowed the captain.
8. Don't forget your key Jeff said Nina.
9. Ron asked Where are you going?
10. Two eggs with bacon shouted the waitress.

B. Follow the directions for Exercise A.

1. Mary said The roof is leaking.
2. Who's there called Michelle.
3. How can you drink so much milk Willie Anita inquired.
4. Those ears of corn look too big for that basket Mr. Valdez remarked.

5. What a tackle shouted David.
6. What was that noise asked my sister.
7. Last call for dinner announced the Amtrak waiter.
8. Kathy's mother said I will help you.
9. Watch out for that truck Manny cried.
10. Heavens to Betsy exclaimed Mrs. Mulligan.

Divided Quotations

Sometimes a quotation is divided. That is, explaining words, like *she said* or *he asked*, come in the middle of the quotation.

"My favorite movie," Lewis said, "is the original *King Kong*."

Divided quotations follow the same capitalization and punctuation rules that you have already studied. Here are three more rules for divided quotations:

1. Use two sets of quotation marks.
2. Use a comma or a period after the explaining words. Use a comma if the second part of the quotation does not begin a new sentence. Use a period if the second part of the quotation is a new sentence.

"I can't go," Frank said. "My homework is not done."

"I believe," said Mona, "that you are wrong."

3. If the second part of the quotation begins a new sentence, capitalize the first word, as in the first example above. Otherwise, do not capitalize the first word.

Exercises   Punctuate divided quotations.

A. Read each divided quotation to yourself. Then copy the sentence, using punctuation marks and capitals correctly.

1. Take the game home Sally said generously you can keep it.

2. How much does this spray cost Bonita inquired is it guaranteed to repel mosquitoes?
3. Are you ready said Bryan I'll time you.
4. The crawl kick isn't hard Judy assured us just keep your knees straight as you swim.
5. What would you do Mr. Rocher asked if the rope broke?
6. Before you leave said Ms. Schafer I want you to finish this assignment.
7. Where did you go Juanita asked I couldn't find you.
8. Look at my watch exclaimed Sam it doesn't even have water in it.
9. You can pet Prince said Louise he won't bite.
10. The other way Hector insisted is much shorter.

B. Follow the directions for Exercise A.

1. Fortunately said Andrea I've got fifty cents.
2. Turn the box over my brother suggested maybe the price is on the bottom.
3. No answered Seth my jacket is blue.
4. If you need more hay said the farmer it's in the barn.
5. Be careful shouted John the canoe will hit bottom.
6. Ask Ms. Mitchell suggested Maureen maybe we can broadcast the announcement.
7. On Saturday Dora said I'll meet you at 8:30.
8. I'm getting cold shivered Robin let's go inside.
9. The most interesting castles Beth said were in Europe.
10. Don't worry said my mother it will wash out.

Dialogue

In writing **dialogue** (conversation), begin a new paragraph every time the speaker changes. Use another set of quotation marks for each new speaker.

"I want to go ice skating this weekend," Thomas said, "but I can't find my skates."

"Can you rent a pair at the rink?" Rosemary asked.

"Yes, I think so," Thomas replied.

Exercise **Punctuate conversation correctly.**

Writing Read and then rewrite the following conversation. Make correct paragraph divisions and use the correct punctuation.

Fay and Alan looked at the lists of ice cream flavors at Swenson's Dairy have you made up your mind yet Fay asked yes Alan said I'm getting strawberry you always get strawberry Fay said why don't you ever try something new I'm trying to decide between chocolate fudge and cherry ripple that's why I always get strawberry Alan said it's so much faster

Using Quotation Marks for Titles

Use quotation marks to enclose chapter titles, titles of magazine articles, titles of short stories or single poems, and titles of songs.

Chapter:	Chapter 9, "State Government Today"
Magazine article:	"Summer Jobs for Teens"
Short Story:	"A Game of Catch"
Poem:	"Out, Out—"
Song:	"Take Me Out to the Ball Game"

Underlining

Underline the titles of books, newspapers, magazines, titles of television programs, and movies.

When you are writing or when you are typing, underline these titles like this: <u>The Contender</u>.

When these titles are printed, they are printed in *italics*, rather than underlined.

Book:	*The Contender*
Newspaper:	*Baltimore Sun*
Magazine:	*Reader's Digest*
Television program:	*Good Morning, America*
Movie:	*The Return of the Jedi*

Exercises Write titles correctly.

A. Number your paper from 1 to 10. Write each of the following titles correctly, either by underlining or using quotation marks.

1. Chariots of Fire (movie)
2. The Ark (book)
3. Boston Globe (newspaper)
4. Child on Top of a Greenhouse (poem)
5. Football's Superstars (magazine article)
6. Field and Stream (magazine)
7. M*A*S*H (television program)
8. The Age of the Glaciers (chapter title)
9. The Battle Hymn of the Republic (song)
10. The Tiger's Heart (short story)

B. Follow the directions for Exercise A.

1. Call It Courage (book)
2. The Diet That's Right for You (magazine article)
3. How the West Was Won (movie)
4. The Outcasts of Poker Flat (short story)
5. I'm Nobody! Who Are You? (poem)
6. The World of Jacques Cousteau (television program)
7. Time (magazine)
8. St. Louis Post-Dispatch (newspaper)
9. America (song)
10. Modern Art (chapter title)

ADDITIONAL EXERCISES

Punctuation

A. **The Period**   Write these items, adding periods wherever necessary.

1. We will attend S E Grover High School after we graduate this spring
2. Meet me at school at 9:00 A M
3. The address is 2025 Touhy Ave, and the ZIP is 60645
4. Dr H L Mason used to live in Washington, D C
5. Lexecon, Inc is located at 140 S Dearborn
6. J B Jones cleared 6 ft 2 in in the high jump
7. Mt Rushmore is in the Black Hills of South Dakota
8. Mail the form to Prizes, Inc, 23 W Harbor Dr, NY, NY
9. (list) Committees for dance
   1 Decorations
   2 Publicity
   3 Band
   4 Clean-up
   5 Tickets
10. (outline) Kinds of dogs
    I Sporting dogs
      A Retrievers
      B Setters
      C Spaniels
    II Hounds
    III Terriers
    IV Working dogs
      A Sheepdogs
      B Husky
      C St Bernard

B. End Marks
Write these sentences, adding the proper end marks.

1. Have you seen Ms. J. L. Pollock
2. Will you read my poem, Mr. Krause
3. Wow That's terrific
4. Dee wallpapered her room
5. Horrors Is that a tarantula
6. May I go to the skating rink tonight
7. Larry's family backpacked through the mountains
8. What a great game that was
9. Steve prefers bratwurst to hamburgers
10. Was the movie exciting

C. The Comma
Write the following sentences, adding commas where they are needed.

1. Melinda said "I rode on the trail near the lake."
2. "Yes I'd like to go to Disney World Vicky."
3. Angie dug the soil and Andy planted the seeds.
4. Dan Pierce the manager flew to Miami Florida.
5. The treaty was signed on December 10 1898.
6. Laura baked a meatloaf potatoes and a cherry pie.
7. When the movie began the talking stopped.
8. "Let's go" said Jerry "before it starts to rain."
9. The plane will arrive in Tokyo Japan tomorrow.
10. "Jack please put the pliers the hammer and the wrench in the toolbox."

D. The Apostrophe
Write each sentence, adding apostrophes where they are needed.

1. Whos pitching for the Cardinals today?
2. Tinas house is farther than yours, isnt it?
3. California hasnt had rain in months.
4. The womens club held its weekly meeting.

5. My two brothers bikes are identical.
6. If its warm enough, well go to the beach.
7. The puppies cries were heard throughout the kennel.
8. Mels chili wasnt very spicy.
9. Theyre waiting at Teds house.
10. Arent the childrens paintings colorful?

E. The Hyphen Copy the following phrases. If you can divide the word in italics into two parts, divide it as you would at the end of a line. Show all the ways the word can be divided. Add any other necessary hyphens to the phrase.

1. twenty one *balloons*
2. sixty two *dollars*
3. thirty three *volumes*
4. eighteen *igloos*
5. the Fourth *Commandment*
6. fifty five *residents*
7. twenty seven *convertibles*
8. one *menu*
9. forty eight *pennies*
10. ninety nine *questions*

F. Quotation Marks Write each sentence, adding quotation marks where they are needed.

1. Carl said, I'll run for office.
2. The man shouted, Get out!
3. Did she say, No one cares?
4. Behind the garage, Dad said, we'll plant a garden.
5. Gail said that she liked the poem The Harbor.
6. What a surprise to see you! exclaimed Rick.
7. I want you, said the coach, to win this game.
8. The first grade class likes to sing London Bridge.
9. Marion asked, Did you remember the potato chips?
10. Well, Dirk said, I guess we're ready.

MIXED REVIEW

Punctuation

A. Using punctuation correctly Copy these sentences, adding end marks, commas, apostrophes, quotation marks, and underlining where necessary.

1. Beth suggested that we sing Auld Lang Syne
2. Erin bring a blanket a flashlight and an alarm clock
3. What time is it asked Marie Doesnt the movie start at 5:30
4. After we took the pictures we developed the film
5. Sam repairs bicycles and his dad repairs cars
6. Mr. Keane assigned the book Sounder
7. Did George Washington say I cannot tell a lie
8. Wow cried Hilary We almost lost an oar
9. On May 29 1917 John F Kennedy the thirty fifth President of the United States was born in Brookline Massachusetts
10. Dr Hills new office isnt far from here

B. Proofreading for correct punctuation Proofread the following letter. Rewrite it, using correct punctuation.

1705 Oak Circle,
St Louis MO
April, 18 1985

Dear Jo

Yes I do like science fiction books now that Ive read some. The list of book titles you gave me helped? Im reading The Martian Chronicles now. Have you kept your part of the deal! I remember Jo, when you said "Ill never read a biography"! Did my suggestions change your mind too.

Your friend
Mara

USING MECHANICS IN WRITING
Punctuation

A. It is twenty years in the future. Your personal robot has spent the day keeping house while you were out in your mini-copter. The robot has left a message for you on your personal computer. You have never succeeded in teaching your robot to punctuate properly, so you must unscramble the message. Rewrite it with correct punctuation.

Dear Owner

I spent the morning in the kitchen What a mess Now the cupboards are in order the dishes are clean and the floor is washed and waxed Please wipe your feet before you walk in I dont want to do that floor again this week This afternoon I washed windows made beds did the laundry vacuumed dusted the furniture and clipped the dog It was all I could do to get him to hold still What would you like me to do tomorrow Do you want me to plan the menu for tomorrow nights barbecue How does steak sound I could also bake my famous Chocomania cake Remember to call your Aunt Gertrude She wants to tell you about her latest trip to the moon It must be nice Dont forget Saturday is my day off Ive earned it

Respectfully
Rob

B. Answer your robot's message. Tell him whether or not he did a good job and what needs improvement. List the things you want him to do tomorrow. Be sure to punctuate correctly.

Spelling

Good spelling skills are valuable. They are important for writing reports in school. They are needed for writing letters. They are vital for filling out forms and applications. As you grow older and write more, they will become even more important. To show people that you are careful and informed, you must be able to spell correctly.

You can become a better speller by learning a few basic rules. These rules will help you to write clearly. In this section, you will learn the most important rules of good spelling. You will also learn how to develop good spelling habits.

How To Become a Better Speller

1. Make a habit of looking at words carefully. Practice seeing every letter. Store the letters in your memory. Many people see a word again and again but don't really look at it. Then they make such mistakes as writing *safty* for *safety* or *sayed* for *said*. When you see a new word or a tricky word, like *necessary*, look at all the letters. To help yourself remember the spelling, write the word several times. You may want to keep a list of the new words for later practice.

2. When you speak, pronounce words carefully. Sometimes people misspell words because they say them incorrectly. Be sure that you are not blending syllables together. For example, you may write *finely* for *finally* if you are mispronouncing it.

3. Find out your own spelling "demons" and attack them. Look over your past papers and make a list of the misspelled words. Study these words until you can spell them correctly.

4. Find memory devices to help with problem spellings. Memory devices link words with their correct spellings. Below are some devices. They may give you ideas for other words.

> bel**ie**ve   There is a *lie* in bel*ie*ve.
> fr**i**end   *I* will be your friend to the *end*.
> emba**rr**a**ss**   I turned *really* red and felt *so silly*.

5. Proofread what you write. To make sure that you have spelled all words correctly, reread your work. Examine it carefully, word for word. Don't let your eyes race over the page and miss misspellings.

6. Use a dictionary. You don't have to know how to spell every word in the English language. No one spells everything correctly all the time. A good dictionary can help you to be a better speller. Use a dictionary whenever you need help.

7. Study the important spelling rules given in this section.

How To Master the Spelling of Specific Words

1. Look at a new or difficult word and say it to yourself. Pronounce it carefully. If it has two or more syllables, say it again, one syllable at a time. Look at each syllable as you say it.

2. Look at the letters and say each one. If the word has two or more syllables, pause between syllables.

3. Without looking at the word, write it.

4. Now look at your book or list and see if you have spelled the word correctly. If you have, write it once more. Compare it with the correct spelling again. Repeat the process again.

5. If you have misspelled the word, notice where the error was. Then repeat steps 3 and 4 until you have spelled the word correctly three times in a row.

Rules for Spelling

The Final Silent e

When a suffix beginning with a vowel is added to a word ending with a silent e, the e is usually dropped.

make + ing = making	expense + ive = expensive
confuse + ion = confusion	believe + able = believable

When a suffix beginning with a consonant is added to a word ending with a silent e, the e is usually kept.

hate + ful = hateful	hope + less = hopeless
bore + dom = boredom	sure + ly = surely

The following words are exceptions:

truly   argument   ninth   wholly

Exercise   Add suffixes correctly.

Find the misspelled words in these sentences and spell them correctly. (In most of the sentences, more than one word is misspelled.)

1. We ordered a flower arrangment of ninty roses.
2. The blazeing fire severly damaged the house.
3. I am hopeing that this game won't remain scoreless.
4. A jack is usful for changeing tires.
5. Ms. Moore's statment was truly moveing.
6. Terence is blameing me for the damage to his bike.
7. Some fameous people are lonly.
8. Why are we haveing this silly arguement?
9. The skill of the dareing acrobats was exciteing.
10. Good writeing skills are a desirable achievment.

Words Ending in y

When a suffix is added to a word that ends with y following a consonant, the y is usually changed to i.

noisy + ly = noisily	carry + age = carriage
happy + est = happiest	fifty + eth = fiftieth
try + ed = tried	heavy + ness = heaviness

Note this exception: When -ing is added, the y remains.

bury + ing = burying	cry + ing = crying
deny + ing = denying	apply + ing = applying

When a suffix is added to a word that ends with y following a vowel, the y usually is not changed.

joy + ful = joyful	pay + ment = payment
stay + ing = staying	annoy + ed = annoyed

The following words are exceptions:

    paid   said   gaily   gaiety

Write words with suffixes and a final _y_.

Add the suffixes as shown and write the new word.

1. employ + er
2. enjoy + able
3. marry + age
4. play + ed
5. carry + ing

6. sneaky + est
7. destroy + er
8. sixty + eth
9. say + ing
10. reply + es

11. hurry + ed
12. holy + ness
13. easy + ly
14. ready + ness
15. boy + ish

The Suffixes _-ly_ and _-ness_

When the suffix _-ly_ is added to a word ending with _l_, both _l_'s are kept. When _-ness_ is added to a word ending in _n_, both _n_'s are kept.

practical + ly = practically
careful + ly = carefully

mean + ness = meanness
open + ness = openness

The Addition of Prefixes

When a prefix is added to a word, the spelling of the word stays the same.

un + named = unnamed
dis + appear = disappear
in + formal = informal
im + mature = immature

re + enter = reenter
un + known = unknown
il + legible = illegible
in + appropriate = inappropriate

Exercise **Write words with prefixes and suffixes.**

Find the misspelled words in these sentences and spell them correctly. Some sentences have more than one.

1. Luis was imobile in a plaster cast.
2. Carolyn likes this meat for its leaness.
3. Sometimes reporters are missinformed.
4. Many students become awfuly unneasy at test time.
5. Mistreating animals should be ilegal.

6. People who write carefuly don't often mispell words.
7. Ken's handwriting is ilegible.
8. Idealy, citizens should not dissobey the law.
9. My mother dissapproves of my stubborness.
10. I realy distrust people who are iresponsible.

Words with the "Seed" Sound

Only one English word ends in *sede: supersede.*
Three words end in *ceed: exceed, proceed, succeed.*
All other words ending in the sound of *seed* are spelled *cede:*

concede   precede   recede   secede

Words with *ie* or *ei*

When the sound is long *e* (*ē*), the word is spelled *ie* except
after *c.*

I Before *E*:

achieve	brief	field	niece	shield
belief	chief	fierce	relieve	yield

Except After *C*:

ceiling   conceited   perceive   receive   receipt

The following words are exceptions:

either	leisure	species
neither	seize	weird

Exercise   **Write words with the "seed" sound and *ie/
ei* words.**

Find the misspelled words in these sentences and spell
them correctly. (In some of the sentences, there is more than
one misspelled word.)

1. Anna recieved an award for her painting.

2. Did the trucker excede the speed limit?
3. Alvarez preceeds Sanders in the batting order.
4. The mayor beleived that she had been wrong.
5. We saw a breif film about making leisure time work.
6. The criminal yeilded after a feirce fight.
7. The outfielder proseded to snatch the line drive.
8. Weird shadows danced on the cieling.
9. Many people succede if they beleive in themselves.
10. The police cheif siezed the thief.

Doubling the Final Consonant

In words of one syllable that end with one consonant following one vowel, double the final consonant before adding *-ing*, *-ed*, or *-er*.

sit + ing = sitting	sad + er = sadder
hop + ed = hopped	stop + ing = stopping
plan + er = planner	trot + ed = trotted
shop + er = shopper	drag + ing = dragging

The final consonant is not doubled when it is preceded by two vowels.

meet + ing = meeting	loan + ed = loaned
break + ing = breaking	train + er = trainer
seem + ed = seemed	soon + er = sooner

Exercise   Double the final consonant.

Decide whether or not the final consonant should be doubled. Then add the suffix as shown and write the new word.

1. leap + ed
2. fat + er
3. beat + ing
4. cool + er
5. chop + er
6. hem + ed
7. scream + ing
8. flap + ed
9. hot + er
10. hug + ing
11. hear + ing
12. trip + ed
13. swim + er
14. leap + ing
15. peek + ed

Words Often Confused

Sometimes you make a mistake in spelling simply because of carelessness or forgetfulness. At other times, however, your problems are caused by the language itself. In English there are many pairs or trios of words that are easily confused. These words sound the same, or nearly the same, but are spelled differently and have different meanings. Words of this type are called **homonyms.**

Here are some examples of homonyms:

do—dew—due
horse—hoarse
pare—pear—pair
tail—tale

When you have problems with homonyms, general spelling rules won't help you. The only solution is to memorize which spelling goes with which meaning.

Here is a list of words frequently used and frequently confused in writing. Study the sets of words, and try to connect each word with its correct meaning. Refer to the list if you have further difficulties with these words.

accept means "to agree to or to receive something willingly."

My brother will *accept* the job the grocer offered him.

except means "to keep out" or "leave out." As a preposition, *except* means "but" or "leaving out."

Overdue books returned to the library today are *excepted* from the usual fines.

Michelle likes every flavor of ice cream *except* pistachio.

already means "previously or before."

The airplane had *already* landed.

all ready means "completely prepared."

The paramedics were *all ready* for the emergency.

capital means "important." It also refers to the city or town that is the official seat of government of a state or nation.

The *capital* of Illinois is the city of Springfield.

capitol is the building where a state legislature meets.

The *capitol* of Illinois is a stately building in Springfield.

the Capitol is the building in Washington, D. C., in which the United States Congress meets.

Senator Wilson arrived at the *Capitol* in time for the vote.

hear means "to listen to."

Every time I *hear* this song, I feel happy.

here means "in this place."

Reference books must remain *here* in the library.

it's is the contraction for *it is* or *it has*.

It's nearly midnight.

its shows ownership or possession.

The boat lost *its* way during the storm.

knew means "understood" or "was familiar with."

The forest ranger *knew* that the fire was out of control.

new is the opposite of *old* and means "fresh or recent."

Old shoes feel more comfortable than *new* ones.

know means "to understand" or "to be familiar with."

Scientists do not *know* the cause of cancer.

no is a negative word meaning "not" or "not any."

This theater has *no* popcorn.

lead (lĕd) is a heavy, gray metal.

Those pipes are made of *lead*.

lead (lēd) means "to go first, to guide."

These signs will *lead* us to the hiking trail.

led (lĕd) is the past tense of lead (lēd).

Bloodhounds *led* the detectives to the scene of the crime.

loose means "free" or "not tight."

A rider keeps the horse's reins *loose*.

lose means "to mislay or suffer the loss of something."

If you *lose* your book, report the loss to the library.

peace is a calm or stillness or the absence of disagreement.

A sunset over the ocean is my idea of *peace*.

piece means "a portion or part."

I have the last *piece* of the puzzle.

plain means "clear or simple." It also refers to an expanse of land.

The judge wanted to know the *plain* truth.

Cattle grazed on the grassy *plain*.

plane refers to a flat surface or a woodworking tool. It is also the short form of *airplane*.

Dad's *plane* landed at La Guardia.

The carpenter used her *plane* to make the door level.

principal means "first or most important." It also refers to the head of a school.

A *principal* export of Brazil is coffee.

Our school *principal* organized a safety council.

principle is a rule, truth, or belief.

One *principle* of science is that all matter occupies space.

quiet means "free from noise or disturbance."

The only time our classroom is *quiet* is when it's empty.

quite means "truly or almost completely."

The aquarium tank is *quite* full.

right means "proper or correct." It also means the opposite of left. It also refers to a just claim.

Emily Post is an expert on the *right* way to behave.

Turn *right* at the second intersection.

A trial by jury is every citizen's *right*.

write refers to forming words with a pen or pencil.

I will *write* a letter to the editor.

there means "at that place."

Please take your books over *there*.

their means "belonging to them."

Our neighbors sold *their* house and moved to a farm.

they're is the contraction for *they are*.

My sisters have never skied, but *they're* willing to try.

to means "in the direction of."

> The surgeon rushed *to* the operating room.

too means "also or very."

> The lights went off, and then the heat went off, *too*.

two is the whole number between one and three.

> Only *two* of the four climbers reached the peak.

weather is the state of the atmosphere, referring to wind, moisture, temperature, and other such conditions.

> Australia has summer *weather* when the United States has winter.

whether indicates a choice or alternative.

> *Whether* we drive or take the train, we will arrive in three hours.

who's is the contraction for *who is* or *who has*.

> *Who's* been chosen to be a crossing guard?

whose is the possessive form of *who*.

> *Whose* bicycle was left on the sidewalk?

your is the possessive form for *you*.

> Please bring *your* sheet music to choir practice.

you're is the contraction of *you are*.

> *You're* going to dance, aren't you?

Exercises   Use words often confused.

A. Write the correct word from the words in parentheses.

1. Is the cast (all ready, already) for the performance?
2. Nobody (knew, new) the answer to the fifth question on the test.
3. (Who's, Whose) bicycle has racing stripes?
4. The twins built (their, there, they're) tree house.
5. The Indian (lead, led) his tribe to the hunting ground.
6. In autumn, many trees (loose, lose) their leaves.
7. One feature of the shark is (its, it's) double row of teeth.

8. Not every problem has only one (right, write) solution.

9. Did Dwayne (accept, except) the invitation to your party?

10. I study best in a well-lit, (quiet, quite) room.

11. The (capital, capitol, Capitol) in Washington, D. C., is built on a hill.

12. The patient is (know, no) better today.

13. Are you taller than (your, you're) sister?

14. We will play the game (weather, whether) it rains or not.

15. A (piece, peace) of fabric was caught in the machine.

B. Write the correct word from the words in parentheses.

1. A fire engine will (lead, led) the parade.

2. Did you (know, no) ants have jaws called mandibles?

3. The (principal, principle) actor in M*A*S*H was Alan Alda.

4. Carlotta ordered a (plain, plane) hamburger.

5. Jaguars seem fierce, but (their, there, they're) afraid of dogs.

6. The teacher asked us to (right, write) our assignment.

7. We had to hunt for the gerbil that got (loose, lose).

8. Although bats don't see well, they (hear, here) well.

9. Does your brother know that (your, you're) planning a surprise party?

10. Ceramics is creative, and it's fun, (to, too, two).

11. Eric is the only batter (who's, whose) left-handed.

12. Her friends taught us the (knew, new) dances.

13. The city of Austin is the (capital, capitol, Capitol) of Texas.

14. Examine the new bike to see whether (its, it's) scratched.

15. Everyone (accept, except) Donna went down the slide.

ADDITIONAL EXERCISES

Spelling

A. Spelling Look at each sentence carefully. Find the misspelled words. Write each word correctly.

1. Bo's dog usualy retreives sticks.
2. Rita spoted the mispelled word.
3. I carryed grocerys in my bike basket.
4. This canoe is realy unnsteady.
5. The meaness of that little dog is surpriseing.
6. Hard work will often succede.
7. A mobile hangs from the cieling.
8. The candidate is very hopful.
9. Have you visited these citys?
10. That shouting is unecessary.

B. Words Often Confused Write the correct word from the words given in parentheses.

1. Will you please (right, write) the answer on the chalkboard?
2. Are you (already, all ready) for the recital?
3. Did you (hear, here) that rumor?
4. The cheerleaders have (knew, new) uniforms.
5. An Indian guide (lead, led) the Pilgrims.
6. That sail is too (loose, lose).
7. I put a monogram on a (plain, plane) red sweater.
8. Everyone (accept, except) John was at practice.
9. The Johnsons opened (their, there, they're) new store.
10. I hope (your, you're) ready for the time trials.

MIXED REVIEW

Spelling

A. Spelling words correctly Number your paper from 1 to 10. Pick out the words that are spelled incorrectly in the following sentences. Write them correctly. If there are no incorrectly spelled words in a sentence, write *Correct*.

1. July is usualy a hot month.
2. The children were makeing a tree house in there yard.
3. If everyone is hear, we will proceed with our meeting.
4. Josh mispelled the title of the movie.
5. The audience claped for each contestant.
6. Are you practiceing you're speech all ready?
7. Everyone accept Sheila recieved an inviteation.
8. The tent shielded us from the fierce winds.
9. These skates are much two loose.
10. Its not likly that Jones will be elected.

B. Proofreading for correct spelling Proofread the following paragraph. Rewrite it, spelling all words correctly.

Did you no that mosquitoes do not actualy bite? Mosquitoes can not open there jaws. However, they do use a needlelike mouth part too stab or sting a victim and draw out it's blood. Some mosquitoes are carryers of diseases. However, most mosquitoes do not sting humans at all. Many species of mosquitoes prefer the hot, damp whether of the tropics, but mosquitoes live everywhere in the world, includeing the Arctic. Sometimes you can here a mosquito even though you cannot see it. The hum that mosquitoes make is the sound of they're wings beatting constantlly. A mosquito can not glide through the air. It must always beat its wings accept when it wants to land.

USING MECHANICS IN WRITING
Spelling

A. Here is a story that was submitted to the school newspaper. Its spelling mistakes need to be corrected before the story is sent to press. Rewrite the story, finding and correcting all spelling errors.

Our club's three-week wilderness adventure last summer was truely fantastic. We did some of the usual outdoors things, like swiming, bikeing, and hiking. We also learned some usful things, to, like makeing a fire without matches and building a bridge across a stream.

There was a lot of sillyness and jokeing around, but we also learned some important things like coperation and shareing work without arguements. Within a few days, even the lazyest campers were carring their share. Its realy surpriseing how much enjoyment you can get from doing hard work! When I got home, my mom said I looked skinnyer and a little dirtyer, but also happyer.

If your interested in finding out about next summer's trip, their is a meeting after school on the nineth of May.

B. Write a letter to the principal of your school. Suggest a class trip to either your state capital or to Washington, D.C. In your letter, use at least five of the following homonyms correctly.

accept	it's	led	right	whether
except	its	piece	write	whose
capital	knew	peace	their	who's
capitol	new	principal	there	your
Capitol	know	principle	to	you're
here	no	quite	too	not
hear	lead	quiet	weather	knot

CUMULATIVE REVIEW
Capitalization, Punctuation, and Spelling

A. Using capitalization, punctuation, and spelling correctly Copy the following sentences, correcting the errors in capitalization, punctuation, and spelling.

1. Id rather see a knew movie than see return of the jedi
2. "is you're brother on vacation in canada asked Lili
3. The train stoped in nashville atlanta and orlando before reaching miami beach
4. mark spitz won seven olympic gold medals in 1972
5. newsweek has an article about british tennis
6. frankfort kentucky is my home town
7. who's dog is that over their asked Fred
8. What a breathtaking veiw it is from the sears tower
9. mr harris recieved The brethren, a book about the supreme court, for his birthday
10. "the baby cryed when she couldnt find you said the babysitter but she stopped write away"

B. Using proofreading skills Proofread the following paragraph. Copy it, correcting the errors in capitalization, punctuation, and spelling.

Are you superstitious. Well my grandmother is. one of my earlyest memories is of my grandmother saying Dont put your shoes on the table because its bad luck" When I droped a fork shed say That means company's comeing. She said my itchy nose meant Your going to kiss a fool." My grandmother did other things, two, to bring us luck. One time, she baked a ring in a loaf of bread. although, I realy dont beleive all of these superstitions it is fun too remember them, and the good times i spent with my grandmother.

A

Apostrophe, 574–577
  in contractions, 575–576
  in possessives, 339–341,
    574–575
Articles, 426, 546
Assignments, understanding,
    234–235
Audience, of a speaker, 274–275,
    284–285
Author card in card catalog, 228
Auxiliaries. *See* Helping verbs.

B

bad/good, 434
Base words, 14–15
be, forms of, 348–349, 355–359,
    372–373. *See also* Irregular
    verbs.
between/*among*, 459–460
Bibliographies, 214–215
Body of business letter, 261–263
Body of composition, 142–143,
    148–149, 164–165, 176–177
Body of friendly letter, 254–255
Body of report, 210–211
Body of speech, 278–279
Books, finding and using in
    library. *See* Library, using the.
Borrowed words, 2
Brainstorming, 70–71
Bread and butter notes, 259–260
Business letters, 261–265

C

Call numbers, of library books,
    225
can/may, 392
capital/capitol, 599
Capitalization, 545–560
  abbreviations, 562
  businesses, 549

clubs, 549
days, 547
direct quotations, 553
first words
  of outlines, 554
  of poetry lines, 551
  of quotations, 553
  of sentences, 551
holidays, 547
I, 556
initials, 546
languages, 549
in letters, 553
months, 547
names, 546
nationalities, 549
organizations, 549
places and things, 548
proper adjectives, 545–546
proper nouns, 545–546
races, 549
religions, 549
titles, of persons and their
    abbreviations, 546
written works, 555
Card catalog, 227–229
Characters, 158–159
Charts. *See* Graphic Aids.
Chronological order
  in narrative compositions, 160
  in paragraphs, 72–73, 92–93,
    96–97
Clauses, 512–513
Closings of letters, 254–256, 263
  commas with, 572
Collier's Encyclopedia, 230
Combining sentence parts, 46–47
Combing sentences, 44–45
Commas, 567–574
  with adjectives, 423
  with appositives, 569
  to avoid confusion, 573

609

Outlines
    capitalization in, 554
    periods in, 564

P

Padded sentences, 42–43
Paragraphs, 49–139
    adjectives in, 108–109
    chronological order in, 72–73,
        92–93, 96–97
    definition of, 50–51
    descriptive, 58–59, 101–109
    details in, 56–57, 72–73, 102,
        124–125. *See also* Details.
    developing, 56–57, 70–71
    ending sentence in, 76–77,
        128–129
    examples in, 56–57
    explanatory, 58–59, 111–139
    facts and figures in, 56–57
    first drafts of, 74–77, 83–84,
        96–97, 106–107, 116–117,
        126–127, 136–137
    first-person point of view in,
        94–95
    general to specific order in,
        72–73
    kinds of, 58–59
    logical order in, 72–73, 92–93,
        96–97, 104–105, 114–115,
        124–125. *See also* Logical
        order.
    main idea in, 50–51
    narrative, 58–59, 89–99. *See
        also* Narrative paragraphs.
    order of importance, 72–73,
        124–125
    organizing, 72–73, 124–125
    point of view in, 94–95
    revising, 62–63, 78–79, 85,
        98–99, 108–109, 118–119,
        128–129, 138–139

    sensory details in, 102, 108–109
    spatial order in, 72–73, 104–105
    step-by-step order in, 114–115
    third-person point of view in,
        94–95
    time sequence in, 72–73
    topic for, narrowing, 66–67
    topic sentence in, 54–55, 116
    transitions in, 96–97, 106–107,
        116–117, 126–127
    unity in, 52–53
Parts of speech, 27–29, 474–481
    definition of, 474
    as shown in dictionary entries,
        26–29
    using words as different,
        476–478
    See also particular parts of
        speech.
Past participle of verbs, 370–371
Past tense of verbs, 359–361
peace/piece, 600
Period, 562–565
    with quotation marks, 579–583
Personal observation to attain in-
    formation, 70–71
Personal point of view. *See* First-
    person point of view.
Phrases and clauses, 515
Phrases, transitional
    in compositions, 168–169
    in paragraphs, 96–97, 106–107,
        116–117, 126–127
piece/peace, 600
plain/plane, 600
Plot in stories, 158–161
Plural forms
    of nouns, 336–339
        shown in dictionary entries,
            338–339
    of pronouns, 486–487
    of verbs, 482–486

Pronouns, 406–420
  as compound objects of preposition, 459
  as compound subjects, 409
  definition of, 407
  after linking verbs, 411–412
  as objects, 412–414
    of prepositions, 459
    of verbs, 412–414
  plural, 486–487
  possessive, 414–415
  predicate, 411–412
  singular forms of, 486–487
  as subjects, 409–410
    agreement with verbs, 486–488
    with point of view
      first-person, 94–95, 162–163
      third-person, 94–95, 162–163
  substituting nouns, 408–409
  we/us, 407–409
Pronunciation of words, as shown in dictionary entries, 26
Proofreading, 85, 592
  symbols, 85
Proper adjectives, 428–430, 546
  capitalization of, 545–546
  definition of, 429
Proper nouns, 334–336
  capitalization of, 334
  definition of, 334
Punctuation, 561–589
  accent mark, 26
  apostrophe, 574–576
  to avoid confusion, 573
  colon, 261
  comma, 567–574
  in compound sentences, 503
  at end of sentence, 562–564

exclamation mark, or point, 566
hyphen, 577–578
in letters, 254, 261, 572
period, 562–564
question mark, 566
quotation marks, 571, 579–583
and underlining, 583

Q

Question mark, 566
  and interrogative sentences, 292
Questions. *See* Interrogative sentences.
quiet/quite, 600
Quotations
  capitalization in, 553
  commas with, 571
  definition of, 579
  direct, 579
  divided, 581
  punctuation, 579–583
Quotation marks, 579–583
  commas with, 571
  in dialogue, 582–583
  with divided quotations, 581
  exclamation marks with, 580
  question marks with, 580
  for titles, 583

R

raise/rise, 395
Real life narrative compositions, 158–159
Real life subjects for paragraphs, 90–91
Regular verbs, 371–372. *See also* Verbs.
Reliable source, 218
Religions, capitalization of, 549
Reports, 203–215

Photographs

Jim Whitmer, ii, 36, 48, 110, 120, 156, 192, 216, 232, 252, 286; James L. Ballard, xvi, 60, 172, 268; Jacqueline Durand, 20, 182, 222; Scott Thode/Click/International Stock Photo, 30, 130; Ray Solowinski/Click/International Stock Photo, 80; Brent Jones, 88; Seena Sussman/Click/International Stock Photo, 100; Barbara Kirk/Click/International Stock Photo, 140; Scott J. Witte/Hillstrom Stock Photo, 202.

Cover

Sinjerli Variation IV, 1977. Frank Stella. Petersburg Press, London and New York. © Vert Foncé, 1977.

Editorial Credits

Editor-in-Chief: Joseph F. Littell
Administrative Editor: Kathleen Laya
Managing Editor: Geraldine Macsai
Senior Editor: Bonnie Dobkin
Editors: James M. LiSacchi, Mary Schafer
Associate Designer: Mary E. MacDonald
Cover Design: Joy Littell, Mary E. MacDonald